North Wal

Mark R

A guidebook to rock climbing in the slate quarries near Llanberis in North Wales

Text and action photography by Mark Reeves
Crag photos and topos by Mark Reeves and Alan James
Other photography as credited
Edited by Alan James and Rebecca Ting
Printed in Europe on behalf of LF Book Services Limited
(ISO 14001 and EMAS certified printers)
Distributed by Cordee (cordee.co.uk)

All maps by ROCKFAX
Some maps based on original
source data from openstreetmap.org

Published by ROCKFAX in September 2018
© ROCKFAX 2018

rockfax.com

This book is printed on FSC-certified paper
made from 100% virgin fibre
sourced from sustainable forestry
 FSC

ISBN 978 1 873341 43 8

This book belongs to:

Cover: Simon Lake on *Goose Creature* (E3) -
p.94 - on Looning The Tube Slab in Australia.
This page: Guess the route?
Photos: Mark Reeves

Bus Stop Quarry
Dali's Hole
California
Australia
Serengeti
Never Never Land
Twll Mawr
Mordor - Lost World
Vivian Quarry
Rainbow Slab Area
Snakes and Ladders
Outlying

'JJ' climbing the first of two contrasting pitches on *Imagine Dragons* (6b) - *p.165* - in Twll Mawr. The first pitch is a short steep climb up the crack in the photo and is followed by a longer slabby and technical pitch with a crux groove.

Bus Stop Quarry
Dali's Hole
California
Australia
Serengeti
Never Never Land
Twll Mawr
Mordor - Lost World
Vivian Quarry
Rainbow Slab Area
Snakes and Ladders
Outlying

Bus Stop Quarry

Dali's Hole

California

Australia

Serengeti

Never Never Land

Twll Mawr

Mordor – Lost World

Vivian Quarry

Rainbow Slab Area

Snakes and Ladders

Outlying

Visiting Kiwi Josh Douglas climbing on *Looning the Tube* (E1 5a) - *p.94* - in Australia. This route was originally a simple shuffle along a pipe fixed to the slab from the bottom left to top right. Over the years it has fallen down, making it more of a climb - imagine how hair-raising the original 'stroll' was! If you would like to try and follow in the pioneers' footsteps, *Exhuming the Tube* pretty much follows the line where the tube was attached.

Slate has often been described as the Marmite of rocks - you either love it or hate it! However, a lot has changed in the quarries since the original boom in the 1980s, so whichever category you fall into, you would be well advised to give the slate another look.

The infamous routes of 'designer danger' and 'run-out rockovers' era will still scare anyone bold enough to step off the ground, but they have been joined by a whole host of sport routes across the grade range. Many of these are on the less slabby sections of the quarry, offering climbing styles other than the customary small edges on slabs. Multi-pitch sport routes and link-ups are another facet to the climbing developed here in recent years. These can offer big full-day expeditions to remote walls and provide a memorable experience.

Part of this experience is the unique nature of much of the climbing. Often you will encounter strange and perplexing crux moves. You can't train for these, so you just have to get yourself on the route and use your strength, balance, technique - and most of all your brain - to solve the puzzle presented. The time you have to figure out the moves usually depends on the angle of the rock. Sometimes the slabs will give you too much time, making commitment to the move difficult. On the steeper routes, lengthy working sessions are often required to decipher the key move.

A lot of routes rely on fixed protection or have lower-offs which need maintaining. In the past 10 years, the North Wales Bolt Fund has been actively re-equipping old routes and helping fund new routes For more information on bolting and how you can help, see page 38.

This guide is a celebration of slate. We hope that it will no longer be a destination to love or loathe, but a place where climbers can become passionate about the unique climbing. There are plenty of routes to enjoy and many dramatic locations to explore in this fascinating post-industrial graveyard - come and see for yourself!

Bus Stop Quarry | Dali's Hole | California | Australia | Serengeti | Never Never Land | Twll Mawr | Mordor - Lost World | Vivian Quarry | Rainbow Slab Area | Snakes and Ladders | Outlying

The geological story of North Wales Slate starts around 500 million years ago, but it wasn't until the last few thousand years that its use as a building material was noticed. Virtually impervious to water, and easily split into tiles, slate became a very desirable roofing product.

Only limited mining occurred in early times - the most notable example of early slate use was on a Roman fort with remains on the outskirts of Caernarfon. Much later slate mining expanded rapidly during the industrial revolution. Factory building and urban growth led to a demand for an effective roofing material and that's where slate, and the Welsh quarries associated with it, came to the fore.

In 1890, the industry peaked with over 17,000 men employed in the mines and quarries of North Wales. The subsequent decline in the industry was to have a major effect on the local workers and economy. In one significant dispute, the quarry owners locked the workers out for nearly a year with no pay in an attempt to disregard new Health and Safety Laws. In the end, after great hardship, the mine owners eventually opened the gates to the capitulating workers, but they only took on half the original workforce.

Another shameful development is only recently coming to light after the Penrhyn family released historic papers. These showed that the owners not only kept the welsh workforce in poverty, but used the ships that transported the slate all over the world to engage in the slave triangle. It was this global transportation that gave birth to some of the names of the areas in the quarries, and though some of these have been misnamed by climbers, the general theme is still there.

After the Second World War, the ceramic tile was born. It was cheaper and easier to manufacture than slate. Despite more mechanization, the quarries went through a steady decline until 1969. At this time the Dinorwig quarries' income had become almost entirely dependent on a single French firm importing all its slate. When this company went bankrupt, all the quarries closed virtually overnight. By the end of the mining in Dinorwig, 362 quarrymen had lost their lives extracting the 'grey gold' - see *362* on p.144.

Bus Stop Quarry · *Dali's Hole* · *California* · *Australia* · *Serengeti* · *Never Never Land* · *Twll Mawr* · *Mordor - Lost World* · *Vivian Quarry* · *Rainbow Slab Area* · *Snakes and Ladders* · *Outlying*

Bus Stop Quarry

Dali's Hole

California

Australia

Serengeti

Never Never Land

Twll Mawr

Mordor - Lost World

Vivian Quarry

Rainbow Slab Area

Snakes and Ladders

Outlying

Rust and ruin high up on the east side of Australia. This old rusting structure strikes a sculptural beauty against the purple/grey backdrop of the slate.

Bus Stop Quarry | Dali's Hole | California | Australia | Serengeti | Never Never Land | Twll Mawr | Mordor - Lost World | Vivian Quarry | Rainbow Slab Area | Snakes and Ladders | Outlying

The Early Climbing Forays

Climbing history started in the quarries in 1969 with the legendary Joe Brown, who seemed to have been waiting for the workers to leave so he could step in. Joe was, of course, a pioneer of steep and intimidating lines up big cliffs throughout the UK and abroad. It seems fitting that he set his sights on the biggest cliff of all, the back wall of Twll Mawr (Big Hole) putting up the compelling and rarely ascended *Opening Gambit*. This route has been greatly altered over the years through small and colossal rockfalls. The route also exacted a high price on two students who fell to their deaths when attempting it - *Opening Gambit* should not be underestimated and, despite the lowly grade of HVS, is probably more of an 'XS'.

Another local legend, Al Harris, whose house on Fachwen overlooked Gideon Quarry, made an early exploration of this slab producing *Gideon*. This smart little HVS was an unusual excursion. The gear is sparse and pushes the limits of friction on what feels like Teflon. Other routes were climbed in these quarries, but they have remained a bit of a backwater that failed to spark the imagination of those that explored the myriad of levels, holes and workings on the other side of the valley.

The Slate Boom and the Birth of the Slatehead

Twelve years after Joe Brown's epic route, it was the rising legend Stevie Haston who was to take up the baton and redefine climbing on the slate with *Comes the Dervish*. Famously cleaned with a 'borrowed knife' from Pete's Eats, *Comes the Dervish* is a route that any wannabe 'Slatehead' needs to put at the top of their ticklist. Originally graded E5, the line has cleaned up and is now one of the best E3s in the UK. If you have not climbed this route then you are not a slate climber, just a climber who has climbed on slate!

For a trend to really take a hold, a single route is not enough - you need a social context to effect a tipping point. *Comes the Dervish* may be said to have sparked the revolution, but it also had as much to do with the socio-economic situation of the times as it did with that clean fresh line on a pure slate blackboard.

The catalyst was the rise of unemployment in the early 1980s. From the unemployed army of 'Maggie's Millions' rose a new boom in the quarries, and this time the boom wasn't from the quarrymen's soft explosives! The 'rock and dole' generation was spawned.

What this meant was that if you were a climber in the early 1980s, and you wanted to live off benefits and climb, the world was your oyster. You could sign on by post, and spend all your available time climbing and engaging in all manner of socially irresponsible activities.

As acres of virgin rock were available to the ballooning population of rock and dolers, climbers migrated to Llanberis to get involved with this new punk-like movement. The stage was set for slate to make a big impact on climbing in the UK, along with mullets and bad moustaches. This was a time of hard men in garish tights. The Slatehead was born - a person whose antics off the rock were just as important as on it. This was a time of hard partying climbers having ample time, not only to push the boundaries of climbing, but also hedonistic behaviour. Perhaps the best account is given in Paul Pritchard's book *Deep Play*, which chronicles the antics of this era.

Bus Stop Quarry
Dali's Hole
California
Australia
Serengeti
Never Never Land
Twll Mawr
Mordor - Lost World
Vivian Quarry
Rainbow Slab Area
Snakes and Ladders
Outlying

Ben Heason pulling through the bulge of the *Comes the Dervish* (E3) - *p.215* - the most famous route on slate. Photo: Simon Carter If you ever walk down the shore of Llyn Padarn and glance across the lake just as the afternoon sun catches the Vivian Quarry, it is easy to understand what prompted Stevie Haston to go over with his 'borrowed' knife and have a look at the tenuous crack that ran up this immaculate slab. Oddly this wasn't even Stevie's first new route in Vivian - the forgettable (and now pretty much defunct) three-pitch *Wendy Doll* takes that honour.

Bus Stop Quarry | Dali's Hole | California | Australia | Serengeti | Never Never Land | Twll Mawr | Mordor - Lost World | Vivian Quarry | Rainbow Slab Area | Snakes and Ladders | Outlying

Designer Danger: Myths and Legends

Stevie Haston had climbed the most conspicuous slab in the quarries. Elsewhere the slabs were devoid of such luxurious cracks, which meant that the ethic quickly turned to bolting. The story is that the new routers of the time, led by the enigmatic John Redhead, applied Joe Brown's 'two pegs per pitch' rule on their new routes on the Rainbow Slab - only this time with bolts. It does not matter whether or not you believe this, or that the hard economic times led to the minimalistic approach to fixed gear. Either way the quarries got was some immaculate routes with astronomical run-outs.

The Sport Climbing Revolution: Slabs are for Softies

If you can turn your brain off and just climb, the slabs of the quarries are likely to feel easier than routes elsewhere of similar grades. It does, however, take a long time and a lot of confidence to train your mind in the ways of the run-out slab. After a while there came a point though when climbers started to look away from the slabs and turn to steeper and blanker rock. Here the pressure of the pump means that mind games become time limited - an altogether scarier and more dangerous proposition.

Many of the top climbers of this period were enjoying the luxury of sport climbing in France whilst collecting their dole money via the post. Upon their return the introduction of the full sport route ethic began to realise the full potential of the quarries.

Three routes stood out and ushered in this new era. In Vivian Quarry, John Redhead sculpted two utterly horrendous routes that suited his height and finger strength. The first, *Manic Strain,* is still considered 7c+ or 8a, whereas the frequently re-named *Misogynist Discharge* is no pushover at 8a+, and features more of a scrape than a chip on its crucial foothold.

Later that year came a four-pitch masterpiece from Johnny Dawes in the form of *The Quarryman*. Its third pitch has now been made famous by his *Stone Monkey* video, where Johnny climbs the gymnastic and powerful groove. A little later, Dawes went on to add the classic *Bobby's Groove* and the ultra technical *Untouchables Arete*.

Another of the main sport climbing activists on the scene was Nick Harms. In 1986 he made the first ascent of *Cwms The Dogfish*, *Tru Clip* and *The Dark Half* - all of which are fantastic high-end sport climbs. None of his routes have diminished in reputation over the years and just a sighting of Nick in the book *The Power of Climbing* will make you realise that, even in those days, the ability to be totally ripped despite rampant hedonism was still possible!

What set many of these routes apart from limestone sport routes elsewhere is the moves. Often a scene of much frustration for the climber, the technical on/off nature of the slate cruxes often have more to do with feet sticking to a hold than the ability to pull hard. This gives slate sport its very own style, where relentless body tension is needed to keep in contact with the tiny holds.

In the years that followed, the Rainbow Slab, Never Never Land, Vivian Quarry and Australia all saw attention with their major lines ascended. Around 80 routes were climbed between 1983 and 1985 of which 30 are now considered classics. Development picked up more speed and in 1986 over 100 new routes were added, around 80 the following year, and over 70 the year after that. Then almost as quickly as it started, the new route boom tailed off as climbers looked elsewhere.

Bus Stop Quarry

Dali's Hole

California

Australia

Serengeti

Never Never Land

Twll Mawr

Mordor - Lost World

Vivian Quarry

Rainbow Slab Area

Snakes and Ladders

Outlying

John Orr making a tenuous move on *The Cure for a Sick Mind* (E6) - *p.245* - on the Rainbow Slab. Photo: Calum Muskett If the thought of fingertip mantels fills you with dread then hard slate slabs are probably not for you. On most of them, matching at least one your hands and feet on the same hold is usually crucial to progress. As the width of the holds get smaller, your calves get more pumped and the grades get higher. Johnny Dawes once said the key to success on slate slabs is learning how to rest on your heels on these tiny ledges. Well it works sometimes!

... and the Beat Goes On

Slate climbing is like flares - if you live long enough then it is going to come back into fashion at some point - and 2006 saw its return to popularity. The resurgence started with the re-equipping many of the classics.

With the re-equipping came some controversial retro-bolting in several forgotten areas that had routes of reasonable quality but a dearth of gear. The ultra classic bold routes were rightly left untouched, but other areas saw plenty of attention from the drill. Those doing the bolting claimed they were bringing these areas "kicking and screaming into the real world of the Noughties". Whatever your opinion, there is no doubt that many of these routes became much more popular going from a couple of ascents in a decade to many ascents a week, just days after they were equipped. The quarries felt alive with climbers again.

A surge of easier sport climbs followed as people starting to clean new routes everywhere. Some were good, others less so, but all were popular. As a result, the quarries really were opened up to everyone. This had a knock on effect in creating access problems, notably at the very public Dali's Hole where the routes became so popular that access to the whole of the quarries was threatened. The original developers took the sensible action of de-bolting these routes to solve this problem. Easy sport routes have subsequently been developed higher up on The Sidings away from the main path through the quarries.

Alongside this 'everyman' revolution, a small number of climbers felt inspired to develop a new set of modern testpieces. None captures the cutting edge of slate climbing more than *The Serpent Vein*, a project that was left uncompleted by the 1990s generation and eventually climbed at 8b by James 'Caff' McHaffie. In 1990, the great Johnny Dawes' last major new route on slate was the magnificent *The Very Big and The Very Small*. At the time this represented the peak of slate slab climbing and still sees few repeats. The one Johnny didn't manage was a project in Twll Mawr that became know as *Meltdown*. In 2012, Caff managed the first ascent of what is currently the hardest route on slate, tentatively graded at 9a.

The slate quarries are far from fully developed. It should also be said that they still have a habit of collapsing from time to time so some new routes become fleeting challenges before huge sections of wall collapse in storms. There is plenty of rock left though and much of this is likely to be developed with new routes - probably sport routes and probably of varying quality. There will be occasional gems in the new routes, but it is safe to say that most of the best lines have been climbed, unless of course something collapses and reveals a new Rainbow Slab - now that would be something!

Bus Stop Quarry

Dali's Hole

California

Australia

Serengeti

Never Never Land

Twll Mawr

Mordor - Lost World

Vivian Quarry

Rainbow Slab Area

Snakes and Ladders

Outlying

Pete Robins climbing *The Very Big and the Very Small*
(8c) - *p.245* - on the Rainbow Slab.
This photo superbly illustrates hard slate - pulling on
a match-edge, reaching for a chalk stain and we can't
even see what he is standing on! Success often depends
on a certain amount of faith - the concentration in Pete's
eyes shows that he believes he can pull it off.

As a fast-developing area, slate has always attracted guidebook writers and a variety of publishers. The first 1986 small book by Perry Hawkins and George Smith was back in the middle of the 80s boom. This guide paved the way for the brilliant 1987 *Llanberis* guide by Paul Williams, published by the Climbers' Club. For many climbers this was their introduction to the slate; written in Paul's inimitable style, this guide inspired a generation of climbers to realise that Llanberis offered more than just 'The Pass'.

Since the 1980s there have been three privately-published guidebooks and the latest one from Ground Up in 2011. A big contribution to this last book was data collected through **wikifoundry.com** - a free open source wiki site set up by Mark Reeves in 2005 to record new routes and re-equipping information. Such has been the development though that even this beautifully produced guidebook is now in need of an update. As an aside, if you are interested in the history of slate, then it is worth tracking down a copy of the 2011 Ground Up guidebook. It is out of print, but there are copies to be found around and it gives much more depth to the characters and development of slate than we have included in this book.

Since 2011, a number of areas have been developed, routes have been re-bolted, new lines have been fitted in and, sadly, a few old buttresses have fallen down. This new Rockfax book brings all these together with an amazing set of new crag shots to illustrate them combined with detailed maps and full route descriptions. It is being published in print and digitally through the Rockfax app. Looking to the future, we have laid the foundation for a sustainable record of climbing in the slate quarries in both print and digital format. All the route descriptions and information are available publicly through the UKClimbing Logbook Database for comments, feedback, grade and star votes, and new routes. The app version will be updated and the new print edition begins being prepared the day after we publish this edition.

Rockfax is very grateful to all the previous authors of guidebooks to North Wales Slate. Without their efforts our job would be much harder. In addition to the list below, Slate has also been included in a number of other selected books from Paul Williams, Ground Up and the Rockfax book North Wales Climbs from 2013.

Guidebooks to North Wales Slate
Dinorwig Slate Quarries (Perry Hawkins, George Smith 1986)
Llanberis (Paul Williams 1987)
Llanberis Slate (Nick Harms 1990)
Slate (Iwan Arfon Jones 1992)
Slate (Iwan Arfon Jones 1999)
Llanberis Slate (Ground Up 2011)
North Wales Slate (Rockfax 2018)

New Routes
Please submit any new routes to the relevant crag on the UKC Logbook Database. These will be checked by the crag moderator and added to the Rockfax app version in future updates.

BETASTICK evo

BETA

CLIMBING DESIGNS

Bus Stop Quarry

Dali's Hole

California

Australia

Serengeti

Never Never Land

Twll Mawr

Mordor - Lost World

Vivian Quarry

Rainbow Slab Area

Snakes and Ladders

Outlying

The Rockfax App brings together all the Rockfax climbing information with UKC Logbooks and presents it in a user-friendly package for use on Apple iOS devices (Android version to follow).

The heart of the app is the Rockfax crag and route information covering individual crags, or bundles of crags, in 'areas' which correspond roughly to printed guidebooks. From the end of 2018, the main data is sold by subscription so that you can purchase access to all the Rockfax guidebook information for a period of time, from 1 month to yearly. Once you are subscribed, you will have access to every digital Rockfax guidebook for the period of your subscription. You can download the main data and store it on your device, so you don't need any signal to be able to read the descriptions and see the topos and maps. There is also plenty of free data available without subscription enabling you to get a really good impression of what the app is like, without shelling out any money.

The Rockfax App itself is a free download and incredibly useful in its own right. It contains a detailed crag map linked to the UKClimbing crags database (currently with basic information and route lists for around 22,000 crags worldwide). The map also displays all the 4,000+ listings from the UKClimbing Directory of climbing walls, outdoor shops, climbing clubs, outdoor-specific accommodation and instructors and guides, amongst others.

To find the app, search for 'Rockfax App' in Google or on the appropriate store.

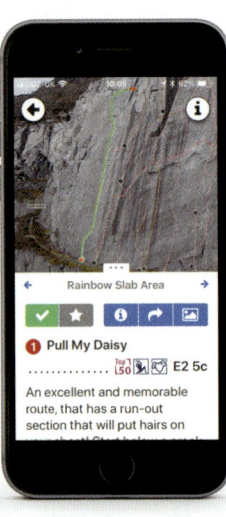

UKC Logbooks

An incredibly popular method of logging your climbing is to use the **UKClimbing.com** logbooks system. This database lists more than 432,000 routes and over 22,000 crags; so far, more than 36,000 users have recorded over 6.1 million ascents! To set up your own logbook all you need to do is register at **UKClimbing.com** and click on the logbook tab. Once set up you will be able to record every ascent you make, when you did it, what style you climbed it in and who you did it with. Each entry has a place for your own notes. You can also add your vote to the grade/star system linked to a database on the Rockfax site used by the guidebook writers. The logbook can be private, public or restricted to your own climbing partners only. The Rockfax App can be linked to your **UKClimbing.com** user account and logbook so that you can record your activity while at the crag and look at photos, comments and votes on the routes. To do this you will need a 3G/4G data connection. You can also look at the UKC logbooks to see if anyone has climbed your chosen route recently to check on conditions.

Route Symbols

🏆1	A good route which is well worth climbing.
🏆2	A very good route, one of the best on the crag.
🏆3	A brilliant route, one of the best in North Wales. (There is no Top50 in this book).
	Technical climbing requiring good balance and technique, or complex and tricky moves.
	Powerful climbing; roofs, steep rock, low lock-offs or long moves off small holds.
	Sustained climbing; either lots of hard moves or steep rock giving pumpy climbing.
	Fingery climbing with significant small holds on the hard sections.
	Fluttery climbing with big fall potential and scary run-outs.
	A long reach is helpful, or even essential, for one or more of the moves.
	A dynamic move is required.
	Graunchy climbing, wide cracks or awkward thrutchy moves.
	Loose rock may be encountered.
🚫	A route which has been de-bolted and is no longer climbable.
	A route which can be deep water soloed.

Crag Symbols

20 mins	Angle of the approach walk to the buttress with approximate time.
Lots of sun	Approximate time that the buttress is in the direct sun (when it is shining).
Sheltered	The buttress can offer shelter from cold winds and it may be a good suntrap in colder weather.
Seepage	The buttress suffers from seepage. It may well be wet and unclimbable after rain.
Abseil in	An abseil approach is required to reach the start of the routes.
Restrictions	Some or all of the routes may be affected by a restriction. Check the crag information for details.
	Deserted - Currently under-used and usually quiet. Less good routes or a remote area.
	Quiet - Less popular sections, or good buttresses with awkward approaches.
	Busy - Places you will seldom be alone. Good routes and easy access.
	Crowded - The most popular sections of the most popular crags which are always busy.

Map and Topo Key

Variation lines on the same route

Abseil point

Crag-top belay

Descent

Lower-off

Approximate vertical height > 30m

Approximate vertical height <30m

30m Ⓐ

18m

Route on a different page

① Trad route (white dash)

② ③ ④

Sport route (yellow dash)

Parking GPS Locations

GPS 53.127975
Ⓟ -4.108359

Parking spots are marked with blue GPS boxes and a QR code. If you scan the QR code with your phone camera, then it should open into a navigation app which will take you straight to the parking. You can also add the coordinates manually if required.

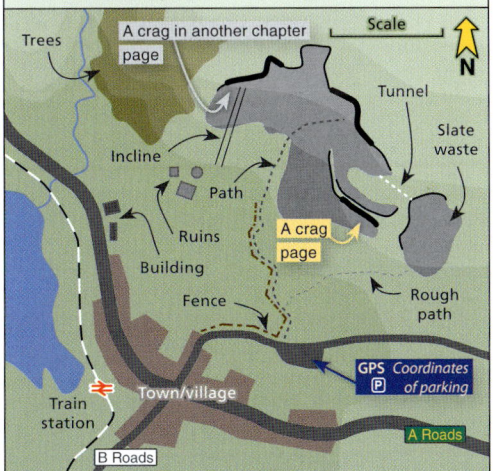

Trees

A crag in another chapter page

Scale

N

Tunnel

Incline

Slate waste

Path

Ruins

Building

Fence

A crag page

Rough path

Train station

Town/village

GPS Ⓟ *Coordinates of parking*

B Roads

A Roads

Bus Stop Quarry | Dali's Hole | California | Australia | Serengeti | Never Never Land | Twll Mawr | Mordor - Lost World | Vivian Quarry | Rainbow Slab Area | Snakes and Ladders | Outlying

Having lived in North Wales since 1995, I am passionate about the climbing we have here. In bringing this book together I have had another amazing opportunity to help sell North Wales and the slate quarries to you, the climbing public at large. This wouldn't have been possible without so many people.

First off the Rockfax team - Alan James for giving me the opportunity to write this book and Rebecca Ting for her eye for detail.

I could not have completed this project without such a good bunch of friends and clients that I have climbed with in the quarries. I hope they know how much they mean to me. In particular four stand out as worthy of a mention.

Simon Lake is all over this guide - his companionship has meant so much to me over the years. At the time of going to print, Simon is recovering from a climbing accident and he does not yet know how much I have missed his company - my thoughts are with you and the family bud!

Llion Morris and I have shared so many great climbing memories with - please don't ask him for truth about what happened on *Fresh Air Crack,* it's too embarassing!

Katie Haston for accompanying us round what once was her back garden.

Dave Evans who has provided fine company on the more adventurous and esoteric routes.

Many of the harder routes were beyond me to climb, but I have been lucky enough to be dragged up some of these classics by James McHaffie, Pete Robins and Dave Rudkin.

We have also been lucky enough to get some great photos from David Simmonite, Simon Carter, David Price, Calum Muskett, Mike Doyle, Tristram Fox, Talo Martin, Mike Hutton, John Bunney, Matt Stygall.

Thanks are also due to two stalwarts of Slate - Neil and Paul Harrison - who have helped at the latter stages by going through the proofs with their eagle-eyes.

In addition to those mentioned above, there are really too many other people to remember; anyone from the list of hundreds of climbers I have had the joy to share a rope with in the quarries from 1995 through to July 2018 when this book went to print have all helped shape me, my knowledge and love for climbing in the slate quarries.

Finally, anyone who has contributed to either the Slate Wiki or added to the UKClimbing database over the years. Your small contributions have been just as important to the final product.

Mark Reeves   July 2018

Bus Stop Quarry

Dali's Hole

California

Australia

Serengeti

Never Never Land

Twll Mawr

Mordor - Lost World

Vivian Quarry

Rainbow Slab Area

Snakes and Ladders

Outlying

Bus Stop Quarry

Dali's Hole

California

Australia

Serengeti

Never Never Land

Twll Mawr

Mordor - Lost World

Vivian Quarry

Rainbow Slab Area

Snakes and Ladders

Outlying

Mark Reeves enjoying an easy day of Australian sport climbing on *Steps of Glory* (5a) - *p.94* - one of the new additions to the Above the Rails area. Photo: David Simmonite

Bus Stop Quarry | Dali's Hole | California | Australia | Serengeti | Never Never Land | Twll Mawr | Mordor – Lost World | Vivian Quarry | Rainbow Slab Area | Snakes and Ladders | Outlying

North Wales Climbs
📖 November 2013

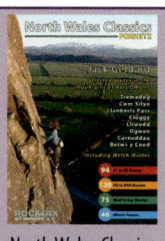

North Wales Classics
📖 April 2010

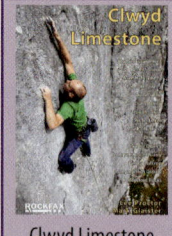
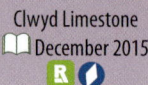

Clwyd Limestone
📖 December 2015

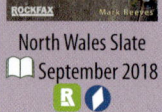

North Wales Slate
📖 September 2018

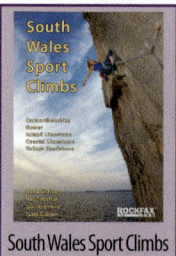

South Wales Sport Climbs
📖 November 2016

Pembroke
R March 2018

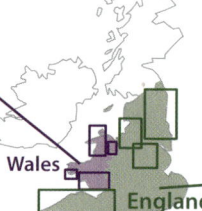
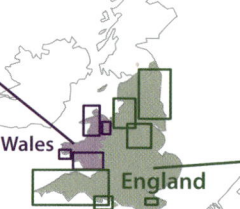

Norway

Wales

England

France

Italy

Greece

	Print version available
R	App version available
⬗	Maps in app version are geo-located
📖+	App version has extra content

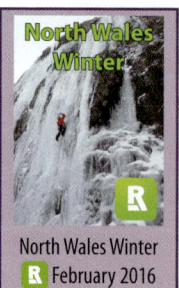

North Wales Winter
R February 2016

Spain

29 titles in print
18 less than 6 years old

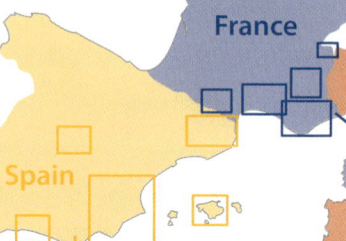

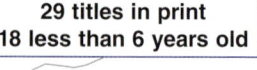

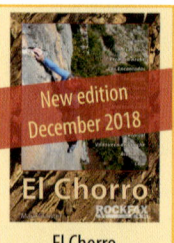

El Chorro
📖 December 2008

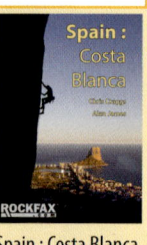

Spain : Costa Blanca
📖 February 2013

Spain : Mallorca
📖 January 2016

Catalunya
R February 2016

Madrid Area
R October 2017

Lofoten Climbs
May 2017

Rjukan
February 2016

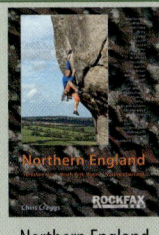

Northern England
February 2008

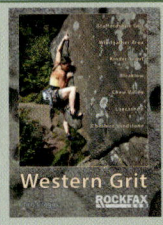

Western Grit
April 2009

Northern Limestone
January 2015

Eastern Grit
April 2015

Peak Limestone
May 2012

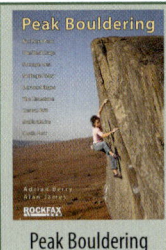

Peak Bouldering
May 2014

Southern Sandstone
September 2017

West Country Climbs
July 2010

The Dolomites
July 2014

Kalymnos
May 2018

Dorset
February 2012

Dorset Bouldering
May 2014

Deep Water
June 2007

**Rockfax produce print and app
guidebooks to areas all over Europe**
rockfax.com

France : Ariege
December 2012

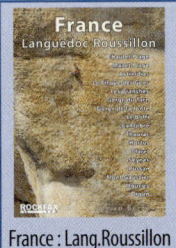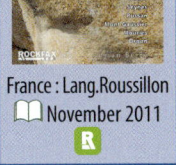

France : Lang.Roussillon
November 2011

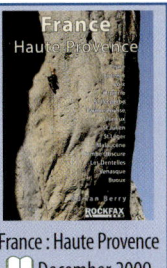

France : Haute Provence
December 2009

France : Côte d'Azur
February 2017

Chamonix
October 2016

Bus Stop Quarry | Dali's Hole | California | Australia | Serengeti | Never Never Land | Twll Mawr | Mordor - Lost World | Vivian Quarry | Rainbow Slab Area | Snakes and Ladders | Outlying

Bus Stop Quarry

Dali's Hole

California

Australia

Serengeti

Never Never Land

Twll Mawr

Mordor - Lost World

Vivian Quarry

Rainbow Slab Area

Snakes and Ladders

Outlying

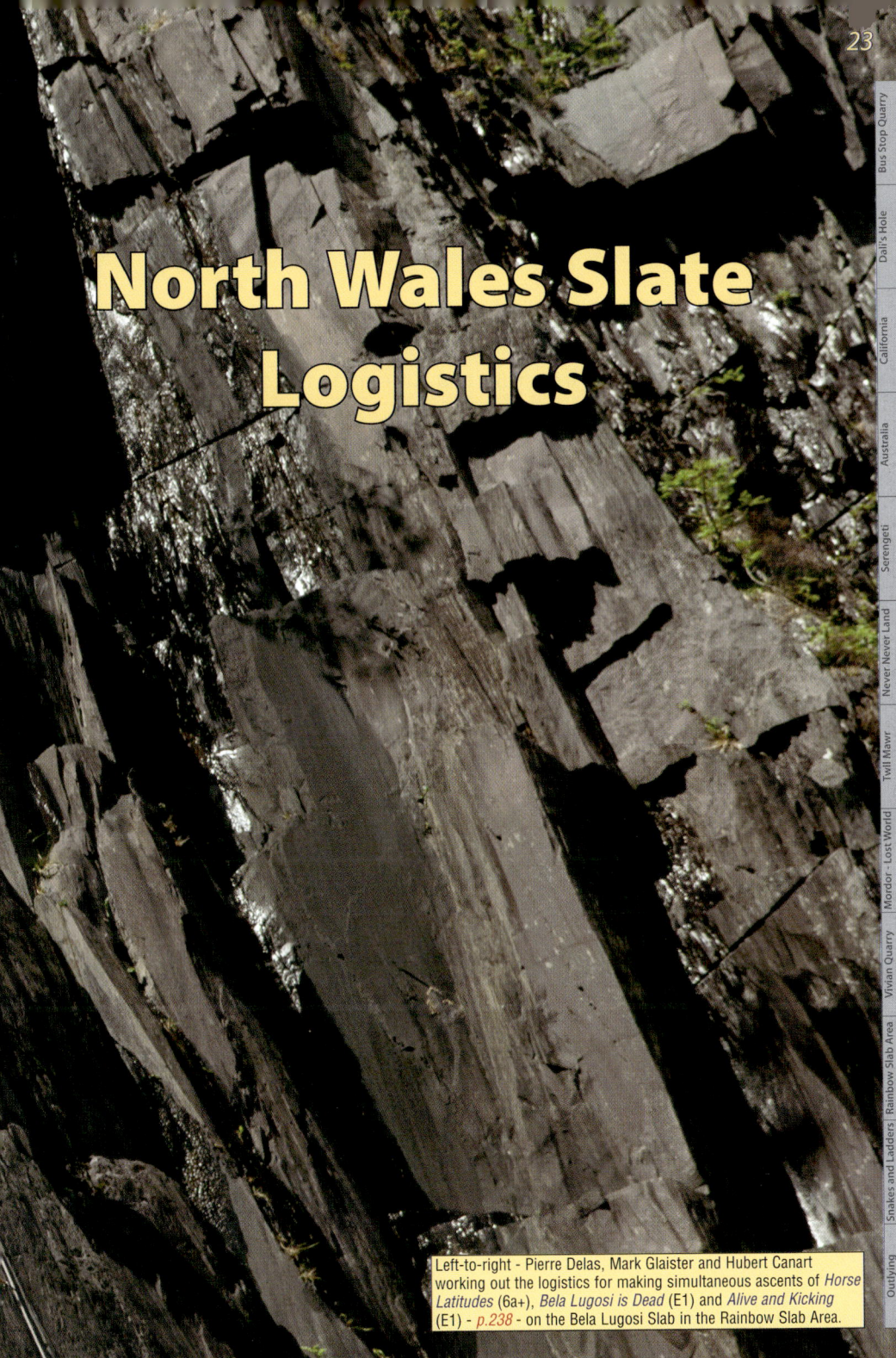

North Wales Slate Logistics

Bus Stop Quarry
Dali's Hole
California
Australia
Serengeti
Never Never Land
Twll Mawr
Mordor- Lost World
Vivian Quarry
Snakes and Ladders/ Rainbow Slab Area
Outlying

Left-to-right - Pierre Delas, Mark Glaister and Hubert Canart working out the logistics for making simultaneous ascents of *Horse Latitudes* (6a+), *Bela Lugosi is Dead* (E1) and *Alive and Kicking* (E1) - *p.238* - on the Bela Lugosi Slab in the Rainbow Slab Area.

Tourist Information Offices

If you are short of ideas for what to do on a wet day or need some accommodation, take a look at the Tourist Information Offices. They contain much more useful information than it is possible to include in these pages.

Llanberis, Electric Mountain. Tel: 01286 870765
nwt.co.uk   visitwales.com   visitsnowdonia.info

When to Go

Temperature ˚C	Jan	Feb	Mar	Apr	May	Jun	Jul	Aug	Sep	Oct	Nov	Dec
Average Max Temp (˚C)	6.8	6.6	8.5	10.8	14.1	16.1	18.1	17.8	15.8	12.5	9.4	7.2
Average Min Temp (˚C)	1.8	1.1	2.8	4.0	6.3	9.2	11.3	11.2	9.2	6.9	4.2	1.9
Average Rain Days/Month	19.6	16.4	17.7	15.1	14.3	13.5	14.5	16.1	14.7	19.3	19.8	18.6

North Wales is often regarded as a year-round climbing venue, despite the fact that it sees pretty high rainfall and is cold in the winter. One of the reasons for this 'year-round' tag is that several venues often seem to be 'in' when the mountain crags are 'out'. The slate quarries are one of these venues. The sheltered south and west-facing aspect of many of the crags means that there are often suntraps in cold weather. The location on the west of the mountains means that it sometimes escapes the worst of the rain. Of course these factors can also combine to make it unbearable in hot weather, though you can usually find shade somewhere. The slabby and vertical nature of most of the crags means that there is almost nowhere to shelter from rain, so if you are perched half way up a bald slab when the clouds open, you'd be well advised to bail out quickly before it becomes a slippery nightmare. That said, the rock dries very quickly on most of the walls, although there is a bit of lingering seepage in places.

Camping

The Listings on **UKClimbing.com** can help you locate a campsite near the area you wish to climb in. Most are happy for you just to turn up without a reservation, except on Bank Holidays. A popular site for climbers is opposite the Vaynol Arms pub in Nant Peris.

Accommodation

There are plenty of small bed and breakfast places, plus some excellent bunk-house style accommodation providers in the area.

Climbing Shops

North Wales has plenty of outdoor shops but not all of them stock climbing gear.

> **Joe Brown Shops**
> High Street, Llanberis, LL55 4HA
> Tel: 01286 870327
> Capel Curig, LL24 0EP
> Tel: 01690 720205
> **joe-brown.com**
> *See advert on back cover*

V12 - High Street, Llanberis.

Pubs

Good pubs are unfortunately quite hard to come by in North Wales, but here are a selection of the better offerings.

Gallt y Glyn, Llanberis - Just west of Llanberis on the main road. It does 'Pizza and Pint'.

The Heights, Llanberis - In the centre of Llanberis. A popular location for climbers offering good food and beer.

Vaynol Arms, Nant Peris - Opposite the campsite. Good beers and a pool table! Can get very crowded on busy weekends.

Plas y Brenin, Capel Curig - The bar in the centre is open in the evenings and has local ales, great food and a stunning lake view.

Cafes

North Wales has a great number of climbers and a high annual rainfall, which means it also has a fair few cafes to retreat to.

> **Lodge Dinorwig**
> Dinorwig, LL55 3EY   Tel: 01286 871632
> Situated near Bus Stop Quarry. Good for a light lunch or coffee and cake
> **lodge-dinorwig.co.uk**
> *See advert on p.25*

Pete's Eats, Llanberis - Well known in this part of the world. A big old school menu with modern alternatives if you don't want everything fried. Whatever you choose, you won't leave hungry!

Caban, Brynrefail - Nice cafe, healthy menu.

Climbing Walls

> **Beacon Climbing Centre**
> Cibyn Estate
> Caernarfon, LL55 2BD   Tel: 0345 4508222
> **beaconclimbing.com**
> *See advert inside front cover*

> **Plas y Brenin**
> Capel Curig, LL24 0ET
> Tel: 01690 720214
> **pyb.co.uk**
> *See advert on p.37*

The Indy Climbing Wall
Llanfairpwllgwyngyll, Angelsey.

More information on
ukclimbing.com/walls/

Guides and Instructors

Snowdonia is a hub of outdoor education. As such you can find many guides, instructors and coaches via internet searches. The Listings on **UKClimbing.com** return 70 Instructors/Guides within 30km of Llanberis.

Hiring a local instructor means that you will have the benefit of their local knowledge for finding the best venue. This can make the most of a day if time is limited or conditions are challenging. Expect to pay between £150 and £250 for a day of 1:1 guiding.

> **Gaia Adventures**
> Llanberis, LL55 4SW   Tel: 07814412439
> **gaiaaddventures.co.uk**
> *See advert on back cover flap*

> **Mark Reeves - Snowdonia Mountain Guides**
> Cwm-y-Glo   Tel: 07872 565225
> **snowdoniamountainguides.com**
> *See advert opposite*

> **Plas y Brenin**
> Capel Curig, LL24 0ET   Tel: 01690 720214
> **pyb.co.uk**
> *See advert on p.37*

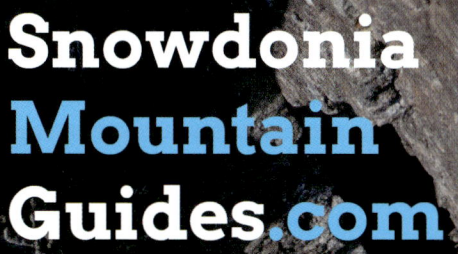

Snowdonia Mountain Guides.com

Classic Routes on
Slate
Gogarth
The Pass
Ogwen
Tremadog
Moelwyns
and beyond

Instruction

Guiding

Coaching

Wales' Premier Coaching Service

Mark Reeves
Qualified Mountaineering Instructor
MSc in Applied Sports Science in Effective Coaching,
Sport Psychology & Performance Physiology
Author of *North Wales Climbs*, *How to Climb Harder* and *Hanging By A Thread*
Mobile: 07872565225 Tel: 01286 870191

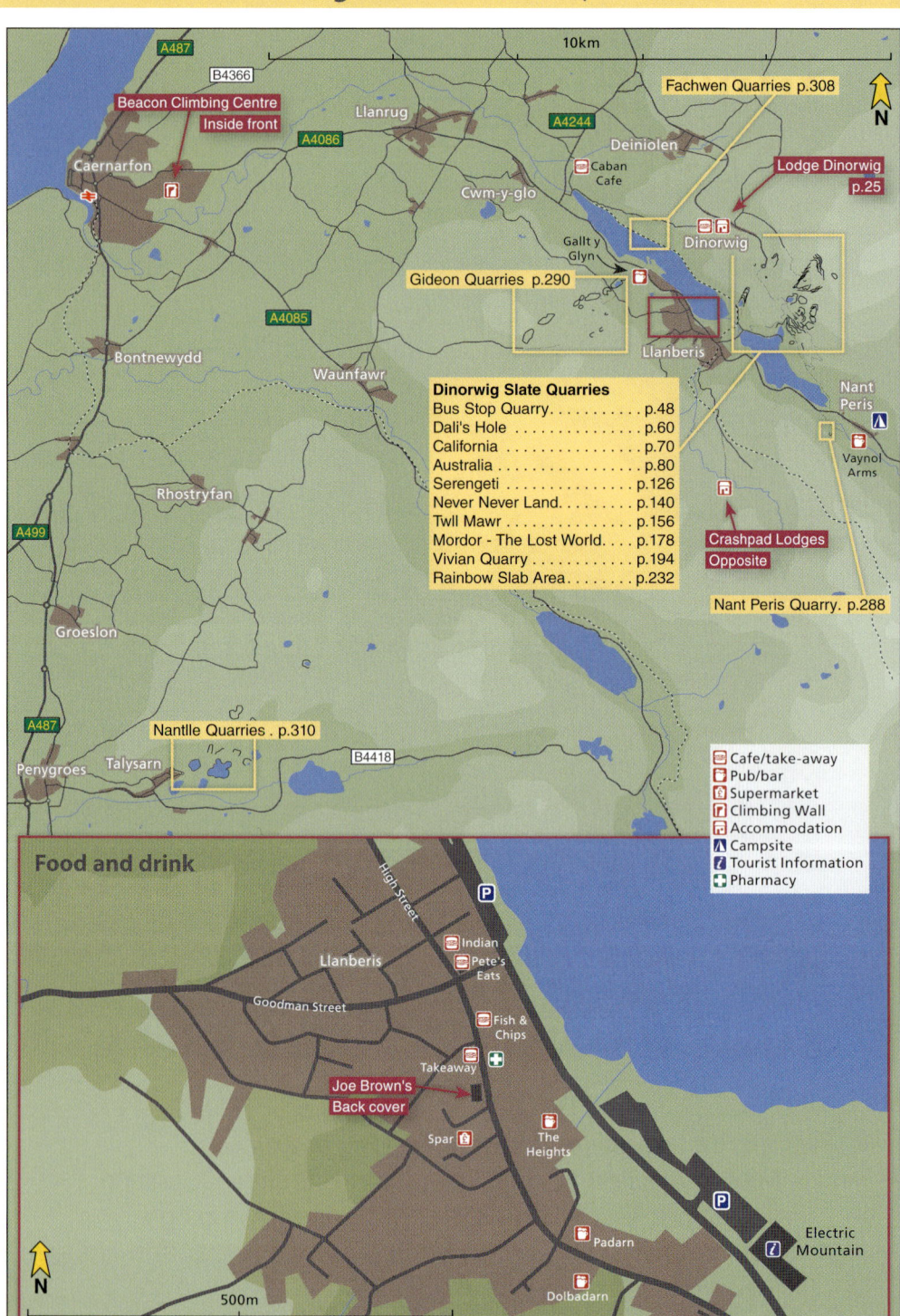

Bus Stop Quarry
Dali's Hole
California
Australia
Serengeti
Never Never Land
Twll Mawr
Mordor – Lost World
Vivian Quarry
Rainbow Slab Area Snakes and Ladders
Outlying

10km

N

A487
B4366
Beacon Climbing Centre
Inside front
Llanrug
A4086
A4244
Caernarfon
Cwm-y-glo
Deiniolen
Caban Cafe
Fachwen Quarries p.308
Lodge Dinorwig
p.25
Dinorwig
Gallt y Glyn
Gideon Quarries p.290
A4085
Llanberis
Nant Peris
Bontnewydd
Waunfawr
Vaynol Arms
Rhostryfan
Crashpad Lodges
Opposite
Nant Peris Quarry. p.288

Dinorwig Slate Quarries
Bus Stop Quarry p.48
Dali's Hole p.60
California p.70
Australia p.80
Serengeti p.126
Never Never Land p.140
Twll Mawr p.156
Mordor - The Lost World. . . . p.178
Vivian Quarry p.194
Rainbow Slab Area p.232

A499
Never Never Land
Groeslon
A487
Nantlle Quarries . p.310
Penygroes Talysarn
B4418

Cafe/take-away
Pub/bar
Supermarket
Climbing Wall
Accommodation
Campsite
Tourist Information
Pharmacy

Food and drink
High Street
P
Indian
Llanberis
Pete's Eats
Goodman Street
Fish & Chips
Takeaway
Joe Brown's
Back cover
Spar
The Heights
P
Padarn
Electric Mountain
Dolbadarn
N
500m

CRASHPAD LODGES

ECO

Yr Helfa   Llanberis

Crashpad is a unique off-grid lodge situated in the heart of the
Snowdonia National Park making it a
perfect base for your climbing getaway in North Wales.
For more information and how to book visit our
website and follow us on the below;-

@CRASHPAD_LODGES
#CRASHPAD_LODGES
WWW.CRASHPADLODGES.COM

Bus Stop Quarry

Dali's Hole

California

Australia

Serengeti

Never Never Land

Twll Mawr

Mordor - Lost World

Vivian Quarry

Rainbow Slab Area

Snakes and Ladders

Outlying

North Wales Slate Climbing

Ben Heason on the immaculate *Splitstream* (E5 6b) - *p.246* - on the stunning Rainbow Slab. Photo: Simon Carter. Undoubtedly the finest slab in Britain with its iconic 'rainbow' ripple. The inspired decision by the original developers to keep the bolting down to a minimum, aiming for only 'two bolts per pitch', has led to routes of real character and line. Despite the high grades and long run-outs there is plenty here to interest many climbers with your main worry often being the length of the fall onto a solid bolt and not if your dubious gear will hold.

Bus Stop Quarry

Dali's Hole

California

Australia

Serengeti

Never Never Land

Twll Mawr

Mordor - Lost World

Vivian Quarry

Rainbow Slab Area

Snakes and Ladders

Outlying

Bus Stop Quarry

Dali's Hole

California

Australia

Serengeti

Never Never Land

Twll Mawr

Mordor - Lost World

Vivian Quarry

Rainbow Slab Area

Snakes and Ladders

Outlying

Mountain Rescue
In the event of a incident requiring assistance in the quarries you need Mountain Rescue:

Dial 112 or 999 and ask for 'POLICE'
then ask for 'MOUNTAIN RESCUE'
North Wales Mountain Rescue Association - **www.nwmra.org**

Rescue Procedure
If you are involved in an incident then give the rescue services as many details as you can. Try to let them know your precise location, crag name and route name. In general it is the Llanberis MRT that will attend a rescue here and they know the quarries well. It may still take a while for the emergency services to reach you so any First Aid you can administer is critical. If a helicopter is called to the scene you need to signal to the pilot by standing with your arms up making a 'Y' shape, if possible with your back to the wind. Once the pilot has seen you, and looks like he is coming in to hover, then move to a safe distance away since they will either come in to land, or send the winchman down. The downdraft is considerable so collect all the bags and loose equipment together and get someone to sit on them to stop them being blown away. Do not approach the helicopter unless directed to do so by the aircrew since the rotating blades are extremely dangerous.

Access
The majority of crags in this book have been climbed on for many years. However, all the climbing basically falls on land owned by First Hydro power and Gwynedd Council, and under the Disused Mines and Quarries Act they need to ensure the areas are 'safe' for the public. This has led to access issues in the past - too many climber were visiting Dali's Hole, which enticed the general public off the main track and into the more dangerous areas of the quarry. As a result, climbers de-bolted this crag. Additionally, a few areas of the quarry have temporary restrictions due to nesting birds, or special approach arrangements. These details are covered in the text.

Apart from this, climbers are generally tolerated in the area although no formal access arrangement exists. In general all that is required to maintain this access is reasonable behaviour: try to leave a place in better shape than you found it; take only pictures and leave only footprints; and abide by the Country Code.

Access arrangements can change and we recommend that, when you are unsure, you use the BMC Regional Access Database to check what the up-to-date situation is. You can check RAD here - **thebmc.co.uk/rad/** or install the BMC RAD app from your iOS or Android app store.

If you do encounter problems then contact the BMC Access and Conservation representative. They are always happy to discuss any problems you encounter and often the BMC's involvement at an early stage can defuse a situation before it develops.

British Mountaineering Council
British Mountaineering Council, 177-179 Burton Road, Manchester, M20 2BB.
Tel: 0870 010 4878
Web: **thebmc.co.uk**
Email: **office@thebmc.co.uk**

Bus Stop Quarry

Dali's Hole

California

Australia

Serengeti

Never Never Land

Twll Mawr

Mordor - Lost World

Vivian Quarry

Rainbow Slab Area

Snakes and Ladders

Outlying

The routes in the slate quarries range from fully bolted sport to full trad. There have different requirements, but with some crossover in standard climbing kit like harness, helmet, rock boots and chalk bag.

Trad Routes

Runners - A typical slate climbing rack will include a double set of wires and a decent set of cams with particular attention on medium to very small cams. For the harder routes a set of microwires is essential. A few of the very hard routes require more specialist protection like skyhooks or hand-placed knifeblade pegs to offer marginal protection. These are described in the text.

Ropes - A pair of double half-ropes is best for the trad routes. 50m will be enough for most pitches and they are also often required for abseil approach or descent.

Extenders - Since the routes often weave around, it is worth taking plenty of extenders (quickdraws) and slings of varying lengths so that you can extend your gear to avoid rope drag.

Other Gear - A belay device that doubles up as an abseil device and a nut key to help remove stubborn pieces when your leader has put them in a little too well.

Sport Routes

For sport climbing you will require a single rope, preferably 60m, although the majority of the routes are possible up and down on a 50m rope. A dozen to fifteen quickdraws will usually suffice - this is slate so some of the sport routes are very 'sporty' by modern standards!

Multi-pitch Sport Routes - Some of the multi-pitch sport routes are better with double 50m half-ropes. This allows abseil escape if the heavens open and leave you marooned deep in Twll Mawr.

Rock Shoes

Any rock shoes will do for the slate, but if you really want to make your life as easy as possible a good pair of edging shoes is advised. Don't underestimate what a new stiff shoe with a sharp edge can do for your climbing, after all, good rock shoes are the only bit of climbing gear that will actually directly improve your climbing. On slate you could gain as much as a grade with the right pair of shoes.

Other Gear

Any day out in the quarries can be a cold and unpleasant experience if you don't have the correct clothing. Waterproofs, warm mid-layers and hats and gloves are worthwhile additions to a pack and might make that two-hour belay stint a little less painful. A golden rule is always have a down jacket with you, wherever you go. Having plenty of warm clothes to hand can be a lifesaver in the event of an accident too. Even in some of the more sheltered areas of the quarries, when the wind blows from the wrong direction it goes right through you.

Some of the approaches and walking descents down from several crags are far more comfortable in trainers than tight climbing shoes. So carry your shoes on the back of your harness or in a small rucksack.

A helmet is recommend in the quarries whether sport climbing or trad climbing. This is both to protect you in the event of a fall, and in case of loose rock coming from above. Take particular care when pulling onto ledges as there is often a lot of loose rock.

crux

specialist equipment for mountaineering
rucksacks . shelters . sleeping bags . apparel

available in Llanberis at

V12 Outdoor
Joe Brown's

The routes in this book are given one of two different grades depending on whether they are a trad route, or a sport route. The table to the right gives a rough comparison of the sport and trad grade with other international grading systems. **Trad routes** are where gear is mostly carried by the lead climber and is hand placed. Many trad routes on slate have some fixed gear from bolts or pegs. **Sport routes** are where all the protection is given by fixed bolts in the rock.

British Trad Grade

1) **Adjectival grade (Diff, VDiff, Severe, Hard Severe (HS), Very Severe (VS), Hard Very Severe (HVS), E1, E2, ... to E10).**
An overall picture of the route including how well protected it is, how sustained and a general indication of the level of difficulty of the whole route.
2) **Technical grade (4a, 4b, 4c,..... to 7b).**
The difficulty of the hardest single move, or short section.

Sport Grade

The sport grade is a measure of how hard it is going to be to get up a certain section of rock. It makes no attempt to tell you how hard the hardest move is, nor how scary a route is.

Colour Coding

The routes are all given a colour-coded dot corresponding to a grade band. The colour represents a level that a climber should be happy at, hence sport routes tend to be technically harder than the equivalent coloured trad routes because the climber doesn't need to worry about the protection.

❶ - Up to Severe / Up to 4+
Mostly good for beginners and those wanting an easy life.

❷ - HS to HVS / 5 to 6a+
General ticking routes for those with more experience.

❸ - E1 to E3 / 6b to 7a
Routes for the experienced climber.

❹ - E4 or 7a+ and above
The really hard stuff.

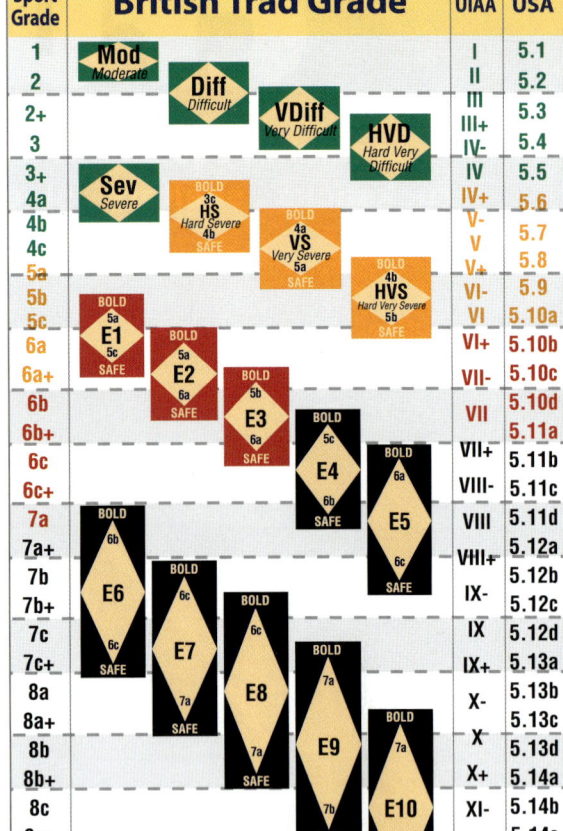

Sport Grade	British Trad Grade	UIAA	USA
1	Mod (Moderate)	I	5.1
2	Diff (Difficult)	II	5.2
2+		III-	5.3
3	VDiff (Very Difficult)	III+	5.4
3+	Sev (Severe) / HVD (Hard Very Difficult)	IV	5.5
4a	HS (Hard Severe) 3c, 4b	IV+	5.6
4b		V-	5.7
4c	VS (Very Severe) 4a, 5a	V	5.8
5a	HVS (Hard Very Severe) 4b, 5b	V+	5.9
5b		VI-	5.10a
5c	E1 5c	VI	5.10b
6a		VI+	5.10c
6a+	E2 6a	VII-	5.10d
6b	E3 5b, 6a	VII	5.11a
6b+		VII+	5.11b
6c	E4 5c, 6b	VIII-	5.11c
6c+		VIII	5.11d
7a	E5 6a, 6c	VIII+	5.12a
7a+		IX-	5.12b
7b	E6 6b, 6c	IX	5.12c
7b+		IX+	5.12d
7c	E7 6c	X-	5.13a
7c+		X	5.13b
8a	E8 7a	X+	5.13c
8a+			5.13d
8b	E9 7a, 7a	XI-	5.14a
8b+			5.14b
8c	E10 7b, 7b	XI	5.14c
8c+		XI+	5.14d
9a			5.15a
9a+			

(Trad grade boxes marked BOLD / SAFE indicate the protection quality of each grade.)

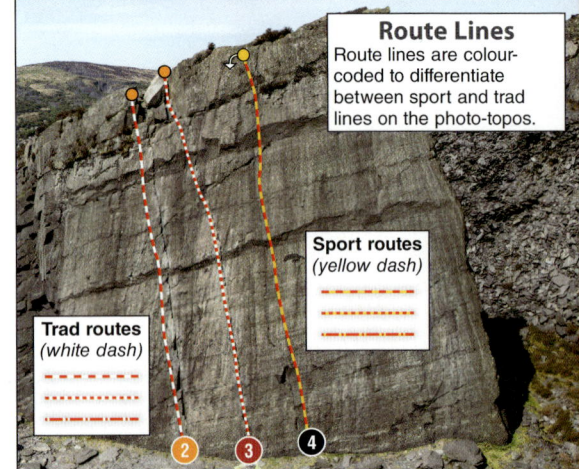

Route Lines
Route lines are colour-coded to differentiate between sport and trad lines on the photo-topos.

Sport routes (yellow dash)

Trad routes (white dash)

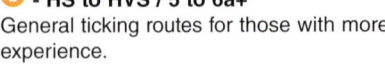

Bus Stop Quarry · Dali's Hole · California · Australia · Serengeti · Never Never Land · Twll Mawr · Mordor - Lost World · Vivian Quarry · Rainbow Slab Area · Snakes and Ladders · Outlying

Bolting in the slate quarries is maintained by a dedicated team of local activists, including the author of this book. This is a time-consuming task since it has been nearly 30 years since the original routes were first bolted and some of the new sport routes have become so popular that lower-offs have needed replacing after just 7 years of use!

A collection of some of the original 6-8mm bolts from the 1980s.

Despite this effort to make the fixed equipment safe, it is worth remembering that bolts can become loose and suffer from rock falls. A further issue on slate has been that the action of lowering off expansion bolts on very popular routes have caused the holes to become oval over time, which makes the bolts move from side to side and then eventually in and out. An effort has been made to place at least one resin anchor where possible on popular lower-offs, but care is needed since not all lower-offs have been replaced so far.

How can you help?

Much of this work is supported by the North Wales Bolt Fund which is run entirely on voluntary donations both of money and time. The main way to help is by making a donation to the North Wales Bolt Fund. The simple gesture of a £10 note in one of the collecting tins in the climbing shops each time you go clipping bolts in North Wales can go a long way to providing the necessary funding. You can also do this online through **UKBoltFund.org**.

If you want to get more involved, there is always a need for volunteers to help with the hard work. Bolting is a difficult and time-consuming activity. If you are an experienced climber, or have a background in rope access, you could be a real asset to supporting the bolting effort in North Wales.

Rockfax supports the bolting efforts in North Wales by providing point-of-sale donations on the Rockfax website and making a financial contribution from sales made direct from the Rockfax website. UKBoltFund.org is maintained by UKClimbing/Rockfax.

Bus Stop Quarry

Dali's Hole

California

Australia

Serengeti

Never Never Land

Twll Mawr

Mordor - Lost World

Vivian Quarry

Rainbow Slab Area

Snakes and Ladders

Outlying

A local instructor getting some professional development in placing bolts. A partnership was set up between the North Wales Bolt Fund (NWBF) and some local instructors to help re-equip the lower-offs on The Sidings which had worn out after only seven years of use. The instructors were shown how to place resin bolts on lower-off anchors and then equalise this with a chain maillion and ring. This is the type of work that requires huge amounts of effort from volunteers, so if you fancy helping re-equip the quarries (or elsewhere in the North Wales area), contact the NWBF, or the BMC regional group.

Photo Page

E8
- *** The Quarryman . . . . *154* . . . 167
- *** Coeur De Lion 167

E7
- *** Dawes of Perception 206
- *** Blockhead 167
- *** Raped By Affection. 247
- ** My Halo 133

E6
- *** The Big Sur 76
- ** Stiff Syd's Cap . . . . *249* . . . 247
- ** Naked Before the Beast 244
- *** Flashdance/Belldance 214
- *** The Wonderful World of Walt Disney 168
- ** Scare City 52
- ** Menstrual Gossip. 214
- ** The Cure for a Sick Mind . . . . *11* . . . 244
- *** Senior Citizen Smith 304
- ** Love Minus Zero 210
- *** Released From Treatment 248
- ** For Whom the Bell Tolls 214
- *** Rainbow of Recalcitrance 248
- ** Dwarf in the Toilet. 209

E5
- *** Shazalzabon 241
- *** Never Never Land 146
- ** The Machine in the Ghost 146
- *** Cystitis By Proxy. . . . . *249* . . . 247
- ** Out of Africa 133
- *** Heading the Shot . . . . *41, 131* . . . 133
- *** Major Headstress 241
- *** Splitstream . . . . *30* . . . 247
- ** Slug Club Special. 133
- *** The Bridge Across Forever. 304
- ** The Book of Brilliant Things 133
- *** Dope on a Rope. . . . . *201* . . . 198
- ** The Long and Winding Road 188
- ** Belldance 214
- ** The Hobbit 72
- ** Unpaid Bills 74
- *** Poetry Pink 244
- *** Central Sadness. 76
- ** Flashdance 214
- ** Tentative Decisions 135
- ** Big Wall Party. 241
- ** Dwarf Shortage 76
- *** Bathtime. 198
- ** Over the Rainbow 252
- *** Waves of Inspiration . . . . *75* . . . 76

E4
- ** The Colour Purple (Twll Mawr). 163
- ** Silver Shadow 265
- ** Moving Being 206
- ** Swan Hunter 95
- ** Shtimuli 72
- ** Menai Vice 95
- *** Jack of Shadows 241
- *** Short Stories 146
- ** Young and Easy Under the Apple Boughs. 212
- *** Ride the Wild Surf . . . . *242* . . . 241
- ** Scheherezade 146
- ** Remain in Light 135
- *** Manatese 268
- ** Soap on a Rope. 198
- ** Men of Leisure 112
- ** Never as Sweet 217
- ** Liquid Armbar. 297
- ** The Sweetest Taboo. 217
- ** The Gorbals 110
- *** Great Balls of Fire 241
- ** The Wow Wow 86
- *** Scarlet Runner 55

- *** The Bone People 304
- *** The Mau Mau. 265
- ** Celestial Inferno 270

E3
- ** The Mancer Direct 297
- *** Colossus 241
- *** Dinorwig Unconquerable 188
- *** Comes the Dervish . . . . *9* . . . 214
- ** See You Bruce 110
- ** Purple Haze 163
- ** Major Whiff 224
- ** Is it a Crime? 217
- ** Ritter Sport. . . . . *222* . . . 224
- ** Goose Creature . . . . *cover* . . . 95
- ** Kubla Khan. 146
- ** Men at Work. 110
- ** Between Here and Now. 96
- *** Off the Beaten Track. . . . . *80, 89* . . . 96

E2
- *** Lethal Injection 163
- *** Pull My Daisy . . . . *230* . . . 244
- ** Turn of the Century 90
- ** The Turkey Chant. . . . . *205* . . . 209
- ** Psychotherapy . . . . *202* . . . 200
- ** Cracking Up 301
- ** Chariots of Fire 270
- ** Rhyfelwr 163
- ** Sylvanian Waters 120
- *** German Schoolgirl . . . . *263* . . . 265
- ** Massambula. . . . . *46* . . . 55
- ** The Madness 224
- ** Solstice Direct 52
- ** Holy, Holy, Holy . . . . *58* . . . 62
- ** The Great Curve 135
- ** Two Tone 224
- *** Last Tango in Peris. 214
- ** Slippery People 135
- ** Angel on Fire 270
- ** Too Bald to Be Bold 209
- ** Bise-Mon-Cul 95

E1
- ** John Verybiglongwords 62
- ** The Monster Kitten . . . . *192* . . . 206
- ** Patellaectomy 152
- ** Gnat Attack. 55
- ** Fool's Gold 52
- ** The Black Gates. 188
- ** Red and Yellow and Pink and Green, Orange. 244
- *** Californian Arete 72
- ** Bela Lugosi is Dead. . . . . *22, 239* . . . 238
- ** Seams the Same . . . . *129, 136* . . . 133
- ** Ruby Marlee Meets Dr Holingsworth 108
- *** Looning the Tube . . . . *4, 78* . . . 95
- ** Combat Rock 163
- ** Alive and Kicking . . . . *22* . . . 238

HVS
- ** Solstice. 52
- ** Razorback 106
- ** Digital Delectation 108
- ** Pandora Plays Sax. 303

VS
- ** Zambesi 62
- ** Mad Dog of the West 108
- ** Equinox 52
- ** Seamstress . . . . *124* . . . 133

M
- *** Snakes and Ladders - The Lost World. . . . . *278* . . . 285
- ** Snakes and Ladders - Australia 283

Graded Lists are compiled from votes on UKClimbing Logbooks.

Bus Stop Quarry · Dali's Hole · California · Australia · Serengeti · Never Never Land · Twll Mawr · Mordor - Lost World · Vivian Quarry · Rainbow Slab Area · Snakes and Ladders · Outlying

Bus Stop Quarry

Dali's Hole

California

Australia

Serengeti

Never Never Land

Twll Mawr

Mordor - Lost World

Vivian Quarry

Rainbow Slab Area

Snakes and Ladders;

Outlying

Tom Livingstone on the brilliant *Heading the Shot* (E5 6b) - *p.132* - on the Seamstress Slab.

Bus Stop Quarry | Dali's Hole | California | Australia | Serengeti | Never Never Land | Twll Mawr | Mordor - Lost World | Vivian Quarry | Rainbow Slab Area | Snakes and Ladders | Outlying

9a
- ☐ *** Meltdown . . . . *157* . . 167

8b+
- ☐ *** The Very Big and the Very Small . . . . *13* . . 244

8b
- ☐ *** Bungles Arete 244
- ☐ ** The New Slatesman . . . . *261* . . 260
- ☐ *** The Serpent Vein 122

8a+
- ☐ ** The Dark Tower 122
- ☐ ** Menopausal Discharge 212

8a
- ☐ ** The Medium 133
- ☐ *** Manic Strain 212
- ☐ *** Cwms the Dogfish 252
- ☐ *** The Dark Half 270
- ☐ *** Bobby's Groove 204

7c+
- ☐ ** Spong 265
- ☐ ** Shoreline 54
- ☐ ** The Mu Mu 257

7c
- ☐ *** Heatseeker 270
- ☐ *** Gin Palace . . . . *213* . . 212
- ☐ *** Chitra 254
- ☐ *** Forsinain Motspur 52
- ☐ *** The Wall Within . . . . *179* . . 186
- ☐ ** Cavity Wall 149

7b+
- ☐ ** Raisin Frumpsnoot 52
- ☐ *** True Clip 265
- ☐ ** Beltane 52
- ☐ *** The Rock Bottom Line 168
- ☐ ** Glasgow Kiss 110
- ☐ ** Satisfying Frank Bruno 259
- ☐ ** Two Bolts or Not to Be 204
- ☐ ** Child's Play 212

7b
- ☐ ** Room with a View 117
- ☐ ** Cig-Arete 257
- ☐ ** Where are my Sensible Shoes? 257
- ☐ ** Race Against the Pump 54
- ☐ ** Ziplock 106

7a+
- ☐ *** Synthetic Life 304
- ☐ *** Black Hole Sun 164
- ☐ ** Slatebite 104
- ☐ ** Rock Yoga 108
- ☐ ** Slabaholics Anonymous 110
- ☐ *** Geordie War Cry 54
- ☐ ** Welcome to the Machine 72
- ☐ ** Cirith Ungol 120

7a
- ☐ ** Tân y Ddraig 170
- ☐ ** L'Allumette 266
- ☐ ** Road to Botany Bay 120
- ☐ ** Honorary Limestone 274
- ☐ ** Saruman 188
- ☐ ** Taken Over By Department 'C' 257
- ☐ ** Beanstalk 106
- ☐ ** Black Holes and Revelations 164
- ☐ ** Walk this way 120
- ☐ ** Great Bores of Today 86
- ☐ ** Chinook Arete 274
- ☐ ** Impact Zone 120
- ☐ *** Supermassive Black Hole . . . . *161* . . 164
- ☐ ** Set the Controls for the Heart of the Sun 164

6c+
- ☐ ** State of the Heart 143
- ☐ ** Gerbil Abuse 253
- ☐ ** Long in the Twll/The North Will Rise Again 168
- ☐ ** The Hand of Morlock 301
- ☐ ** The Porphyry Chair 183
- ☐ ** Ayers and Graces 119
- ☐ ** Minder 64
- ☐ ** The Carbon Stage 146
- ☐ *** Zut Alors 99
- ☐ ** Lucky Break 118

6c
- ☐ ** Wave Rock 120
- ☐ ** The Desolation of Smaug! 170
- ☐ *** G'Day Arete . . . . *123* . . 120
- ☐ ** Crazy Train 96
- ☐ ** Sleight of Hand 257
- ☐ ** Y Rhaffwr 99
- ☐ ** Island of Stability 174
- ☐ ** Manimal . . . . *227* . . 218

6b+
- ☐ ** A Little Pail 152
- ☐ ** Gadaffi Duck 90
- ☐ ** Truffle Hunter's Roof . . . . *221* . . 220
- ☐ ** Put it on the Slate Waiter 108
- ☐ ** Olympic Torch 110
- ☐ ** A Grand Day Out 114
- ☐ *** Slab Rog 110
- ☐ ** No Feart of the Boaby 112
- ☐ ** Red Throated Diver 96
- ☐ ** Scarface Claw 96

6b
- ☐ ** Imagine Dragons . . . . *3* . . 164
- ☐ ** A Brucie Bonus 118
- ☐ ** To Infinity and Beyond! 120
- ☐ ** Slab Slayer 108
- ☐ ** Teenage Dreams 273

6a+
- ☐ ** Harder than it Looks 104
- ☐ ** In Loving Memory 100
- ☐ ** Celtic Warrior 273
- ☐ ** Peter Pan 130
- ☐ ** Orangutang Overhang 95
- ☐ ** Journey to the Centre of the Earth 183
- ☐ ** Obsession 148
- ☐ ** Kata Tjuta Rib 119
- ☐ ** Horse Latitudes . . . . *22, 232* . . 238
- ☐ ** Gwion's Groove 257

6a
- ☐ ** The Gravity Hill . . . . *185* . . 190
- ☐ ** Overtaken by Department 'C' 257
- ☐ ** The Railway Children 100
- ☐ ** White Tiger 273
- ☐ ** We Speak No Americano! . . . . *68* . . 72
- ☐ ** Fresh Air . . . . *138* . . 143
- ☐ ** Plastic Soldier 108
- ☐ ** Clash of the Titans 108
- ☐ ** Slate Ninja 273

5c
- ☐ ** Carpe Diem 273
- ☐ ** Hawkeye . . . . *140* . . 143
- ☐ ** Operation Zig-Zag 146

5b
- ☐ ** Jugs Bach . . . . *276* . . 274
- ☐ ** Octogenarian 144

5a
- ☐ ** Learning to Fly 144
- ☐ ** A Grand Day Out Pitch 2 100
- ☐ ** Steps of Glory . . . . *19* . . 95

Simon Lake tackling the technical *Cig-Arete* (7b) -
p.132 - in the Rainbow Slab Area. Photo: Matt Stygall

Bus Stop Quarry

Dali's Hole

California

Australia

Serengeti

Never Never Land

Twll Mawr

Mordor - Lost World

Vivian Quarry

Rainbow Slab Area

Snakes and Ladders

Outlying

	Routes	Sport Routes				Trad Routes			
		up to 4c	5a to 6a+	6b to 7a	7a+ up	up to S	HS to HVS	E1 to E3	E4 up
Bus Stop Quarry	55	3	6	5	9	1	7	15	9
Dali's Hole	65	–	2	6	2	1	7	21	8
California	36	1	1	1	2	–	1	9	20
Australia	244	6	46	47	18	2	36	56	29
Serengeti	48	1	3	3	3	–	6	14	18
Never Never Land	65	1	13	15	1	1	3	13	8
Twll Mawr	69	–	1	11	7	–	3	19	26
Mordor - The Lost World	49	–	13	5	4	–	4	10	13
Vivian Quarry	144	–	2	6	12	–	21	52	49
Rainbow Slab Area	168	1	13	14	25	1	23	43	48
Snakes and Ladders	3	–	–	–	–	2	1	–	–
Outlying — Nant Peris Quarry	6	–	–	–	–	–	–	4	2
Outlying — Gideon Quarries	60	–	2	5	3	–	12	20	15
Outlying — Fachwen Quarries	7	–	–	–	–	–	2	5	–
Outlying — Nantlle Valley	5	–	–	–	–	–	2	1	2
TOTALS	1028	18	113	117	86	8	130	284	247

Approach	Sun	Weather	Multi-pitch	Abseil in	Restrictions	Summary		
1 - 4 min	Sun and shade	Sheltered				Easy access with popular quality trad and sport routes on offer. Great for a quick hit. Some very good bold routes on the big Rippled Slab. Catches plenty of sun and is sheltered.	50	Bus Stop Quarry
16 - 18 min	Sun and shade	Sheltered			Restricted	A small area above an often-dry pool that resembles a Dali painting. Many of the easy sport routes have now been de-bolted giving the area much less appeal. There are still a few good trad routes worth seeking out.	62	Dali's Hole
20 - 22 min	Morning	Sheltered	Multi-pitch			A big hole reached through a tunnel. It is home to one of the finest slabs on slate which has some amazing hard trad challenges. The more shady south wall has some good new sport routes and a bold slate classic.	72	California
18 - 40 min	Sun and shade	Sheltered	Multi-pitch	Abseil in		A vast excavation. It is conveniently supplied with distinct levels giving access to many different walls. Mostly slab climbing with plenty of good sport routes across the grades, and some popular trad climbing as well.	87	
22 - 24 min	Morning	Sheltered				An attractive area with the famous Seamstress Slab and lesser-known Yellow Wall. Mostly trad routes from the mid-to-hard grades. Reasonably sheltered with shade on some walls in the afternoon.	130	Australia
21 - 24 min	Morning	Sheltered				A big slab with several smaller areas around it offering a variety of climbing. Some bold trad slabs, some sport walls, some loose routes and some dry tool routes in one quarry.	143	Serengeti
22 - 38 min	Sun and shade		Multi-pitch	Abseil in		The deepest hole in the quarries with three amazing walls. Some brilliant multi-pitch routes both sport and trad, plus the famous Quarryman Wall with its iconic routes. Difficult access. Most routes are major undertakings.	160	Never Never Land
35 - 55 min	Sun and shade		Multi-pitch	Abseil in		The most remote section of the quarries is prone to rockfalls. It is worth exploring and recent additions have extended the area - The Balcony and The Cutting having good mid-grade sport routes.	182	Twll Mawr
2 - 30 min	Sun and shade	Sheltered	Multi-pitch	Abseil in	Restricted	A famous quarry in clear view of Llanberis and with slate's most iconic route, *Comes the Dervish*. Easy access and plenty to explore on the different levels. Mostly trad climbing but some hard sport as well.	197	Mordor - Lost World
20 - 35 min	Sun and shade	Sheltered		Abseil in		A vast area with some brilliant routes and the Rainbow - one of the finest slabs on British rock. Plenty of variety across the grades, but the real quality is in the hard trad routes which are world class.	238	
20 min	Sun and shade					This popular tour takes in several of the quarries by way of ladders, abseils, walking and tunnels. It can be done in different sections and is a good wet weather activity for experienced climbers.	282	Vivian Quarry
20 min	Not much sun					A poor quarry above Nant Peris with some old routes that see little attention. Much loose rock, best avoided.	289	
10 - 25 min	Sun and shade	Sheltered	Multi-pitch	Abseil in		A smaller complex of quarries to the south of Llanberis. Four main holes with a small set of routes each. The biggest Gideon Quarry has two excellent walls and is worth a look for any mid-to-hard grade trad climber.	297	Snakes and Ladders Rainbow Slab Area
5 - 20 min	Sun and shade					Four small quarries above the lakeside railway. Overgrown with loose rock and nothing of any real quality.	309	
2 - 14 min	Morning	Sheltered		Abseil in		An area further to the south near the famous Dorethea Quarry pool. A few routes but nothing of note. Possible potential for new routes only. Popular with scuba divers.	311	Outlying

Faded symbol means that only some of the routes - are multi-pitch / require abseil approach / restricted

Bus Stop Quarry

Dali's Hole

California

Australia

Serengeti

Never Never Land

Twll Mawr

Mordor - Lost World

Vivian Quarry

Rainbow Slab Area

Snakes and Ladders

Outlying

The bold and run-out finale to *Massambula* (E2 5b) - *p.54*.
This slab captures something of the original slateheads'
minimalistic bolting! Though most of the routes are within
the physical limits of most climbers, it is the head game on
the run-out that determines success.

Bus Stop Quarry

Bus Stop Quarry

Dali's Hole

California

Australia

Serengeti

Never Never Land

Twll Mawr

Mordor - Lost World

Vivian Quarry

Rainbow Slab Area

Snakes and Ladders

Outlying

	No star	✪	✪✪	✪✪✪
Mod to S / 4c	1	3	-	-
HS-HVS / 5a-6a+	6	5	2	-
E1-E3 / 6b-7a	8	8	4	-
E4 / 7a+ and up	2	7	6	3

One of the more popular areas in the Upper Dinorwig Quarries, Bus Stop Quarry offers a variety of climbing styles. These range from the great trad line of *Fool's Gold*, through the run-out 'traditionally' bolted routes on the Rippled Slab, to sport routes both easy and hard. While previous generations were introduced to slate climbing by top roping *Equinox* and *Solstice*, today's climber often experiences the sport routes *First Stop*, *Jagged Face* or *Comfort Zone* before venturing deeper into the quarries. New sport routes such as these have revitalised slate climbing, also allowing climbers to master the skills required safely before graduating to the run-out slabs of *Scarlet Runner*, *Massambula* and *Gnat Attack*.

For the mid-grade sport climber, there are a few 6th grade routes around such as *Bosch Stop*, *Wizz Bang* and *My Hovercraft...* In the 7th grade are the brilliant *Geordie War Cry*, *Beltane* and *Forsinain Motspur*. As such, Bus Stop Quarry really does seem to have something for everyone, which, combined with ease of access, has made it one of the most frequented areas on slate.

Conditions

The quarry has a mainly southerly aspect - at least one area will be in the sun. Some of the routes suffer from seepage due to the vegetation above. The worst affected are *Massambula* and *Geordie War Cry,* two of the area's classics.

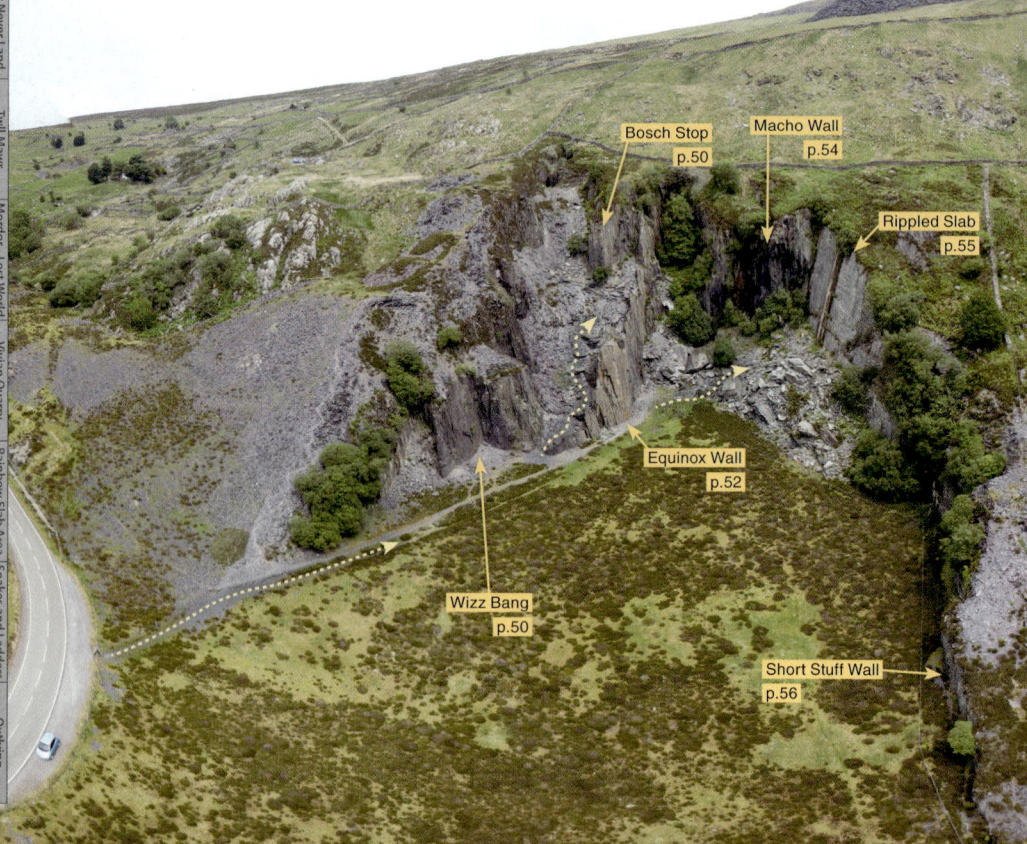

Bosch Stop p.50

Macho Wall p.54

Rippled Slab p.55

Equinox Wall p.52

Wizz Bang p.50

Short Stuff Wall p.56

Bus Stop Quarry | Dali's Hole | California | Australia | Serengeti | Never Never Land | Twll Mawr | Mordor - Lost World | Vivian Quarry | Rainbow Slab Area | Snakes and Ladders | Outlying

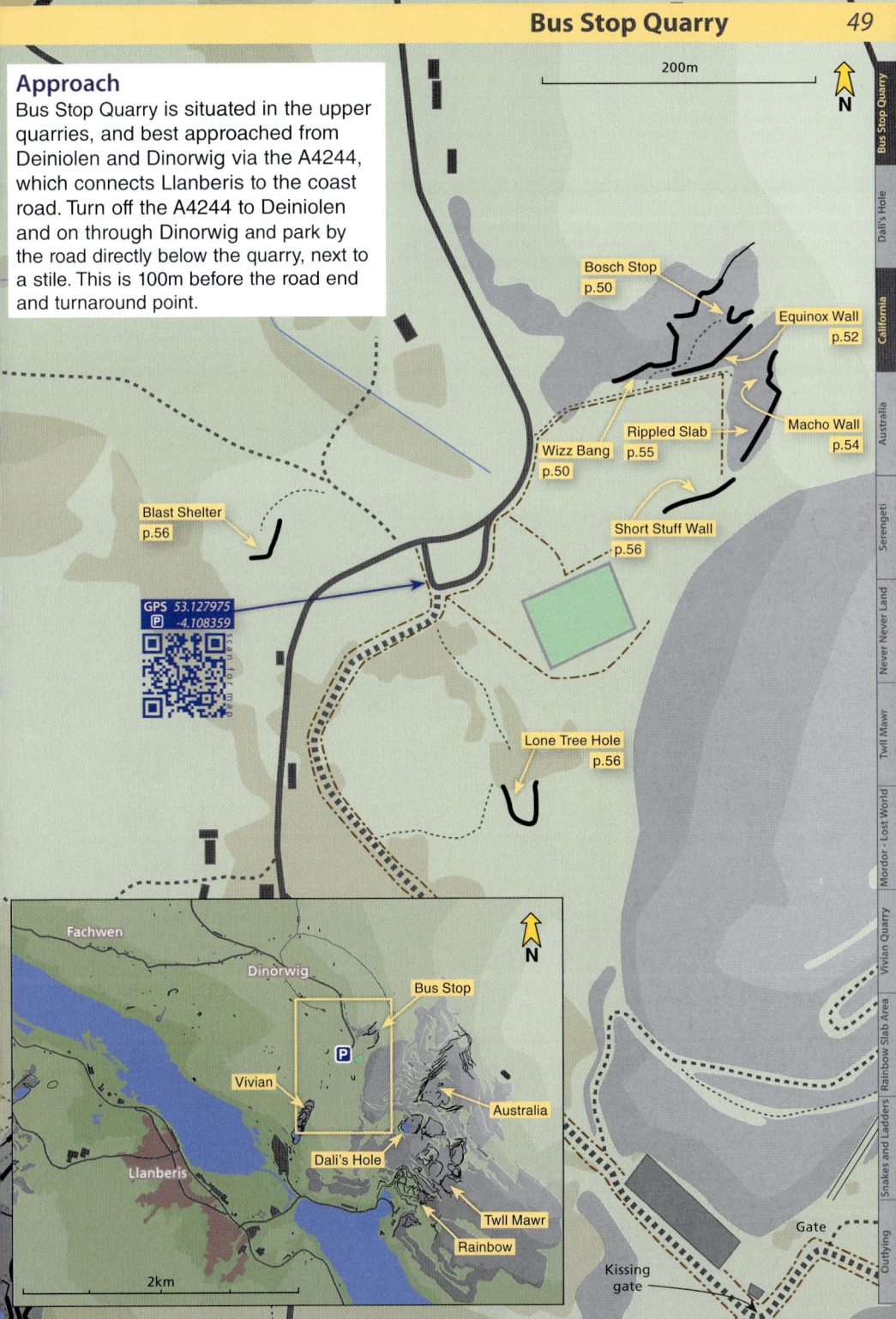

Approach

Bus Stop Quarry is situated in the upper quarries, and best approached from Deiniolen and Dinorwig via the A4244, which connects Llanberis to the coast road. Turn off the A4244 to Deiniolen and on through Dinorwig and park by the road directly below the quarry, next to a stile. This is 100m before the road end and turnaround point.

200m

N

Bosch Stop
p.50

Equinox Wall
p.52

Macho Wall
p.54

Rippled Slab
p.55

Wizz Bang
p.50

Short Stuff Wall
p.56

Blast Shelter
p.56

GPS 53.127975
P -4.108359
scan for map

Lone Tree Hole
p.56

Fachwen

Dinorwig

Bus Stop

P

Vivian

Australia

Dali's Hole

Llanberis

Twll Mawr

Rainbow

N

Kissing gate

Gate

2km

Bus Stop Quarry
Dali's Hole
California
Australia
Serengeti
Never Never Land
Twll Mawr
Mordor - Lost World
Vivian Quarry
Rainbow Slab Area
Snakes and Ladders
Outlying

Bus Stop Quarry

Dali's Hole

California

Australia

Serengeti

Never Never Land

Twll Mawr

Mordor - Lost World

Vivian Quarry

Rainbow Slab Area

Snakes and Ladders

Outlying

Wizz Bang to Bosch Stop

The pleasant buttress on the left as you approach the quarry has lots of easy sport routes, as well as the extended bolted boulder problem of *Wizz Bang* for those wanting something more challenging.

Approach (map p.49, overview p.48) - From the stile, follow the fence up for 30m until below the crag.

🚫 **Access -** Check the BMC RAD, as nesting ravens can mean there are temporary restrictions from time to time. A notice may be displayed when this is the case.

1 First Stop . . . . 🔟 ⬜ 5a
A pleasant and easy route.
FA. Colin Goodey, S.Trainer 8.10.2009

2 Septuagenarian . . . . 🅱️ ⬜ 6a
Sadly now a poor route that has seen a rockfall(s). The lower-off is now in a potentially dangerous state.
FA. Colin Goodey, Sue Goodey 11.8.2009

3 Mudslide Slim . . . . 🔟 🅱️ ⬜ HS 4a
A trad climb up the corner to the lower-off.
FA. Franco Ferrero, Donald King 5.9.1986

4 Wizz Bang . . . . 🔟 ⬜ 6c
A highball boulder problem with bolts. It sees many failures due to most people following the more obvious line to a dead end.
FA. Craig Smith, Paul Doyle 28.1.1994

5 The Big Easy . . . . 🔟 🧗 ⬜ 4b
A pleasant route up the left edge of the slab.
FA. Phil Targett 2.3.2008

6 Jagged Face . . . . 🔟 🧗 ⬜ 4a
A more popular and logical line than its neighbour.
Photo on p.57.
FA. Martin Hurst, Bret Wedley, Timothy Muller, Michael Hurst 21.5.2008

7 Comfort Zone . . . . 🔟 ⬜ 5a
A hard start leads to easy climbing up the stairs to a lower-off.
FA. Colin Goodey, Sue Goodey 8.10.2009

8 Finatic . . . . 🔟 ⬜ 6c
At the back of the bay. Take a line between two fins of rock, passing three bolts, to a lower-off.
FA. Ian Lloyd-Jones, Phil Targett 15.12.2007

14m

9 Bish Bash Bosch . . . . . . ⬡ 🔧 ▭ **6a+**
A rather testing climb, though not as testing as its neighbour.
FA. Ian Lloyd-Jones 14.12.2007

10 Bosch Stop Quarry . . . . . ⬡ 🔧 ▭ **6a+**
Tricky moves.
FA. Ian Lloyd-Jones 13.12.2007

11 Jenga . . . . ⬡ ▭ **4c**
Head round to the right from *Bish Bash Bosch* and climb the
bolted corner. High above the quarry and with good climbing.
FA. Ian Lloyd-Jones 13.12.2007

Equinox Wall
p.52

Bus Stop Quarry

Dali's Hole

California

Australia

Serengeti

Never Never Land

Twll Mawr

Mordor - Lost World

Vivian Quarry

Rainbow Slab Area

Snakes and Ladders

Outlying

Equinox Wall

A great little buttress with a variety of excellent trad and sport routes. The crag gets the sun until the evening. *Fool's Gold*, *Equinox* and *Solstice* are all classic and reasonable trad routes, whilst *Scare City* and *1000 Tons...* are real slate testpieces. The recently developed *Beltane* and *Raisin Frumpsnoot* are perfect sporting companions to *Forsinain Motspur*.

Approach (map p.49, overview p.48) - From the stile, follow the fence up to the bottom of the crag.

Descent - From the top of your route either lower off or walk to the top of *Solstice* and *Equinox* and follow a path back left to the base of the crag.

Walk back down

18m

Dali's Hole
California
Australia
Serengeti
Never Never Land
Twll Mawr
Mordor - Lost World
Vivian Quarry
Rainbow Slab Area
Snakes and Ladders
Outlying

1 Guillotine . . . . HVS 4c
Aptly named. Climb the left-slanting flaky crack 3m left of *Fool's Gold*. Follow this to the top of a pinnacle, then move right to a crack/groove and up to a ledge. Move left gingerly to escape.
FA. Terry Taylor, Alan Whittall 18.6.1985

2 Wusty Woof. E1 5c
Follows *Fool's Gold* to the roof and finish up left over loose terrain.
FA. Al George, Terry Taylor 23.6.1985

3 Fool's Gold E1 5c
Climb the groove just left of the thin crack that leads to the roof. Move onto the arete and make a hard but well-protected pull into the crack, then power up to the small ledge. Follow the crack more easily to a two-bolt belay on the ledge.
FA. Phil George, Al George 24.6.1985

4 1000 Tons of Chicken Shit. . . E5 6a
An interesting flake feature 4m right of *Fool's Gold*. Climb up around the blunt arete to gain the thin flake and a spike (first real gear). Follow the flake left into *Fool's Gold* and finish up this.
FA. Stevie Haston (solo) 10.6.1986

5 Scare City E6 6a
A good route, but it is poorly protected until you reach the letter box at two-thirds height. Start as for *1000 Tons...* and follow this to the spike. Move up and right, past very poor gear, onto the wall to gain a prominent letter box - good small cams. Head up and slightly left to a bold finish.
FA. Tony Kay, Paul Pritchard 28.9.1987

6 Raisin Frumpsnoot . . . . 7b+
A desperate and thin route up the blunt rib to a small overlap. Above, it joins the last few hard moves of *Forsinain Motspur*.
FA. Adam Wainwright 5.5.2007

7 Forsinain Motspur Direct . . . 7c+
Start at the left-hand side of the small roof. A hard boulder problem (f7A+) leads to the first bolt, then continue up the route as normal.
FA. Calum Muskett 5.2010

8 Forsinain Motspur Superdirect 8a
Start as for *Forsinain Motspur Direct*. Clip the right-hand bolt on the headwall and then climb the final section of *Beltane*.
FA. Calum Muskett 16.10.2010

9 Forsinain Motspur 7c
A powerful and technical route that has some great climbing weaving between the bolts. Gain the first bolt from the left. From an undercut in the overlap, make a powerful move up and right to a side-pull. Big moves on good holds lead to the second roof (possible knee bar/rest). Move up to the bolts on the headwall and then traverse left to a hard pull onto a ledge. A desperate slab move leads up to the lower-off.
FA. Trevor Hodgson, S.Jones 23.6.1988

10 Jól . . . . 8a+
Climb to the first bolt on *Forsinain Motspur*, and then tackle a short boulder problem (f7B) on crimps to gain *Beltane*, which is followed to the top.
FA. Calum Muskett 2014

11 Beltane . . . . 7b+
Easier and better than *Raisin Frumpsnoot*, but it still packs a big punch. Maybe 7b for the tall.
FA. Adam Wainwright 30.5.2007

12 Solstice . . . . HVS 5a
Start below the crack and climb easily up to a small ledge. Above is a sustained section of laybacking to reach a good hold. From here, follow the flake-line rightwards more easily to a junction with *Equinox*. It is best finished up the crack leading up and left, which was the original finish to *Equinox*.
FA. Al George, Terry Taylor 23.6.1985

13 Solstice Direct. E2 5c
Follow *Solstice* to where it moves right after its crux and make a tough pull to gain a hanging groove. Follow this to the top via some good moves and small gear.

14 Equinox Direct. E1 5a
A poor eliminate up the centre of the wall. Climb up to the left of the ledge at 3m on *Equinox*, then make a committing move to climb the line of small loose holds. These lead directly up, to join *Equinox* and *Solstice* where they meet.

15 Equinox . . . . VS 4c
Start below the line of weakness that leads diagonally up and left across the wall. Climb this easily with very little in the way of obvious gear until near the top. From the junction with *Solstice*, step right and finish on large positive holds (this was the original finish to *Solstice*).
FA. Terry Taylor, Al George 24.6.1985

16 Sterling Silver E2 5c
Climb a series of cracks and flakes right of *Solstice* and *Equinox*. A route that demands concentration as many of the flakes are of questionable attachment to the rest of the crag. It used to get two stars but it is no longer recommended after some rockfall activity in recent years.
FA. J.Banks, L.Naylor, D.Clark 4.7.1986

17 Demolition Derby. E1 5a
A poor route that goes up the slab 8m right of *Sterling Silver*. Pick your way up the slightly more solid bits of rubble, or climb any one of the more appealing routes in this quarry!
FA. Paul Jenkinson, Mark Boniface 23.3.1988

18 Equinox Wall Girdle . E6 6b
One of the few crags that was awaiting a girdle has finally got one! Start as for *Fool's Gold* up to the flake of *1000 Tons...*. Traverse right and follow *Scare City* up to the cam slot. Continue across the sport routes at this level with some difficulty before finishing up *Solstice*.
FA. Calum Muskett 10.2013

Bus Stop Quarry
Dali's Hole
California
Australia
Serengeti
Never Never Land
Twll Mawr
Mordor - Lost World
Vivian Quarry
Rainbow Slab Area
Snakes and Ladders
Outlying

Bus Stop Quarry

Doll's Hole

California

Australia

Serengeti

Never Never Land

Twll Mawr

Mordor - Lost World

Vivian Quarry

Rainbow Slab Area

Snakes and Ladders

Outlying

❶ Hasta La Vista Baby . . . . ☆1   **E3 6a**
Start up the arete in order to reach the prominent crack. Follow the crack to a large cleft and a lower-off.
FA. Francis Haden, Malcolm Davies 18.7.1994

❷ Race Against the Pump. . ☆2   **7b**
Start up *Hasta La Vista Baby* and gain the crack. Place some cams here and move right to gain the first bolt. Reaching the next bolt is problematic, but it is essential to clip it as it protects the desperate and powerful crux. Carry on up past a third bolt to reach the lower-off.
FA. Francis Haden 21.7.1994

❸ Shoreline . . . . ☆2   **7c+**
The direct version of *Geordie War Cry* is sadly often damp and has not been re-equipped. It does look good though.
FA. Stevie Haston 4.1990

❹ Geordie War Cry . ☆3   **7a+**
Steep, pumpy and awesome. This route takes on the steeper side of slate, and it is obligatory to shout 'Whey aye man' from the lower-off, or scream in frustration should you fail. Start up either the slab or the steep wall, to reach a bolt at the top of the slab. An exciting traverse right gains the niche, before a hard move left past another bolt provides the first crux and leads to the pumpy headwall. From a large flat hold, make a difficult move up and right to the arete before the heading back left to the lower-off.
FA. Bill Wayman, Dave Kirton, Martin Barnicott 11.10.1987

❺ Mildly Macho . . . . ☆1   **E5 6b**
A seriously macho leader (or a psychopath) is required for this one. Start 5m left of the damp corner where Macho Wall and Rippled Slab meet. Head up the groove and hand traverse right onto a ledge. Take the groove up to the large loose flake, then climb the ferocious finger-crack to another 'booming' flake. Scary moves on slate fins attain the top via corniced vegetation.
FA. Stevie Haston, G.Jones 5.1987

Rippled Slab

❻ Scarlet Runner Direct
. . . . ☆1   **E3 6a**
A safer but harder direct start to *Scarlet Runner*, although some holds are a little creaky.
FA. Francis Haden, Malcolm Davies 22.7.1994

❼ Scarlet Runner . ☆3   **E4 5c**
A scary route. A bold and nerve-wracking start leads to the first bolt at about 10m - reaching it is only **5b** though! Above, sustained slab climbing weaves between the now ample bolts.
FA. Bill Wayman, Paul Williams 28.6.1985

❽ Breakdance . . . .   **VS 4a**
The rising traverse line across the slab from left to right is not actually that pleasing to climb because of loose and vegetated sections. Start up *Scarlet Runner* and head right along a low break to reach the higher break just after the intersection with *Massambula*. From *Gnat Attack*, continue right through a moss-covered slab to belay on a large rowan tree.
FA. Franco Ferrero, Donald King 12.9.1986

❾ Buzz Stop . . . . ☆1   **E3 6a**
Just left of the line of damp vegetation is a line of bolts that often remains damp. Although bolted, it isn't a sport route. This has also been climbed in winter as a thin ice smear.
FA. Berwin Jones, Pete Trewin 20.6.2002

❿ Virgin on the Ridiculous . . . . ☆1   **E4 6a**
This is virtually overgrown from years of neglect. The moss cornice does little to help. Although this was a good route, it now needs a good clean and a drought to make it climbable.
FA. Bill Wayman, Paul Williams 3.7.1985

⓫ Massambula . . . ☆2   **E2 5b**
Climb up the well-worn slab to the groove and first gear. Move up to reach the break, where more gear can be arranged - a skyhook is particularly good here! Mantel up and traverse the break to the first bolt on the route. Move past this with difficulty to reach the second bolt. Above this the climbing is easy, but you have to run it out a long way before you find the lower-off.
Photo on p.46.
FA. Paul Williams, Bill Wayman 3.7.1985

Macho Wall
The steep wall is home to the classic *Geordie War Cry*. It suffers from seepage for a few days after rain, but can offer shade for much of the day in hot weather.
Approach (map p.49, overview p.48) - From the stile, follow the fence up to below Equinox Wall, then make your way up one of several indistinct tracks through scree to the base of the routes.
🚫 **Access -** Check with the BMC RAD, as *Hasta La Vista Baby* and *Race Against The Pump* have previously had a temporary restriction due to nesting ravens. *Geordie War Cry* is not affected.

Rippled Slab

A great slab with several run-out bolted slab climbs including the popular *Massambula*. It suffers from seepage for a few days after rain, but can offer shade for much of the day in hot weather.

Approach (map p.49, overview p.48) - From the stile, follow the fence up to below Equinox Wall, then make your way up one of several indistinct tracks through scree to the base of the routes.

⑫ Meltdown . . . . 🔲 E4 6a
Follow *Gnat Attack* to the ledge and move left along the break to reach the first of two bolts. Climb past these direct to join *Gnat Attack* near its top.
FA. Terry Taylor, A.Burton 28.4.1991

⑬ Walking Out . . . . 🔲 E5 6b
An eliminate up the wall between *Meltdown* and *Gnat Attack*. Climb up and clip the first bolt on *Gnat Attack*, then traverse left to below a blank wall. Climb up between the two routes to reach 'thank god' holds on the foot-traverse of *Gnat Attack*, which is followed to the top.
FA. Jacob Shieldhouse-Hadley 23.4.2015

⑭ Gnat Attack . . . . 🔲 E1 5c
A great introduction to the type of climbing you find on the run-out slabs in the quarries. Solo up to the first bolt (at 12m!), and make a desperate move to reach the second bolt. Above this, a small terrace leads up and left like a stairway to the stars. Enjoy the easy and run-out climbing above until you have a nervous moment moving back right to reach the lower-off.
FA. Andy Newton, R.Newton 31.7.1985

⑮ Blue Horizon . . . . 🔲 S
Another vertical garden. Climb direct to the large rowan tree at the end of *Breakdance*, passing a lone bolt. If someone cleans and re-bolts this line, maybe it will be worth climbing?
FA. Franco Ferrero, Donald King 12.9.1986

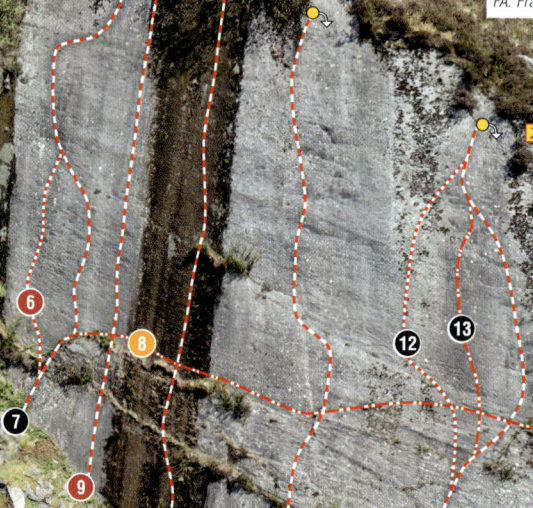

Bus Stop Quarry · Dali's Hole · California · Australia · Serengeti · Never Never Land · Twll Mawr · Mordor - Lost World · Vivian Quarry · Rainbow Slab Area · Snakes and Ladders · Outlying

Short Stuff Wall

This wall to the right of the Rippled Slab is only short but has reasonable climbing.
Approach (map p.49, overview p.48) - Opposite the Bus Stop Wall, gained by walking around from Equinox Wall or straight across from the parking.

Routes have been claimed on the Butterfly Slab down and right of the Rippled Slab. They are completely overgrown. The routes are **Casual Man, E1 5b, The Casual Plan, HVS 5b, Tiny Little Elephants, HS 4a, Nose Bleed Section, E4 5c** (all FA. Jacob Shieldhouse-Hadley 3.2015)

1 My Hovercraft is Full of Eels 6b
The steep broken arete.
FA. Rob Mirfin, Sarah Daniels 22.8.2006

2 Mini Bus Stop 6a
The right arete of the thin groove provides some assistance before the route moves left to the lower-off.
FA. Ian Lloyd-Jones, Lucy Body, Ian Martin 22.5.2007

3 Fridge .... 6b+
The technical little groove leads to a lower-off.
FA. Paul Doyle, Craig Smith 26.2.1993

4 Freezer................. 6b+
Short and sweet apparently, but mostly just short. Climb up to the overlap and move onto the 'headwall' to a lower-off.
FA. Phil Targett 26.5.2007

Lone Tree Hole

This hole is between the football pitch and the main track into the quarry.
Approach (map p.49, overview p.48) - From the bottom of the field, head into the wooded area on a vague path. Alternatively, walk up the main footpath into the quarries. After 300m (when the path straightens out after a left turn) a path leads into the wooded area towards the hole.

5 So this is Living........... E2 5a
The vegetated slabby left-hand corner of the hole is just right of an unclimbed arete. Climb it to a tricky finish.
FA. Cliff Phillips 8.5.1984

6 Malice In Wonderland E2 5b
The unprotected slab to the right of *So this is Living*.
FA. Will Perrin 1990s

7 As the Sun Sets in the West ... E4 5c
The vegetated right-hand corner of the hole.
FA. Cliff Phillips 8.5.1984

8 Wond .... VS 4c
The blocky arete on the right of the quarry.
FA. Cliff Phillips 8.5.1984

11 Stand to your Rights......... VS 4c
The right-hand corner of the slab.
FA. Cliff Phillips 8.5.1985

Blast Shelter

This small area has a pleasant slab and is much quieter than the main quarry - a nice place for a picnic.
Approach (map p.49, overview p.48) - From the Bus Stop turnaround take the gravel track that leads down an open hillside. Just before the track forks after 100m, take a vague path left into a bay with a blast shelter.

9 Biggles Flies Undone E1 5b
Start just to the left of the left-leaning slab. Follow the edge up to just above a peg where you break out onto the slab before following a grassy crack to the top.
FA. Cliff Phillips 15.5.1985

10 Reclaim Your Mind E3 5c
An eliminate to the crack at the top (first gear). If you are able to place any runners in *Biggles*... then you are too far left.
FA. Jacob Shieldhouse-Hadley 2.6.2015

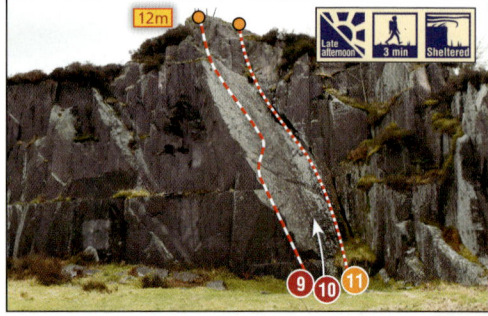

Bus Stop Quarry

Dali's Hole

California

Australia

Serengeti

Never Never Land

Twll Mawr

Mordor - Lost World

Vivian Quarry

Rainbow Slab Area

Snakes and Ladders

Outlying

The modern classic *Jagged Face* (4a) - *p.50* - at Bus Stop Quarry.

Bus Stop Quarry

Dali's Hole

California

Australia

Serengeti

Never Never Land

Twll Mawr

Mordor - Lost World

Vivian Quarry

Rainbow Slab Area

Snakes and Ladders

Outlying

Hazel Robson on the sustained layback crack of *Holy, Holy, Holy* (E2 5c) - *p.63* - in Dali's Hole.
This area was the birthplace of the modern slate sport climbing boom. Sadly it was a victim of its own success and was eventually de-bolted by the climbers that developed most of the routes. Fortunately some of the original lines (like this trad layback) are still climbable.

Dali's Hole

Bus Stop Quarry

Dali's Hole

California

Australia

Serengeti

Never Never Land

Twll Mawr

Mordor - Lost World

Vivian Quarry

Rainbow Slab Area

Snakes and Ladders

Outlying

	No star	✹1	✹2	✹3
Mod to S / 4c	1	-	-	-
HS-HVS / 5a-6a+	5	3	1	-
E1-E3 / 6b-7a	12	10	4	-
E4 / 7a+ and up	3	7	1	-

Dali's Hole became synonymous with easy sport climbing as soon as it was developed, quickly acquiring the nickname 'Costa del Dali'. Sadly the area became a victim of its own success and the crowds turned this into an access flashpoint which has ended with many routes being de-bolted. We have included all the routes here for the record but many are obsolete now. Despite this, there are still some good routes in this area: *John Verybiglongwords* is a great deep water solo in the right conditions; *Zambesi* and *Holy, Holy Holy* offer some great trad climbing; *Launching Pad* is a more old-school run-out slab and *Minder* is a superb sport route on Hidden Wall.

Hop over gate

Up one level

Hidden Wall
p.64

Main Area
p.62

DO NOT
cross this
fence

Path around back
of the hole

Bus Stop Quarry

Dali's Hole

California

Australia

Serengeti

Never Never Land

Twll Mawr

Mordor - Lost World

Vivian Quarry

Rainbow Slab Area

Snakes and Ladders

Outlying

Conditions
The area is sunken and relatively sheltered making it a morning suntrap. There is a section of north-facing wall that offers shade if required.

Access
Only use the described approach. No attempt should be made to climb, damage or cross the fence. Access is very sensitive so please go elsewhere if it is busy.

To Pen Garret hut

Stairs of Cirith Ungol

Australia p.80

Dali's Wall p.65

Tunnel of Love to Australia

Dali's Slab p.64

California Side p.66

Carry on along the path past the tunnel to reach Dali's Hole

Tunnel to California - p.70

Bus Stop Quarry | Dali's Hole | California | Australia | Serengeti | Never Never Land | Twll Mawr | Mordor - Lost World | Vivian Quarry | Rainbow Slab Area | Snakes and Ladders | Outlying

Approach   See map on page 71
Dali's Hole is situated in the upper quarries, and best approached from Deiniolen and Dinorwig via the A4244, which connects Llanberis to the coast road. Turn off the A4244 to Deiniolen and on through Dinorwig to parking at the road end near Bus Stop Quarry. Head along the main track until it opens out by a large cutting shed on the left and continue to a kissing gate by a left bend in the track. Pass through here and follow the main track towards a large incline. Where the track bends right, hop over the gate in front of you and follow the path up and right for one level, Dali's Hole is down and to your right. Traverse around to the opposite side of the hole and follow a small track back down into the hole by a tunnel that leads through to California.

Main Area

Although most of the easier sport routes have been de-bolted, there are still a few trad and sport lines worthy of attention.

Approach (map p.71, overview p.60) - From the kissing gate, walk on to a bend in the track and hop over the gate. Go rightwards towards Dali's Hole and up one level. Follow a track round to the opposite side of the hole, where a small path leads down past the tunnel to California. Continue down until you can walk back across to the wall having completed a circuit of the hole.

🚫 **Access -** Do not cross the big fence. Use only the circular approach described. Most of the sport routes right of *At the Cost of a Rope* have had their hangers removed.

Approach to Lower Tier - *Abseil in to gain the starts. These can be covered when the water is high. Conversely, it is sometimes possible to walk in to the base when the pool is dry.*

❶ A Good Slate Roof/Tribulation to

Bob Marley and Peter Tosh . . . . . 🎗️ ☐ **E3 6a**
Climb the crack that goes through the 'Good Slate' roof to a hold on the left. Turn the bulge and take the crack to a ledge. Move right to another crack and follow this to the top.
FA. (A Good Slate Roof) R.Newcombe, Harold Walmsley 6.1989
FA. (Tribulation...) Mark Boniface, A.Shaw 3.9.1988

❷ Mu Hat Mu Ganja . . . . 🎗️ ☐ **E1 5b**
The corner has two bolts.
FA. Mark Boniface 4.1989

❸ Twm Dre (Monkey on a Stick)

. . . . 🎗️ 🐏 ☐ **E6 6b**
The thin groove high up is the only hope of climbing this blank wall; it gives bold and tricky climbing.
FA. (some aid) Martin Barnicott, Bill Wayman 10.1986
FFA. Shane Ohly, S.Warren 2000

❹ Le Cochon . . . . 🎗️ ☐ **HVS 5b**
The pinnacle that rises above the rim of the hole, adjacent to *Holy, Holy, Holy*. Start from the bottom of the hole and move up past an old bolt, then continue up right to a ledge. Take the crack to the mini tunnel and drop down the far side to belay on the *Holy, Holy, Holy* wall.
FA. A.Maddison, Jonny Martin 29.9.1987

❺ Simion Street . . . . ☐ **E2 5c**
Just left of the prominent fin of *John Verybiglongwords* is a corner with a bolt to its left. Head up to the bolt, move right into the corner and climb past another bolt to the top.
FA. A.Maddison, Jonny Martin 29.9.1987

❻ John Verybiglongwords. . . 🎗️ 🐏 ☐ **E1 5a**
A stunning fin that can be approached by abseiling from near *Holy, Holy, Holy*. When the water level is high, this is an amazing deep water solo.
FA. Paul Williams, Steve Howe 6.10.1986

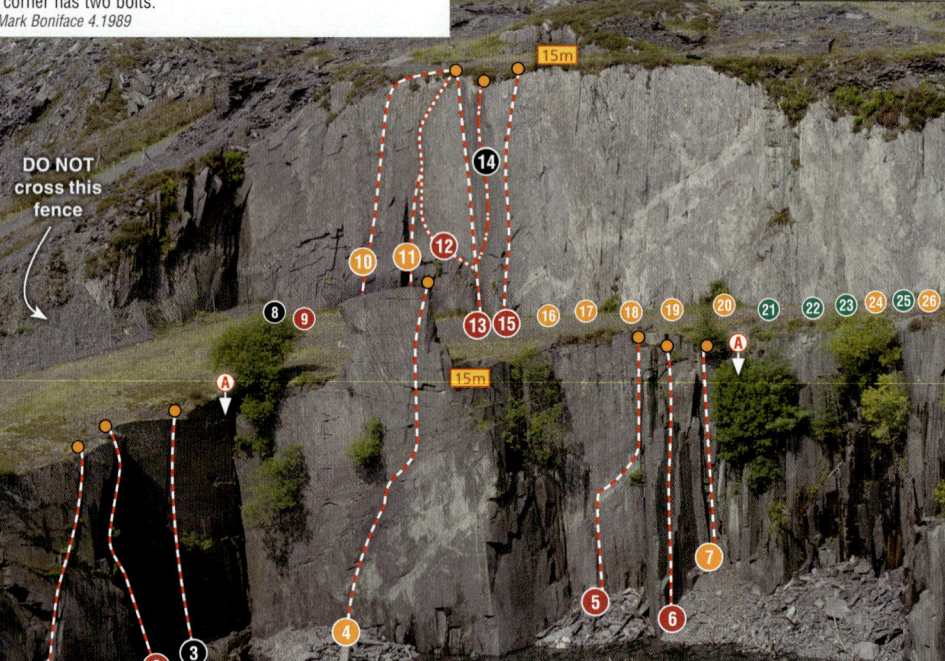

7 Velvet Walk . . . . ▣ [ ] **VS 4c**
Sadly now overgrown. Start below the twin cracks just right of the fin of *John Verybiglongwords*. Climb these to the top.
FA. A.Maddison, Jonny Martin 27.9.1987

Back up on the main level.

8 Lob Scouse . . . . ⊖ [ ] **E4 6b**
The wall above the fence past a rod and bolt - now defunct.
FA. Andy Woodward, Clive Stephenson, Danny Dutton 10.1989

9 Escape From Coldbitz . . . . . . ⊖ [ ] **6c+**
A defunct sport route left of *Zambesi*.
FA. Lucian Cottle, Jim Kelly 10.2009

10 Zambesi . . . . ⭐⭐ [ ] **VS 4c**
A nice route, although the gear is hard to arrange and the climbing somewhat awkward at the top. Belay off the wobbly spike and bolts way back.
FA. Terry Taylor (solo) 5.6.1986

11 Harvey's Brassed off Team . . ⭐ [ ] **HVS 5c**
Move up to gain a ledge and the arete. A hard groove above leads to the arete proper. Follow this to the top.
FA. Andy Cummings, M.Adams 1.10.1988

Walk all the way round to descend

Hidden Wall
p.64

Immac Groove - p.64

28 29 30 31 32 33

12 Launching Pad . . . . ⭐ [ ] **E1 5b**
A good route, if a little polished. Climb the corner of *Holy, Holy, Holy* for a few metres and arrange high runners. Make an exciting traverse left to reach the first bolt, climb up to the second and head straight up to the top. Belay well back on bolts.
FA. Mark Boniface 1988

13 Holy, Holy, Holy . . . . ⭐⭐ [ ] **E2 5c**
A great route, which tackles the corner. It is harder than it looks and the crack can sometimes hold a bit of moisture. Belay well back on bolts. *Photo on p.58.*
FA. Cliff Phillips (solo) 28.5.1984

14 The Chiselling . . . . ⭐ 🔧 [ ] **E4 6a**
A strenuous undertaking. Bridge up *Holy, Holy, Holy* until you can gain the crack in the right wall. Fire up this with all guns blazing until it eases near the top.
FA. Nick Harms, Mo Anthoine 27.2.1987

15 At the Cost of a Rope . . . . . . ⭐ [ ] **E1 5b**
A rather scrappy line which requires a steady head and a good eye for runners. Follow the crack that starts on the left of the arete and moves around it at the top.
FA. Mark Boniface 1988

The next routes have all been de-bolted.

16 La Grendre . . . . ⊖ [ ] **6a+**
17 Mon Amie . . . . ⊖ [ ] **5a**
18 Tolerance . . . . ⊖ [ ] **5b**
19 Le Grandpere . . . . ⊖ [ ] **5c**
20 Pour Tout Le Monde . . . . . . ⊖ [ ] **6a**
21 Departure Lounge . . . . ⊖ [ ] **3c**
22 Kinder Sport . . . . ⊖ [ ] **3c**
23 Emerald Dyke . . . . ⊖ [ ] **4a**
24 La Grandmere . . . . ⊖ [ ] **5a**
25 La Famille . . . . ⊖ [ ] **4c**
26 Binky Bonk Central . . . . ⊖ [ ] **6a+**
27 My Wife's An Alien . . . . ⊖ [ ] **5a**
28 Captain Slog . . . . ⊖ [ ] **4c**
29 Le Petit Pois . . . . ⊖ [ ] **6a+**
30 Slate Arrivals . . . . ⊖ [ ] **5b**
31 Telescopic Stem Master . . . . ⭐⭐ [ ] **6b+**
More of an extended boulder problem, but very tricky.
FA. Nick Harms 28.2.1987

32 Aardman Productions . . . . . . ⊖ [ ] **6a**

33 Tower of Laughter . . . . . ⭐ 💙 [ ] **E1 6a**
A good route. Reaching the first bolt is a little worrying, but there is a convenient one by the crux. Belay off a concreted-in telegraph pole.
FA. Ian Lloyd-Jones, Chris Jex 19.7.1991

Bus Stop Quarry
Dali's Hole
California
Australia
Serengeti
Never Never Land
Twll Mawr
Mordor - Lost World
Vivian Quarry
Rainbow Slab Area
Snakes and Ladders
Outlying

Hidden Wall and Dali's Slab

A quiet section of Dali's Hole with a few good routes.
Approach (map p.71, overview p.60) - From the top of the Main Wall, go up one level and walk round on the track that descends down to the tunnel to California. As soon as you can, drop down a rather active scree slope to the base of either crag.

1 Immac Groove . . . . ☐ **E2 6a**
Climb the groove down and left, nearly by the water.
FA. Chris Davies, Phil Targett, Clive Stephenson 14.10.1989

2 Mfecane . . . . ☐ ☐ **7b**
A fierce pitch. Start up the groove, then make a campus-style move through the roof before continuing to a lower-off.
FA. Danny Dutton, P.Smith 9.9.1993

3 Her Indoors . . . . ☐ ☐ **E3 5c**
After a friable start, the slab above is enjoyable. Take some gear to protect the initial crack before you reach the first bolt.
FA. Mick Hardwick, Martin Barnicott, Bill Wayman 10.1986

To mid afternoon | 16 min | Sheltered

Dali's Wall

22m | 18m | 15m

4 Yuk Hunter . . . . ☐ ☐ **E4 6a**
The smooth corner above a ledge requires a series of reaches.
FA. Martin Barnicott, G.Barnicott 20.11.1986

5 Minder . . . . ☐ ☐ ☐ **6c+**
An amazing route described as the poor man's *Bungles Arete* by someone who has climbed both!
FA. Bill Wayman, Mick Hardwick, Martin Barnicott 10.1986

6 Arthur Dali . . . . ☐ ☐ **E3 6b**
The main corner offers some problematic climbing.
FA. Martin Barnicott, Bill Wayman 10.1986

7 Come off it Arfer . . . . ☐ **VS 4c**
The prominent arete on the right-hand side of the wall. Move slightly right at the top.
FA. G.Barnicott, Martin Barnicott 3.11.1986

8 Rycott. . . . . ☐ ☐ **E3 5c**
A broken climb! Start just right of the arete and climb up into the corner/groove and follow it to the top. The peg is missing.
FA. Martin Barnicott, G.Barnicott 3.11.1986

9 Schmitt Hammer . . . . ☐ ☐ **S**
The loose left arete/edge of the tower. Beware of the rock as a rockfall has affected the shared finish with *Medicine Show*.

10 Medicine Show . . . . ☐ ☐ ☐ **HVS 5b**
Climb up the slab past a bolt and make a traverse of the ridge to a belay on the right. Care is needed with loose rock.
FA. Andy Newton, Kath Griffiths, I.MacMillan 19.4.1988

11 When the Winds Blows . . . . . ☐ ☐ **7a**
Start below three bolts. Climb to the first and then move out to the second, before continuing to the top.
FA. Perry Hawkins, Al George 29.1.1987

12 Toad in Toad Hall . . . . . . ☐ ☐ ☐ **7a**
A direct on *When the Wind Blows* has thin and desperate moves to the second bolt before finishing up that route.
FA. Phil Targett, Clive Stephenson 20.11.1990

Dali's Wall

This wall is a little scrappy. *Grandad's Rib* and *Dali Mirror* are the best of the easy routes.

Approach (map p.71, overview p.60) - Go up one level and Dali's Wall is on the left.

13 First and Last . . . . `6b+`
The short wall, past a bolt, to a lower-off.

14 The Hemulin . . . . `E2 5c`
Climb the groove past a bolt to the top.

15 Rock Video . . . . `E2 6a`
Another groove. An old peg protects at the top.

16 Grandad's Rib . . . . `E2 5b`
The green rib has a low bolt and pleasant climbing above.
FA. Martin Crook, Bill Wayman 11.10.1986

17 Coy Mistress . . . . `E1 5c`
The V-groove is unstable at present and best avoided.
FA. Bill Wayman, Martin Crook 11.10.1986

18 The Dude in the Orange Hat
. . . . `XS 5c`
Climb the remains of the rockfall, which may still be active!
FA. N.Bradford 3.2007

19 Salvador . . . . `E5 6a`
Another unstable groove and a missing peg.
FA. Bill Wayman, Martin Crook 11.10.1986

20 Moth to the Flame . . . . `E3 6b`
A boulder problem start gains a low ledge. Climb the finger crack above to the top.
FA. Andy Woodward 6.11.1987

21 Dali Mirror . . . . `E2 5c`
Ascend the groove, with the crux passing a bolt, to reach another groove system and ledges above.
FA. Bill Wayman, Martin Crook 12.10.1986

22 Dali Express . . . . `E3 6a`
The suspended groove. Climb the crack past a peg. Move left then right to gain a ledge. Grope upwards into the groove, which eases towards the top.
FA. Bill Wayman, Martin Crook 12.10.1986

Below the scree cone at the base of *Dali's Dihedral* is the hidden *Tunnel of Love* to the bottom of Australia.

23 Dali's Dihedral . . . . `E5 6b`
The serious groove/pod at the top of the scree cone has a hard start, an easier middle and a desperate crux right at the top.
FA. Martin Crook, John Tombs 28.3.1987

24 Return of the Visitor . . . . `E5 6b`
The arching overlap gives an intense outing. Climb up to a bolt - difficult to pass - and enter the groove. Move onto the wall on the right and pass two more bolts to the top.
FA. Perry Hawkins, George Smith 22.2.1987

25 Cuts like a Knife . . . . . . `E5 6a`
The finger-crack past a peg.
FA. Bill Wayman, Jon deMontjoye 12.10.1986

26 Making Plans for Nigel . . . . . `E1 5c`
The right-hand crack. Ignore the bolt in the wall right of *Cuts Like A Knife* and gain the crack from the right. Climb the crack with difficulty to a shot-hole thread. Scramble or abseil off.
FA. Martin Crook, John Tombs, Mark Boniface 21.3.1987

27 Con Quista Dors . . . . `7b`
The route up the greenstone pillar is unusual since it relies on friction. Follow the wandering line of bolts.
FA. Bill Wayman, Jon deMontjoye 3.12.1987

28 Stretch Class . . . . `E4 6a`
Flexibility of the lower limbs is required for this bridging testpiece - two bolts and a peg.
FA. G.Landless, Bill Wayman, M.Rudolph, Dave Kirton 3.10.1987

Bus Stop Quarry | Dali's Hole | California | Australia | Serengeti | Never Never Land | Twll Mawr | Mordor - Lost World | Vivian Quarry | Snakes and Ladders | Rainbow Slab Area | Outlying

California Side

The west-facing side of the quarry has mostly loose or small walls. Four routes have been developed, but nothing of any great quality.

Approach (map p.71, overview p.60) - From the gate, follow the track then go up one level and walk round to the track that descends to the tunnel. The first two routes are found just before the California tunnel. For the last two routes, descend towards Dali's Hole.

1 **Slip Not** . . . . 6a+
The left-hand line of bolts up the slab.
FA. Ian Lloyd-Jones 16.11.2007

2 **Why Knot?** . . . . 6a+
Start up *Slip Not* and move right to the edge.
FA. Ian Lloyd-Jones 16.11.2007

3 **Jex's Fumble Clipping Arete** . HVS 5a
The juggy arete looks great but appears totally detached and is best avoided.
FA. Ian Lloyd-Jones, Chris Jex, Phil Targett 19.5.1991

4 **Dali's Lemming Ducklings** . . E3 6b
Again, rather detached and best avoided. A crack up the right side of *Jex's...* is climbed to a good hold where you can escape left into *Jex's...* .
FA. Ian Lloyd-Jones 7.6.1991

Afternoon 17 min Sheltered

8m

2

1

Tunnel to California - p.70

12m

3 4

Path to Main Area

A slackliner above Dali's Hole - one of the many possible high-lines in the quarries.

Bus Stop Quarry

Dali's Hole

California

Australia

Serengeti

Never Never Land

Twll Mawr

Mordor - Lost World

Vivian Quarry

Rainbow Slab Area

Snakes and Ladders

Outlying

Bus Stop Quarry

Dali's Hole

California

Australia

Serengeti

Never Never Land

Twll Mawr

Mordor - Lost World

Vivian Quarry

Rainbow Slab Area

Snakes and Ladders

Outlying

California

Terry Walker on *We Speak No Americano!* (5b, 6a) - *p.72* - California, a good two-pitch sport route. Photo: David Simmonite
One of a growing number of great multi-pitch sport routes in the quarries, this line is particularly popular as a result of its ease of access and the steady grade.

Bus Stop Quarry

Dali's Hole

California

Australia

Serengeti

Never Never Land

Twll Mawr

Mordor - Lost World

Vivian Quarry

Rainbow Slab Area

Snakes and Ladders

Outlying

		No star	⚜	⚜	⚜
Mod to S / 4c		-	1	-	-
HS-HVS / 5a-6a+		1	-	1	-
E1-E3 / 6b-7a		7	1	-	1
E4 / 7a+ and up		4	6	8	6

California has historically been a playground for the big boys and girls, with most routes being serious undertakings. The only mid-grade route of quality used to be *Californian Arete* at E1 - a 35m solo! The routes on the main wall are amazing, with *Central Sadness* and *Waves of Inspiration* being two of the best E5s in the quarries. More recently, the addition of *We Speak No Americano!* has added to the appeal for the mid-grade climber. For those in search of esoteria, there is even some aid climbing hidden amongst the routes, some of it very demanding in nature.

Conditions

California offers more shelter than most of the other slate quarries, though it only gets a bit of sunshine in the morning and can remain damp.

Approach

California is situated in the upper quarries, and best approached from Deiniolen and Dinorwig via the A4244, which connects Llanberis to the coast road. Turn off the A4244 to Deiniolen and on through Dinorwig to parking at the road end near Bus Stop Quarry. Head along the main track until it opens out by a large cutting shed on the left and continue to a kissing gate by a left bend in the track. Pass through here and follow the main track towards a large incline. Where the track bends right, hop over the gate in front of you and follow the path up and right for one level, Dali's Hole is down and to your right. Traverse around to the opposite side of Dali's Hole and follow a small track back down into the hole to a tunnel on the left (see p.66). Walk through this and follow a narrow path to a second tunnel, bringing you out into the expanse of California.

Dali's Hole
p.60

Higher tunnel
from Serengeti

California
Express -
p.72

Californian
Arete - p.73

From approach
tunnels

Californian Arete Area
p.72

California Wall
p.74

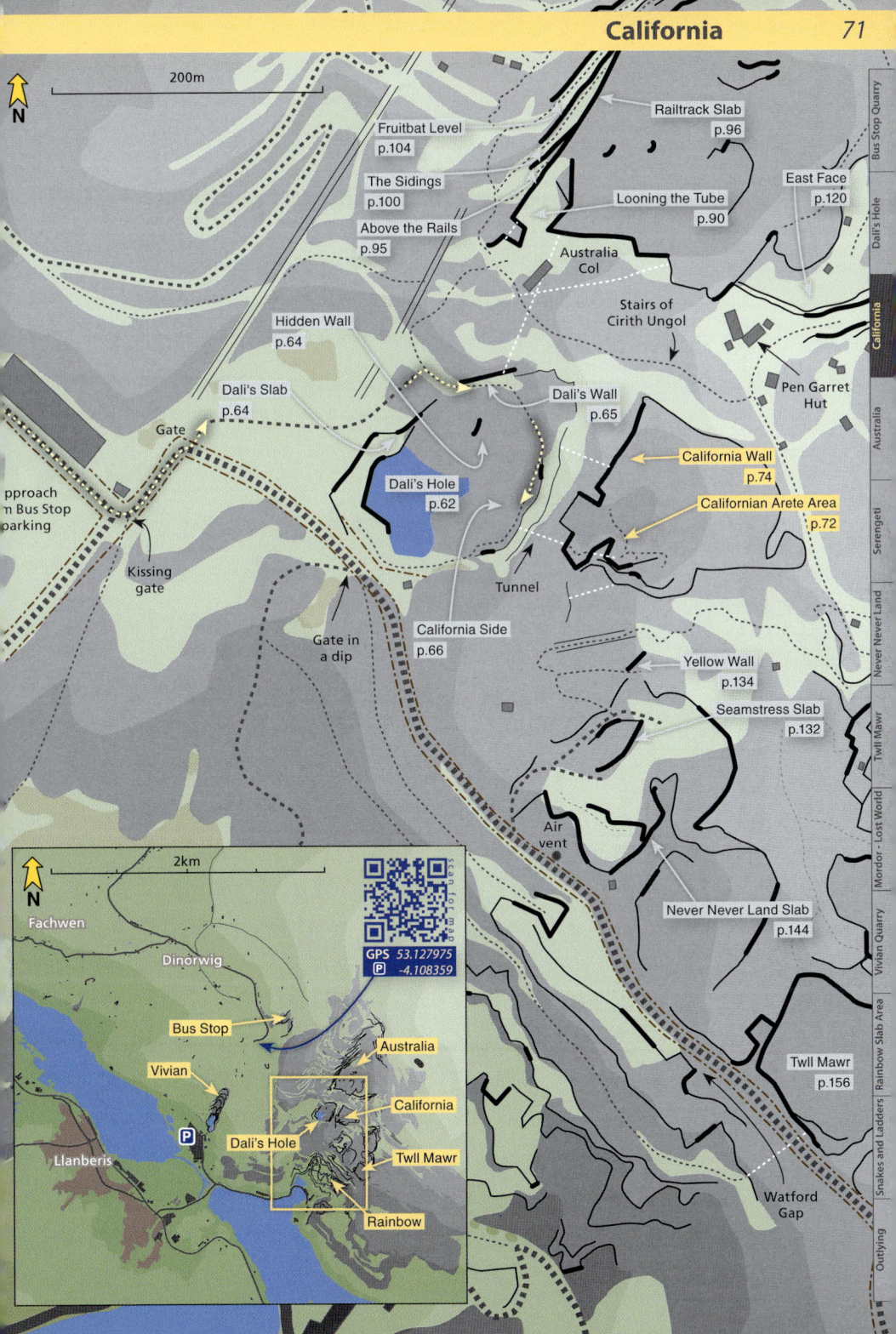

200m

N

Railtrack Slab
p.96

Fruitbat Level
p.104

East Face
p.120

The Sidings
p.100

Looning the Tube
p.90

Above the Rails
p.95

Australia
Col

Stairs of
Cirith Ungol

Hidden Wall
p.64

Pen Garret
Hut

Dali's Slab
p.64

Dali's Wall
p.65

Gate

California Wall
p.74

Dali's Hole
p.62

Californian Arete Area
p.72

Approach
m Bus Stop
parking

Kissing
gate

Tunnel

Gate in
a dip

California Side
p.66

Yellow Wall
p.134

Seamstress Slab
p.132

Air
vent

Never Never Land Slab
p.144

Twll Mawr
p.156

Watford
Gap

N

2km

Fachwen

Dinorwig

GPS 53.127975
-4.108359

Bus Stop

Australia

Vivian

California

Dali's Hole

Llanberis

Twll Mawr

Rainbow

Bus Stop Quarry | Dali's Hole | California | Australia | Serengeti | Never Never Land | Twll Mawr | Mordor - Lost World | Vivian Quarry | Rainbow Slab Area | Snakes and Ladders | Outlying

Californian Arete Area

A shady wall that sees little traffic mainly because the routes are either hard, or bold, or both. The superb E1 solo of *Californian Arete* is worth a look if you are confident. *We Speak No Americano!* is an excellent sport route that has added to the appeal of the area.

Approach (map p.71, overview p.70) - Walk through the tunnel and follow the narrow path round below *The Hobbit* to another tunnel. Upon exiting, marvel at the mighty and cavernous excavation.

Descent - Abseil from above *Californian Arete*. Alternatively, scramble leftwards across a narrow ledge and go out through a tunnel which leads to just above Yellow Wall (p.134).

❶ The California Express . . . . . 🌟1 [___] **3c**
From the tunnel, walk up the scree and head back across a vegetated level between two trees - one is a memorial to Will Perrin. Walk up the slate stairs and climb the bolted arete.

❷ Welcome to the Machine 🌟2 ⚡ [___] **7a+**
A technical start leads to a flake then back right to a ledge. Climb a groove above then move up left to another groove.
FA. Ian Lloyd-Jones 21.6.2018

❸ Tambourine Man . . . 🌟2 ⚡⚡ [___] **8a**
The extremely technical groove.
FA. Pete Robins 16.4.2007

❹ We Speak No Americano! . . . 🌟2 [___] **6a**
A great route up the wall which can be done in two pitches. Climb the blocky groove to the grassy ledge (**5b** - possible belay). A tricky move to the ledges leads to interesting climbing up the line of weakness above. *Photo on p.68.*
FA. Celt Lloyd-Jones (aged 8), Tesni Lloyd-Jones (aged 11) 27.8.2010

❺ A Pair of Six . . . . . . 🌟1 ⚡⚡ [___] **E3 5c**
Climb past a bolt to the ledge. Follow the crack above to a tree.
FA. Chris Davies, Mark Williams, Ian Lloyd-Jones 5.6.2010

Morning | 20 min | Sheltered

Tunnel

Alternative hair-raising scramble out to Serengeti, through a tunnel

35m

30m

6 Slabs 'R' Us . . . .  7b
A tough line, with tricky, technical moves up to and past the third bolt. Above, the climbing eases.
FA. Ian Lloyd-Jones, Sion McGuinness 11.6.2010

7 Shtimuli E4 6a
The arete is only just protected by the bolts. Climb up past the first bolt and a small cam to the second bolt. Continue past another two bolts above, or move across and gain the lower-off on *Slabs 'R' Us*.
FA. Chris Dale, A.Dale, P.Colquohoun 5.1989

8 Aultimers Groove E2 5c
The corner groove is steep at the start.
FA. Kath Goodey, Colin Goodey 11.1989

Not much sun | 20 min | Sheltered

35m

27m

9 Californian Arete E1 4c
A classic of the quarries, and a must for any wannabe Slatehead. There is a poor lonely wire above the hard climbing and an even worse sling. From the blast shelter through the base of the arete, mantel onto the roof and follow a line of juggy hand holds out right to gain the arete. Once on the arete, compose yourself and climb up to reach a heart-stoppingly airy high step. After this the climbing eases and the route switches to the opposite side of the arete. Finish up a short groove on the left side of the arete from a ledge near to the top. Trail a rope up to abseil off, although you will need two to reach the ground unless using a 70m.
FA. Cliff Phillips (solo) 16.6.1986

10 Wedlock Holiday E5 6c
The smooth wavy groove to the right of *Californian Arete* is desperate. From the blast shelter make your way up the groove, past a bolt to a roof. You can step left and rest here before making more demanding moves rightwards below the roof (another bolt) and on to the top.
FA. Graham McMahon, Chris Dale 17.7.1989

11 Classy Situations E2 5a
The left-facing groove gives reasonable climbing and a steady head will get you up the upper wall.
FA. Cliff Phillips 16.6.1984

12 Pitch Two E4 6b
An alternative finish to *Classy Situations* up the shallow groove. Three bolts and a peg protect this desperate line.
FA. Chris Parkin, George Smith 3.1987

13 Midnight Flier E5 6b
Start at a bolt belay on the exposed ledge and take the delicate flake-line. This requires plenty of thin slings, small wires, superglue and a prayer should you blow it.
FA. Bill Wayman, G.Landless 12.8.1987

14 NYQUIST A3
Bat hooks and bolts to the left-hand finish.
FA. D.Williams, M.Ryan, Mark Hanford 1998

15 Happy Hooking A3
More bat hooks and bolts!
FA. D.Williams, M.Ryan, Mark Hanford 1998

16 The Hobbit E5 6b
A brilliant but damp and dirty line up the bolt-protected flake-line. More like a *7b*, but take wires for the run-out to the belay.
FA. Bill Gregory, Jon Barton 20.5.1990

17 The Sneaking E4 5c
The damp wall to the right of *The Hobbit* has some spaced bolts.
FA. Jon Barton, Bill Gregory 19.5.1990

18 Ya Twistin Ma Melon Man E3 6a
Climb the corner past three bolts and some extra gear. Just before the top move left into *The Sneaking* to finish.
FA. Mark Boniface, A.Shaw 5.1990

19 New Rays from an Ancient Sun. A2
An aid route left of the tunnel. Lethally loose at the top.
FA. J.Howel 1993

20 Old Fart A3
An aid route up the edge of the lower cave.
FA. D.Williams, M.Ryan 1998

Approach through tunnels

Bus Stop Quarry · Dali's Hole · California · Australia · Serengeti · Never Never Land · Twll Mawr · Mordor - Lost World · Vivian Quarry · Rainbow Slab Area · Snakes and Ladders · Outlying

California Wall

California Wall is one of the main trad areas on slate, with routes like *Central Sadness* and *Waves of Inspiration* among the best E5s in the quarries. There is no easy ride here - expect thin climbing on run-out slabs.

Approach (map p.71, overview p.70) - Follow the Dali's Hole approach and, as you descend back to the hole, there is a tunnel to your left. Walk through this and follow the narrow path to another tunnel. Upon exiting, marvel at the mighty and cavernous excavation. Walk and scramble across to the base of the wall.

To reach routes 5 to 7 it is possible to scramble up from the Dali's Hole Approach just before you drop down towards the California Tunnel and scramble up to a tree and the far side of the tunnel that *Snakes and Ladder Approach* climbs to.

Descent - Walk left to the huge chain which is the abseil point.

Morning | 22 min | Sheltered

Abseil descent

45m

20m

❶ The Wooley (or Won't He) Jumper ⬜ **E3 6a**
Start from the scree terrace to the left of *Unpaid Bills*.
1) 4c, 10m. Climb the loose groove system until you can move out right onto the wall and up to a ledge - poor belay.
2) 6a, 20m. Ascend the crack-line above with difficulty, until a hand-traverse leads right to a vegetated top-out.
FA. J.Webb, Mark Boniface 1991

❷ Unpaid Bills . . . . ⬜ **E5 6b**
The amazing green pillar in two pitches.
1) 5c, 17m. Feels like trad E3. **2) 6b**, 22m. Feels like bold **7b**.
FA. Jon Barton 2000. A combination of two other routes.

❸ Primal Ice Cream . . . . . . ⬜ **E3 5b**
The corner is ridiculously run out in places, but never really desperate. Any hard moves are near gear, although there is a hair-raising mantelshelf onto a jug near the top.
FA. Chris Dale, John Silvester 10.4.1986

❹ Snakes and Ladders Approach . . ⬜ **HVS 5a**
Make a hard move to the chain and pull up this. For the full adventure see p.282.

❺ Espirit De Corpse . . . ⬜ **E4 6a**
The finger-crack is amazing and sustained, though getting there from the tunnel is somewhat alarming due to some hollow flakes that you have pull on and put gear behind.
FA. John Silvester, Chris Dale 12.4.1986

❻ Simply Peach . . . . . ⬜ **E5 6b**
The wall right of the tunnel is sustained. Start on the ledge just right of the tunnel and follow a thin crack to a bolt. Up and right is a bolt shared with *Sad Old Red* - clip this and then head back up and left to a third bolt. A few desperate moves past this lead to easier ground and the top.
FA. George Smith, Chris Parkin, Dave O'Dowd 21.9.1986

❼ Sad Old Red . . . . ⬜ **E4 6a**
Climb to a bolt before moving up past a flake to another bolt (shared with *Simply Peach*). Move right by a spike into the flake-line and finish up easier ground.
FA. Chris Dale, John Silvester 10.4.1986

Bus Stop Quarry | Dali's Hole | California | Australia | Serengeti | Never Never Land | Twll Mawr | Mordor - Lost World | Vivian Quarry | Rainbow Slab Area | Snakes and Ladders | Outlying

Lee Roberts experiencing some *Waves of Inspiration* (E5 6a) - *p.76* - a belting route up the centre of California Wall. California Wall is one of the great slabs of Slate and has some ferocious outings that played a big part in establishing the mythology of hard slate slab climbing. The long sustained nature of the climbing gives the routes their character, combined with a spicy mix of bolts where you need them, some trad gear to fill in the gaps and good old fashioned grit when you have neither!

8 The Madcap Laughs E3 6a
The loose and hideous groove is best avoided.

9 Spider Pants E6 6b
As girdles go this is something of a classic. The first pitch is worth it in its own right. Start below the tapering groove that dreams are made of.
1) 6b, 30m. Gain the flake and follow it as it becomes the groove. Make some shapes to reach a ledge at its top, then move up and right to the *Central Sadness* belay.
2) 5c, 10m. Climb *Central Sadness* to the perched flake at the base of the finger-crack and belay.
3) 6b, 47m. Traverse right to the bolt on *Sombre Music* then climb up to gain further protection 3m above before descending again to the bolt. Move right again, past a bolt, to gain *The Big Sur*. Move up to another bolt and a brief respite, then drop down and move right below an overlap to gain *Waves of Inspiration* and another bolt. Move right for 3m and then up *Waves of Inspiration*. At the break 6m below the top, head up and rightwards on jugs to the top.
FA. George Smith, Dave O'Dowd 20.5.1987

10 Central Sadness E5 6a
Possibly the best route of its grade in the quarries. Start below a thin crack to the right of a tapering groove. Often described as one pitch for the hero and another for the married man.
1) 6a, 25m. The bold first pitch starts with a tricky move to gain the crack; follow it more easily to a ledge below a recess. Move up the recess on slopers to a spike (sling), and then commit to gaining the wall above. Head up this, moving right near the top, to a two-bolt belay.
2) 6a, 32m. The better protected second pitch moves up and right from the belay towards a crack. Once gained, follow it in an amazing position, past very small cams, until a difficult move gains a larger crack that leads up and right to the top.
FA. John Silvester, Chris Dale 5.5.1986

11 Dwarf Shortage E5 6a
A sustained pitch. Start just to the right of the crack of *Central Sadness* and climb past two bolts - both are hard to clip and the consequences of not doing so would be painful. Move up and right to gain the top of the groove, from which easy climbing leads to the next bolt. Sustained but never desperate climbing leads to a junction with *Central Sadness* at the finger crack. Follow this to the top.
FA. Owen Barnicott 5.8.2010

12 Sombre Music E6 6b
Another cracking pitch. From the left-hand end of the ledge that *Waves of Inspiration* starts from, climb the thin crack past a bolt and small cam placement. Now move up and left towards a juggy break and follow this left to another crack and good gear. Climb the crack past two more bolts to the hanging bay then scramble out to the top.
FA. George Smith, Perry Hawkins 12.4.1987

13 The Big Sur E6 6b
Another classic, though being tall is helpful (if not essential) for the crux. Start as for *Waves of Inspiration* and at 6m swerve left past a bolt. A desperate series of moves gains a finger-hold. More challenging climbing is needed to pass the next bolt. Step up and then move left to the good crack and another bolt. Move up the crack passing a bolt out left where another tricky sequence leads to a large flat hold. Finally, move up directly past the last bolt to the top.
FA. John Silvester, Chris Dale 5.5.1986

14 Waves of Inspiration . . . E5 6a
A long pitch that keeps coming at you to the final move. Start at a bolt belay. Move up and left to gain a crack/break. Follow this rightwards past small wires and a bolt to gain the vertical crack on the right. Follow this past another bolt, to a position about 3m below a third bolt. Place a wire below this and traverse left for 3m past a small cam-slot to gain the base of a steep flake/groove. Climb this on good holds to a triangular ledge, with a bolt on the right. Move right past the bolt and head up past another bolt, crux, to gain a diagonal crack above. Head more-or-less direct to the top. The belay bolts are a little hidden.
Photo on p.75.
FA. Chris Parkin, Perry Hawkins, George Smith 4.8.1986

15 Stairway to Silence . . . E7 6b
A desperate hard route on the right-hand edge of the slab. Start at a fixed belay on a ledge. Skyhooks are required for protection.
1) 6b, 10m. Move up left to a hole. Easier ground leads to a bolt and a belay.
2) 6b, 30m. Climb up past a jug to a bolt. Continue to a break and some marginal gear. Move up to good holds which lead boldly to the top.
FA. John Silvester, Chris Dale 5.5.1986

16 Fruit of the Gloom . . . . . XS 5b
To the right of California Wall is a loose disgusting-looking wall. If you go high enough up the base of it you will see an off-width, chimney slot that breaks through it. Having made the harrowing scramble past the base of this crack, make a belay of sorts. The leader now shuffles leftwards to gain the base of the hideous beast and battles upwards. The hope is that the upwards momentum of the climber beats the downwards momentum of the crag.
FA. Will Perrin, Dave Rudkin 2000

*Snakes and Ladders
Approach - p.74*

Snakes and Ladders Approach - p.74

Abseil descent
to the left

50m

Bus Stop Quarry

Dali's Hole

California

Australia

Serengeti

Never Never Land

Twll Mawr

Mordor – Lost World

Vivian Quarry

Rainbow Slab Area

Snakes and Ladders

Outlying

Australia

Bus Stop Quarry

Dali's Hole

California

Australia

Serengeti

Never Never Land

Twll Mawr

Mordor - Lost World

Vivian Quarry

Rainbow Slab Area

Snakes and Ladders

Outlying

Neil Trumper on the initial rising traverse of *Looning the Tube* (E1 5a) - *p.94* - on the Looning the Tube Slab. Photo: David Price
The original description for this in Paul Williams' 1987 CC guide was:
"Shuffle along to the end of the pipe and step across to the foot of the crack. The crack has its moments ... and so will you! Slightly loose!" - E1 4c, no stars.
Well the tube fell down many years ago, and the crack became much less loose, turning this wobbly excursion into something of a slate classic. The remains of part of the tube and the chain that held it in place are visible in this photo.

	No star	☆	☆☆	☆☆☆
Mod to S / 4c	4	4	-	-
HS-HVS / 5a-6a+	34	35	14	-
E1-E3 / 6b-7a	29	39	31	5
E4 / 7a+ and up	18	13	18	2

Bus Stop Quarry

Dali's Hole

California

Australia

Serengeti

Never Never Land

Twll Mawr

Mordor - Lost World

Vivian Quarry

Rainbow Slab Area

Snakes and Ladders

Outlying

Australia is the largest single working in the Dinorwig Quarries, consisting of a vast open cwm high on the side of Elidir Fawr. The quarrymen thoughtfully developed the area in tiers, giving walls of around 30m in height and allowing relatively easy access to the various sections along terraces. Most of the best walls are on the west side where there are around six or seven tiers of quality walls and slabs. The north side and east walls have less to offer, but still feature the odd decent bit of rock. In the late noughties this area saw a boom in easy sport climbing. The Sidings is one of the best areas in the quarries for low-grade clip-ups, although there are many other routes in this area that cover the full spectrum of the slate experience. Australia has become a very popular place to sport climb, although there are some excellent trad lines to be found as well, and some that blur the lines between the two. The nature of the walls on the western side means that it is possible to climb routes on successive tiers creating some enjoyable long link-ups - see p.114.

Conditions

The open aspect means that Australia can catch the wind, though it will get shelter from westerlies. Sun and shade can be found due to the many walls although the majority of the climbing faces southeast and catches the sun until mid-afternoon. On the lower walls this is likely to be a bit of a suntrap if out of the wind. There is little seepage to be found except on the very low north-facing walls.

James Oswald reaching up for another positive edge on *Off the Beaten Track* (E3 5c) - *p.97* - in Australia. The Railtrack Slab was largely ignored for years after an initial wave of new routes. Twenty years the remains of the old pegs and bolts had become too manky for anyone to bother climbing. It was re-equipped in 2006 as part of a major effort across the quarries. With the first ascensionists' permission, several had an extra bolt or two added. Many of the routes are still not full sport routes, but they have found a new lease of life as well-equipped trad routes. *Off The Beaten Track* is a great example of this. Having had virtually no ascents for years, within a week of it being re-equipped with an extra lower bolt, people were almost queuing for it and it is now regarded as a classic. This 2006 retro-bolting was limited to a few areas in the quarry, and the clean slabs like California Wall and Rainbow Slab were carefully re-equipped to maintain the classic 'designer danger' that the first ascensionist crafted.

Bus Stop Quarry | Dali's Hole | California | Australia | Serengeti | Never Never Land | Twll Mawr | Mordor - Lost World | Vivian Quarry | Rainbow Slab Area | Snakes and Ladders | Outlying

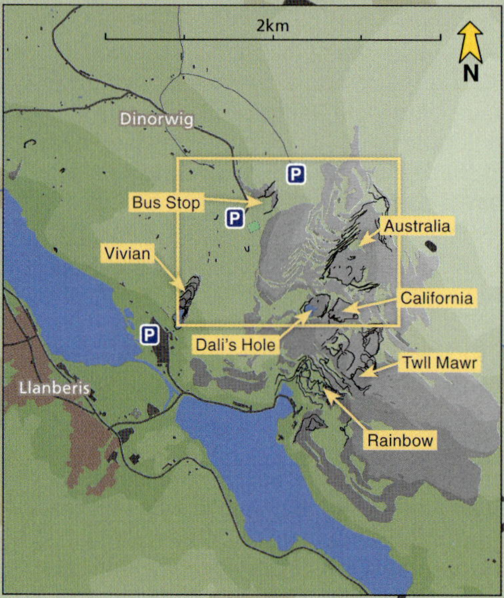

2km

N

200m

N

Dinorwig

Bus Stop

Australia

Vivian

California

Dali's Hole

Twll Mawr

Llanberis

Rainbow

Bus Stop Quarry
p.48

GPS *53.127975*
      -4.108359

Approach

Australia is situated in the upper quarries, and best approached from Deiniolen and Dinorwig via the A4244, which connects Llanberis to the coast road. Turn off the A4244 to Deiniolen and on through Dinorwig to parking at the road end near Bus Stop Quarry. Head along the main track until it opens out by a large cutting shed on the left and continue to a kissing gate by a left bend in the track. Pass through here and follow the main track towards a large incline. Where the track bends right, hop over the gate in front of you and follow the path up three levels to the 'Australia Col' and the lip of the Australia bowl. It is possible to access every level by following a small track up the left-hand side of the quarry from here, or the East Face and The Dark Tower via the Stairs of Cirith Ungol on the right.

The upper walls in Australia are better approached from a higher parking spot. This is the last sharp turning when leaving Dinorwig, but is easier to find by driving back from the Bus Stop turnaround for 1km to the first road on the right up the hill, then the first right again up a small track. There is limited parking at the end of this road by a gate. Head over the gate and continue along the track to a level at the top of the main upper incline. Cross the fence and continue to a tunnel - this is the entrance to The Gorbals.

Gate

Kissing
gate

Bus Stop Quarry

Dali's Hole

California

Australia

Serengeti

Never Never Land

Twll Mawr

Mordor - Lost World

Vivian Quarry

Rainbow Slab Area

Snakes and Ladders

Outlying

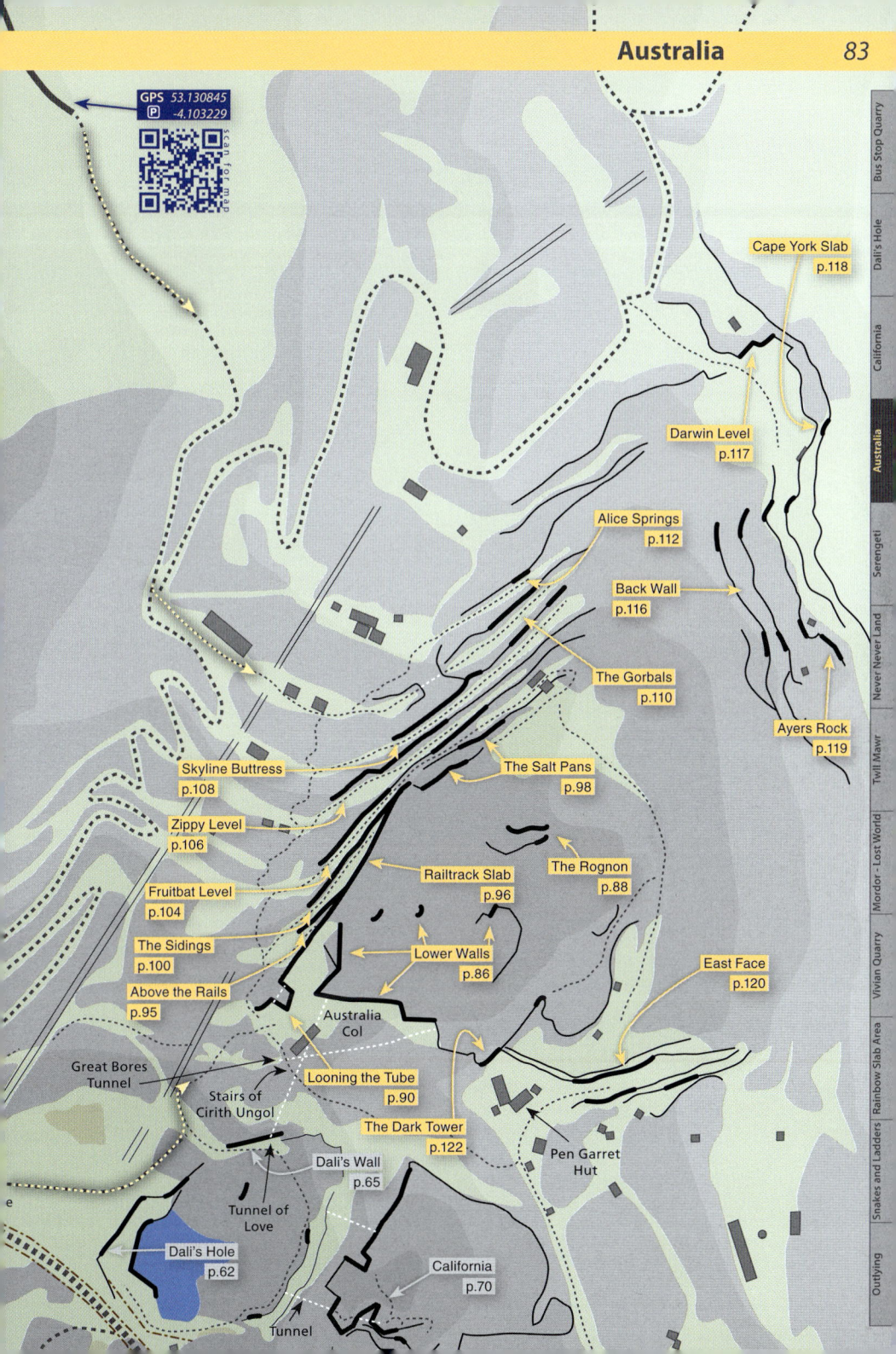

GPS 53.130845
P -4.103229

scan for map

Cape York Slab
p.118

Darwin Level
p.117

Alice Springs
p.112

Back Wall
p.116

The Gorbals
p.110

Ayers Rock
p.119

The Salt Pans
p.98

Skyline Buttress
p.108

Zippy Level
p.106

The Rognon
p.88

Railtrack Slab
p.96

Fruitbat Level
p.104

The Sidings
p.100

Lower Walls
p.86

Above the Rails
p.95

East Face
p.120

Australia
Col

Great Bores
Tunnel

Looning the Tube
p.90

Stairs of
Cirith Ungol

The Dark Tower
p.122

Pen Garret
Hut

Dali's Wall
p.65

Tunnel of
Love

Dali's Hole
p.62

California
p.70

Tunnel

Bus Stop Quarry

Dali's Hole

California

Australia

Serengeti

Never Never Land

Twll Mawr

Mordor - Lost World

Vivian Quarry

Rainbow Slab Area

Snakes and Ladders

Outlying

Bus Stop Quarry

Dali's Hole

California

Australia

Serengeti

Never Never Land

Twll Mawr

Mordor - Lost World

Vivian Quarry

Rainbow Slab Area

Snakes and Ladders

Outlying

Pen Garret hut and East Face

Lost World approach

Stairs of Cirith Ungol

Australia Col

Tunnel of Love entrance

Great Bores Tunnel entrance

Tunnel to halfway up California Wall

California Tunnel

Dali's Hole p.60

Dali's Hole approach

From Bus Stop parking

Looning the Tut p.90

Great Bores Tunnel entrance

Australia Col

Stairs of Cirith Ungol

Bus Stop Quarry

Dali's Hole

California

Australia

Serengeti

Never Never Land

Twll Mawr

Mordor - Lost World

Vivian Quarry

Rainbow Slab Area

Snakes and Ladders

Outlying

Darwin Level
p.117

Alice Springs
p.112

The Gorbals
p.110

From higher
parking

Skyline Buttress
p.108

Zippy Level
p.106

Fruitbat Level
p.104

The Sidings
p.100

The Salt Pans
p.98

To East Face

Above the Rails
p.95

Railtrack Slab
p.96

The Rognon
p.88

Temple of Boom
p.87

Lower Walls
p.86

Tasmania
p.87

Lower Walls

An area probably admired by many climbers but rarely visited. The various sections all have their own names, with Billabong being the shady north-facing wall below the col, Temple of Boom the bulging buttress on the west side, and Tasmania the isolated hole at the base with a decent slab. This area is often damp. It is also quite lichenous and mossy due to its northern aspect.

Approach (map p.83, overview p.84) - From the gate, follow a path up one level and walk to the base of Dali's Wall. Below *Dali's Dihedral* is a cone of scree. At the top of this is a secret tunnel through to the bottom of Australia - The 'Tunnel of Love'. This leads to the base of *Darkness Visible*. Alternatively, head up one more level from Dali's Wall where there are three tunnels leading into the hillside. Take the right-hand of these and then the right fork. This is the Great Bores Tunnel. This leads to a fall-out zone - head down and left past *Great Bores...* and *The Wow Wow*.

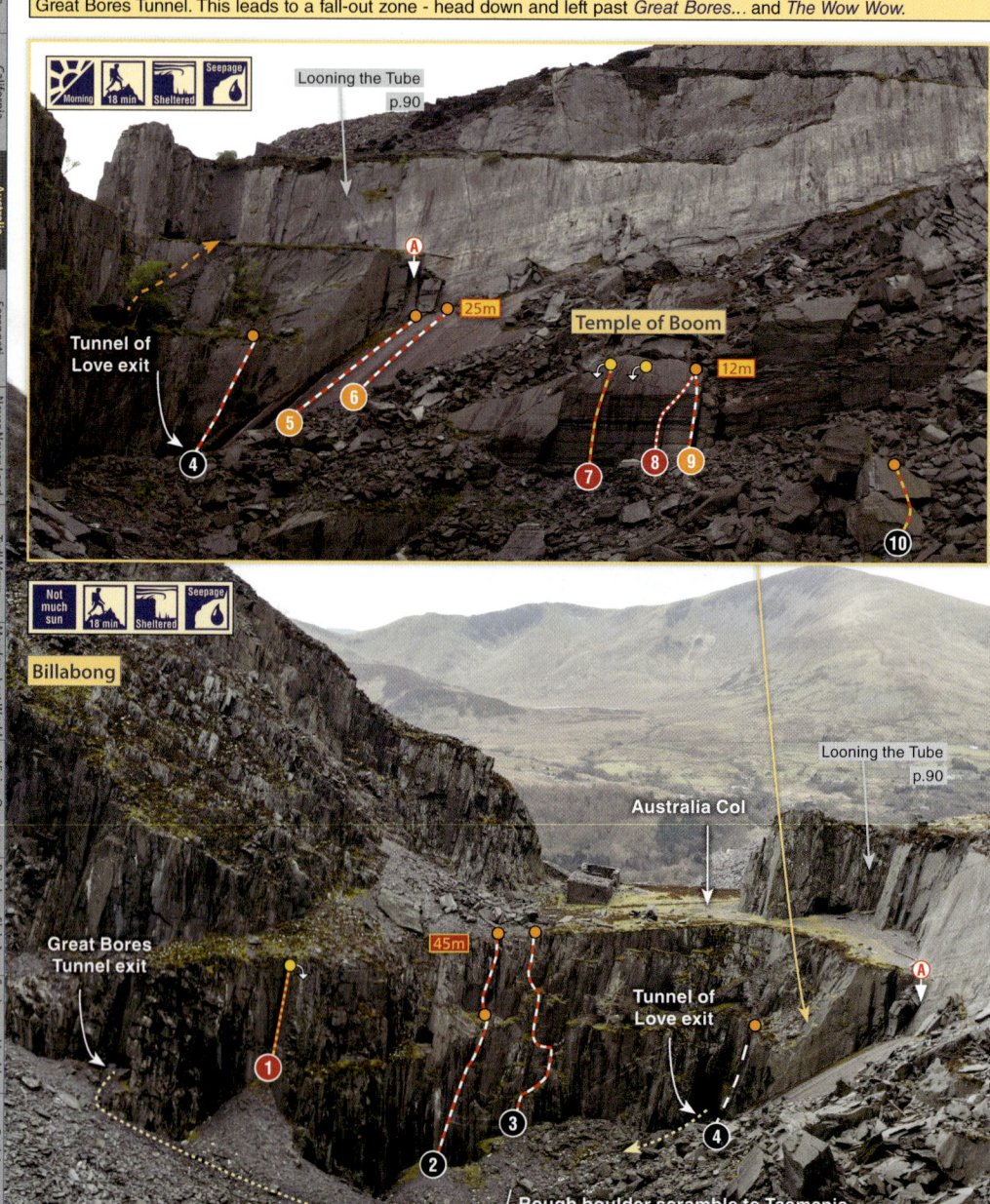

Looning the Tube p.90

Tunnel of Love exit

Temple of Boom

25m

12m

Billabong

Looning the Tube p.90

Australia Col

Great Bores Tunnel exit

45m

Tunnel of Love exit

Rough boulder scramble to Tasmania

Billabong

1 Great Bores of Today 7a
An entertaining route which starts delicately up the perched metal tube to the wall. An initial tricky pull gains the wall and eventually the line of bore-holes, which are usually filled with water. An access bolt above allows you to abseil down and dry them out with a rag.
FA. Jon Ratcliffe 27.3.2008

2 The Wow Wow. E4 6a
A diagonal crack-line makes up the meat of this route and eats cams of all sizes (best to double up if possible).
1) 6a, 27m. Climb the crack with difficulty to reach a 'good' hold. More sustained climbing leads onto a ledge. Despite the crack being easier above, it is also considerably wider, with all the issues that come with that. There is a bolt belay 3m back.
2) 5b, 18m. The crack is followed again, but before it peters out, move left to good holds and follow them to a bolt. Mantel up into the groove and continue to the tree and belay on a boulder.
FA. Jon Ratcliffe, Steve Franklin 9.6.2009

3 The Dunlop Green Flash . . . . . . XS
A random solo exploit up the line of least resistance, that generally follows vegetated ledges. Maybe best avoided, or at least don't tell your mum you did it!
FA. Mark Dicken 2003

4 Darkness Visible E4 6a
The enticing slab below *Looning the Tube* is split by a narrow crack. Climb this to a bolt near the top and belay on blocks and a bolt to the right.
FA. George Smith, Dave O'Dowd 1986

The right arete, however tempting, does not climb independently of *Darkness Visible*. The easy-angled slab to the right has a couple of claimed routes, although it is barely more than a walk.

5 Illegal Smeagol. . . . . VS 4a
Close to the waterfall is an interesting route.
FA. Jacob Shieldhouse-Hadley, J.Dawson-Cluff 8.3.2015

6 Runup . . . . VS 4a
A lower start to *Bise-Mon-Cul* (p.94). Start between the two cracks and pad up to the only gear (two downwards-pointing metal spikes at two-thirds height) and finish easily. Belay on the anchors as for *Bise-Mon-Cul*.
FA. Jacob Shieldhouse-Hadley 28.2.2015

Temple of Boom

7 Dekophobia. 7a
FA. Mark Dicken 8.2006

The lower-off to the right is an abandoned project.

8 Son of Rabbit E2 5c
The crack-line right of *Dekophobia* is climbed with difficulty to a wobbly block. Follow the crack right towards the scree above.
FA. Mark Dicken 2006

9 Temple of Boom . . . . HVS
Expect to be schooled on this off-width - a car jack can protect the wide crack.
FA. Mark Dicken, R.Huws 2006

10 My Secret Garden 7b
FA. Mark Dicken, Gruff Owen 4.5.2007

Tasmania
This really is the pit of the quarry. With very little to entice you there other than curiosity, it is destined to remain a quiet backwater. As you come out into the belly of Australia, descend the scree quickly before any more joins the slope from above. Walk along the base of the scree-filled hole to a hidden slab at the lowest point. All rather tedious.

11 Arnie Meets the Swamp Monster E1 5a
Head up just left of the slab, passing loose blocks, to gain a large side-pull/flake. Take the wide crack and make a series of mantelshelves before hand traversing left to the arete. From the ledge, continue up the arete to the top.
FA. Chris Jex, Nigel Manning 3.7.1990

12 Toilet Trouble E2 5c
Climb the centre of the slab past a bolt - crux. A crack leads on to the top.
FA. Nick Butterworth, Chris Jex 3.7.1990

13 Stinky Boots E2 5b
Start left of the corner. Climb up to some ledges and a bolt, which protects the next section. Keep right of *Toilet Trouble*, with possible protection in the corner on the right.
FA. Nigel Manning, Nick Butterworth 3.7.1990

Skyline Buttress
p.108

Fruitbat Level
p.104

The Salt Pans
p.98

15m

12m

④ ⑤ ⑥ ⑦ ② ③ ①

The Rognon

This island of rock in a sea of scree sees little attention. It has a long approach and is a bit loose and adventurous.
Approach (map p.83, overview p.84) - The Rognon can be approached from the Lower Walls (p.86). From the Tunnel of Love exit below *Darkness Visible,* scramble across the scree to the base.
Alternatively, head up to the Fruitbat Level, walk to its end and descend to The Salt Pans (p.98), then descend to The Rognon from here.

❶ **Joie De Vivre** . . . . 🔲 **HS 4a**

❷ **Theftus Maximus** . . . . 🔲 **E1 5b**
3m left of the broken corner.
FA. K.Strange 15.5.1986

❸ **Little Mo.** . . . . 🔲 **HS 4a**
2m left of the broken corner.

The Upper Tier is a little more inviting.

❹ **Abattoir Blues** . . . . 🔲 **E2 5c**
The fine arete is exposed in places. Climb up past a bolt, then go 'au cheval' to reach a second bolt - hard to clip. Above this, move onto the front face and up to the top.
FA. Mark Dicken 2007

❺ **Genital Persuasion.** . . . . 🔲 **E3 5c**
Start below a groove with a bonsai tree growing from its top. Head up past a shot-hole and three bolts.
FA. A.Jackson, Nick Biven 26.4.1986

❻ **Single Factor.** . . . . 🔲 **E2 5c**
Start just right of *Genital Persuasion*. Ascend direct to a high bolt at 10m, then move into the crack on the right. At a good foothold, head straight up past a second bolt.
FA. Nick Biven, A.Jackson 26.4.1986

❼ **Second Thoughts** . . . . . . 🔲 **VS 4b**
The blunt friable right-hand rib is best avoided.

Bus Stop Quarry

Dali's Hole

California

Australia

Serengeti

Never Never Land

Twll Mawr

Mordor - Lost World

Vivian Quarry

Rainbow Slab Area

Snakes and Ladders

Outlying

James Oswald eyeing up the finishing hold on *Off The Beaten Track* (E3 5c) - *p.97* - on the aptly named Railtrack Slab.

Looning the Tube

The area around *Looning the Tube* has a good mix of sport, trad and run-out bolted climbs and is very popular. Areas of sun and shade can be found throughout the day, although it is mostly a morning sun wall.

Approach (map p.83, overview p.84) - This area is on the west side of the col, immediately left on the approach.

1 Puddy Kat 5a
Climb the flake/groove, with a tricky move up the cleaned slab above. Two bolts to a lower-off.
FA. Jim Kelly, Julia Kelly 14.5.2009

2 Just for Fun E2 5c
Bridge up the corner, reaching out to clip the bolt, and make hard moves up the slab on the right to reach the ledge and bolt. Follow the flake to the top, or use the lower-off to the left.
FA. Ian Lloyd-Jones, Chris Davies (both led) 21.4.1991

3 The Burning . . . . . . 6b+
The sustained and pumpy groove passing a number of bolts.
FA. Mike Turner, Clive Stephenson 8.8.1991

4 The Deceptive Dyke 5c
The pleasant dolerite pillar. Make bold moves up to gain the ledge and first bolt, then follow the pillar and bolts to the lower-off. *Photo on p.92.*
FA. Mark Reeves, Llion Morris 9.2006

5 1066 . . . . 6b
A very contrived line up the bolted wall right of *Deceptive Dyke*. Avoid following the groove!
FA. Phil Targett, Tony Hughes 27.8.2008

6 N.E. Spur E3 5c
The arete is bold and seldom climbed.
FA. Chris Parkin, Wynn Rees 13.7.1986

7 Loony Toons . . . E3 5c
The technical wall past three bolts has some long reaches, and is quite scary.
FA. S.Puroy, C.Fowler, E.Thomas 13.9.1990

8 Brief Encounter . . . . HVS 5a
A mix of trad and bolts. Climb up to a ledge below a groove. A long reach and hard pull to the first bolt gain the wall above. Sustained climbing then leads past two more bolts to a lower-off.
FA. Ian Lloyd-Jones, Bob Llewelyn 20.4.1991

9 Astroman from the Planet Zzzoink E3 6a
Very dirty and needs re-bolting. Best avoided. The arete to the right is slightly easier but not independent.
FA. Nigel Manning 5.7.1991

10 The Man Who Fell to Earth E2 5c
Also very dirty and in need of re-bolting.
FA. Ian Lloyd-Jones 29.6.1991

11 Donald Duck 6c

A trick start leads to easier climbing higher up. The spaced bolts make it feel exciting - it might be better viewed as an E3.
FA. Rob Deane, Perry Hawkins 5.8.1986

12 Gadaffi Duck . . . . 6b+

The groove has a hard start, but eases shortly after the second bolt, to give nice sustained climbing.
FA. Rob Deane, Perry Hawkins 5.8.1986

13 Sad Man Who's Sane . . . VS 4c

The slab with two bolts. A wire can be placed to protect the move onto the central ledge.
FA. Mark Reeves, Brian Wills 9.2006

14 U.B.L. . . . . HS 4b

Similar to its left-hand neighbour but slightly easier. There is a long reach to gain the lower-off. About sport **4c** with a single cam placement.
FA. Mark Reeves, Brian Wills 9.2006

15 Hyperfly . . . . 6a+

Bridge up the groove to the left of the square-cut corner of *Turn of the Century.*
FA. Phil Targett, Ian Lloyd-Jones 23.8.2007

16 Turn of the Century E2 5c

The square-cut corner gives technical climbing past two bolts and some trad gear to a lower-off.
FA. Perry Hawkins, George Smith 12.8.1986

17 Maximum Tariff 6b

Technical and sustained climbing up the wall.
FA. Phil Targett. Ian Lloyd-Jones. P.Walley 7.9.2007

18 Buffalo Smashed in Head Jump

. . . . E4 5c

A harrowing lead. Move up to gain the groove capped by an overlap. Difficult and poorly-protected moves lead to ledges and the *Maximum Tariff* lower-off.

19 Dried Mouth Sesame Seed . . 5c

Climb the groove, passing a bolt and a bolt stud.
FA. K.Turner, L.Dow 20.8.1991

20 Technical Hamster 6c

It is also possible to climb the left side of the little arete.
FA. Phil Targett, Tony Hughes 6.8.2007

21 Technical Hamster Dance . . . . . HVS 4b

An eliminate up the right side of the arete.
FA. Phil Targett 6.8.2007

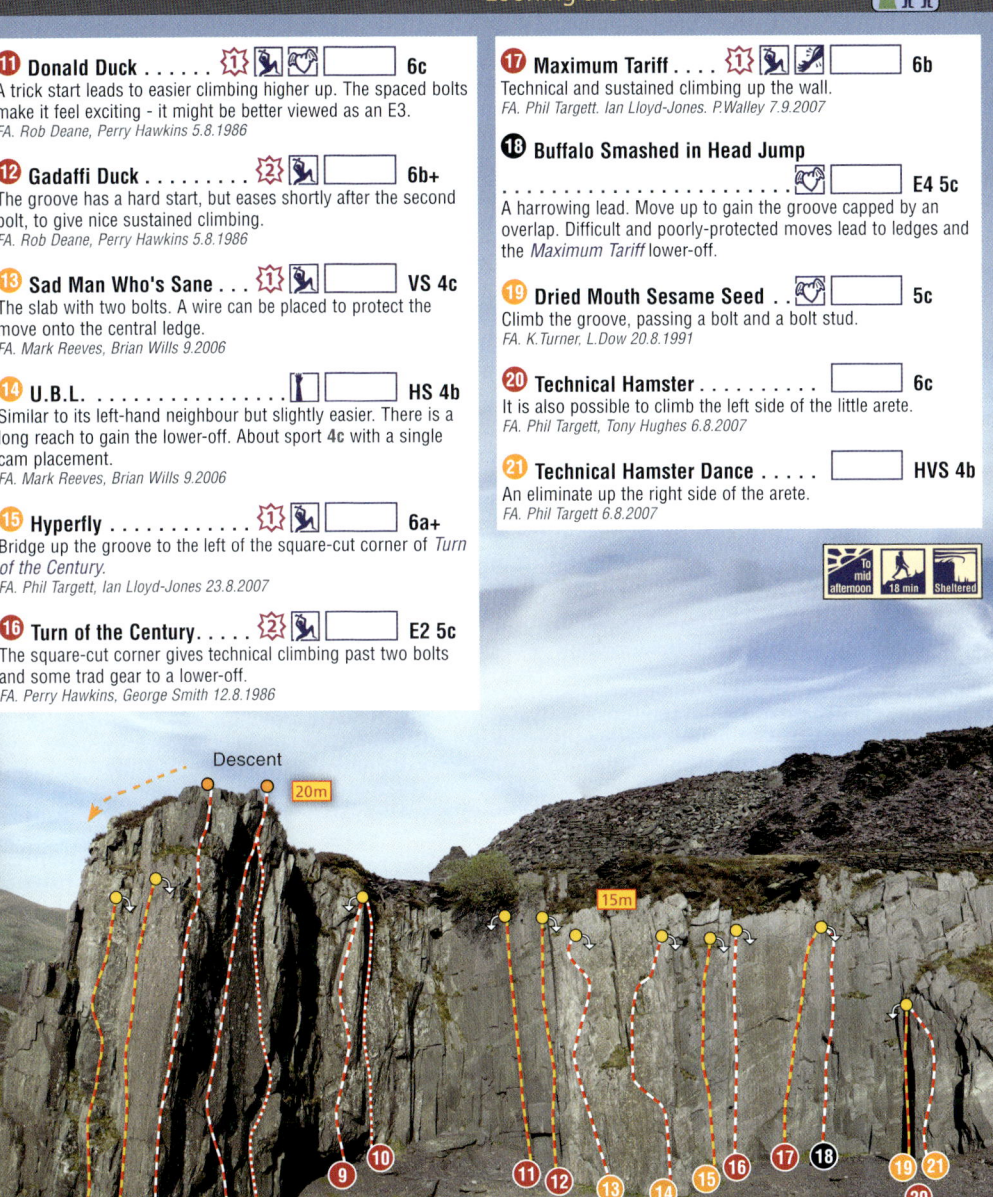

Bus Stop Quarry

Dali's Hole

California

Australia

Serengeti

Never Never Land

Twll Mawr

Mordor - Lost World

Vivian Quarry

Rainbow Slab Area

Snakes and Ladders

Outlying

James McMahon on *The Deceptive Dyke* (5b) - *p.90* - on the Looning the Tube area of Australia.
Some see slate as a monoculture of slab climbing, but there are many angles to slate and it has a natural grain to it. These variables mean it offers many different styles of climbing. One feature of the slate quarries is dolerite veins or 'dykes' of rock. These volcanic intrusions might have ruined the surrounding rock for the quarrymen, but they often make great rock climbs.

Bus Stop Quarry

Dali's Hole

California

Australia

Serengeti

Never Never Land

Twll Mawr

Mordor - Lost World

Vivian Quarry

Rainbow Slab Area

Snakes and Ladders

Outlying

Bus Stop Quarry

Dali's Hole

California

Australia

Serengeti

Never Never Land

Twll Mawr

Mordor - Lost World

Vivian Quarry

Rainbow Slab Area

Snakes and Ladders

Outlying

22 Dried Mouth Frog . . . . ☐ **HS 4a**
The groove on the left edge of the slab is short, reasonably straightforward and protected by small wires. Exit by meandering up loose ledges and gaining the level above to belay as for *Looning the Tube* on a bolt at the base of the slab above.
FA. K.Turner, L.Dow 20.8.1991

23 Swan Hunter . . . . . . ☐ **E4 6b**
A bold route. Head up the arete to the break and make a detour to clip the bolt on *Goose Creature*. Move back out to the arete to make the alarming crux moves. It has been climbed direct, without the side runner, at E6.
FA. Andy Swann 20.4.1986. FA. (Direct) J. Shieldhouse Hadley 28.3.2016

24 Goose Creature . ☐ **E3 6a**
A great route with a hard rockover. Climb up to a small ledge, then foot traverse the break until you can climb up past a bolt to a second break. Mantel this and clip a bolt on the right, then traverse left to another bolt, and make a hard move past it. A further thin move leads to jugs and the lower-off.
Photo on cover.
FA. Andy Swann 20.4.1986

25 Menai Vice . . . . ☐ **E4 6c**
Make a direct start to the first bolt on *Goose Creature*, then break out slightly right to clip a second bolt. Passing this to reach a third bolt is desperate. Move onto the top and belay as for *Looning the Tube*.
FA. George Smith, Wynn Rees 12.7.1986

26 Looning the Tube . . . ☐ **E1 5a**
The original line of this wall used to start up the tube... until it fell down! Traverse out across the slab passing a bolt before moving up and right to the rusty spike. From here, follow the groove up and left past a cam slot. A hard move past a bolt leads to easier climbing to the level above. Belay way back off a spike and bolt at the base of the wall. *Photos on p.4 and p.78.*
FA. Cliff Phillips (roped solo) 19.6.1984

27 Hysterectomy . . . . ☐ **E5 5c**
Follow *Looning the Tube* to the bolt and then head straight up the slab following the line of weakness, past a good skyhook below half-height. Maintain your composure to eventually reach a bolt just before you top out.
FA. Andy Swann, Dave O'Dowd 20.4.1986

28 Zzzooming the Tube . ☐ **E3 6a**
Follow *Looning the Tube* to the metal spike. Move right and then make something of a desperate heart-in-your-mouth pull to clip the first bolt. Move up and make another desperate clip before carrying on to the lower-off.
FA. Ian Lloyd-Jones, Tony Hughes 21.8.1984

29 Pruning the Tube . . . . ☐ **E2 5c**
Follow *Looning the Tube* to the rusty spike. Continue along the break until you reach a bolt by your ankles. Clip this and make a small move right. Finish straight up to the right of a small tree.
FA. Nick Walton 26.4.1986

30 Exhuming the Tube . . . . . ☐ **E3 5c**
This route follows the original line, from when the tube extended all the way to the next level. Follow *Pruning the Tube* to the bolt at ankle height, then continue along the rising break-line past another bolt. Carry on along the break, clipping a bolt just before the top, and climb up onto the next level.
FA. Mark Reeves, Llion Morris 2010

31 Bise-Mon-Cul . . . . ☐ **E2 5c**
A lower start to *Looning the Tube* reached either from below or by a short abseil from above to a bolt belay. Climb the slab past some bolts to join *Looning...*
FA. Jim Kelly, John Redhead 27.3.2010

32 Mad on the Metro . . ☐ **E4 5c**
A nice route, run-out but steady. Start below a bolt and a ring above a small blocky pinnacle. Climb up to the first bolt, then carry on up easier terrain to a second. Move up and left to a third and then make a trickier move up and right to a single-bolt lower-off.
FA. Chris Davies, Matt Wells 6.1993

33 Gerboa Racer . . . . ☐ **E4 5c**
The slab is thin, run out and friable. Care is needed throughout, and it is not to be mistaken for *Fcuk Les Clotures*.
FA. Rob Mirfin, B.Crampton 2002

34 Fcuk Les Clotures . . . . ☐ **5a**
Just to the left of the unstable looking pillar is a well-cleaned slab with five bolts leading to a shared lower-off with *Gerboa Racer*.
FA. Jim Kelly, John Redhead 16.6.2010

35 A Selfish Act of Loonacy . ☐ **6b**
Follow *Fcuk Les Clotures* to the third bolt, then move right across the thin slab and up past two more bolts.
FA. Jim Kelly, John Redhead 27.3.2010

Above the Rails

36 Sport 4 All . . . . ☐ **5a**
Climb the groove on the left of the wall.
FA. Ian Lloyd-Jones 2.10.2007

37 Kinder Surprise . . . . ☐ **5a**
Climb the slanting line to the right of *Sport 4 All*.
FA. Ian Lloyd-Jones, Phil Targett 7.9.2007

38 Surprise Surprise . . . . ☐ **6a**
A tricky start leads to delicate and balancy climbing above.
FA. Ian Lloyd-Jones 11.9.2007

39 Shorty's Dyno . . . . ☐ **6a**
A great dyno for the short (probably worth 6c+)...a straightforward reach for the tall.
FA. Ian Lloyd-Jones, Phil Targett (both led) 13.9.2007

40 Orangutang Overhang . . . ☐ **6a+**
A technical groove followed by an entertaining roof.
FA. Ian Lloyd-Jones, Tony Hughes, Phil Targett 28.8.2007

41 Cyber World Sl@te Heads
. . . . ☐ **6a+**
Climb the groove up to the right-hand side of the large roof and continue to a lower-off on the large flake.
FA. Ian Lloyd-Jones, Phil Targett, Tony Hughes 27.8.2007

42 Steps of Glory . . . . ☐ **5a**
Climb the slabby wall to the right of *Cyber World Sl@te Heads*. Some nice stepped edges lead to a lower-off. *Photo on p.19.*
FA. Mark Chambers, Christian Roots, Ian Pagano (all led) 2.3.2008

Above the Rails

A short level with some nice sport routes, the best of which are *Steps of Glory* and *Orangutang Overhang*.
Approach (map p.83, overview p.84) - From the Australia Col, head left of the Looning the Tube area and follow the incline up one level.

To mid afternoon | 20 min | Sheltered

The Sidings
p.100

Approach one level up from Australia Col

17m

15m

36 37 38 39 40 41 42

28 29 30

35

27

Railtrack Slab
p.96

22

Approach from Australia Col

23 24 25 26

32 33 34

A

Approach to Railtrack Slab

31

Approach to routes on the right-hand side

Lower Walls
p.86

Illegal Smeagol - p.87

Runup - p.87

Bus Stop Quarry | Dali's Hole | California | Australia | Serengeti | Never Never Land | Twll Mawr | Mordor - Lost World | Vivian Quarry | Rainbow Slab Area | Snakes and Ladders | Outlying

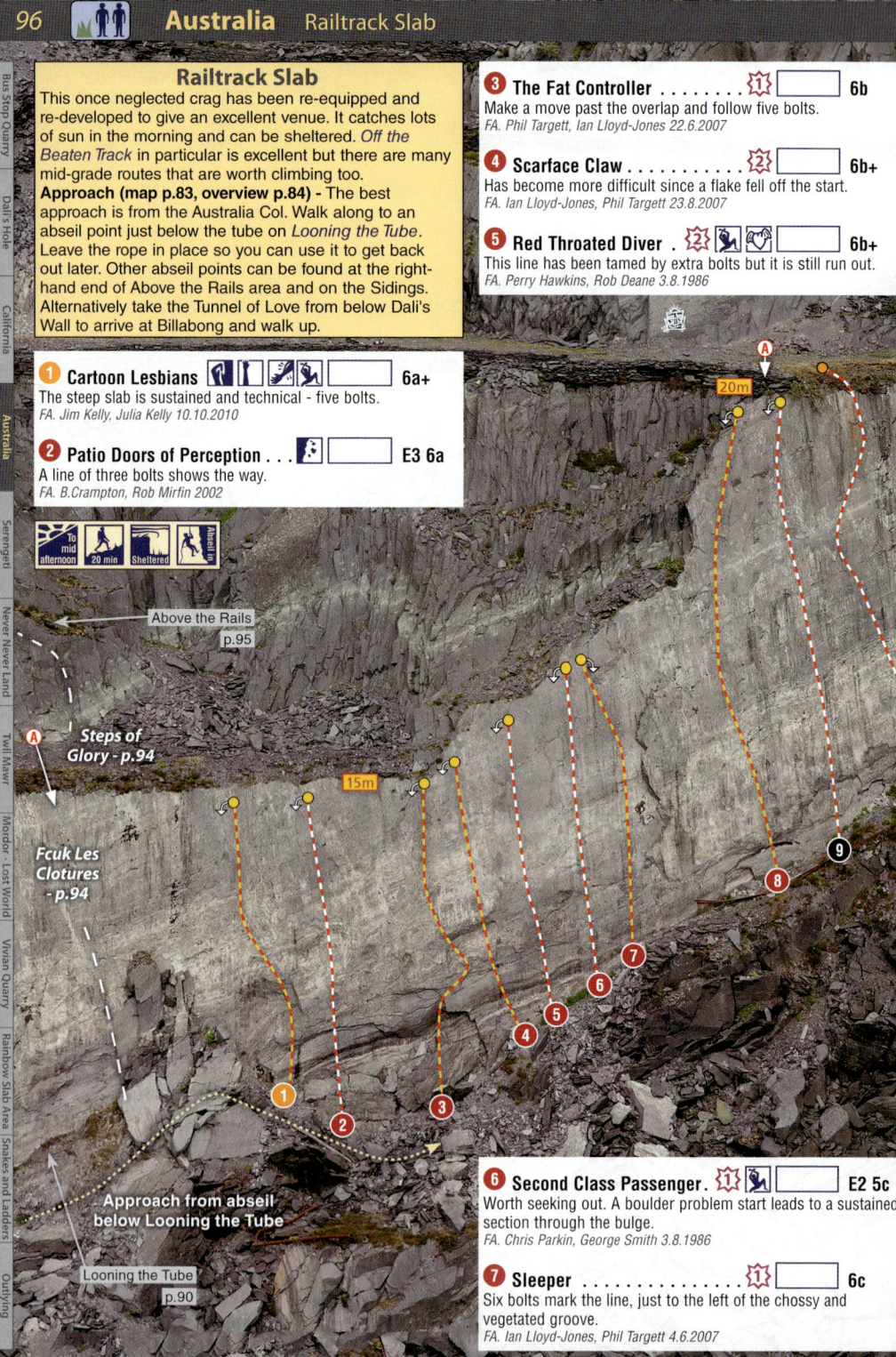

Railtrack Slab

This once neglected crag has been re-equipped and re-developed to give an excellent venue. It catches lots of sun in the morning and can be sheltered. *Off the Beaten Track* in particular is excellent but there are many mid-grade routes that are worth climbing too.

Approach (map p.83, overview p.84) - The best approach is from the Australia Col. Walk along to an abseil point just below the tube on *Looning the Tube*. Leave the rope in place so you can use it to get back out later. Other abseil points can be found at the right-hand end of Above the Rails area and on the Sidings. Alternatively take the Tunnel of Love from below Dali's Wall to arrive at Billabong and walk up.

❶ Cartoon Lesbians .... 6a+
The steep slab is sustained and technical - five bolts.
FA. Jim Kelly, Julia Kelly 10.10.2010

❷ Patio Doors of Perception ... E3 6a
A line of three bolts shows the way.
FA. B.Crampton, Rob Mirfin 2002

❸ The Fat Controller 6b
Make a move past the overlap and follow five bolts.
FA. Phil Targett, Ian Lloyd-Jones 22.6.2007

❹ Scarface Claw .... 6b+
Has become more difficult since a flake fell off the start.
FA. Ian Lloyd-Jones, Phil Targett 23.8.2007

❺ Red Throated Diver . 6b+
This line has been tamed by extra bolts but it is still run out.
FA. Perry Hawkins, Rob Deane 3.8.1986

20m

15m

Above the Rails
p.95

A Steps of Glory - p.94

Fcuk Les Clotures - p.94

Approach from abseil below Looning the Tube

Looning the Tube
p.90

❻ Second Class Passenger . E2 5c
Worth seeking out. A boulder problem start leads to a sustained section through the bulge.
FA. Chris Parkin, George Smith 3.8.1986

❼ Sleeper 6c
Six bolts mark the line, just to the left of the chossy and vegetated groove.
FA. Ian Lloyd-Jones, Phil Targett 4.6.2007

A Grand Day Out Pitch 2 - p.101

The Australian - p.99

The Sidings p.100

The Salt Pans p.98

Bus Stop Quarry | Dali's Hole | California | Australia | Serengeti | Never Never Land | Twll Mawr | Mordor - Lost World | Vivian Quarry | Rainbow Slab Area | Snakes and Ladders | Outlying

8 Crazy Train 6c
Sustained climbing following the line of eight bolts. Either top out or traverse across right to the lower-off on *Ancestral Vices*.
FA. Ian Lloyd-Jones, Phil Targett 22.6.2007

9 Ancestral Vices . . E4 6b
Sustained climbing up the wall which is tricky, especially if the holds are damp (they often are). The crux at the top is avoidable.
FA. Paul Williams, Neil Carson, D.Carson, S.Kerr 5.4.1988

10 Off the Beaten Track E3 5c
An amazing route with spaced bolts. Moving past the first bolt to gain the wobbly flake is the crux - you might want a sling to loop over a small spike to reach the second. A steady approach above this brings you to a dramatic top-out on the rails. Belay on the Sidings level. *Photos on p.80 and p.89*.
FA. Chris Parkin, Perry Hawkins, George Smith 2.8.1986

11 Uncle Nick's Broken Toe . E5 6b
A bold direct to *Here to Stay, Gone Tomorrow*. There is no gear.
FA. Calum Muskett 9.2009

12 Here to Stay, Gone Tomorrow E3 6a
Start up *Between Here and Now* and move out left to gain the top bolted section of the original route. This makes it a safe and enjoyable outing.
FA. George Smith, Chris Parkin, Perry Hawkins 2.8.1986. A different line.

13 Between Here and Now E3 6a
Nearly as good as *Off the Beaten Track*. Start below a line of well-spaced bolts and climb delicately to reach the lower-off.
FA. George Smith, Perry Hawkins, Rob Deane 4.8.1986

14 The Toms Approach E4 5c
The diagonal crack has little in the way of protection. One of the early lines here, but seldom climbed these days.
FA. Bob Drury 7.9.1986

15 Now or Never Never E5 5c
A very bold line up the slab. Trend rightwards at first then back left. A single skyhook is the only possible protection.
FA. George Smith 12.8.1986

16 A Grand Day Out Pitch 1 . . . . 6a
Pitch 1 of a wandering sport route that makes it way to the very top of this side of Australia. This first pitch is poor and has some loose rock near its top.
FA. George Smith, Perry Hawkins, Rob Deane 4.8.1986

17 Psychodelicate 7c
A technical masterpiece but rarely climbed. A delicate traverse across the roof leads to a stopper move to gain the slab. It is run out above this and certainly no pushover.
FA. George Smith, Chris Parkin 6.12.1986

18 The Ghan 6b
Head up the corner at the right-hand end of the slab, to a ledge. Climb the left edge of the slab above to reach the main slab. Follow a line of weakness diagonally across this to the lower-off.
FA. Harold Walmsley, Colin Struthers 16.4.2014

The Salt Pans

The Salt Pans offer secluded climbing with some nice new sport routes. The best lines are the three outstanding aretes of *The Australian, Zut Alors* and *Y Rhaffwr,* though the other routes in the area are worth a look.

Approach (map p.83, overview p.84) - From the Australia Col, head up three levels, walk along the Fruitbat Level and descend the Oil Drum Glacier at the end to The Salt Pans. Alternatively, scramble rightwards from the base of Railtrack Slab.

Three levels up from the Australia Col, past the Fruitbat Level - p.104
Bad Step
6
7
15m
1
2
3
4
5
Approach from Railtrack Slab - p.96

To mid afternoon | 30 min | Sheltered

15m

Drop down onto the
Oil Drum Glacier

8

9

Bus Stop Quarry
Dali's Hole
California
Australia
Serengeti
Never Never Land
Twll Mawr
Mordor - Lost World
Vivian Quarry
Rainbow Slab Area
Snakes and Ladders
Outlying

❹ The Rack . . . . 🏛1 📙 ⬜ **6b+**
Start at a groove and climb it and a ramp. Mantel and continue
up the wall (a little less reachy than *Stretched to the Limit*). At
the last bolt, step left and finish up *Stretched to the Limit*.
FA. Colin Struthers, Harold Walmsley 12.11.2013

❺ Narcolepsy . . . . 🏛1 📗🧗🤾 📙 ⬜ **7a+**
A steep slab with technical and thin climbing
FA. Rob Mirfin 2002

❻ The Australian . . . . 🏛2 🤾 ⬜ **6b**
This arete overlooks the Railtrack Slab and is on a level above
Zut Alors and *Y Rhaffwr*. Don't fluff the first clip!
FA. Chris Davies, Phil Targett, Matt Wells 21.10.1989

❼ Jenny Wren . . . . ⬜ **VD**
Start 10m or so right of *The Australian* and about 10m left of
a pipe crossing a gap in the level above. Climb the deep hand-
width crack with good protection.
FA. Philip Biglands 24.10.2013

❽ The Stream of Obscenity . . . . 🏛1 ⬜ **7a**
A lone sport route through some stepped bulges.
FA. Mark Dicken 2007

❾ Kosciusko . . . . 🏛1 ⬜ **VS 4b**
The curving arete leads to a hand-traverse as it arcs over. Top
out by the perched block.

❶ Zut Alors . . . . 🏛3 🤾🤾 ⬜ **6c+**
The furthest left arete of the level. Follow the sharp arete on its
right-hand side with occasional excursions right onto the slab.
Finish with unusual moves in a fine position on the very crest of
the undercut upper arete.
FA. Colin Struthers, Harold Walmsley 10.11.2013

❷ Y Rhaffwr . . . . 🏛2 🤾 ⬜ **6c**
A nice arete with unusual moves.
FA. Ian Lloyd-Jones, Chris Davies 18.12.2009

❸ Stretched to the Limit . . . 🏛1 📙 ⬜ **6c+**
The blunt arete between *Narcolepsy* and *Y Raffwr*. Start on its
left side then transfer to the right by the first bolt and climb past
a very long reach and a tricky sequence until the angle eases.
FA. Harold Walmsley 12.11.2013

The Sidings

Although only short in length, The Sidings has some good easy sport routes. Most of them were developed by Josie Ball and her brother Archie, who were about 11 and 7 at the time - their father bolted the lines up for them. The area offers the best easy sport routes in the quarries and is very popular.

Approach (map p.83, overview p.84) - From the Australia Col, head to the left of the Looning the Tube area and follow the incline up one level. From here take a small track on the left up to another level. The Sidings are along this level.

1 **Puffing Billy** . . . . [   ] S 4a
Climb the corner.
FA. Charlie Jordan 30.8.2008

2 **Not Known** . . . . [   ] 6a
FA. [route symbols]

3 **Glass Axe** . . . . [   ] E5 7a
The groove/arete between *Not Known* and *N'Gauge*.
FA. Andy Woodward 1986

4 **'N' Gauge** . . . . [   ] 5c
Follow the narrow pillar at the left-hand end of the level. The top move is very hard.
FA. Josie Ball 11.2007

5 **Side Line** . . . . [   ] 4c
Climb out right from first bolt of *'N' Gauge*.
FA. Josie Ball 27.1.2008

6 **Derailed** . . . . [   ] 4a
A good route that follows the corner up and right to a lower-off.
FA. Josie Ball 27.1.2008

[icons: To mid afternoon / 25 min]

7 **Thomas the Tank** . . . . [   ] 4a
A slabby line.
FA. Archie Ball 16.12.2007

8 **Rack and Pin** . . . . [   ] 5c
Start up the corner on the left-hand side of the clean slab.
FA. Josie Ball 16.12.2007

9 **Sodor** . . . . [   ] 6a
The hairline crack left of the centre of the slab. Where the crack terminates at the horizontal feature, continue straight up on pronounced holds to the lower-off.
FA. Josie Ball 13.10.2007

Above the Line, HVS, *was the original line of the slab. It has been superseded by these sport routes.*

10 **The Mallard** . . . . . . [   ] 5c
The thin slab.
FA. Josie Ball 16.12.2007

11 **The Polar Express** . . [   ] 5c
The route on the right-hand side of the slab, just before the base gets broken and the height decreases. *Photo on p.102.*
FA. Josie Ball 13.10.2007

Approach two levels up from the Australia Col

9m

Above the Rails p.95

12 Ivor the Engine . . . . ⚹ [ ] **5a**
Climb the initial broken slab to the cleaner slab at the top.
FA. Josie Ball 27.1.2008

13 Gordon . . . . ⚹ [ ] **3c**
A nice and easy route up the slab and corner on the right-hand side of the face.
FA. Archie Ball 16.12.2007

14 The Level Crossing . ⚹ 🧗⚒ [ ] **5c**
A traverse of the slab following the distinct break. Start up *Rack and Pin*, then follow the break to finish at *Ivor the Engine*.
FA. Josie Ball 27.1.2008

15 Being a Bob . . . . ⚹ [ ] **5a**
FA. Mark Reeves, Simon Geering 27.3.2017. Retro-bolted by Mark Reeves.

16 'Those who climb...' . . . . . . ⚹ [ ] **5c**
The groove, 10m right of *Gordon*. Soloed in August 1986 but not claimed at the time.
FA. Chris Parkin 2.8.1986. Equipped in 2008. The more complete name is 'Those who climb clearly marked projects are the kind of people who would steal the chocolate bar from a kid's lunch box....' with some abuse at the end.

17 Choo Choo . . . . ⚹ [ ] **5c**
The arete and groove. One of the final jugs is loose!
FA. Josie Ball 28.2.2008

18 Hogwarts Express . . . . ⚹ [ ] **5c**
Climb the stepped corner 4m right of *Choo Choo*, with the crux at the top.
FA. Josie Ball 27.1.2008

19 The Railway Children ⚹⚹ 🧗❙ [ ] **6a**
Climb the bouldery wall to good jugs, then move right onto a neat wall.
FA. Josie Ball 15.2.2008

20 In Loving Memory . . . . . ⚹ 🧗 [ ] **6a+**
Climb rightwards beneath the hanging groove, then head left above it to the lower-off.
FA. Josie Ball 14.4.2008

21 A Grand Day Out Pitch 2 . ⚹⚹ 🧗 [ ] **5a**
Originally pitch two of *A Grand Day Out* started here. Owing to rockfall below, it is worth now starting the whole route from here and omitting pitch 1.
FA. The Balls 2010

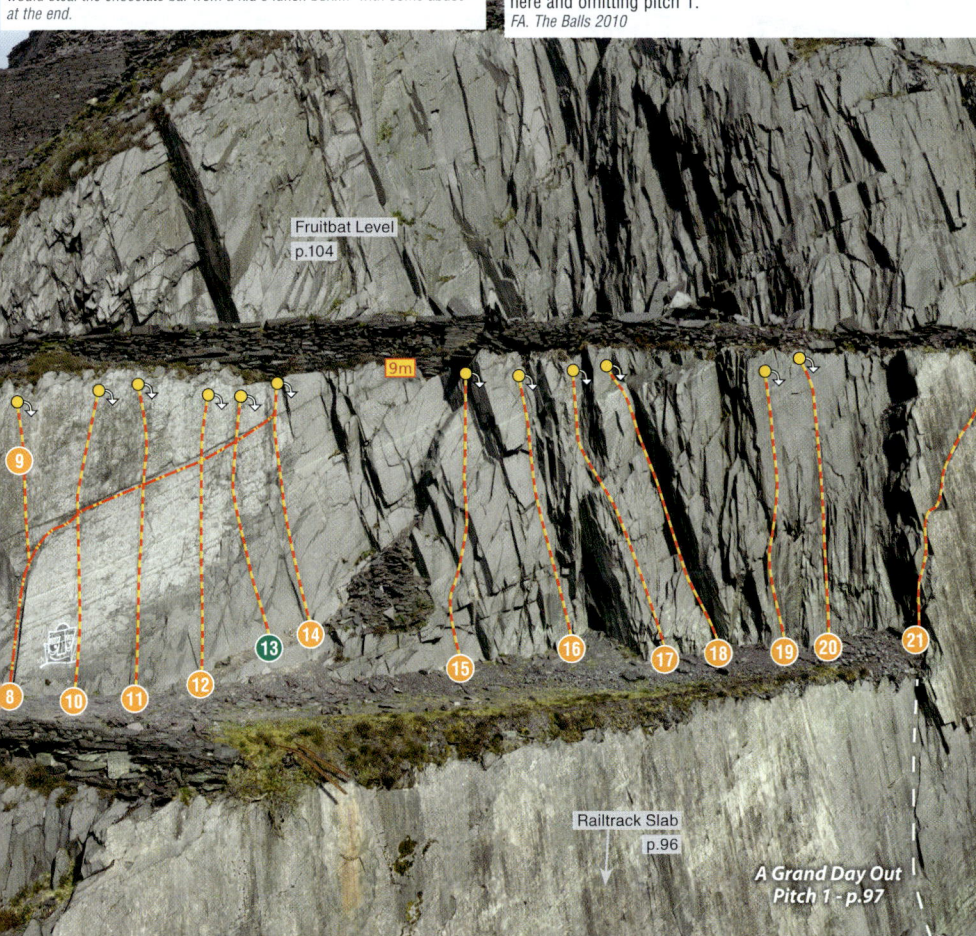

Fruitbat Level
p.104

9m

Railtrack Slab
p.96

*A Grand Day Out
Pitch 1 - p.97*

Bus Stop Quarry
Dali's Hole
California
Australia
Serengeti
Never Never Land
Twll Mawr
Mordor - Lost World
Vivian Quarry
Rainbow Slab Area
Snakes and Ladders
Outlying

Bus Stop Quarry

Dali's Hole

California

Australia

Serengeti

Never Never Land

Twll Mawr

Mordor – Lost World

Vivian Quarry

Rainbow Slab Area

Snakes and Ladders

Outlying

William Adams on the pleasant *Polar Express* (5b) - *p.100* - at The Sidings.
Love it or hate it, easy sport climbing in the quarries is here to stay. The
Sidings is among the most popular venues, along with other areas of
Australia. The area was developed by Fraser Ball and his kids Josie and Archie.
Despite the routes being short and friendly, the views are pretty spectacular.

Bus Stop Quarry

Dali's Hole

California

Australia

Serengeti

Never Never Land

Twll Mawr

Mordor – Lost World

Vivian Quarry

Rainbow Slab Area

Snakes and Ladders

Outlying

Bus Stop Quarry

Dali's Hole

California

Australia

Serengeti

Never Never Land

Twll Mawr

Mordor - Lost World

Vivian Quarry

Rainbow Slab Area

Snakes and Ladders

Outlying

Fruitbat Level

The Fruitbat Level has a few quality sections of rock spread out along the level. There are several decent routes but nothing of any real quality.

Approach (map p.83, overview p.84) - From the Australia Col, scramble up a good path on the left side of the working. The Fruitbat Level is the third level up, just above The Sidings.

1 Solitude Standing E3 6a
A bold but short route up the inverted V-groove - skyhook useful. A tricky start leads to an overlap 7m up. Belay off a block up and left.
FA. Phil Targett, Danny Dutton, Clive Stephenson 25.11.1989

2 Eric the Fruitbat E3 5c
A tenuous pitch. The initial moves up the slab are poorly protected by cams. A long and harrowing reach for the bolt follows, although you might be able to lasso it before making more difficult moves past it. Belay off the birch tree above.
FA. Danny Dutton, Danny Dutton, Clive Stephenson 25.11.1989

3 Harder than it Looks . . . . 6a+
About 25m along the level is a bolted line which is also pitch 3 of *A Grand Day Out*. It is a great **6a+** in its own right.
FA. Josie Ball, Archie Ball, Fraser Ball 8.2010

4 M.I.L Arete E1 5b
The arete with a big droopy bar in its upper section - steady as you go! Climb the slab easily to below the droopy bar. Slinging this and passing it is the crux.
FA. Phil Targett, Chris Davies 21.10.1989

5 Genevive E2 5c
To the left of the greenstone arete is a corner groove. Climb up this past a low ledge. Continue with care past a peg and some friable rock to the top.
FA. Phil Targett, Chris Davies 21.10.1989

6 Rory's Unfinished Business . . . . HVS 4c
Just to the right of the corner of *Genevive* is a distinct groove, which offers some independent climbing.
FA. Jamie MacDonald, Rory Shaw 17.4.2015

7 Pontiac Arete . . . . VS 4c
The crack in the greenstone arete is loose at its top.
FA. Clive Allen, Rob Wright 16.2.1991

To mid afternoon | 30 min

Zippy Level
p.106

Walk off leftwards

14m

The Sidings
p.100

A Grand Day Out
Pitch 1 - p.97

Tricky path -
take care

Railtrack Slab
p.96

8 **Stretched Limo** 1 E2 5c
The pleasant groove to the right of the arete. Climb the groove to a ledge at 4m. Carry on up the groove via a series of reaches past a peg.
FA. Clive Allen, Rob Wright 16.2.1991

9 **Gymnastic Fantastic** . 6c+
The steep tower, passing four bolts to a lower-off. After a reachy start head right to a textbook slate move. Either make a difficult stretch back left into the flake, or continue straight up.
FA. Nick Sharpe, G.Jones 20.9.2010

10 **Slatebite** . . . . 2 7a+
Start up the groove, then make awkward moves to the tall pocket out right. Rock into this and make a burly move up to gain the fourth bolt, then on to the top.
FA. Chris Davies 6.2.2010

11 **The Christening of New Boots** . . E1 5b
20m before you reach the huts is a corner. Start 1m left of this and move up and right into the corner. Climb back out, then head up and left to reach a diagonal roof. Move right round this and head straight up to the top.
FA. Matt Wells, I.Hill 5.6.1993

12 **Rock Athlete's Day Off** . . . . . . HVS 5b
From the base of the corner avoided by *The Christening of New Boots*, move up and right to a ledge at the base of a groove. Climb the left arete of the groove to the top.
FA. I.Hill 5.6.1993

14m

Project

5 6 7 8 9 10 11 12

The Salt Pans
p.98

Bus Stop Quarry

Dali's Hole

California

Australia

Serengeti

Never Never Land

Twll Mawr

Mordor – Lost World

Vivian Quarry

Rainbow Slab Area

Snakes and Ladders

Outlying

Bus Stop Quarry / Dali's Hole / California / Australia / Serengeti / Never Never Land / Twll Mawr / Mordor - Lost World / Vivian Quarry / Rainbow Slab Area / Snakes and Ladders / Outlying

1 Jepp the Knave . . . . 🔲🔲🔲 [ ] 7b+
Make a hard rockover leftwards past the first bolt to reach a
good rest. Step right and layaway up the steep rib to a sloper. A
hard sequence to stand on this allows you to reach better holds
and a ledge.
FA. Phil Targett, Chris Davies 28.10.2009

2 Thumberlina . . . . . . 🔲🔲🔲 [ ] 7c
Climb up to the base of the grove left by the massive flake.
'Quarryman style' climbing up this leads to a jug, a long move
up and left to a corner and left to a ledge before you reach the lower-off.
*FA. James Docherty, Jo Docherty and Luke Dudill 14.7.2018. Two days
before this book went to the printers.*

3 Last Chance for a Slow Dance . . [ ] E3 5b
The cleaned flake-line on the right side of the steep wall. Climb
direct to the start of the flake-line, then continue (with improving
gear) to a blunt spike at its apex. From here traverse right into
the bay and finish up the groove as for *...and a Pen Please*.
FA. Mark Dicken 2.11.2007

4 In on the Kill Taker . . . . 🔲 [ ] E5 6b
Climb *Last Chance for a Slow Dance* to the blunt spike. Make
a reach for the bolt and commit to the headwall via a series of
desperate moves and possible BIG air!
FA. Mark Dicken, Mark Reeves 8.8.2008

5 Beanstalk . . . . 🔲 [ ] 7a
A brilliant line with three distinct difficult sections. Climb up and
right, passing two bolts to a jug, and the third bolt. Move back
left and up to the fourth bolt. There is a sling placement if you
want it where the route crosses *Last Chance For a Slow Dance*,
then continue past the fifth bolt to the double lower-off.
FA. Chris Davies, Phil Targett 7.10.2009

6 ...and a Pen Please . . . . . . 🔲 [ ] HVS 5a
Climb the broken crack on the left side of the slab. This leads to
a corner which is climbed to the top.
FA. Paul Woodhouse, Keith Archer 7.7.2003

7 Boulevard of Broken Dreams . 🔲 [ ] 6c+
Start at the square-cut flake left of *Rastaman Vibration*. Ascend
the flake to a good rockover which gives access to a blank slab.
A thin move past the third bolt gains easier ground to the roof.
The roof is not as straightforward as it appears; the lack of
footholds and friction makes it very easy to fall.
FA. Tesni Lloyd-Jones, Ian Lloyd-Jones 16.7.2013

8 Rastaman Vibration . . . . 🔲 [ ] E2 6a
Start below two bolts, and make some thin moves to pass them.
Continue direct to the roof, moving through this with care.
FA. Mark Boniface 1988

9 Razorback . . . . 🔲 [ ] HVS 5a
The crack-line provides an entertaining climb.
FA. Mark Boniface 1988

To mid afternoon / 32 min

Walk off
leftwards

14m

Skyline Buttress
p.108

Zippy Level
The Zippy Level is similar to the Fruitbat Level - plenty of
routes but nothing of outstanding quality. Many routes are
seeing more attention since being re-bolted.
Approach (map p.83, overview p.84) - From the Australia
Col, scramble up the left side of the working for four levels.
The Zippy Level is above the Fruitbat Level.

10 Putting on Ayres E4 6c
Two bolts lead the way, although the climbing is perplexing and utterly desperate. Pass the first bolt on the left, and if you reach the break, traverse right to the second bolt. The direct method requires an all-out leap of faith!
FA. Danny Dutton 26.3.1989

11 Feeling Rusty? . . . . 6b+
The rusty streak to the right is climbed past five bolts. Although the good footholds to the right are in, the short will be faced with a desperate reach at the top.
FA. Clive Allen, Rob Wright 16.2.1991

12 Zippy's First Acid Trip E1 5c
Climb up the slabby left arete of the corner before moving right into the corner itself. Head out right just below the top.
FA. Mark Boniface 5.1.1988

13 Your Ma E1 5c
The corner-crack right of *Zippy's First Acid Trip*. Be careful topping out, as there are several bits of rock that could fall down on your belayer.
FA. C.Murphy, P.Collins 13.3.2013

14 Ziplock 7b
Left of a project bolt-line. An obstinate lower groove leads to the crux, with easier climbing above.
FA. Ian Lloyd-Jones, Phil Targett 17.9.2009

15 Indiana Jasmine and the Topple of Doom!
. . . . 5c
The wall and arete. Nice solid climbing past three spaced bolts to a top-out. Belay off the metal posts.
FA. Chris Davies, Ian Lloyd-Jones 24.9.2009

16 Second's Chance . . . . VS 4c
The slabby wall with a slight bulge at half-height.
FA. Mark Dicken 2.11.2007

17 Cross Eyed Tammy . . . . HVS 5a
The corner is more awkward than it first appears. Turn the initial bulge on the right, then make your way out right to the arete and the top.
FA. Mark Dicken 16.11.2002

18 Resurrection Shuffle E4 6b
Start about 1m in from the left arete, to the left of the hairline crack. Climb up and then move rightwards towards a larger hold and onto the halfway ledge. Finish up the fine finger/hand-crack.
FA. Andy Woodward, Danny Dutton 1987

19 The Samba Drum . . . E3 5c
Climb the crack-line 3m to the right of *Resurrection Shuffle* to reach a ledge at half-height. Climb the crack above, via some long and tenuous moves over some suspect rock, to the top.
FA. Keith Archer, Paul Woodhouse 5.7.2003

20 Pulverised 7b
The vertical wall to the right of *The Samba Dance*. A thin crimpy crux provides the entertainment. Six bolts lead to a lower-off.
FA. Ian Lloyd-Jones 24.9.2009

21 De Nouement 7b
Climb the right-hand line of bolts in the wall right of *The Samba Drum*. Six bolts lead to a resin lower-off. Moves passing the second and fifth bolts provide the spice.
FA. Phil Targett, Owain Jones 7.10.2009

Bus Stop Quarry · Dali's Hole · California · Australia · Serengeti · Never Never Land · Twll Mawr · Mordor - Lost World · Vivian Quarry · Rainbow Slab Area · Snakes and Ladders · Outlying

Bus Stop Quarry

Dali's Hole

California

Australia

Serengeti

Never Never Land

Twll Mawr

Mordor - Lost World

Vivian Quarry

Rainbow Slab Area

Snakes and Ladders

Outlying

1 Digital Delectation . . . . . ⚁ 🧗 ▢ HVS 5a
A great route up the left-hand side of the slab. Follow the poorly-defined crack, which requires care to protect, to a ledge at about half-height. Move left and finish up another crack.
FA. Lew Hardy, G.Parfitt 1.5.1986

2 Good Afternoon Constable . . . 🧗 ▢ VS 4c
The incipient cracks give decent climbing, but not much gear.
FA. Ian Wilson, Tim Downes 6.10.1985

3 Dolmen . . . . 🧗 ▢ HVS 5a
The stepped groove leads up and rightwards to join *Menhir*.
FA. Joe Brown, Jim Lyon 2.2.2002

4 Menhir . . . . 🧗 ▢ VS 4c
Just to the left of the blunt rib is a left-trending groove.
FA. Joe Brown, Jim Lyon 2.2.2002

5 The Skyline Club . . . ⚀ 🧗 🧗 ▢ E2 5c
Climb the blunt rib left of *Act Naturally* past three chopped bolts. Two pegs may help guide you up and right towards the upper hanging arete. Step right over the roof and clip the bolt. Up past the next two bolts to the top - bolt belay.
FA. Chris Davies, Phil Targett 1.10.2009

6 Antiquity . . . . ⚀ 🧗 🧗 ▢ E1 5a
A route that was originally graded VS, which is pretty outrageous given the terrain. Start up the groove of *Act Naturally* and, after 7m, traverse out on jugs to the arete. Climb past two pegs and the bolt studs. Finish straight up, 1m right of a groove.
FA. Joe Brown, Jim Lyon 26.2.2002. It has been retro-bolted twice, once to replace the peg and once because it was thought the line traversed in higher and The Skyline Club was the first route to ascend this area of rock.

7 Act Naturally . . . . ⚀ 🧗 ▢ VS 4b
Reasonable climbing with okay gear. Tackle the right-slanting groove with a large stepped ledge in the middle.
FA. Cliff Phillips (solo) 19.6.1984

8 Ruby Marlee Meets Dr Holingsworth
. . . . ⚁ ▢ E1 5b
A big, safe climb with atmosphere. Start up *Act Naturally* - you will need some gear to reach the final well-bolted slab above the ramp. For the upper section, sustained but straightforward climbing leads past a large number of bolts to the top.
FA. Chris Davies, Ian Lloyd-Jones 16.6.2009

Walk off the back

32m

14m

Approach tunnel to The Gorbals

Skyline Buttress
Unsurprisingly, this crag dominates the Australia skyline. It has a mix of trad and sport, some of which is reasonable and some classic.
Approach (map p.83, overview p.84) - From the Australia Col, head to the left and follow the path up the edge of the quarry for five levels to the massive Skyline Buttress.

9 Ronald Reagan meets Doctor Strangelove

. . . . **E2 5b**

An exciting climb in a great position, it is not for the faint-hearted, best described as a bit of an adventure. Climb a scoop in the wall to reach a crack. Ascend this to easier ground at the halfway ledge. Then take the crack left of the main groove.
FA. Lew Hardy, Martin Crook 23.4.1986

10 Lindy Lou . . . . **HVS 4b**

A harrowing lead. Climb the loose groove just to the left of the tower that splits the buttress to the edge of the halfway ledge, then climb the right arete of the main groove, also loose!
FA. Cliff Phillips (solo) 19.6.1984

11 Plastic Soldier **6a**

To the right of a shattered pillar leaning against the crag is a large cleaned slab. This route follows the left side of the slab, and is pitch 4 of *A Grand Day Out*.
FA. Ian Lloyd-Jones, Phil Targett, Sam Beesley (all led) 15.4.2009

12 Clash of the Titans **6a**

Climb the right-hand side of the large slab.
FA. Ian Lloyd-Jones, Chris Davies (both led) 16.6.2009

13 The Dreaming **E1 5b**

A poor old route taking the chossy groove then the diagonal crack leftwards across the buttress. Best ignored.
FA. R.Ebbs, S.Parker 2.11.1993

14 Mad Dog of the West . . . . . . **VS 5a**

A fantastic trad line, which is about 10m right of the base of *Clash of the Titans*, in a small bay. Climb up into a cleft to where a crack leads up a slab to the level above.
FA. Perry Hawkins, J.Elliot, R.Caves 19.4.1986

15 The Methane Monster **E1 5b**

Climb a groove and then a hanging crack above. When it eases, climb the area on the right. Bolt belay.
FA. Chris Davies, Matt Wells 23.9.1989

16 Binwomen . . . . **VS 4b**

Climb the left edge of the slabby front face. Friable in places.
FA. Martin Crook 6.5.1986

17 Up the Garden Path . . . . . . **HS 4b**

An eliminate up the gardened slab just to the right of the arete.
FA. Rob Wright, Clive Allen 1989

18 Billy Two Tokes **E1 5b**

Climb suspect holds to reach a bolt. From here, continue to the top on even more worrying holds.
FA. Martin Crook, Noel Craine 6.5.1986

19 Youthslayer . . . . **VS 5a**

Climb the thin crack - lots of microwires - in the white slab, then take the crack above.
FA. Lew Hardy, G.Parfitt, S.Anderson 5.5.1986

20 Slab Slayer **6b**

Climb the cleaned line right of *Youthslayer*. A rockover on small holds is followed by easier climbing. Four bolts to a lower-off.
FA. Sam Beesley, Ian Lloyd-Jones, Chris Davies 27.3.2010

21 Harri Bach Llanrug **6a**

Start by the flake-crack. Six bolts lead to a lower-off.
Photo on p.113.
FA. Ian Lloyd-Jones, Chris Davies 12.11.2009. Named after the first ascensionist's great grandfather who spent 54 years working as a quarryman. His name is etched into the Pen Garret Hut wall.

22 Rock Yoga . . . . **7a+**

The second line of six bolts is very technical. Expect thin holds and rockovers with a high stepping and yoga-esque crux sequence. Traverse up and left to a lower-off.
FA. Sam Beesley, Ian Lloyd-Jones, Chris Davies 27.3.2010

23 Put it on the Slate Waiter . . . . . **6b+**

A blank slab. Long reaches between good holds.
FA. Clive Allen, Rob Wright 18.6.89

24 Toe Be or not Toe Be **7b**

Thin and painful climbing up the clean slab. Mantelshelf to get established on the slab. Easier climbing leads to the stopper crux (possibly f7A) by the final bolt.
FA. Ian Lloyd-Jones 16.6.1989

The Gorbals
p.110

12m

The Gorbals p.110

Bus Stop Quarry
Dali's Hole
California
Australia
Serengeti
Never Never Land
Twll Mawr
Mordor - Lost World
Vivian Quarry
Rainbow Slab Area
Snakes and Ladders
Outlying

Bus Stop Quarry

Dali's Hole

California

Australia

Serengeti

Never Never Land

Twll Mawr

Mordor - Lost World

Vivian Quarry

Rainbow Slab Area

Snakes and Ladders

Outlying

The Gorbals

Higher even than the Skyline Buttress is another level with some good slabs. Although the routes are generally quite hard, there are some nice sport routes here.
Approach (map p.83, overview p.84) - This area is best approached from the upper parking spot (p.82). Walk along into the quarry and follow the path to a tunnel that leads through to the Gorbals level.
Alternatively, go up six levels from the Australia Col to reach the same tunnel.

1 Mynd am Aur 7a
The thin route on the left of the slab.
FA. Tesni Lloyd-Jones, Ian Lloyd-Jones 27.7.2012

2 Slab Rog . . . . 6b+
Good climbing up the centre of the slab, glu-in bolts.
FA. Ian Lloyd-Jones, (solo) 4.12.2009

3 Olympic Torch . . . . 6b+
The right-hand side of the slab goes to a shared lower-off.
FA. Tesni Lloyd-Jones, Ian Lloyd-Jones 27.7.2012

4 The Shining . . . . VS 4c
The loose groove.
FA. Clive Allen, Rob Wright 18.6.1989

5 Mister Blister 7a
Good moves up the black streak.
FA. Ian Lloyd-Jones, Chris Davies 10.4.2010

6 Men at Work E3 6a
A scary start leads to the first of four bolts right of the black streak.
FA. Chris Davies, Phil Targett 1.10.2009

7 The North Face of the Aga E3 6a
Start below and left of the glu-in bolt shared with *Filler* move up and right to clip it. Move up and left to the second glu-in bolt and carry on past the third bolt to a lower off.
FA. K.Simpson, S.Winstanley, Clive Stevenson, Robert Pink 1.4.1989

8 Filler E3 6a
An eliminate with a tricky independent finish. Start left of the first bolt on *Sprint Finish*. Climb up and right to clip it before moving left to clip the second bolt on the *The North Face of the Aga*. Zag back to the top bolt on *Sprint Finish*. Move up and left to clip an independent bolt to reach the top.
FA. Mark Reeves, Llion Morris 2010

9 Sprint Finish 6a
Start 4m right of *The North Face...* below a glue-in bolt. Continue up past another two glue-in bolts to the top.
FA. Clive Allen, Rob Wright 18.6.1989

10 Old and Complicated under the Oak Tree
. . . . 5b
Climb up the right-hand side of the slab past three bolts.
FA. Mark Reeves, Llion Morris 2010

11 Youthanasia E2 5b
The chossy groove is best avoided. If you feel you can't, then climb up to the roof, peg, turn this on the left and then head up and right past some more gear to the top.
FA. Matt Podd, Len Lovatt 17.7.1989

12 See You Bruce E3 5b
A classic route with some great climbing and exposure. Head up the left side of the slab past a bolt to a ledge. Move out right to regain the slab near the arete. Climb the slab and arete boldly, passing spaced bolts to a great finale and lower-off.
FA. Len Lovatt, Matt Podd, Phil Warsop 9.1989

13 Glasgow Kiss . . . . . 7b+
A line of bolts leads to a rather intense finish.
FA. Ian Lloyd-Jones, Sion McGuinness 22.4.2010

14 The Gorbals E4 6a
The original line of the cliff. From just above the step, climb up easy ground to gain a flake on the right. Arrange gear here and make committing moves up to clip the first bolt. Continue up, passing another bolt, and move up to a good ledge. Up and left is another bolt - the crux is making your way up the thin crack above to the lower-off.
FA. Chris Parkin, Perry Hawkins 25.4.1986

Walk off leftwards, down the back of Skyline Buttress and back through the tunnel

To mid afternoon   12 min

18m

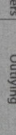

15 **Slabaholics Anonymous** . . . 7a+

More bolts lead up the slab just right of *The Gorbals*.
FA. Ian Lloyd-Jones 6.6.2011

16 **Black Daisies for the Bride** . . E5 6b

Out of keeping with the routes on this slab now, as the overly bold starts puts people off, but it does give some nice climbing. Start just left of the perched boulder and climb past three lonely bolts to the top.
FA. Paul Doyle, Craig Smith, Ben Smith 10.8.1993

17 **Slabology** 7a

A line up and right on the wall. More technical rockovers.
FA. Ian Lloyd-Jones, Sam Beesley 11.3.2010

18 **Fetzer.** E2 5b

Start just in from the edge of the slab. Briefly climb a crack, until after 2m you can move up and right to clip a lone bolt. Continue direct to the ledge, then move out left to the arete and finish up this past another bolt.
FA. I.Hassell, J.Smithies 19.8.1988

19 **Tennent's Creek** E2 5b

A more direct start to *Fetzer*. Continue up the crack with poor gear, then rejoin *Fetzer* for the final arete.
FA. I.Hassell, J.Smithies 18.9.1988

20 **Franzia** E2 5b

Start just to the left of the large flake of *Turkey Trot*, moving out left slightly to clip a bolt shared with *Fetzer*. Continue up to rejoin *Turkey Trot* at the large halfway ledge. Move up and right across scree to a large blocky corner, as for *Turkey Trot*.
FA. I.Hassell, J.Smithies 18.9.1988

21 **Turkey Trot** . . . . VS 4c

Start at the large flake and climb it to the halfway ledge. Move up and right across scree to finish up the blocky corner.
FA. Paul Williams 14.5.1986

22 **A Swarm of Green Parrots** . . . VS 4c

At the end of this level (by the Oil Drum Glacier) is another broken slab of loose rock.
FA. S.Parker, R.Ebbs 2.11.1993

Bus Stop Quarry · Dali's Hole · California · Australia · Serengeti · Never Never Land · Twll Mawr · Mordor - Lost World · Vivian Quarry · Rainbow Slab Area · Snakes and Ladders · Outlying

Bus Stop Quarry
Dali's Hole
California
Australia
Serengeti
Never Never Land
Twll Mawr
Mordor - Lost World
Vivian Quarry
Rainbow Slab Area
Snakes and Ladders
Outlying

Alice Springs

Miles away from anywhere, just like its namesake. This out-of-the-way level above the Gorbals Level has a few good routes that are worth going walkabout up here. The area's eponymous route fell down some time ago.
Approach (map p.83, overview p.84) - From the higher parking (p.82) follow the path through the workings towards the Gorbals tunnel. Go up onto the next level via a path up the scree on the left before the tunnel. It can also be reached from the Australia Col but this is a really long walk up seven levels.

A route called **Koala Bare, E2 5b,** *(FA. Trevor Hodgson 29.11.1987) takes a line somewhere up the wall here.*

1 **The Ghostly Hipster** . . . . 🛡 [____] **5b**
The left hand line of bolts, through a steep groove.
FA. Duncan Spencer, Mark Reeves 4.7.2018

2 **The Last Ammendment** . . . . . 🛡 [____] **5b**
A right-hand line.
FA. Mark Reeves, Duncan Spencer 4.7.2018

3 **Bear Knee Cessity** . . 🛡 🧗 🪨 [____] **6a+**
Start to the right of an embedded flake and climb up just left of the bolt to reach a ramp-line that leads up to a third bolt. A tricky move left gains a jug on the arete. Follow this past bolts to a final move to gain another ramp-line just below the lower-off.
FA. Mark Reeves, Duncan Spencer 4.7.2018

4 **Men of Leisure** . . . . 🛡 🪝🔨 💢 [____] **E4 6a**
Another of the great slate slab pitches, albeit a slightly esoteric one and a bit loose. Reaching the first bolt is bold - a lonely skyhook might help. Sustained climbing leads past the second bolt, where a run-out gains the less-than-positive break - cams. Move up and right to a bolt that is off to the side of *No Feart...* before heading back up left to the lower-off.
FA. R.Tompsett, P.Dobbs, T.Clements 28.9.1993

5 **No Feart of the Boaby** . . . 🛡 🧗 [____] **6b+**
A technical climb.
FA. Colin Struthers, Mark Hounslea 29.4.2012

6 **Celtic Blood** . . . . 🛡 [____] **6a**
The groove on the right-hand side of the slab.
FA. Celt Lloyd-Jones 27.11.2011

7 **Flying Death Fin (or is it Dutch?)**
. . . . 🔨 🪨 [____] **HVS 4c**
The thin crack just to the right of the *Celtic Blood* groove leads up to small pyramid of rock. From here climb the arete boldly to the top, finishing close to *Goblin Party*.

8 **Captain Condom and the Mothers of Prevention**
. . . . 🧗 🪨 [____] **E3 6b**
A direct boulder problem start to *Flying Death Fin...* .
FA. Nick Harms 21.4.1987

9 **Eyes Wide Shut** . . . . . . 🛡 🪨 [____] **E5 6b**
Straight up from *Captain...* Climb just to the left of the arete to the line of what you hope are jugs (but are actually side-pull slopers) to a very precarious barn door move. This gains a positive hold before things ease at 7m.
FA. Jacob Shieldhouse-Hadley (on-sight solo) 29.9.2015

10 **Where is My Mind** . . . . . 🛡 🪨 [____] **E6 6b**
A bold eliminate up the slab. Climb up the slab avoiding holds on the loose pillar of *Goblin Party*. Solo to the ledge at 13m - no runners and a bad landing, but escapable.
FA. Jacob Shieldhouse-Hadley 30.1.2016

11 **Goblin Party** . . . . . . 🛡 🔨 🧗 [____] **VS 4b**
The prominent dyke feature needs a steady head and hand.
FA. Paul Williams 10.5.1986

Two levels above Alice Springs is a small buttress with two short easy sport routes.

12 **Out There Left** . [____] **5b**

13 **Out There Right** [____] **5b**

Bus Stop Quarry

Dali's Hole

California

Australia

Serengeti

Never Never Land

Twll Mawr

Mordor - Lost World

Vivian Quarry

Rainbow Slab Area

Snakes and Ladders

Outlying

Liz Hewitt on *Harri Bach Llanrug* (6a) -
p.109 - Skyline Buttress. Photo: Mike Doyle

Grand Days Out

Australia's multi-tiered layout lends itself to the enchainment of routes up each level. The first of these was *A Grand Day Out*. Continuing this idea we have suggested a couple more link-up possibilities. Many others are available and it really does come down to your own imagination. The same linking up of levels is possible in other areas of the quarries like Rainbow Wall and Vivian Quarry.

Zippy Level
p.106

Fruitbat Level
p.104

The Sidings
p.100

Above the Rails
p.95

Railtrack Slab
p.96

Skyline Buttress
p.108

Alice Springs
p.112

The Gorbals
p.110

Bus Stop Quarry
Dali's Hole
California
Australia
Serengeti
Never Never Land
Twll Mawr
Mordor - Lost World
Vivian Quarry
Rainbow Slab Area
Snakes and Ladders
Outlying

❷ An Extreme Day Out . . . . 🏕🐑⬜ E4

For those looking for something a little harder this set gives a series of routes up to E3 which are probably worth E4 if you connect them all in a single day.
1) **E3 5c. Off the Beaten Track** (p.97). A brilliant bold start.
2) **6a. Sodor** (p.100). A sporty connection - alternatives are available.
3) **E2 5c. Genevive** (p.104). This is not the best level for trad pitches - an alternative is *Stretched Limo*.
4) **E2 6a. Rastaman Vibrations** (p.106). Only short but with some thin climbing.
5) **E2 5c. Ronald Reagan Meets Dr Strangelove** (p.109). A great long pitch with some bold climbing.
6) **E3 6a. Men at Work** (p.110). Possibly the hardest for last. Bold to start but bolts above that.

❶ A Very Trad Day Out . . . . . . 🏕⬜ E1 5b

This combination of routes gets you from the very base pretty much to the very top, up a reasonable set of trad pitches with a couple of sport connections.
1) **VS 4c. Runup** (p.87). Start from way down in the base. Belay at the top or continue to the belay below the next pitch.
2) **E1 5a. Looning The Tube** (p.94). The best pitch.
3) **5a. Steps of Glory** (p.94). A sport connection.
4) **6a. Sodor** (p.100). A sport connection - alternatives exist.
5) **E1 5b. M.I.L. Arete** (p.104). A nice arete.
6) **HVS 5a. Razorback** (p.106). The crack.
7) **HVS 5a. Digital Delection** (p.108). A great climb. Drop down and go through the tunnel for the next one.
8) **VS 4c. The Shining** (p.110). Not the best pitch. The two easy sport routes to the right are alternatives.
9) **VS 4b. Goblin Party** (p.112). A fine finish virtually at the top of the vast bowl.

❸ A Grand Day Out . . . . . . 🏕🧗⬜ 6b+

A great long adventure which is proving popular. The top of the first pitch has a lot of loose rock and is best avoided by starting from The Sidings.
1) **6a. A Grand Day Out Pitch 1** (p.97). This is the old first pitch which is now best avoided, due to some rockfall. Belay at the end of the Sidings level instead.
2) **5a. A Grand Day Out Pitch 2** (p.101). Move out right in a great position and climb to the level above.
3) **6a+. Harder than it Looks** (p.104). Almost directly opposite is another good one.
4) **6b+. Feeling Rusty?** (p.107). The hardest pitch. *Indiana Jasmine...* to the right provides an easier alternative to bring the overall grade down a bit.
5) **6a. Plastic Soldier** (p.109). Great climbing on the Skyline.

Bus Stop Quarry

Dali's Hole

California

Australia

Serengeti

Never Never Land

Twll Mawr

Mordor - Lost World

Vivian Quarry

Rainbow Slab Area

Snakes and Ladders

Outlying

Back Wall

Something of an acquired taste, the routes here are very adventurous and they all involve much loose rock. The descriptions here are unchecked and the route lines approximate. The most prominent feature is *Big Thursday* up the continuous line of greenstone pillars.
Approach (map p.83, overview p.84) - *Big Thursday* is best approached from the Alice Springs Level by crossing the Oil Drum Glacier. For the other two routes approach from The Salt Pans and scramble up the scree.

❶ Big Thursday . . . . 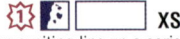 **XS**

For those that like it loose, this is an exciting line up a series of greenstone pillars separated by large levels on which you can recompose yourself, or escape!
1) 4c. The pillar is often greasy and always loose.
2) 4c. Head up the groove and slabby green pillar.
3) 5c. *The Wrist Cutter Crack.* Step off the block into the suicidally loose crack.
4) 5a. *The Next 1.* Virtually no pro and terminal rock.
5) 5b. Overhanging suspect flakes to a corner and loose pillar.
6) 5b. *The Crux.* Stand on the rim of the slate crevasse, step on, get into the groove, climb grim rock and razor fins to an easier slab. Ace.
7) 4c. *The Remains of the Day.* Climb the easy-looking remains of the pillar with a couple of weird moves. Great.
FA. Martin Crook, Nick Walton 5.1994

❷ If You Kill People They Die . . 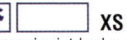 **XS**

Best avoided, but one assumes the first ascensionist had a death wish this day, or no friends to play with.
1) 60m. Follow the groove to the vertical shale band and cross this to solid rock. Then follow the most solid rock to the next level.
2) 5b, 12m. To the left of a prominent smooth brown overhanging wall is an arete/groove. Climb this on wobbly holds to an arete.
3) 4c. 12m. The V-groove on the right of the arete of the small wall. A chain is draped over the buttress.
4) 4c, 30m. The blocky arete left of the big bay behind the groove. Climb this until it is possible to traverse rightwards to easy ground at the back of the bay.
5) 4c, 30m. The prominent arete split by a chimney. Climb the right arete until it is possible to traverse into the chimney. Scramble up to the next level (hanging pipe) and walk off.
FA. Mark Dicken 14.10.2002

❸ Conquistadors of the Useless **ABO**

A winter/alpine line up the rubble gully at the right side of Upper Dinorwig. Not recommended!
FA. Martin Crook 1994

Darwin Level
p.117

Cape York Slab
p.118

Ayers Rock
p.119

**Approach to
Ayers Rock**

❶

**The lines are approximations
as the routes have suffered
rockfalls since their first ascents**

❷

❸

Darwin Level

Way up high at the very top of the Australia bowl is this excellent wall. There are a couple of great sport routes here, *Wish You Were Here* being a classic. The nearby Cape York Slab and Ayers Rock now make this part of the quarries worthwhile for the sport climber.

Approach (map p.83, overview p.84) - Approach from the upper parking spot (p.82). Hop over the gate and follow the continuation of the track up past another gate where the track veers right. Where the track turns back left onto a level, turn off left and follow a number of zig-zags up until you can walk onto the level, about 20 minutes from the parking.

Another Wasted Journey is in a bay to the right of the tunnel. *Easy Routes Can Have Bolts Too!* is found by walking around the outcrop, or through the tunnel. To the right of this is the larger Darwin Level wall.

4 Another Wasted Journey . . . . ▢▢ **E1 4c**
Start on the right of the first bay encountered to the right of the tunnel. The decomposing arete is climbed past an iron spike. Belay well back on another spike.
FA. Paul Jenkinson, Jules McKim, Guy Howard 20.2.1988

5 Easy Routes Can Have Bolts Too! ▢▢ **5c**
The wall to the right of the small tunnel on the left as you enter the level.
FA. Simon Beal 31.3.2007

Further right you can see a larger wall. An old route **Don't Look Back in Bangor**, *E3 5b, tackled a good jamming crack, but it has fallen down.*

6 Room with a View . . ▢▢▢▢ **7b**
A 'French start' (your partner's shoulder) leads to a technical and sustained lower wall. Move left to gain the crack. Head up this to a rock scar, then exit rightwards via long pulls.
FA. Jon Ratcliffe, Rob Lamey 14.6.2008

7 The Faffer . . . . ▢▢▢ **E6 6b**
A powerful route up the diagonal crack. The initial wall is technical and includes a crucial and hard-to-place wire. The gear improves above the break.
FA. Jon Ratcliffe 11.6.2008

8 The Very Old and the Very New . ▢▢ **A3**
A clean aid route taking the hairline crack to the left of *Wish You Were Here*. There are a couple of bolts to protect the fragile lower gear placements and a very thin finish.
FA. Simon Beal 17.2.2007

9 Wish You Were Here
. . . . ▢▢▢▢▢ **7c**
One of the best sport routes in the quarries. A bouldery start leads to more sustained difficulties and a powerful fight with a flake feature. The route eases at two-thirds height.
FA. Jon Ratcliffe 31.3.2007

To mid afternoon | 30 min

20m

Cape York Slab - 50m

Bus Stop Quarry
Dali's Hole
California
Australia
Serengeti
Never Never Land
Twll Mawr
Mordor - Lost World
Vivian Quarry
Rainbow Slab Area
Snakes and Ladders
Outlying

Cape York Slab

The current upper limit of development takes a bit of getting to but has a couple of decent sport routes and a few other offerings. Before undertaking routes that start up anywhere near the huge perched flake, you might want to have a look at what it is balanced upon!

Approach (map p.83, overview p.84) - As for Darwin Level (p.117) then walk across the plateau to reach the bolted approach climb.

Descent - Abseil off the lower-off on the top of the *Cape York Approach*, or from the abseil point on the level above the Cape York slab if your route tops out.

1 Cape York Approach . . . . . . 🎿 [____] **4b**
A mossy left-slanting ramp up the left end of a vegetated slab which is about 30m right of the hydro tunnel entrance on the Darwin Level. There are sound holds for all moves, but also fragile alternatives that must be avoided - careful climbing is needed. Belay on the lower-off before the top and scramble out. This is also the abseil back down, care is needed to reach it!
FA. Harold Walmsley 17.6.2014

2 Lucky Break . . . . 🔯 [____] **6c+**
Excellent and continuously interesting climbing following the line of least resistance up the smooth slab left of *Cape York Crack*.
FA. Harold Walmsley, Colin Struthers 14.8.2014

3 Cape York Traverse . . . . 🔯 🎿 [____] **6a+**
Climb *Cape York Crack* (care needed with large flake) to just after the second overlap. Make an exposed traverse left to a flake/block near the left arete. Surmount the step above and exit up the groove on the left, finishing with an awkward mantel and an easy scree/grass slope. Walk right to the abseil point.
FA. Harold Walmsley (self-belayed) 20.7.2014

4 Cape York Crack . . . . . . 🎿🎿 [____] **6a+**
The fault-line that starts just in from the left end of the level has a couple of balancy and delicate moves. Care is needed with the initial moves up the left side of the massive perched flake.
FA. Harold Walmsley (self-belayed) 13.7.2014

5 High Stakes. . . . . 🎿 [____] **6b+**
Link three diagonal right-facing flake-grooves just right of *Cape York Crack*. Care is needed with the massive perched block when you start laybacking up.
FA. Harold Walmsley, Colin Struthers, 5.8.2014

6 A Brucie Bonus . . . . 🔯 🎿🎿 [____] **6b**
Climb a slabby rib to the overlap, leaning left to clip the bolts on *High Stakes*. Find holds over the centre of the overlap; tall people can just reach up for jugs while the short will have a tussle on their hands and have to rock over a high foot on the lip for the same jugs. Carry on up to the *High Stakes* lower-off.
FA. Harold Walmsley, Colin Struthers, 14.8.2014

7 Cape York Slab . . . . 🎿 [____] **VS 4b**
Above some blocks about 25m left of the top of *Cape York Approach* lies a slab that is very mossy on its right and cleaner on its left. Start at the left edge of the slab base. Pad up a ramp, continue left just above the rim of the leaning lower wall, then go up to a ledge in a shallow depression. From the right side of the ledge, follow a shallow groove more easily to the top (block belays behind).
FA. Harold Walmsley (solo) 17.6.2014

Ayers Rock

A very distant development currently with a trio of great sport routes. All the routes are worth doing. Although *Ayers and Graces* is the best, its start can suffer from seepage after rain.

Approach (map p.83, overview p.84) - The easiest approach is from the Darwin Level (p.117). From near the concrete blocks on the edge of the Darwin plateau, about 100m before the big gated hydro tunnel, descend diagonally down to a faint level. Follow the track left towards a some big boulders. Pass above these and continue with your heart in your mouth across grass and scree to a boulder field, where the level opens out again on the Ayers Rock level. Descend the boulder scree and traverse the level proper to a nice grassy spot near a ruined hut with fabulous views of the rest of Australia. The routes start up the scree slope beyond the hut.

⑧ Ayer Head . . . .  **6c+**
Good moves and positions on the right-facing corner/ramp mostly via its left rib. A stopper move just left of the rock scar is the crux and care is needed with loose rock.
FA. Colin Struthers, Harold Walmsley 4.7.2013

⑨ Kata Tjuta Rib . . . . **6a+**
An interesting route, mostly on good rock. Climb to a high bolt. Move right along the ledge and climb the stepped, low-relief rib up the back wall of the bay. A direct start is possible at **6c**, but you need to pre-thread the bore hole prior to leading it, unless it is in place.
FA. Harold Walmsley 24.7.2014

⑩ Ayers and Graces . . . **6c+**
A superb pitch with unusual moves on excellent slate. From a block, reach left to a ledge on the left. Swing left and gain the ledge on the left of the arete. Continue up the arete with difficulty until the angle eases. Easier climbing leads to a delicate finish.
FA. Harold Walmsley, Colin Struthers 25.6.2013

20m

Bus Stop Quarry

Dali's Hole

California

Australia

Serengeti

Never Never Land

Twll Mawr

Mordor - Lost World

Vivian Quarry

Rainbow Slab Area

Snakes and Ladders

Outlying

The lowest level with climbing is the **Botany Bay Level**.

1 **Road to Botany Bay** . . . . 🔩 ☐ **7a**
The left arete of the buttress is a classic worth seeking out.
FA. Mike Turner, Colin Goodey 24.8.1987

2 **Impact Zone** . . . . . 🔩 ☐ **7a**
Follow *Wave Rock* to the fourth bolt before breaking left out of
the groove to another line of bolts.
FA. Ian Lloyd-Jones, Phil Targett (both led) 6.3.2009

3 **Wave Rock** . . . . 🔩 ☐ **6c**
Climbs the attractive 'Wave' feature on the steep wall between
Sylvanian Waters and *Road to Botany Bay*.
FA. Ian Lloyd-Jones 21.2.2009

Evening | 35 min

4 **Sylvanian Waters** . . . . 🔩 ☐ **E2 5c**
Good climbing up the wavy slab. Climb up to the first bolt and
make hard moves up and left to the second. Move up right to
the third and on to the top.
FA. Matt Wells, Chris Davies 23.6.1993

5 **The Garet Slide** . . . . ☐ **4a**
Climb the slabby feature.
FA. Ian Lloyd-Jones 29.1.2009

6 **Birthday Girl** . . . . 🔩 ☐ **7b**
The attractive flake-line on the wall to the right of the ladders.
FA. Jon Ratcliffe 16.3.2010

The next level up is know as the **G'Day Arete Level**.

7 **Spicy Little Octopus** . . . . . . 🔩 ☐ **6a+**
Start by the ruined building furthest along the level, beneath a
short wall and corner with a tree at the top.
FA. Keith Archer, M.Farram 4.5.2013

East Face
The east side of the quarry has been developed with
a lot of sport routes spread over the three main levels.
Road to Botany Bay, *G'Day Arete* and *Cirith Ungol* are
excellent. You can also get quick access to The Cutting
and Balcony areas at the top of The Lost World (p.190)
giving a good day's climbing. The two ladders are an
integral part of the infamous Snakes and Ladders tour of
the Quarries.
Approach (map p.83, overview p.84) - The best
approach is from the Australia Col and then up the stairs
of Cirith Ungol to the Pen Garret Hut, where you arrive
on the G'Day Level by the *G'Day Arete* arete.
Alternatively, approach from The Salt Pans (p.98), cross
the base of the quarry and climb the ladder to the Botany
Bay Level.

Ladder for approach from The
Salt Pans. This is how Snakes and
Ladders (p.284) gets out of Australia

8 Walk this way 7a
Climb the tricky/reachy shallow groove to gain the ledge. Foot traverse across the face using tiny (but positive) handholds for balance until a better hold and a precarious stride gains the arete. Continue up the slab with some tricky moves to gain the lower-off above.
FA. Ian Lloyd-Jones, Sam Beesley 2.6.2008

9 Hogiau Pen Garet. . . . . 6a+
Start to the right of the rusty pipe and cable.
FA. Ian Lloyd-Jones, Phil Targett (both led) 21.4.2008

10 The Koala Brothers 6b
Climb the dolerite dyke above the shed 100m left of *G'Day Arete*. The leader starts off the shed which is collapsing, so take care!
FA. Josie Ball 19.5.2008

11 G'Day Arete. 6c
The spankingly good square-cut arete. *Photo on p.123.*
FA. Mike Turner, Colin Goodey 24.8.1987

12 Jack the Ripper E4 6a
The corner right of *G'Day Arete.*
FA. J.Jackson 3.9.1987

The top level is called the **Far Out Level**.

13 Far From the Madding Crowd E4 6a
At the far end of this level, beyond the blast shelter and the pipe leaning against the wall, is a striking layback feature. Avoid the initial lower flake by climbing up just right of a ledge at the base of the main flake. Now climb the flake to the top and continue up the slab above to a metal spike on the left.
FA. Paul Jenkinson, P.Hiscock 23.4.1988

14 The Curious Incident 6a
The slabby side of the arete left of *To Infinity and Beyond!*
FA. Ian Lloyd-Jones, Phil Targett (both led) 2.5.2008

15 To Infinity and Beyond! 6b
Climb up the main slab/wall left of the dolerite vein.
FA. Ian Lloyd-Jones, Sam Beesley 22.4.2008

16 Ride Like the wind! . . . . 6b+
A sweeping line. Start up *To Infinity and Beyond!* to the second bolt, then move right and climb to the lower-off.
FA. Ian Lloyd-Jones, Phil Targett 4.5.2008

17 Cirith Ungol. . . . . 7a+
An intricate and sequency line up the steep dolerite vein.
FA. Ian Lloyd-Jones, Phil Targett 2.5.2008

18 Atticus Finch 6c
Climb the groove in the arete. An easy stepped start leads to a unique finish. There is a project to the left.
FA. Phil Targett, Ian Lloyd-Jones 4.5.2008

25m

Pen Garret Hut

Ladder

Bus Stop Quarry · Dali's Hole · California · Australia · Serengeti · Never Never Land · Twll Mawr · Mordor - Lost World · Vivian Quarry · Rainbow Slab Area · Snakes and Ladders · Outlying

The Dark Tower

Some big numbers are found here with two outstanding hard sport routes.

Approach (map p.83, overview p.84) - The first two routes are best approached from The Salt Pans (p.98). Descend one level and approach through a gorge made by a fallen slab of rock to arrive below the East Face. *The Dark Tower* is also best approached from The Salt Pans but you don't need to drop down one level.
The Serpent Vein is best approached by abseil.
Buffer in a Crack House requires you to run the gauntlet from the Billabong area via loose scree and rock - good luck and may the force be with you!

❶ Not Quite Snakes and Ladders   **HVS**
The chimney climb to the left of *Where the Green Ants Dream* is not very appealing.
FA. Ewan Russell 2010

❷ Where the Green Ants Dream   **E5 6a**
The narrow prow provides a challenge. Easy climbing at first is followed by bold committing climbing to a flat jug. Get stood on this and continue to the top.
FA. Ed Stone 20.4.1988

❸ The Dark Tower . . . .   **8a+**
The left arete of east wall, left of *The Serpent Vein* is gained by stepping off the edge of The Salt Pans.
FA. Pete Robins 2012

❹ The Serpent Vein   **8b**
The beautiful dolerite ladder feature up the wall gives an outstanding route. Abseil in from behind the Pen Garret Hut. Some ironmongery gets you over the edge where a two-bolt belay 6m lower can be seen and used to descend 30m to a hanging belay near the base of the cliff.
FA. James McHaffie 2008

❺ Buffer in a Crack House .   **XS**
The appalling chimney is classic Kay/Crook territory. It has probably fallen down several times since the first ascent and will continue to do so - not recommended.
1) 4b, 40m. Climb the appalling looking cracked pillar to a cleft. Kevlar umbrella essential for belayer.
2) 5b, 40m. Bridge up with a feeling of impending doom. Pass stacked blocks with trepidation (more for the belayer), then make a final mantel onto scree and head up it quicker than it is raining down on your belayer!
FA. Martin Crook, Ray Kay 9.1998

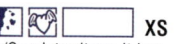

Pen Garret Hut

Ⓐ
36m to belay

❸

❹

❺

❶ 18m

❷

Bus Stop Quarry

Dali's Hole

California

Australia

Serengeti

Never Never Land

Twll Mawr

Mordor – Lost World

Vivian Quarry

Rainbow Slab Area

Snakes and Ladders

Outlying

Matt Thompson on the awesome *G'Day Arete* (6c) -
p.121 - on Australia's East Face. Photo: Tristram Fox

Serengeti

Bus Stop Quarry

Dali's Hole

California

Australia

Serengeti

Never Never Land

Twll Mawr

Mordor – Lost World

Vivian Quarry

Rainbow Slab Area

Snakes and Ladders

Outlying

Josh Douglas enjoys one of the most popular slate trad routes
Seamstress (VS) - *p.132* - on the beautiful Serengeti Plain.

Bus Stop Quarry

Dali's Hole

California

Australia

Serengeti

Never Never Land

Twll Mawr

Mordor – Lost World

Vivian Quarry

Rainbow Slab Area

Snakes and Ladders

Outlying

	No star	☆	☆☆	☆☆☆
Mod to S / 4c	-	*1*	-	-
HS-HVS / 5a-6a+	*4*	*3*	*2*	-
E1-E3 / 6b-7a	*8*	*6*	*3*	-
E4 / 7a+ and up	*4*	*9*	*7*	*1*

Serengeti has several areas with an excellent variety of climbing styles, as well as some popular classic routes. Nearly all the routes on the compact Seamstress Butte are worth climbing, *Seamstress* and *Seams the Same* being two of the most popular trad climbs in the whole of the quarries. The significantly harder *Heading the Shot* is one of the more popular E5s on slate, while scattered around are a nice selection of sport routes like *Peter Pan*, *Quelle Surprise* and *Exploding Goats*. Routes like *Slippery People*, *Remain in Light* and *The Great Curve* make Yellow Wall worthy of a trip for the extreme climber.

Conditions

The area can be exposed to the weather, especially Serengeti Plain which catches any wind whistling up or down The Pass. However, there are areas of shelter and the many different aspects mean sun or shade can be found throughout the day.

Approach

Serengeti is situated in the upper quarries, and best approached from Deiniolen and Dinorwig via the A4244, which connects Llanberis to the coast road. Turn off the A4244 to Deiniolen and on through Dinorwig to parking at the road end near Bus Stop Quarry. Follow the main track through the quarries until you reach the bottom of a dip - Dali's Hole is fenced off to your left. Carry on up the other the side of the dip. About 50m after the track levels off is a stile (about 30m before the round air-vent). Hop over the fence here and follow the small path up one level. Round to the right past a small rectangular building is the Serengeti Plain. Yellow Wall can be seen set back and to the right of the Seamstress Butte when looking at *Heading the Shot*.

GPS 53.127975 -4.108359

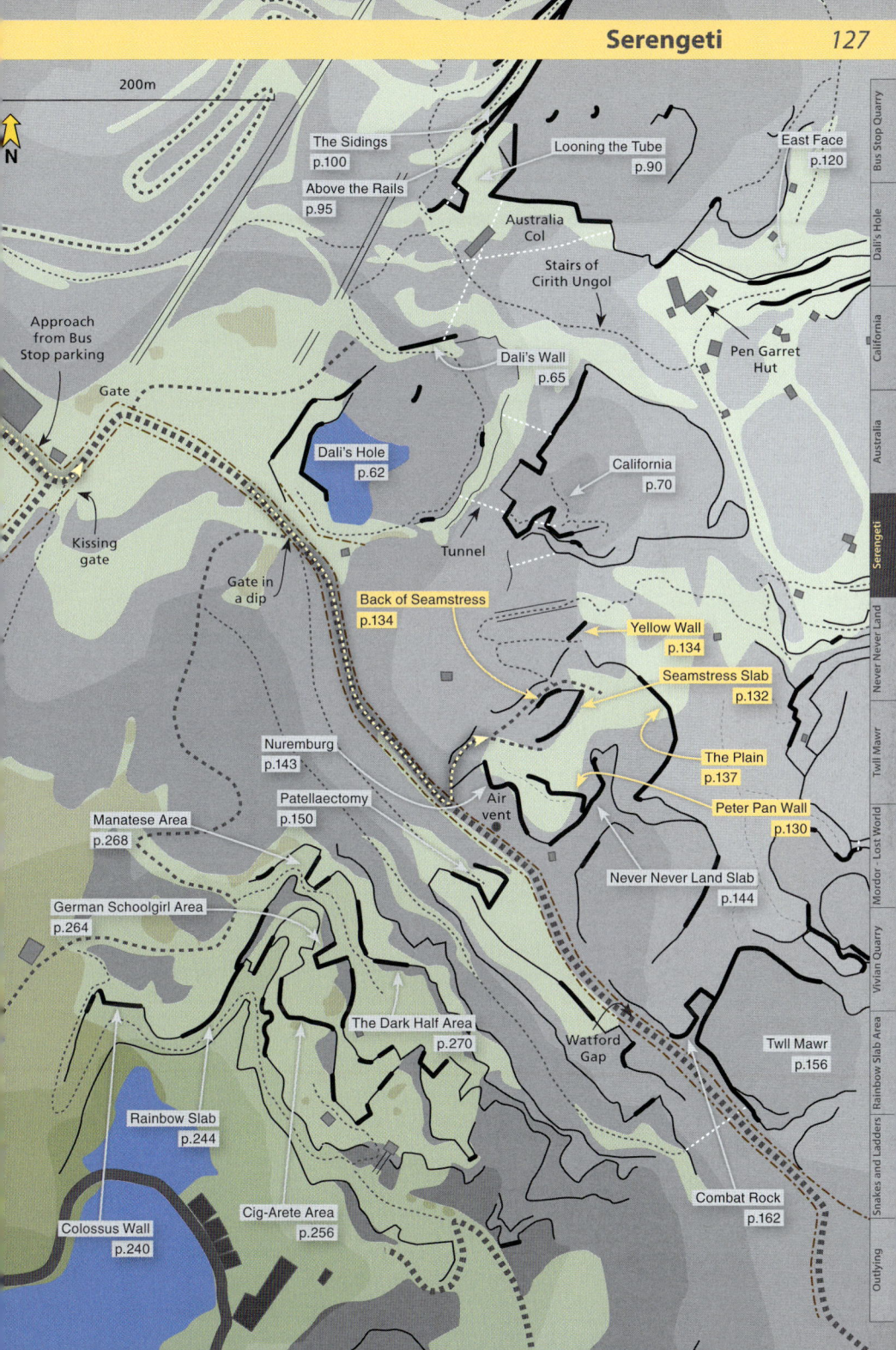

200m

N

The Sidings
p.100

Looning the Tube
p.90

East Face
p.120

Above the Rails
p.95

Australia
Col

Stairs of
Cirith Ungol

Approach
from Bus
Stop parking

Pen Garret
Hut

Gate

Dali's Wall
p.65

Dali's Hole
p.62

California
p.70

Kissing
gate

Tunnel

Gate in
a dip

Back of Seamstress
p.134

Yellow Wall
p.134

Seamstress Slab
p.132

Nuremburg
p.143

The Plain
p.137

Patellaectomy
p.150

Air
vent

Peter Pan Wall
p.130

Manatese Area
p.268

Never Never Land Slab
p.144

German Schoolgirl Area
p.264

The Dark Half Area
p.270

Watford
Gap

Twll Mawr
p.156

Rainbow Slab
p.244

Cig-Arete Area
p.256

Combat Rock
p.162

Colossus Wall
p.240

Bus Stop Quarry

Dali's Hole

California

Australia

Serengeti

Never Never Land

Twll Mawr

Mordor - Lost World

Vivian Quarry

Rainbow Slab Area

Snakes and Ladders

Outlying

Bus Stop Quarry

Dali's Hole

California

Australia

Serengeti

Never Never Land

Twll Mawr

Mordor - Lost World

Vivian Quarry

Rainbow Slab Area

Snakes and Ladders

Outlying

Australia
p.80

Pen Garret Hut

The Cutting
p.191

The Balcony
p.190

California
p.70

The Plain
p.137

Yellow Wall
p.134

Back of Seamstress
p.134

Peter Pan Wall
p.130

Never Never Land Slab
p.144

Seamstress Slab
p.132

Lower Tier
p.148

Nuremburg
p.143

Patellaectomy
p.150

Bus Stop Quarry
Dali's Hole
California
Australia
Serengeti
Never Never Land
Twll Mawr
Mordor - Lost World
Vivian Quarry
Rainbow Slab Area
Snakes and Ladders
Outlying

Kate Carrothers tackling the beautiful thin crack of *Seams the Same* (E1 5b) - *p.132* - on the Seamstress Slab. This is one of the most popular trad routes in the quarries and rightly so. The slab is also home to many classic routes across the grades.

Peter Pan Wall

This wall is opposite the Seamstress Slab. The first routes are actually at the top of the Never Never Land Slab, but are reached from this level.

Approach (map p.127, overview p.128) - Follow the main track through the upper quarries, past the Dali's Hole dip. As you ascend the track up from the dip, the path levels off. Go over the stile just before the circular air-vent. From here, head up the narrow track that winds up through scree. At the first level, head right towards a building and carry on to the Serengeti Plain. The Peter Pan Wall is on your right as you enter the level, just past a building.

Bus Stop Quarry · Dali's Hole · California · Australia · Serengeti · Never Never Land · Twll Mawr · Mordor - Lost World · Vivian Quarry · Rainbow Slab Area · Snakes and Ladders · Outlying

Never Never Land Slab
p.144

Walk off descent

❶ Igam-Ogam E4 6a
Exposed climbing starting from the far left edge of the ledge. The translation from Welsh is 'Not Straight' - a bit of beta?
FA. Ian Lloyd-Jones, Chris Davies 7.10.1990

❷ Squashing the Acropods .   E1 5b
A bold outing up the rib past a bolt.
FA. Chris Davies, Ian Lloyd-Jones 7.10.1990

❸ Kookaburra Waltz E4 6a
A poor eliminate squeezed in between *Squashing the Acropods* and *Watch Me...* Climb up the rib to reach the bolt on the right. Head straight up to reach an awkward mantel to clip the next bolt. A wire is needed to sling the next bolt.
FA. Danny Dutton, Clive Stephenson 10.1989

❹ Watch Me Wallaby Wank, Frank
. . . .   E4 6a
A good route. Start by the block on the terrace. Climb the slab past two bolts to a ledge. Pass the first bolt then move right towards the arete past the second. From the ledge, make a hard move past another bolt to reach the lower-off.
FA. Nick Harms, Graeme Alderson 3.8.1986

❺ Unsexual E2 5a
The arete has little in the way of gear meaning that it is feels like a solo... eek!
FA. Cliff Phillips 23.5.1984

❻ Peter Pan . . . .   6a+
A great route. Ascend the stepped groove to a ledge below the final wall. Make a perplexing move to the left of the final bolt to reach the lower-off.
FA. Martin Crook, Cliff Phillips 20.5.1984

❼ Nick the Chisel . . . .   7b+
A boulder-problem start leads to an easier finish.
FA. Trevor Hodgson (solo) 20.5.1987

Bus Stop Quarry

Dali's Hole

California

Australia

Serengeti

Never Never Land

Twll Mawr

Mordor - Lost World

Vivian Quarry

Rainbow Slab Area

Snakes and Ladders

Outlying

Simon Lake showing full concentration on the thin *Heading the Shot* (E5 6b) - *p.132* - on the Seamstress Slab. This route became infamous for its homemade bolt hangers which could only be clipped with the smallest carabiners. The bolts sprouted ugly clipping slings for several years. When the route was finally re-equipped in 2006 it caused some controversy. However, given the ease with which the old bolts sheared off with a swift blow from a hammer, it really was about time! Though some people think it is 7a+, it really feels every bit of E5 6b.

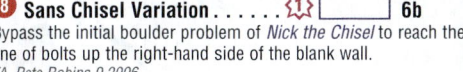

8 Sans Chisel Variation . . . . . . ⚡ [___] **6b**
Bypass the initial boulder problem of *Nick the Chisel* to reach the line of bolts up the right-hand side of the blank wall.
FA. Pete Robins 9.2006

9 Hole in One . . . . [___] **VS 4c**
A line superseded by *Sans Chisel*... Essentially the dirty corner and V-groove.
FA. Cliff Phillips 23.5.1984

10 Walking Pneumonia . . . . [___] **VS 5a**
The groove starting just left of *Stick's Groove* soon degenerates into a heathery scramble.
FA. Cliff Phillips 8.6.1984

11 Stick's Groove . . . . [___] **VS 4b**
The clean-cut corner may need a clean before climbing.
FA. Nick Walton 20.5.1984

12 Stuck up Fruhstuck . . . . [___] **E1 5c**
The groove right of *Stick's Groove* is gained from the rib on the right.
FA. Cliff Phillips 8.6.1984

Seamstress Slab

The central section of the complex Serengeti area has some excellent slab climbing, and *Seamstress* is one of the most climbed routes in the quarries. There are also some very challenging slab routes, *My Halo* being bold, whilst *Windows of Perception* and *The Medium* are just hard. For the middle ground (in that it is hard and bold, but never seemingly impossible or death-defyingly so), there is the excellent *Heading the Shot*.

Approach (map p.127, overview p.128) - Follow the track through the upper quarries, past the Dali's Hole dip and up to where the path levels off. Go over the stile just before the circular air-vent. Head up the narrow track that winds up through scree. At the first level, head right towards a building and carry on to the Serengeti Plain.

1 Karabiner Cruise **6c**
The bolts are rotten, but the line can be bouldered at f6B.
FA. Phil Targett 7.1991

2 Diagonal Dilemma . . **7b**
Climb up to gain the thin diagonal crack which leads (with difficulty) to a junction with *Y Gwaedlyd*.
FA. Ian Lloyd-Jones 7.1991. Originally a trad route at E5 6c.

3 No Problem **E4 6b**
The steep diagonal groove is desperate.
FA. Ian Lloyd-Jones 6.7.1991

4 Y Gwaedlyd **7a**
Climb to a niche then continue to an overlap. Finish up right.
FA. Ian Lloyd-Jones, Elfyn Jones 20.5.1991

5 Silent Homecoming **E2 5c**
After a desperate start to pass the first bolt, head up and right to a juggy rail. Now go back left to the next bolt before easier ground is reached out right near the arete.
FA. Phil Targett, Ian Lloyd-Jones 21.5.1991

6 The Other Medium **E3 6c**
Squeezed in between *Silent Homecoming* and *Neat Arete*. Gain the 'obvious' gaston crimp, pass this with difficulty and then make a lunge for a flatty. Finish as for *Neat Arete*.
FA. Jacob Shieldhouse-Hadley 30.4.2016

7 Neat Arete . . . . **HVS 5b**
Boulder up to gain the undercut arete - large cam in the crack. A difficult move leads to improving holds. Belay well back.
FA. Cliff Phillips 8.6.1984

*A bolted route **Broken Memories, E5 6a**, used to be on this section but has now fallen down.*

8 Jim Symon 11 Frobisher Close . . **HS**
A blocky and virtually unprotected line up the loose wall.
FA. Duncan Lee, Gary Thornhill 1987. Claimed again in 2010.

9 Balance of Power **E4 6a**
Climb to the first bolt and then swing up to the arete. Continue up reaching out to clip the bolt on *Out of Africa*.
FA. Chris Davies, Ben Davies 29.12.1989

10 Out of Africa **E5 6b**
Climb up the slab just in from the arete. Move along the break and make a committing move to the bolt. Finish up the groove.
FA. Danny Dutton, Clive Stephenson, S.Winstanley 4.1988

11 The Book of Brilliant Things
. . . . **E5 6a**
An epic traverse of the slab, with ground sweeping pendulum potential for all involved. Start up *Out of Africa* and make bold moves right into *Stack of Nudebooks* - have the spike lassoed or clipped in some way before leaving the ground. Move across the *Seamstress* routes below the overlap to reach a good ledge above the crux of *Windows...* - bolt by foot. Continue rightwards, with an anxious moment, to gain *Heading the Shot* and clip its bolts. Move out right and finish up *The Stick Up*.
FA. Gwion Hughes, Iwan Jones, Mel Roberts 5.4.1986

12 Slug Club Special . . **E5 6a**
A bold route. To earn the grade you must do it ground up, although many lasso the metal spike from *Seamstress* reducing it to E3/4. Climb up to the spike and continue direct up a faint groove past a bolt.
FA. Gwion Hughes, Iwan Jones, Mel Roberts 8.8.1986

13 Stack of Nudebooks Meets the Stickman
. . . . **E4 6a**
As for *Slug Club Special*, but escape into *Seamstress*.
FA. Nick Walton, Martin Crook 4.1984

14 Seamstress . . . . **VS 4c**
A great trad route. Climb the left-hand of the two parallel cracks to a large spike belay. *Photo on p.124.*
FA. Stevie Haston (solo) 6.1983

15 Seam Stress **E6 6a**
A bold eliminate up the shallow slabby groove between *Seamstress* and *Seams the Same*. No side runners at this grade.
FA. Ian Lloyd-Jones, Sion McGuinness 20.9.2010

16 Seams the Same . . . **E1 5b**
Follow the right-hand of the two parallel cracks. The gear and climbing are thin above the overlap. *Photos on p.129 and p.136.*
FA. Stevie Haston (solo) 6.1983

17 My Halo **E7 6b**
A bouldery and poorly-protected line up the vague groove. The first real gear is on the ledge at about half-height.
FA. Nick Dixon 5.1987

18 Windows of Perception . . **E6 7a**
A bold start to the first bolt, where the hardest rockover in the world awaits the contortionist. From the ledge, head up to join *My Halo*.
FA. Johnny Dawes 24.10.1985

19 The Medium . . . **8a**
Climb the vague groove up the slab past two bolts. Passing the second is the crux - a dyno for a three-finger edge. From here, move into the top of *Heading the Shot*.
FA. Johnny Dawes 24.7.1986

20 Heading the Shot **E5 6b**
A classic - hard, technical and sustained. Follow the line of bolts up the slab. Reach the overlap and the main difficulties are behind you. Hand traverse left into the groove and finish up this. **7a+** if you pre-place the quickdraws. *Photo on p.131 and p.41.*
FA. Stevie Haston, Nick Walton 8.1984

21 The Stick Up **E2 5b**
The bold arete has a sawn slot for a sling - a very thin one!
FA. Nick Walton 23.5.1984

Bus Stop Quarry · Dali's Hole · California · Australia · Serengeti · Never Never Land · Twll Mawr · Mordor - Lost World · Vivian Quarry · Rainbow Slab Area · Snakes and Ladders · Outlying

Morning
22 min
Sheltered
12m
1
2
3
4
5
6
7
8
9

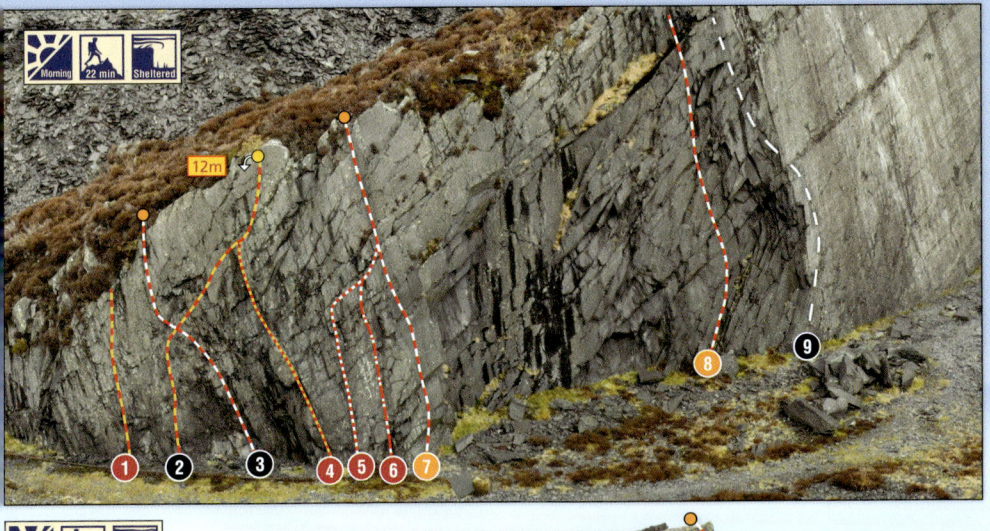

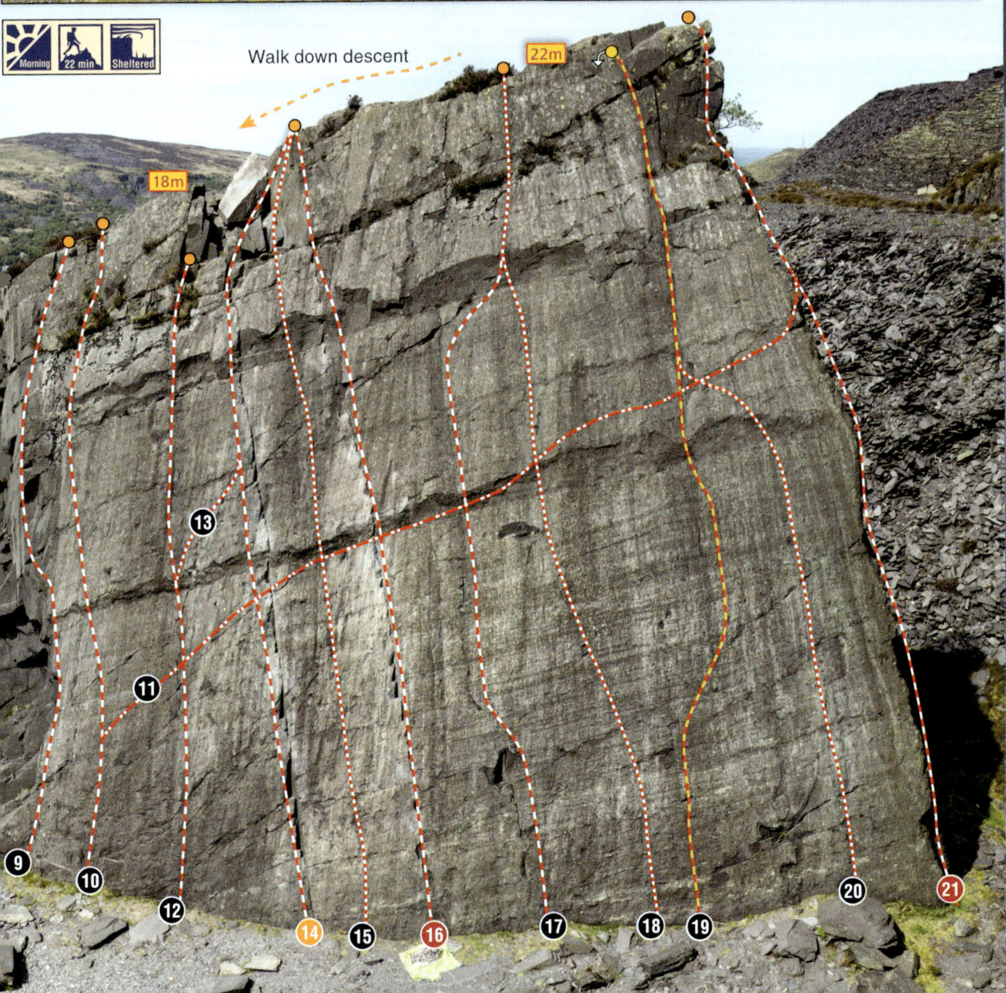
Morning
22 min
Sheltered
Walk down descent
22m
18m
9
10
11
12
13
14
15
16
17
18
19
20
21

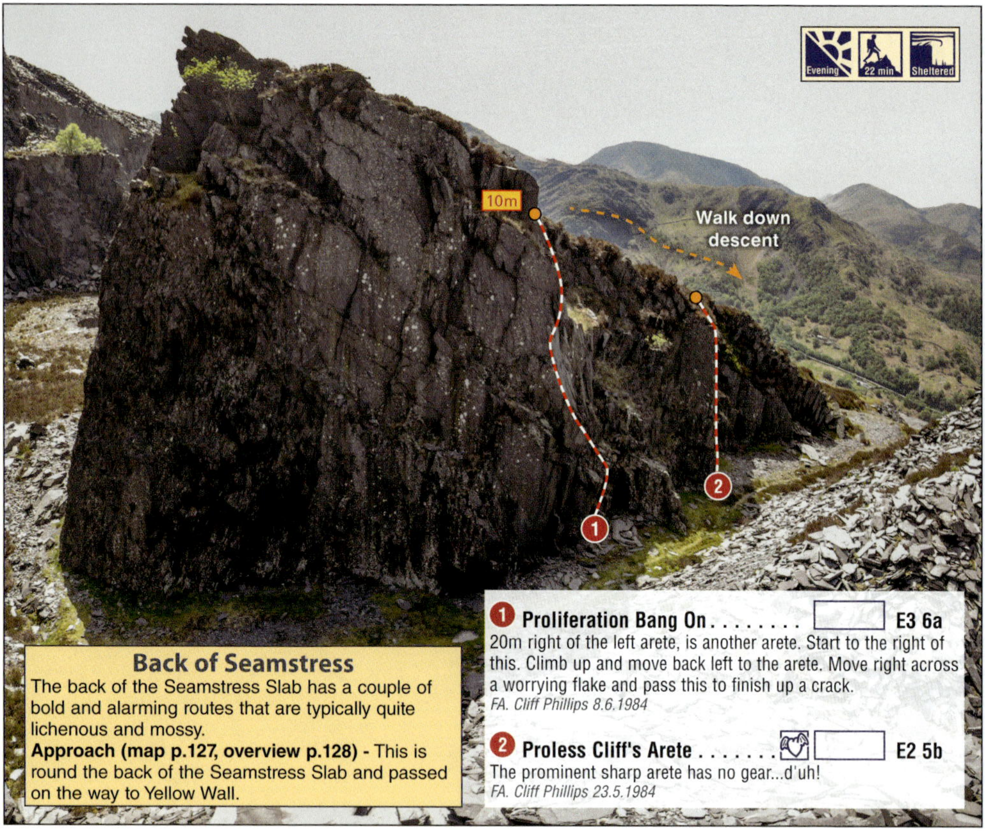

Evening | 22 min | Sheltered

10m

Walk down descent

Back of Seamstress
The back of the Seamstress Slab has a couple of bold and alarming routes that are typically quite lichenous and mossy.
Approach (map p.127, overview p.128) - This is round the back of the Seamstress Slab and passed on the way to Yellow Wall.

❶ Proliferation Bang On . . . . ☐ **E3 6a**
20m right of the left arete, is another arete. Start to the right of this. Climb up and move back left to the arete. Move right across a worrying flake and pass this to finish up a crack.
FA. Cliff Phillips 8.6.1984

❷ Proless Cliff's Arete . . . . 🗨☐ **E2 5b**
The prominent sharp arete has no gear...d'uh!
FA. Cliff Phillips 23.5.1984

Yellow Wall
A nice buttress featuring a few good lines including the classic *Slippery People*, *The Great Curve* and *Remain in Light*. It faces east and gets the morning sun.
Approach (map p.127, overview p.128) - Follow the track through the upper quarries, past the Dali's Hole dip and up to where the path levels off. Go over the stile just before the circular air-vent. Head up the narrow track that winds up through scree. Either head right round the front of the Seamstress Butte then round its far side, or walk left behind it. You will see the buttress ahead up a level. Walk up through the scree gully to the crag.

❸ Short Staircase to the Stars
. . . . ⚀🗨▮☐ **E3 6a**
The direct start to *Slippery People* is bouldery and sure to get your pulse racing. Climb the arete to the bolt at 5m, then move up to a bolt on *Slippery People* and follow this to the lower-off.
FA. Danny Dutton 10.1989

❹ Slippery People . . . . ⚁🗲▮☐ **E2 5c**
A great route that goes up near the left-hand arete. Climb up easily to below and right of the first bolt. A 'gripper clipper' and a long reach left help pass it. Climb up past the second bolt to a lower-off.
FA. Perry Hawkins, Dave Cuthbertson, John Silvester 11.4.1986

❺ Tentative Decisions . ⚡🗲▮☐ **E5 6a**
A good route with some bold climbing both below and above its lone bolt. Climb the more featured rock just right of *Slippery People* until a committing move can be made to clip the bolt. Climb past this to gain the crack and some gear. Move slightly right towards the top.
FA. Chris Davies, Phil Targett 23.12.1989

❻ Loved by A Sneer . . . . 🗨☐ **E4 5c**
Not a great route, but it certainly is a bold one. Climb up to a flake and then move up and right until a few metres below the top were you can move back left at an easing in the climbing.
FA. Bob Drury 24.4.1986

❼ Spirit Level . . . . ⚡🗲🗨☐ **E7 6b**
Bold and technical climbing protected mainly by your wits, although micro cams and microwires do somehow keep you going. Make your way up to where there used to be a small peg. Move past this with difficulty (crux), to reach some microwire placements within spitting distance of the top.
FA. Mark Katz 1998

8 The Great Curve....... E2 5b
The arcing flake-line is reached by climbing up to a ledge and bolt at 5m. Move up to gain the flake. Good climbing leads past a bolt and into easier ground on *Long Distance Runner*. Step up and left to a crack - the lower-off is on the right at its top.
FA. Richie Brookes, R.Austin 20.2.1987

9 Remain in Light.... E4 6a
A pleasant route that goes directly through *The Great Curve* and feels more like **6c** than E4 once you reach the fixed gear. Start right of *The Great Curve* and gain the ledge and bolt at 5m. Move directly up into *The Great Curve* and clip its bolt, then head straight up the wall passing a few more bolts.
FA. R.Austin, Richie Brookes 16.2.1987

10 Long Distance Runner E3 5c
A poor route up the line of weakness on the right side of the slab, just in from the corner. Traverse in from the left to gain the ledge at 5m. Continue up clipping some of the gear on *The Great Curve*, before heading right past an independent bolt to the lower-off.
FA. M.Murray, R.Austin 11.2.1987

Morning | 24 min | Sheltered

Walk down descent

22m

20m

3 4 5 6 7 8 9 10

Bus Stop Quarry | Dali's Hole | California | Australia | Serengeti | Never Never Land | Twll Mawr | Mordor - Lost World | Vivian Quarry | Rainbow Slab Area | Snakes and Ladders | Outlying

Bus Stop Quarry

Dali's Hole

California

Australia

Serengeti

Never Never Land

Twll Mawr

Mordor - Lost World

Vivian Quarry

Rainbow Slab Area

Snakes and Ladders

Outlying

Josh Douglas crimping his way up the thin *Seams The Same* (E1 5b) - *p.132* - one of the classic routes on the Seamstress Slab.

The Plain

The Plain is the area on the far side of the Serengeti Plain. The walls are fairly broken with little to offer apart from the odd decent feature. It faces south and is unlikely to be busy.

Approach (map p.127, overview p.128) - Follow the track through the upper quarries, past the Dali's Hole dip and up to where the path levels off. Go over the stile just before the circular air-vent. Head up the narrow track that winds up through scree. Go to the right of the Seamstress Butte. *Quelle Surprise* is adjacent to the slab. The rest of the routes are found on the continuation of that wall rightwards, all the way round to *Exploding Goats*, which overlooks Never Never Land.

1 Quelle Surprise 5a
On a broken wall to the right of Seamstress Slab across a ditch. Follow bolts up the clean slabby ramp with a distinct left-to-right finger-crack.
FA. Colin Goodey, Sue Goodey 16.8.2010

2 Laund Arete E4 6b
The short sharp arete is an excellent E4 providing it is dry and you are able to unlock the sequence. Around 7a.
FA. Nick Harms 2.4.1987

3 The Mark of Thor E3 5c
The prominent layback flake/crack that leads to a ledge on the right.
FA. Nick Walton, S.Jones 20.12.1991

4 Exploding Goats 4c
The left-hand route on the slabby pillar.
FA. Mark Dicken 1998

5 All For One 5a
The right-hand route on the pillar.
FA. M.Goodsmith, Colin Goodey, Del Smith 5.5.2008

Bus Stop Quarry

Dali's Hole

California

Australia

Serengeti

Never Never Land

Twll Mawr

Mordor – Lost World

Vivian Quarry

Rainbow Slab Area Snakes and Ladders

Outlying

Never Never Land

Bus Stop Quarry

Dali's Hole

California

Australia

Serengeti

Never Never Land

Twll Mawr

Mordor - Lost World

Vivian Quarry

Rainbow Slab Area

Snakes and Ladders

Outlying

Both photos: Max Hausle on *Fresh Air* (6a) - *p.143* - at the Nuremburg area of Never Never Land. This route was originally two routes - one went up the arete and one up the slab. On an early attempt at repeating the original slab route, the author headed up the slab with a full trad rack. At half-height he reached a reasonable ledge and found the stud of an old hand-drilled bolt from the 1980s, but it wasn't clippable. With no gear up to this point he dropped his ropes to be rescued. Thankfully someone bolted this route and it is now one of the better and more popular mid-grade sport routes in the quarries.

	No star	☆	☆☆	☆☆☆
Mod to S / 4c	1	1	-	-
HS-HVS / 5a-6a+	4	6	6	-
E1-E3 / 6b-7a	13	11	5	-
E4 / 7a+ and up	5	2	7	4

Bus Stop Quarry
Dali's Hole
California
Australia
Serengeti
Never Never Land
Twll Mawr
Mordor – Lost World
Vivian Quarry
Rainbow Slab Area
Snakes and Ladders
Outlying

Anita Grey climbing *Hawkeye* (5c) - *p.143* - at the Nuremburg area of Never Never Land. Photo: Mike Hutton

Never Never Land has been a major venue in the quarries for some time, with its eponymous slab offering some quintessential slate frighteners. Whilst the area has kept these bold routes, recent development has added a flourish of new sport routes across the grades.

Hawkeye and *Fresh Air* are gentle introductory routes. If you want something more demanding then it is worth looking at *State of the Heart*. Never Never Land has many worthwhile routes from 4 to 7a, as well as some bold offerings like *Kubla Khan*, *Short Stories* and, of course, *Never Never Land*. A new area since the last guide is Over There Land which has a couple of good hard sport routes, the best of which is *Cavity Wall*. Finally, *Patellaectomy* is classic (if a little bizarre) and some newer sport routes like *A Little Pale* and *Offa's* are worth a look. There are even some totally out there dry tooling routes for snow-sick winter climbers to enjoy!

Conditions

The area can be exposed to the weather as the wind whips through the Watford Gap on its way up or down the Llanberis Pass. However, several areas offer some shelter from the wind and the Nuremburg side is blessed by the sun, if it is out.

Bus Stop Quarry | Dali's Hole | California | Australia | Serengeti | Never Never Land | Twll Mawr | Mordor - Lost World | Vivian Quarry | Rainbow Slab Area | Snakes and Ladders | Outlying

Bus Stop Quarry
Dali's Hole
California
Australia
Serengeti
Never Never Land
Twll Mawr
Mordor - Lost World
Vivian Quarry
Rainbow Slab Area
Snakes and Ladders
Outlying

Approach

Never Never Land is situated in the upper quarries, and best approached from Deiniolen and Dinorwig. Drive through Dinorwig to parking at the road end near Bus Stop Quarry. Follow the main track through the quarries until you reach the bottom of a dip - Dali's Hole is fenced off to your left. At the dip carry on up the track until it flattens off. Just beyond this a circular air-vent is seen on the left - this is Nuremburg. 50m right of Nuremburg in the bay on the left is the Never Never Land Slab. When you are looking straight at the Slab, the Shame and Embarassment Wall is directly behind you. Over There Land is further along the main track, just past and on the opposite side of the track to Never Never Land.

The Patellaectomy area is found below Nuremburg on the opposite side of the track reached by climbing over the gate when at the dip by Dali's Hole on the main approach. Walk along a level that leads below the main path to the areas.

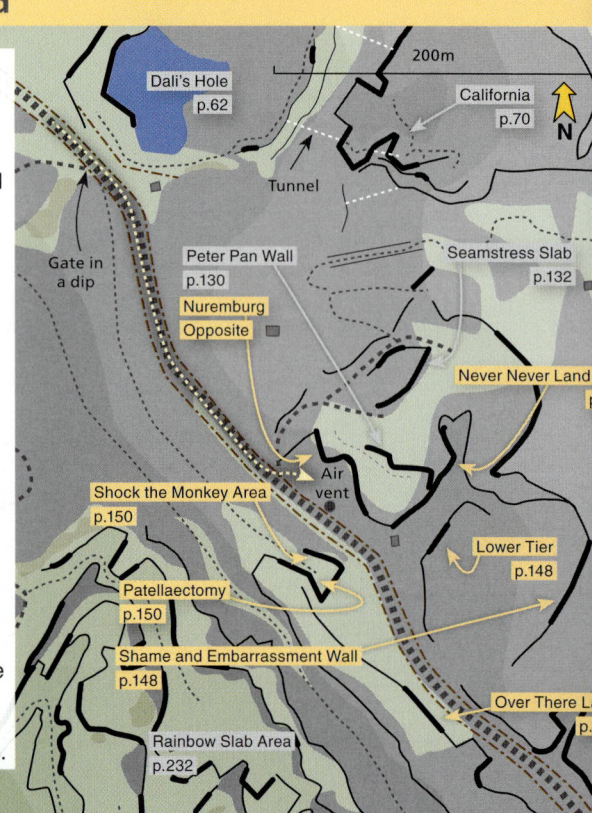

200m

Dali's Hole
p.62

California
p.70

N

Tunnel

Gate in
a dip

Peter Pan Wall
p.130

Seamstress Slab
p.132

Nuremburg
Opposite

Never Never Land

Shock the Monkey Area
p.150

Air
vent

Lower Tier
p.148

Patellaectomy
p.150

Shame and Embarrassment Wall
p.148

Over There L
p.

Rainbow Slab Area
p.232

Yellow Wall
p.134

Seamstress Slab
p.132

Nuremburg
Opposite

Never Never Land Slab
p.144

Shame and Embarrassment Wall
p.148

Patellaectomy
p.150

Lower Tier
p.148

Over There Land
p.149

Nuremburg

A great area with some good sport routes that have superseded the older bold routes. *Fresh Air* is possibly the area's best route. *Hawkeye* is also popular as is the much harder *Slate of the Heart*. The area faces southwest and gets plenty of sun.

Approach - Follow the main track through the quarries until you reach the bottom of a dip - Dali's Hole is fenced off to your left. Carry on up the other the side of the dip to just after the track levels off. Hop over the stile about 30m before the round air-vent. Nuremburg is behind the air-vent.

① **Macsen** . . . . 🔲 ▨ ▭ 6a
A nice route just to the left of *Hawkeye*.
FA. Colin Goodey, Sue Goodey, Sue Trainer, Mark Hellewell, Graham Sutton 19.6.2007

② **Hawkeye** . . . . 🔲 ▨ ▭ 5c
A pleasant and popular route up the arete. *Photo on p.140.*
FA. Ian Lloyd-Jones, Colin Goodey 19.6.2007

③ **Fresh Air** . . . . 🔲 ▨ ▨ ▭ 6a
Great open climbing. Ascend the line of bolts on the left of the slab to a lower-off. *Photos on p.138.*
FA. Colin Goodey, Kath Goodey 19.7.2007. A combination of Breaking Wind, HVS, and Hot Air Crack, HVS, (both FA. John Tombs).

④ **Swiss Air** . . . . 🔲 ▨ ▨ ▭ 6c
Just to the right of *Fresh Air*. Often damp.
FA. Tim Mueller, Ian Lloyd-Jones 6.3.2011

⑤ **State of the Heart** 🔲 ▨ ▨ ▨ ▭ 6c+
A technical route on weird angles and slopers with some sharp rock. Probably **7a+** if you can't do the reach.
FA. Mike Raine 22.3.2008

⑥ **Yossarian** . . . . 🔲 ▭ 6b+
Climb the overlapping slab between the two aretes.
FA. Phil Targett, Ian Lloyd-Jones 29.5.2008

⑦ **Steps of Escher** . . . . 🔲 ▨ ▭ 6c
The hanging arete. Pad up the black slab to the foot of the V-groove. Swing up and left and follow the line of bolts to a lower-off.
FA. Phil Targett, Ian Lloyd-Jones 14.6.2008

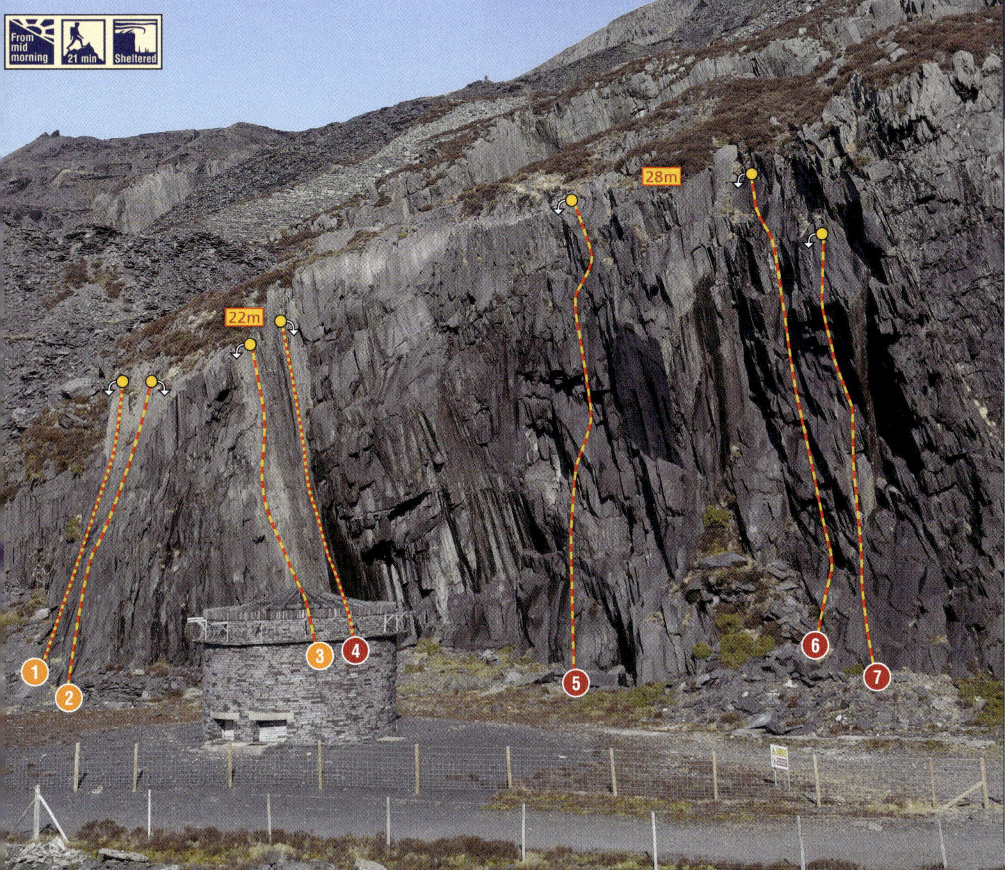

From mid morning | 21 min | Sheltered

Bus Stop Quarry

Dali's Hole

California

Australia

Serengeti

Never Never Land

Twll Mawr

Mordor - Lost World

Vivian Quarry

Rainbow Slab Area

Snakes and Ladders

Outlying

Never Never Land Slab

A great area with some good sport routes and older run-out slabs. The slab faces southeast and gets morning sun. It dries quickly and is well sheltered.

Approach (map and overview p.142) - Follow the track through the upper quarries, past the Dali's Hole dip, to a circular air-vent just after the path flattens off. Hop over the gate just past the air-vent and head to the right past a building to the slab.

① Tomb Raider . . . . ☆1 ☐ **6a**

A good two-pitch sport route. Start left of the main slab, just to the right of a concrete slab.

1) 5+, 25m. Climb directly up the slab to where it meets an overlap. A hard move rightwards past this gains the main wall. A series of mantelshelves leads past four bolts to a ledge (possible belay). Traverse right along Dandelion Ledge to a bolt belay.

2) 6a, 15m. Climb the corner to below the roof. Either climb directly over the roof (hard), or move left round the bulge. Continue up the corner to a good stance and bolt belay.

Descent - Walk down the grassy plateau back towards the approach to Seamstress Slab.

FA. Colin Goodey, Sue Goodey, Bryn Williams 19.10.2007

② Back in the Saddle . . . . ☆1 ☐ **6b+**

Start up *Tomb Raider* and then take the much more challenging and intricate line through the overlaps to the left.

FA. Chris Davies, Ian Lloyd-Jones 28.5.2009

③ Octogenarian . . . . ☆2 ☐ **5b**

This easy sport line is a pleasant addition to the area. Start just to the left of the arete of *362*, below a line of bolts. The crux is high up, where all the holds face the wrong way!

FA. Celt Lloyd-Jones, Colin Goodey, Ian Lloyd-Jones 8.9.2015

④ Learning to Fly . . . . ☆2 ☐ **5a**

Clip the first bolt, shared with *Octogenarian*. The route is meant to step immediately left, but the more logical line is to continue up to the second bolt and then trend across to follow the independent line of bolts to a lower-off.

FA. Celt Lloyd-Jones, Ian Lloyd-Jones 15.8.2016

Two routes took wandering lines up here. **Road to Nowhere, VD,** *was a serious ramble.* **Rodent to Nowhere, E1 5a,** *started left of 362 and took a line across the slabs up and right.*

⑤ 362 . . . . ☆1 🏃 ☐ **6a**

A decent three-pitch sport route. The name refers to the number of quarrymen who died working in the Dinorwig Quarry.
Photo opposite.

1) 5a, 16m. Follow the line of bolts up the left edge.
2) 5c, 7m. Step up the steep wall behind the belay to a good ledge. Harder moves up left gain better holds and the ledge.
3) 6a, 15m. As for pitch 2 of *Tomb Raider*.

FA. Bryn Williams, Colin Goodey 29.10.2007

Dandelion Ledge

Bus Stop Quarry

Dali's Hole

California

Australia

Serengeti

Never Never Land

Twll Mawr

Mordor - Lost World

Vivian Quarry

Snakes and Ladders Rainbow Slab Area

Outlying

Claire Henriette on the first pitch of the excellent *362* (6a)
- *opposite* - on the edge of the Never Never Land Slab.

6 Scheherezade E4 6b
A technical route with a tough low crux followed by thin sustained moves above bolts higher up. Can feel more like a 7a+ sport route.
FA. Nick Harms, Clive Stephenson 11.1988

7 Pipers at the Gates of Dawn . E5 6b
A bold and dangerous and wandering girdle. Head up *Scheherezade* to the third bolt, then down and across to the third bolt of *The Machine in the Ghost*. Move down to a foothold, then up briefly to lasso a spike for protection before dropping down further to move into the groove of *Never Never Land*. Head up and right to the bolt on *Kubla Khan*. Clip this, then traverse right for 10m to a large ledge in the groove. Head up the loose groove of *Andy Pandy* to the top.
FA. T.Forster 3.9.1989

8 The Machine in the Ghost
. . . . E5 6b
Thinner, more technical and much bolder than *Scheherezade*.
FA. Andy Woodward 10.8.1986

9 Never Never Land E5 6a
A great route; one of the better E5s in the quarries, though still a serious one. Start below the stepped roofs and ascend the groove under them until you can make a move left to go up to an iron spike. Gain and follow the sustained flake until bolts can be seen above and right on *Igam-Ogam* (p.130). Either move out to these and climb to the top (safe but hard), or continue up to a rest and poor gear. Trend up and left to a sloping ledge on the edge of the buttress and make your way very boldly to the top.
FA. Martin Crook, Nick Walton, Andy Newton 2.1984

Descent (map and overview p.142) - Walk across to Seamstress and reverse the approach to this.

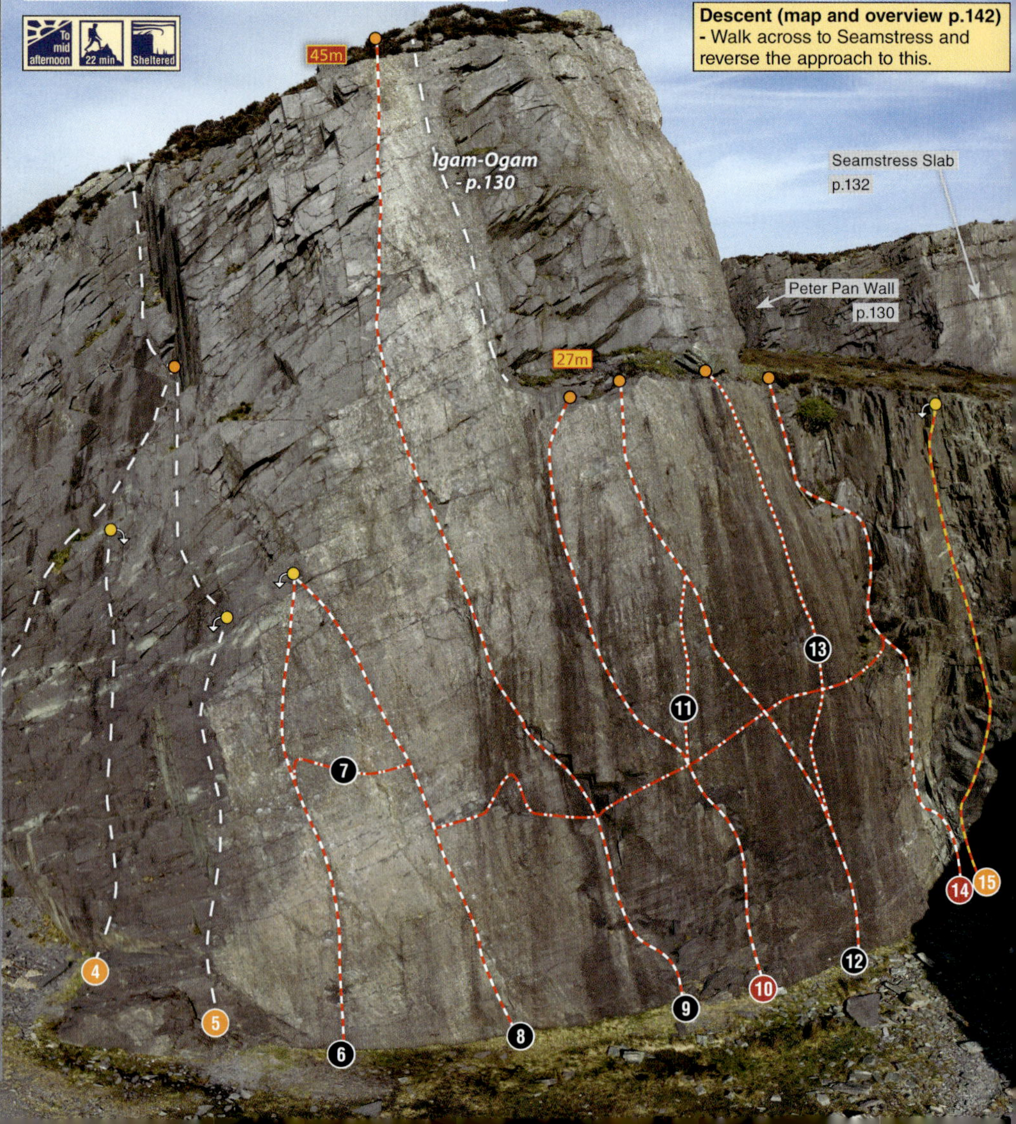

10 Kubla Khan . . . . ⚄ 🧗 🪓 ☐ **E3 6b**

A great route with a desperate crux. Climb up to the bolt easily, pass it directly with difficulty and then move left into the cracked groove. The gear soon runs out, so place it while you can. A large metal spike protects the moves to the belay ledge out right.
FA. Martin Crook, Andy Newton 3.1985.
FA. (Direct) Malcolm Campbell, Ian Fox 1985

11 Dark and Scary Stories . . . . . ⚄ ☐ **E5 6b**

A direct variant of *Kubla Khan*, low in the grade. Climb *Kubla Khan* to the bolt, then sprint up the slab via some bold climbing to reach the third bolt of *Short Stories*. Finish up this.
FA. Calum Muskett, Tony Pearson 9.2009

12 Short Stories . . . ⚄ 🧗 ✒ 🪝 ☐ **E4 6a**

Glue-in bolts lead you up a lonely line on this slab. Technical, sustained and run out, with a sting in the tail!
FA. Steve Howe, Sue Harland 2.4.1987

13 Ghengis . . . . ✒ 🪝 ☐ **E6 6a**

A hard route which is bolder since losing its peg and flake. The route can still be done protected by a "nest of skyhooks". Alternatively, for a less bold alternative, clip the second bolt on *Short Stories* and traverse in.
FA. Steve Howe, Sue Harland 2.4.1987

14 Andy Pandy . . . . ☐ **E1 5a**

A poor route. Climb the groove to gain the faint crack on the right of the slab and follow it to the loose groove. Climb this up to the Serengeti level. The direct start is **The Ascent of the Vikings, E1 6a**.
FA. Mel Roberts, Martin Crook 23.5.1984
FA. (Direct start) A.Winterbottom, B.Cralis 24.5.1984

15 Dog and Bone . . . . . ⚄ 🧗 🪓 ☐ **6a**

Start with delicate moves up clean rock right of the slab, then weave your way up the left-hand side of the tower.
FA. Mark Hellewell, Graham Sutton 18.9.2013

16 Operation Zig-Zag . . . . ⚄ ☐ **5c**

The blunt arete. Positive holds and interesting moves.
FA. Graham Sutton, Mark Hellewell 17.9.2013

17 Release the Kraken . . . . ⚄ 🧗 ☐ **6b+**

A nice bolted route.
FA. Ian Lloyd-Jones 18.11.2011

18 The Carbon Stage . . ⚄ 🧗 🪒 ☐ **6c+**

A good route, although eliminate low down. High up it is more independent, with a jump for the short, or a long stretch for the tall, to reach the final ledge. Glue-in bolts.
FA. M.Jones 19.8.1994

19 Zeus . . . . ⚄ ✒ ☐ **6a+**

The steep blocky bulges to a small shelf. Make a tricky mantel onto this and continue to the lower-off.
FA. Mark Hellewell, Colin Goodey 2010

20 Titan . . . . ⚄ ☐ **4c**

On the very edge of the buttress is this easy, long and exciting route. After a rockover to the left, the route moves right onto the edge and goes steeply up past bolts to a chain lower-off.
FA. Colin Goodey, Mark Hellewell, Sue Trainer 2010

21 Graze Anatomy . . . . 📖 ☐ **6a+**

Start off the scree slope right of *Titan*. There is a difficult mantel by the first bolt.
FA. Graham Sutton, Mark Hellewell 18.9.2013

Bus Stop Quarry | Dali's Hole | California | Australia | Serengeti | Never Never Land | Twll Mawr | Mordor - Lost World | Vivian Quarry | Rainbow Slab Area | Snakes and Ladders | Outlying

1 **Snap** . . . . ☐ **E1 5a**
The left-hand line of weakness past a bore-hole.
FA. Mel Roberts (solo) 2.4.1984

2 **Alpen** . . . . ☐ **E1 5b**
An eliminate. Climb direct to a ledge at 6m, finish up and left.

3 **Free Gift** . . . . ☐ **S**
The right-facing flake-line.
FA. Philip Biglands 2.10.2011

4 **Crackle** . . . . 🧗 ☐ **VS 4c**
A virtual solo up to a choice of loose cracks.
FA. Mel Roberts (solo) 2.4.1984

5 **Pop** . . . . ☐ **HVS 5b**
Climb the right-hand weakness of the slab, just left of a crack.
FA. Mel Roberts (solo) 2.4.1984

Lower Tier

This very small slab is situated directly below the Never Never Land Slab. The routes are short and have some loose rock.
Approach (map and overview p.142) - Scramble down from Never Never Land.

Shame and Embarrassment Wall

A large and loose section of wall that has a tendency to fall down. This is the third topo shot in as many years - be warned! The sport routes on the left are more stable.
Approach (map and overview p.142) - The wall is opposite the Never Never Land Slab. Scramble across the scree to the base.
Descent - For the routes which top out, it is safest to head up and right around the back of Serengeti, then down the incline above Yellow Wall.

6 **The Gargoyle** . . . . 🧗 ☐ **6a+**
The narrow slab which climbs up to a steep arete.
FA. Kath Goodey, Colin Goodey, Del Smith 14.8.2008

7 **Obsession** . . . . 🧗🧗 🧗 ☐ **6a+**
A fantastic route that is prone to rockfall from above - best avoided in high winds, when small shards of slate can rain down on you. A couple of the bolts are damaged, but the route is still very good and climbable.
FA. Colin Goodey, Mark Hellewell 6.6.2008

Right of Obsession was **Fear of Rejection E4 5c, 5c** *- a Stevie Haston crack route with death potential. It has fallen down as has most of the wall to the right. This is a common occurrence, so much so that a topo photo is a just snapshot! Please treat these descriptions with suspicion.*

8 Stairlift to Heaven . . . .  **E1 5a**
The second half of the second pitch of this route has NO protection and is very loose. The route is best avoided.
1) 4c, 30m. Climb up the leftward-leaning blocky ramp to a ledge system. Follow this back right to a belay by a large flake.
2) 5a, 30m. Pad up the hanging slab with the first runner at the triangular niche. Top out over scree and belay well back on a drystone wall.
FA. Mark Dicken, C.Neale 11.5.2003

9 Stannah to Hell . . . . **XS 5c**
If *Stairlift to Heaven* was not exciting enough for you, then this trip up a tottering ramp-line across the wall should suffice.
1) 5c, 10m. Follow *Shame and Embarrassment* to its first bolt.
2) 4c, 55m. Pick your way leftwards along the ramp to a cluster of rubble (though this might be on the ground by now).
3) 5a, 30m. Finish up *Stairlift to Heaven.*
FA. Calum Muskett, Mark Dicken 10.4.2010

10 Shame and Embarrassment. . **E5 6b**
A worrying line which tackles the curving flake-crack. Climb up 6m to a slabby ledge and a bolt. Reluctantly move up and right before stepping back left to another bolt. Now gain and climb the flake-line.
FA. Johnny Dawes, Trevor Hodgson 14.9.1986

11 Hollow Heart **E2 5b**
The flake-line left of *Bar of Soap.*
FA. Richie Brookes 13.5.1987

12 Bar of Soap **E1 5b**
The short crack right of *Shame and Embarrassment* just to the left of the high point of the scree cone. Poor and slippery!
FA. Stevie Haston, Martin Crook 6.1983

Further right was an arete called **Suspension of Disbelief, E4 6a***. The bolts on this have now corroded to nothing.*

Over There Land
This wall has recently been developed as a sport climbing venue, with a few 7th grade routes. *Cavity Wall* is superb.
Approach (map and overview p.142) - Head along the main track. Over There Land is past the Never Never Land Slab on the right-hand side just before the Watford Gap.

13 Name Unknown **E3 6a**
The greenstone pillar originally had three bolts and some fixed wires. It was considered too unstable for re-equipping.

14 Cavity Wall **7c**
Excellent and sustained slate pocket pulling with a couple of really cool rockovers. It may be tricky to on-sight, but with its ease of access and number of bolts it would make a good redpoint project.
FA. Ian Lloyd-Jones 14.6.2012

15 Let Yourself Go! **7a**
Climb the bolted groove left of the old fallen down fence. Six bolts protect the technical groove. A battle between 'slate weirdness' versus 'lateral thinking', climbs much better than it looks. Take care to avoid the big block when lowering down.
FA. Tesni Lloyd-Jones, Ian Lloyd-Jones 9.7.2013

16 Super Slinky **7a**
Climb the bolted groove right of *Let Yourself Go!*, just right of the old fallen down fence. Five bolts lead the way up the frictionless groove.
FA. Celt Lloyd-Jones (11), Ian Lloyd-Jones 12.7.2013

17 Easy for Caterpillars **7a**
The concave slab on the far right of the wall is easy to start. A good short technical crux in the middle is followed by some dynamic / long reaches.
FA. Ian Lloyd-Jones 25.6.2012

Bus Stop Quarry | Dali's Hole | California | Australia | Serengeti | Never Never Land | Twll Mawr | Mordor - Lost World | Vivian Quarry | Rainbow Slab Area | Snakes and Ladders | Outlying

Bus Stop Quarry

Dali's Hole

California

Australia

Serengeti

Never Never Land

Twll Mawr

Mordor - Lost World

Vivian Quarry

Rainbow Slab Area

Snakes and Ladders

Outlying

Air vent

Never Never Land p.140

Shock the Monkey Area

Patellaectomy p.152

Patellaectomy - Shock the Monkey Area

Tucked away in a cul-de-sac, this area is easy to miss. While the main adjacent sector's eponymous route *Patellaectomy* is a major attraction, the new dry tooling routes here really are worth a visit if that is your cup of tea. At M6+ *The Monkey Bar Kid* is the easiest route in this area, while *One Hundred Words for No Snow* at M9+ is a real challenge for the modern mixed climber during the 'off-season'.

Approach (map and overview p.142) - Follow the main track through the upper quarries, past the gate below Australia and on to another gate on the right by the Dali's Hole dip. Go over the gate and turn left onto a path which leads directly into this secluded bay.

Lots of sun | 20 min | Sheltered

14m

1

2

3

❶ Cry Wolf . . . . ⟨3⟩ [____] **M9**
Take the left-hand ramp-line, via a difficult start, to the niche of
One Hundred Words... Climb the wall left of the niche to join *One
Hundred Words...* above, finishing up the challenging headwall.
FA. Pete Harrison 12.2.2012

❷ One Hundred Words for No Snow
. . . . ⟨3⟩ [____] **M9+**
The left-hand side of the tall wall on the left side of the bay
as you walk in features mostly natural placements. Climb the
diagonal seam to a breather in the niche. A drilled pocket above
gives access to the upper wall where torques, stein pulls, a dyno
and some footless matching lead to a couple of very thin moves
rightwards. A cruxy move up with tricky feet gains a pocket and
the upper crack. Follow this with interest to the lower-off.
FA. Pete Harrison 1.2012

❸ Shock the Monkey . . . . [____] **HVS 5a**
Climb the slabby side of the arete past four bolts.
FA. Ian Lloyd-Jones, Nigel Manning 6.4.1993

❹ Rastamouse . . . . ⟨2⟩ [____] **M7+**
The left-hand corner of the wall has excellent technical climbing.
FA. Torquil Bennett 27.12.2011

❺ Monkey-Bar Kid . . . . ⟨2⟩ [____] **M6+**
Start on the ledge left of *The Deerhunter*. Good hooks, no big
reaches, few hand changes and close bolts make this about as
easy as a route on this wall will get.
FA. Torquil Bennett 6.12.2011

❻ The Deerhunter . . . . ⟨1⟩ [____] **M7**
Start in the short corner 5m to the left of *Bambi*. Fairly
straightforward but sustained climbing leads to a more technical
and powerful crux between the last two bolts, including a dry
tool take on the slate high-step.
FA. Torquil Bennett 11.2011

❼ Bambi . . . . ⟨2⟩ [____] **M9+**
Climb the wall left of *Ibex* past double bolts at half-height - clip
both.
FA. Rob Gibson 24.11.2010

❽ Ibex Direct . . . . [____] **M8**
Traverse across the cave to the line of bolts between *Ibex* and
Bambi. Join *Ibex* towards the top and follow it to lower-off.
FA. Rob Greenwood 2012

❾ Ibex . . . . ⟨2⟩ [____] **M7**
Sustained climbing with fun moves and a crux near the top.
The route is on the back wall, just right of the tunnel. A clipstick
helps reach the first bolt.
*FA. Pete Harrison 19.2.2009. The route was the first on this wall and was
created by Owen Samuel and Rocio Siemens*

❿ Rest in Pete's Eats . . . . [____] **E1 5a**
At the back of the bay. Climb a crack to loose flakes, then
head up on the left-hand side of the flakes to a broken corner.
Traverse left on the steep ramp to the top.
Descent - Walk back down the main track to gate by Dali's Hole
on the approach.
FA. R.Liddle, L.Dow 23.4.1993

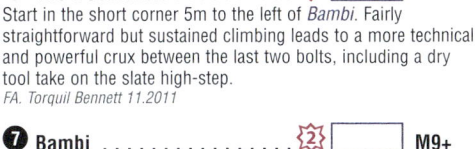

Patellaectomy

Tucked away in a cul-de-sac, this area is easy to miss. *Patellaectomy* itself is a must, if only for total slate madness. There are also some great sport and dry tooling routes in the area.

Approach (map and overview p.142) - Follow the main access track through the upper quarries until you get to the bottom of a dip by Dali's Hole. Cross the gate on the right of the track and follow a path along a flat level into a secluded bay.

Descent - Either abseil from a bolt belay, or make the long walk back round via the Dali's Hole gate

1 Home Run. . . . . ⚑ [ ] E2 6a

Start below an overhang 3m left of *Patellaectomy*. Make tricky moves up and right past the first high bolt. Carry on past two more until easier (but still sustained) climbing leads to the top and the belay.

FA. Jan Bowman, Andy Bowman 6.7.1993

2 Monkey See, Monkey Do . . . 🧗 [ ] E2?

A major section has fallen down leaving a deep V-groove and the route hasn't yet been reclimbed. It used to start 2m left of *Patellaectomy* and climbed direct through the overhang with gear where the block has fallen out to arrive at a horizontal break on top of the now missing block. It is finished up a small crack system.

FA. Simon Beal, Andy Scott, Nick Harford 23.6.2008

3 Patellaectomy . . . . 🏵️ 🗝️ [ ] E1 5c

An awesome route that utilises all available ironmongery. Gain the chimney and a bolt. Bridge up this to reach the bars on the right. Mantel these and move up the wall passing another bar and bolt to the top.

FA. Chris Parkin, M.Robinson 23.4.1992

Early morning | 20 min | Sheltered

4 Pail Rider . . . . 1 6c+
Start at the four shot-holes at the base of the wall - use these with caution as they are little reservoirs of water. Gain the right-hand flakes and follow them to a small ledge by the third bolt. Technical moves on side-pulls and a giant step out right gain the flake near the arete, with a small ledge and bolt. Ascend the short crack to an awkward mantel onto the ledge below the final arete. A fierce pull out left past the last bolt leads up the wall/arete to the lower-off.
FA. Andy Scott, Jon Ratcliffe 24.6.2008

5 Beyond the Pail 1 7a
Start as for *Pail Rider* at the four shot-holes in the base of the wall and follow it to the third bolt. Make a precarious step left to the first shot-hole under the bars. Hard moves from here lead to a dramatic rockover to grab the right-hand bar. Mantel this and head diagonally right to another bolt. More thin moves lead out to the last bolt near the arete on *Pail Rider*, which is joined for its final moves.
FA. Andy Scott, Jon Ratcliffe 25.6.2008

6 A Little Pail . . . . 2 6b+
Start a couple of metres right of *Pail Rider*. Climb the delicate shallow groove to a niche. Pull into this and make your way up to the base of a short crack on the left - junction with *Pail Rider*. Follow this to its lower-off.
FA. Jon Ratcliffe, Andy Scott 25.6.2008

7 Donkey Rider E1 5a
The wall and crack system left of *Dyke Rider*. Climb boldly up the lower wall to reach a collection of spikes (sling) and a good wire slot above. Step left to a good crack and climb to the top with one hand in the crack and the other on the edge of broken ground to the right. At the top, sling a good block then traverse right to the *Dyke Rider* lower-off.
FA. Graham Desroy, Simon Panton 28.4.2010

8 Dyke Rider E2 5b
As you enter the bay, a mini dyke on the right next to a tunnel stands out. Climb this pleasantly past two bolts, to a point where an obvious tricky section looms. Press on through to big holds and a lower-off
FA. Simon Beal, Andy Scott, Jon Ratcliffe (all led) 25.6.2008

9 Penblwydd Hapus(i fi) 6c
The bolted route to the right of *Dyke Rider*. Climb the hanging groove above the tunnel mouth to a bold finish up easier ground. Shares the same lower-off as the previous route.
FA. Simon Panton 1.5.2010

10 Offa's 1 6b
The first line on the right as you enter the bay, up the middle of the steep wall that faces into the bay. Five bolts to a chain lower-off. The crux is passing the overlap.
FA. Chris Davies, Mark Williams 8.5.2010

Not much sun | 20 min | Sheltered

Bus Stop Quarry
Dali's Hole
California
Australia
Serengeti
Never Never Land
Twll Mawr
Mordor - Lost World
Vivian Quarry
Rainbow Slab Area
Snakes and Ladders
Outlying

Twll Mawr

Bus Stop Quarry

Dali's Hole

California

Australia

Serengeti

Never Never Land

Twll Mawr

Mordor - Lost World

Vivian Quarry

Rainbow Slab Area

Snakes and Ladders

Outlying

Bus Stop Quarry

Dali's Hole

California

Australia

Serengeti

Never Never Land

Twll Mawr

Mordor - Lost World

Vivian Quarry

Rainbow Slab Area

Snakes and Ladders

Outlying

Caroline Ciavaldini on the amazing *The Quarryman* (E8)- *p.166* - in Twll Mawr. Photo: David Simmonite
The route was immortalised when Johnny Dawes was filmed making an ascent of the infamous groove pitch in the 80s classic Stone Monkey video. It is essentially a 7c sport pitch up a blank groove with few holds forcing the climber into flamboyant and wild bridging positions in order to edge their way up. Oddly the technical crux is actually the top pitch which sees less attention than the iconic groove. Caroline climbed the whole route on her ascent in 2018.

	No star	⚜	⚜	⚜
Mod to S / 4c	-	-	-	-
HS-HVS / 5a-6a+	1	3	-	-
E1-E3 / 6b-7a	8	10	10	2
E4 / 7a+ and up	5	12	10	8

Twll Mawr translates as 'Big Hole' and lives up to its name. Although it was first developed way back in 1971 by the legendary Joe Brown with the route *Opening Gambit*, it really saw little attention until the 1980s when a mini-boom followed Johnny Dawes' ascent of *The Quarryman*. More recently a series of long sport routes has transformed this area into a place where any 6c/7a climber can have a great adventurous day out on well-bolted multi-pitch routes. These routes can feel committing but most of the belays are rigged for abseil, so twin ropes will help you retreat if you are caught out.

Conditions

The routes on the South Wall are well worth considering in hot weather as they are in the shade from early morning onwards. It does take a while to dry though and some are prone to seepage which is hard to bypass. The routes on the Quarryman and North Walls range from hard trad classics and super sport routes, to loose and seldom repeated adventures - choose your route with care! They can be climbed almost year round in sunny conditions. If you are not looking for a big day out, there are some excellent single-pitch routes in the main hole and the Combat Rock area.

Ignacio Mulero making the coveted second of *Meltdown* (9a) - *p.166* - in Twll Mawr. Photo: Talo Martin
This route has a long history dating way back to the halcyon days of slate in the 1980s. It was first established as a project by Johnny Dawes and attempted by both him and Jerry Moffatt in their prime, but neither managed to complete it. The route lay forgotten for many years until James 'Caff' McHaffie finally succeeded on it in 2012. The first repeat took another six years and is pictured here.

Bus Stop Quarry | Dali's Hole | California | Australia | Serengeti | Never Never Land | Twll Mawr | Mordor - Lost World | Vivian Quarry | Rainbow Slab Area | Snakes and Ladders | Outlying

Bus Stop Quarry

Dali's Hole

California

Australia

Serengeti

Never Never Land

Twll Mawr

Mordor - Lost World

Vivian Quarry

Rainbow Slab Area

Snakes and Ladders

Outlying

Approach

Twll Mawr is situated in the upper quarries, and best approached from Deiniolen and Dinorwig via the A4244, which connects Llanberis to the coast road. Turn off the A4244 to Deiniolen and on through Dinorwig to parking at the road end near Bus Stop Quarry.

North and South Walls - Walk along the main footpath/track through the quarries. At the dip by Dali's Hole, go over the gate on the right. Head down the track one level and then walk left along a long level. This is the once-banned Peregrine Walls, but access to the level is now allowed as long as you don't linger. The RSPB have asked that we look out for nesting peregrines across the quarries and give any a wide berth. At the end of this long level at Golgotha (or 'Place of the Skull'), where a tunnel leads into Twll Mawr, the right fork leads through to below the South Wall. To reach the base of the South and North Walls, carry on along to the scree slope and walk across to the bottom of your chosen route.

Combat Rock and Quarryman Wall - Walk on along the main track through the quarries, past Never Never Land and through the 'Watford Gap'. Combat Rock is on the other side of the gap on the left and the abseil to the Quarryman Wall is gained by a difficult scramble under Combat Rock to the far side of 'The Alcove' - rope advised.

Seamstress Slab
p.132

Yellow Wall
p.134

Walk
off the
top

Mordor - The Lost World
p.178

Never Never Land
p.140

Gate in
a dip

Peregrine
Walls

Watford
Gap

The
Alcove

North Wall
p.170

Climber

Quarryman Wall
p.166

Combat Rock
p.162

South Wall
p.164

Golgotha
p.160

Tunnel entrance to
South Wall

Bus Stop Quarry

Dali's Hole

California

Australia

Serengeti

Never Never Land

Twll Mawr

Mordor - Lost World

Vivian Quarry

Rainbow Slab Area Snakes and Ladders

Outlying

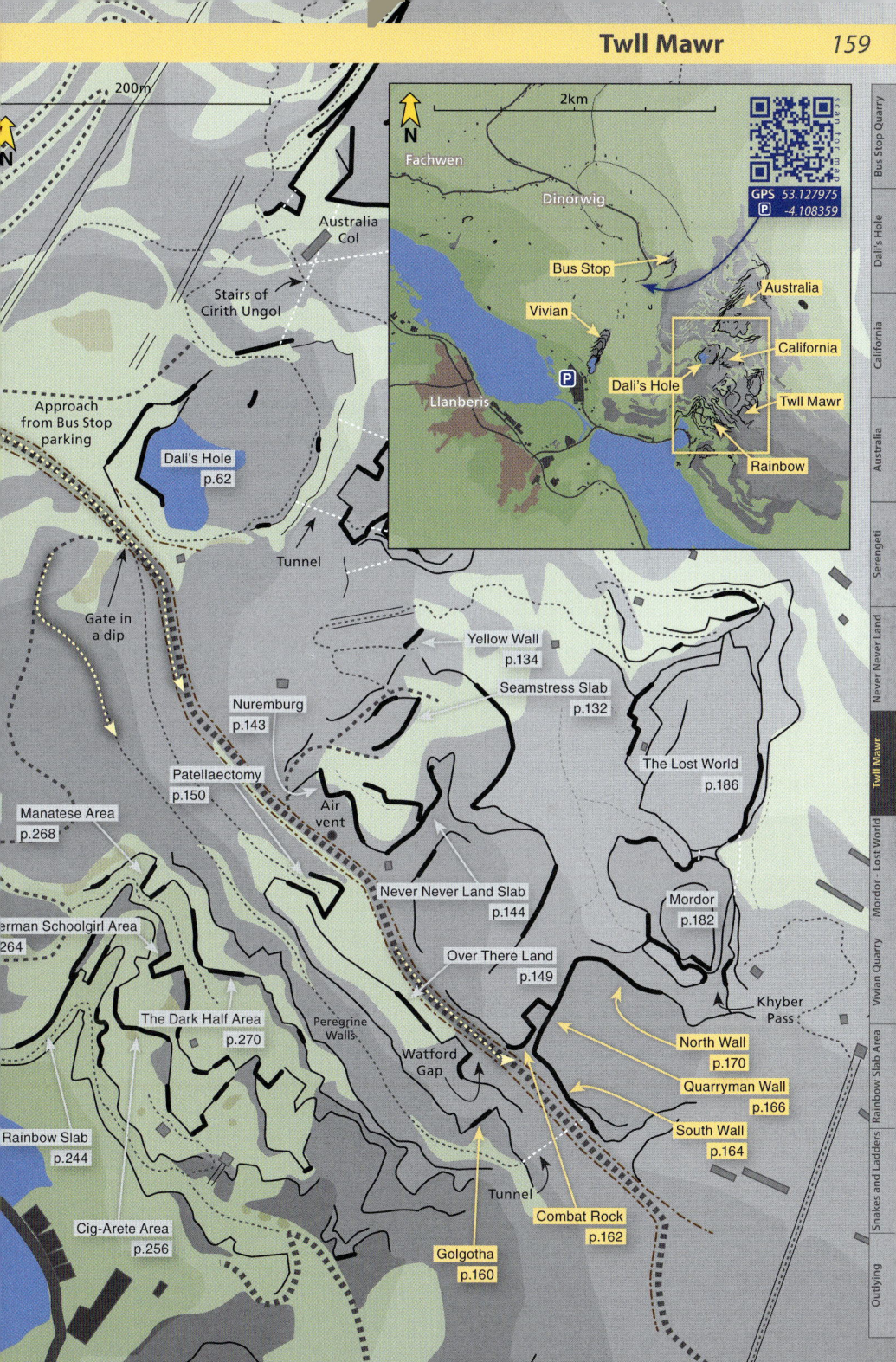

200m

N

Australia Col

Stairs of Cirith Ungol

Approach from Bus Stop parking

Dali's Hole
p.62

Tunnel

Gate in a dip

Nuremburg
p.143

Patellaectomy
p.150

Manatese Area
p.268

German Schoolgirl Area
264

The Dark Half Area
p.270

Rainbow Slab
p.244

Cig-Arete Area
p.256

Air vent

Never Never Land Slab
p.144

Peregrine Walls

Watford Gap

Over There Land
p.149

Tunnel

Golgotha
p.160

Combat Rock
p.162

Yellow Wall
p.134

Seamstress Slab
p.132

The Lost World
p.186

Mordor
p.182

Khyber Pass

North Wall
p.170

Quarryman Wall
p.166

South Wall
p.164

Inset map:

2km

N

Fachwen

Dinorwig

Bus Stop

Vivian

Australia

California

Dali's Hole

Twll Mawr

Rainbow

Llanberis

GPS 53.127975
-4.108359

Side tabs (right margin):
Bus Stop Quarry · Dali's Hole · California · Australia · Serengeti · Never Never Land · Twll Mawr · Mordor - Lost World · Vivian Quarry · Rainbow Slab Area · Snakes and Ladders · Outlying

Golgotha

This wall could be considered as Upper Rainbow Area but is passed on one of the approaches to Twll Mawr so has been included here. The best routes are on the clean slab, although there is a more adventurous route around the skull-like configuration of tunnel mouths.

Approach (map p.159, overview p.158) - Follow the main track through the upper quarries, to the dip by Dali's Hole. Head over a gate on the right and down towards the Rainbow Slab Area. Go down one level and follow this leftwards towards Llanberis Pass. After a few hundred metres turn a corner - there is a clean slab on your left and skull-like tunnel mouths to the right.

🚫 **Access -** In the past this area had a voluntary climbing ban to protect nesting birds. This has been lifted since it was thought that the limited climbing had no effect on the birds. Occasionally you will hear their shrill call or the whoosh as they dive past you.

Despite this, it is important that climbers don't disturb wildlife in the quarries. Please don't prospect for new routes close to bird nests, especially between April and June. If you do find a nest, don't loiter, pass quietly by and contact the RSPB.

❶ The Daddy Club . . . . 🪨 [____] **E1 5b**
The groove on the left side of the dolerite prow is climbed to a bolt. Head up until forced onto the arete on the left. Wires and cams protect the next moves rightwards to the lower-off.
FA. Mark Dicken, Paul Jenkinson, Calum Muskett 22.8.2008

❷ Green Slip . . . . 🪨 [____] **7a**
The direct line up the dolerite tower to join *The Daddy Club*.
FA. Calum Muskett 11.2010

❸ Slip of the Tongue . . . . . 🔟 🪨 [____] **E6 6c**
Three bolts and some thin wires protect this technical offering. Head straight up to the first bolt and then enter the slim groove which goes left at the final bolt to finish direct.
FA. Pete Robins 11.2010

❹ Slip Sliding Away. . . 🔟 🪨 🪨 [____] **E5 6b**
The smooth groove to the right of *Slip of the Tongue*. Climb this with a lot of effort to gain the right-trending finish. This is easier but much looser.
FA. Calum Muskett, Johnny Dawes 9.2009

❺ Split Decision . . . . . 🔟 🪨 🪨 [____] **E6 6c**
A crack-line is followed with great technical effort to reach a sloping hold. Finish up *Slip Sliding Away*.
FA. Calum Muskett 11.2010

❻ Tales of the Golden Monkey . 🔟 [____] **E2 5c**
A unique route that traverses from one quarry to another via a half-height tunnel.
1) 4c, 20m. Start on the Golgotha side, right of the mouth of the skull. Scramble then climb directly into the right eye socket. Follow the tunnel to the Twll Mawr side.
2) 5c, 20m. See topo on - p.164. Exit left, looking out, to find the groove round the corner. Climb this on small to very small gear (with much head scratching) to a ledge. A continuation groove staggers right above and spits you out onto the path.
FA. Mark Dicken, Fraser Ball 13.7.2011

Ian Lloyd-Jones, a descendant of a local quarryman, on his own creation *Supermassive Black Hole* (7a) - *p.165* - one of a new set of multi-pitch sport routes in Twll Mawr. Photo: David Simmonite

Bus Stop Quarry

Dali's Hole

California

Australia

Serengeti

Never Never Land

Twll Mawr

Mordor - Lost World

Vivian Quarry

Rainbow Slab Area

Snakes and Ladders

Outlying

Bus Stop Quarry

Dali's Hole

California

Australia

Serengeti

Never Never Land

Twll Mawr

Mordor - Lost World

Vivian Quarry

Rainbow Slab Area

Snakes and Ladders

Outlying

Combat Rock

The massive and impressive hole of Twll Mawr is famous for its hard routes. Combat Rock is more pedestrian in nature and has a few good trad and semi-bolted routes.
Approach (map p.159, overview p.158) - Follow the main track through the upper quarries to the dip by Dali's Hole. Carry on along the main track through the prominent 'Watford Gap', just past Never Never Land, until the giant hole is visible on your left. The wall is immediately on the left.
Descent (Routes 1 to 3) - Walk back along the ridge parallel to the main track until above *Patellalectomy*, then walk back along the main path and through the Watford Gap.

1 In Between Red and Green .... ☐ E1 5a
The left-hand of the three cracks leads to the cracked headwall.
FA. B.Lillington, J.Teed 26.3.2003

2 Snoring Exploring .... ☐ E1 5b
The wider right-hand crack leads to a corner and headwall.
FA. B.Lillington 26.3.2003

3 Watford Gap West .... ☐ VS 4b
Start on the left side of the pillar. Head up the corner to a tricky slump onto an overhanging boulder. Climb the wall above to gain a heathery groove. Awkward climbing up this leads to the top. Belay way back on a rubble thread.
FA. Cliff Phillips (solo) 19.5.1984

4 Combat Rock .... ☒ ☐ E1 5a
A good route that follows the crack-line out from the left-hand side of the tunnel mouth. Follow it to the lower-off.
FA. Paul Trower, A.Howard 20.4.1984

5 Rhyfelwr .... ☒ 🧗 ☐ E2 5b
The crack that runs parallel to *Combat Rock* out of the right side of the tunnel is a little harder and bolder.
FA. Ian Lloyd-Jones, Steve Slater 24.9.1989

6 Teenage Kicks .... 🧗 ☐ E4 6a
A meandering line up the wall and thin seam/crack - microwires. Move left at the top to the *Combat Rock* lower-off.
FA. Duncan Lee, John Warburton 5.5.2005

7 Purple Haze .... ☒ 🧗 ☐ E3 5a
An entertaining route with massive exposure. Start from the bolted abseil station at the base of *Teenage Kicks*. Move right along the ledge to the flake. Follow this up past some hollow tombstones to a ledge below the steep groove of *The Colour Purple*. Most people will want to clip the first bolt on this before committing to the swing out right to climb up the bold and exposed prow to the lower-off.
FA. Paul Trower, Ian Wilson 4.4.1986

8 The Colour Purple .. ☒ 🧗 🧗 ☐ E4 6b
Climb *Purple Haze* to the steep groove and then the groove. Passing the first bolt is easy compared to the move past the second!
FA. Chris Parkin, J.Smallwood 29.4.1992

9 Cyclone B .... ☒ 🧗 🧗 ☐ E3 6a
The flake and groove system to the right of *Purple Haze*. Climb up past a couple of bolts to a bolt belay on the prow. It is possible to combine this with *The Colour Purple* for a longer outing.
FA. Fraser Ball, Chris Parkin 26.4.1992

This area is accessed via an exposed traverse below the Combat Rock wall to the hanging bay to its right - rope up for this.

10 Lethal Injection E2 5c
Start at the belay just as you enter 'The Alcove'. Weave up the left arete to 'the Podium'. Clip the belay on *Cyclone B*, then move right to a crack - gear. Above this, gain the slim groove of *Legal Murders* and a bolt. At the next bolt, traverse left back to the arete and the shared finish with *Purple Haze*.
FA. Chris Parkin, J.Smallwood 29.4.1992

11 Legal Murders E3 6a
Start a little way up 'The Alcove' below a wide flake-crack that tapers out at 7m. Climb this until it heads right. A delicate dance leftwards past a bolt gains a flake. Head up this past two bolts, until you can make an escape leftwards to the arete and a shared lower-off with *Purple Haze*.
FA. Chris Parkin, Fraser Ball 26.4.1992

12 Top Gear E1 5b
The corner-crack is climbed to a lower-off.
FA. Chris Parkin, Keith Robertson 6.6.1997

13 Drunken Laughs E2 5b
A game of 'three halves' up the back wall of The Alcove - a boulder problem to the ledge; crack climbing to a slab; bold climbing up the slab. Finish at full-time on a lower-off.
FA. Matt Pugh, Mark Dicken 14.2.2007

Bus Stop Quarry

Dali's Hole

California

Australia

Serengeti

Never Never Land

Twll Mawr

Mordor - Lost World

Vivian Quarry

Rainbow Slab Area

Snakes and Ladders

Outlying

45m

20m

75m

A

Comba
Rock abs
point

*Tales of the Golden
Monkey - p.160*

**Right-fork of
tunnel from
Golgotha**

Early
morning

28 min

14

13

6

1 2 3

4

5

7

8 9

10

11 12

South Wall

This is an amazing area, with recent
developments transforming it into a multi-pitch
sport climbing paradise for the 7a climber.
The wall faces northeast and only gets a little
morning sunshine. It is well sheltered and can
be cool in hot weather.

Approach (map p.159, overview p.158)
- Follow the main track through the upper
quarries to the dip by Dali's Hole. Head over
a gate on the right and down towards the
Rainbow Slab Area. Go down one level and
follow this leftwards towards the Llanberis Pass.
At its end, take the right tunnel and right fork
into Twll Mawr (routes 1-6 start from here). To
reach the base of routes 7-12 carry on, then
scramble down into the depths of the giant hole.
It is worth stashing your bags near the start of
the level or planning to climb with them because
most routes top out.

The route **Practically Esoteric** *(FA. Nick Dixon, Andy Popp 1986) used to be found around here before it fell down.*

❶ Booooom, Blast and Ruin 🗯️ 👆 ☐ **VS 4c**
Classic thrutching up the twin crack-line just left of the bolted slabby arete of *Dark Side of the Moon*. Layback, udge or jam your way up past plentiful wide gear to gain the bolt lower-off on the grassy pedestal.
FA. Ian Lloyd-Jones, Sion McGuinness 4.7.2013

❷ Dark Side of the Moon 🗯️ 👆 👆 ☐ **7b**
Desperate climbing up the thin and technical slabby arete. It features a unique rockover that turns into a knee-bar low down, then a sustained fingery arete above.
FA. Ian Lloyd-Jones 4.7.2013

❸ Set the Controls for the Heart of the Sun
.... 🗯️ 👆 ☐ **7a**
The striking right arete is very tricky past the first four bolts. It relents to give fantastic climbing higher up.
FA. Ian Lloyd-Jones 18.6.2013

❹ Imagine Dragons .... 🗯️ ☐ **6b**
An adventurous sport route. Start on a vegetated ledge by a tree.
Photo on p.3.
1) 6b, 20m. Follow the line of bolts steeply up a line of cracks behind the tree. Belay on the ledge above.
2) 6b, 25m. Head left to the first bolt and follow the line of bolts to a groove. Make technical moves up this to a bolt belay below the top. Alternatively, top out and belay off the fence posts.
FA. Tesni Lloyd-Jones, Celt Lloyd-Jones 18.6.2013

❺ Lost in the Echo .... 🗯️ 👆 🔥 ☐ **E2 5b**
Climb the cleaned crack up the groove with the unusual 'criss cross' patterned rock just a few metres from the right-hand fork of the access tunnel. The continuous crack-line takes loads of gear. Belay as for *Imagine Dragons*.
FA. Ian Lloyd-Jones, Celt Lloyd-Jones 27.6.2015

❻ Champagne Supernova .. 🗯️ 👆 ☐ **7b**
A massive pitch with 20 bolts and three contrasting technical grooves! Start from the end of left fork of the Twll Mawr entrance tunnel. Follow bolts to join the final corner of *Black Holes and Revelations*. Only 7a+ if you use the ladder.
FA. Ian Lloyd-Jones 3.7.2017

❼ Cam-ikaze Corner ..... 🗯️ 👆 ☐ **E3 6a**
An off-width corner-crack which will appeal to some who enjoy the perverse pleasure of jamming, thrutching and squirming up these things. Take plenty of large cams.
FA. Ian Lloyd-Jones 18.8.2014

❽ Black Holes and Revelations
.... 🗯️ 👆 ☐ **7a**
A great two-pitch expedition up the full height of the wall. The first pitch is enough for many. Start below a bolted slanting groove.
1) 6b, 25m. (a.k.a. The Wobbly Ladder Pitch) Climb up the groove heading for the hanging ladder. From a good foothold, jump for the ladder or make a traverse across on bore-holes. Scamper up the ladder to a bolt belay by the tunnel.
2) 7a, 50m. A beast of a pitch. Head up towards the wavy groove capped by a square block. Some traditional thrutching up this leads to easier ground and the base of a square-cut groove. This proves trickier than it appears. Belay on a bolt/thread on the viewing platform above.
FA. Ian Lloyd-Jones, Sion McGuinness 2011

❾ In The Line of Fire .... ☐ **7c+**
An old route that can now be considered an open project since a rockfall destroyed some of the original bolts and holds!
FA. Steve Mayers 1993

❿ Supermassive Black Hole
.... 🗯️ 🔥 🧗 ☐ **7a**
A stellar line up this wall gives something of a safe adventure. Start below a bolted groove. *Photo on p.161.*
1) 7a, 25m. Climb the groove past many bolts. When the holds run out, make a move right onto the blank wall. A crucial foothold here can remain damp, but the bolt can provide aid past it. Regain the groove above and pull onto the ledge to belay.
2) 6b, 12m. A short pitch that heads up and right, past bolts, to a second groove.
3) 6c, 25m. The second groove looks just as hard as the first, but is a little easier. As with the first pitch, a step right bypasses a blank section before regaining the groove again and following it to the belay below a final dolerite slab.
4) 6b, 12m. Follow the bolts up the slab via some quartz pockets. Belay off fence posts and a thread.
FA. Ian Lloyd-Jones, Sion McGuinness 2011

⓫ Running Scared . 🗯️ 👆 👆 🔥 ☐ **7c+**
A desperate pitch. Climb fairly easily up to a rest on the left. Thin climbing above this is the meat of the route.
FA. Steve Mayers 1993

⓬ Black Hole Sun .... 🗯️ 🔥 👆 ☐ **7a+**
A belter of a route, possibly the best on this wall.
1) 7a+, 25m. Climb the blocky start to a ledge. A crack-line points the way with increasing difficulty to a ledge below a V-groove. Ascend the groove on the left arete to a bolt belay on a ledge below the next pitch.
2) 7a, 25m. Follow the arete via some technical moves and long reaches.
3) 7a, 25m. The stunning arete is a cracking pitch and gives a fitting finale to this amazing route.
FA. Ian Lloyd-Jones, Sion McGuinness, Phil Dowthwaite, Andy Schofield 14.7.2011

⓭ Black Hole of Calcutta ..... 🗯️ ☐ **7a**
A great route, although many people may wish to abseil in from the top of the fin to savour the easier pitch two. To gain the base of the route, it is best to abseil from the belay station below Combat Rock - p.162.
1) 7a, 25m. Climb the attractive well-bolted slab/groove to the right of the second arete pitch of *Black Hole Sun* to a bolt belay on a ledge. An easy scramble leads up to the bolt belay of *Black Hole Sun*.
2) 6a+, 30m. Climb the groove to the left of the top arete pitch of *Black Hole Sun*, to reach a bolt belay on top of the fin of rock.
FA. Ian Lloyd-Jones, Callum Nelson 15.3.2015

⓮ Black Hole of Calcutta (P2) .. 🗯️ ☐ **6a+**
Worth doing on its own and easily reached by abseil from above. Climb the groove to the left of the top arete pitch of *Black Hole Sun* to a bolt belay on top of the fin.
FA. Ian Lloyd-Jones, Callum Nelson 15.3.2015

Bus Stop Quarry
Dali's Hole
California
Australia
Serengeti
Never Never Land
Twll Mawr
Mordor - Lost World
Vivian Quarry
Rainbow Slab Area
Snakes and Ladders
Outlying

Quarryman Wall

The massive and impressive hole of Twll Mawr was originally made famous by its hard routes on the Quarryman Wall. The eponymous groove was immortalised in the Stone Monkey video by a flamboyant Johnny Dawes. It is still mainly a playground for the elite. It faces west and gets plenty of sun and is well sheltered.
Approach (map p.159, overview p.158) - For the Quarryman Wall, just head along the main track, through the Watford Gap, until the giant hole is visible on your left. Combat Rock is immediately above you on the left here. For the first three routes, abseil down the wall here to ledges. For the rest of the routes, make an alarming traverse (most people do this roped) along ledges from Combat Rock and up into 'The Alcove'. Walk across this to the other side from where an abseil from a bolted anchor leads to terraces at the base of the wall.

❶ Wolfhound **E4 6a**
The hanging finger-crack requires a skyhook for protection to reach it.
FA. Perry Hawkins, Rob Deane 10.5.1986

❷ Birdman of Cae'r Berllan **E2 5c**
The wide crack is something of a tussle at the top.
FA. Perry Hawkins, Rob Deane 10.5.1986

❸ A Winter's Tale **6b**
Meander up the wall taking care with some fragile holds.
FA. Harold Walmsley, Mark Hounslea 15.12.2016

❹ The Hunted **E7 6c**
The thin crack and wall directly beneath the centre of 'The Alcove'. Start just down and left of the Quarryman Wall, beneath a bolt, next to the hairline crack. Difficult moves lead up past the bolt to some good wires in the crack. Easier climbing brings you to a good ledge and a second bolt. The wall above is much easier.
FA. Calum Muskett 2012

❺ Fleur-de-Lis **E6 6c**
Climb the initial easy groove to the top of a large flake on the left of *Coeur de Lion*, with tricky moves traversing back right to join that route at its second bolt. Climb direct to another bolt before easier moves left along a hollow flake - wires and a step right - bring you directly under a final bolt. A difficult move brings good holds and a scary but steady rockover to clip the bolt. The crux is gaining a two-finger pocket, above which a final lunge for the square-cut top remains.
FA. Calum Muskett, Rob Greenwood 2011

❻ Beijqueiro **E4 6b**
An adventure route and not really the clip-up you might expect.
1) 5c, 25m. From the abseil bolts, make a committing step onto a notch in the arete. Carry on up the arete to a sloping ledge and a peg. A groove on the left leads to another peg, before moving back right to a ledge - peg. Above are two grooves in the arete. Start up the right groove, pass a bolt, then move left into the other groove to reach the 'Rome' belay.
2) 6b, 28m. Move out to the arete and clip a bolt round on the face. Then, most likely, you will step back and forth several times before you commit to the powerful move off a lonely undercut. Scrabble round the next arete to arrive at the base of the corner. Climb this with comparative ease to the top.
FA. Johnny Dawes 25.4.1988

❼ Coeur De Lion . . **E8 7a**
A desperate route which has seen one repeat in 30 years. Only a minimal description is included here.
1) 7a, 25m. Extremely thin and bold climbing up the wall to the 'London' belay.
2) 6c, 30m. Follow the crack above, then move left across the desperately technical wall to the 'Rome' belay on the arete.
3) 6b, 21m. The pillar on the right leads to the top.
FA. Johnny Dawes, John Tombs 28.3.87

❽ Blockhead **E7 6c**
A quality direct finish up the twin cracks above the 'London' belay ledge.
1) 6c, 25m. Pitch 1 of *The Quarryman* up the wall.
2) 6c, 10m. Climb twin cracks to easier ground.
3) 6a, 20m. The wall above past two bolts.
FA. Adam Wainwright, Mike Thomas 1992

❾ The Quarryman . . **E8 7a**
This extraordinary outing sees few ascents as a complete route. Some abseil in to attempt the iconic groove pitch on its own.
Photo on p.154.
1) 6c, 25m. A great pitch up the wall.
2) 6b, 10m. Traverse right along the break to the 'Paris' belay.
3) 6c, 18m. The groove starts smooth and wide and gets smoother and wider before a few holds appear and it eases slightly near the top.
4) 7a, 25m. For those who have climbed the groove, the disappointingly hard top pitch still needs to be done, although it is only desperate for a short section.
FA. Johnny Dawes 10/11.9.1986

❿ Meltdown . . **9a**
The 9a slab that escaped the great Johnny Dawes was mopped up after a prolonged effort by Caff. *Photo on p.157.*
FA. James McHaffie 7.2012. Repeated by Ignacio Mulero 5.2018.

⓫ King of the Mezz **E7 6c**
A bold and challenging addition to the wall. From the 'New York' belay follow *The Fire Escape* to the first bolts, then drop down below the line of overhangs (crux) until you can climb around them and up into *Blockhead*. Belay and finish up *Blockhead*.
FA. Johnny Dawes, Neil Dyer, O.Anderson 5.2011

⓬ The Fire Escape . **E7 6c**
The ultimate in designer climbs, especially since the top peg is no longer there! From the 'New York' belay move out left to two bolts. Clip these and head up to the roof. Move through this leftwards with some effort, then continue to the top without any more runners! The design is for a potential 50m lob should you blow the run-out!
FA. Johnny Dawes 22.9.1988

⓭ Phil's Harmonica . . . **E6 6c**
Another alternative top pitch to *The Quarryman*. From the 'New York' belay, move left into the sentry box below a flake. Follow it to a peg, move up to a bolt and pass it leftwards to a friction groove. Climb the groove to a pinch and a bolt, then finish up the groove to the right of *The Fire Escape*.
FA. Johnny Dawes 26.4.1988

⓮ Mike's Trombone **E6 6b**
The groove that *The Quarryman* avoided is bold. It is best not to contemplate the consequences of failure as the ledges below are likely to 'break your fall'.
FA. Calum Muskett, Rob Greenwood 9.2011

Bus Stop Quarry | Dali's Hole | California | Australia | Serengeti | Never Never Land | Twll Mawr | Mordor - Lost World | Vivian Quarry | Rainbow Slab Area | Snakes and Ladders | Outlying

Combat Rock
p.162

The
Alcove

Rome

London

New
York

Paris

Morning 25 min Abseil in

m to ledge

South Wall
p.164

Descent (map p.159, overview p.158) - From the top of the wall, walk over rough ground up to a grassy plateau between Twll Mawr and Mordor. Head upwards from here to pick up a rough track which leads to the approach path for Heaven Walls. Turn leftwards down the slope here to wind down through Serengeti and back to the main track.

Bus Stop Quarry
Dali's Hole
California
Australia
Serengeti
Never Never Land
Twll Mawr
Mordor - Lost World
Vivian Quarry
Rainbow Slab Area
Snakes and Ladders
Outlying

⑮ The Wonderful World of Walt Disney

. . . . E6 6b

A fantastic outing up the cliff and the easiest route on the Quarryman Wall. Approach as for *The Quarryman*.

1) 6a, 30m. Climb the corner/groove past a stud and three bolts to below *The Quarryman* groove pitch.

2) 6b, 20m. Climb easily right over ledges and around the arete, then move up to a small roof (bolt). Rock up right then back left above the roof and follow the arete past a bolt to a ledge. Use flakes on the right to gain the next bolt, then climb leftwards to the next ledge.

3) 6b, 20m. Climb easily rightwards up ledges, then traverse right to the ledge on the edge - bolt. Make one tricky move onto a foothold then jump across the corner to jugs. Continue to the belay.

4) 6a, 20m. The Scoop Dragon. Climb the groove past three bolts and a peg to the top.

FA. Bob Drury, Johnny Dawes, Andy Popp, Mike Thomas 2.7.1987

⑯ Disney Pixar . E7 6c

A brilliant and tougher variation of *The Wonderful World of Walt Disney*.

1) 6a, 35m. As for *Wonderful World...*

2) 6b, 20m. As for *Wonderful World...* to the rest at the top of the arete. From here, climb up and right with difficulty, passing a bolt to gain the jump move on pitch 3 of *Wonderful World...* Leap across the groove to belay.

3) 6a, 18m. Finish up *The Dyke*.

FA. Calum Muskett, Emma Twyford 11.2015

⑰ The Dyke E6 6a

Climb the seam diagonally up and left across the wall past a couple of bolts. Bold wall climbing.

FA. Johnny Dawes, Mike Raine 11.4.1988

Approach (Routes 18, 20 and 21) - *Approach as for the South wall through the tunnel by Golgotha - p.158*

⑱ Opening Gambit. . . . . . . XS

One of Joe Brown's original forays into the quarries shows just how bold they were back then. Given how frequently this area of rock exfoliates itself, it is a wonder if any of the original line actually exists.

1) 45m. Pick your way up scree-covered ledges to reach the base of *The Quarryman* where the bolt belay at the start of *Wonderful World...* is.

2) 4c, 27m. Traverse rightwards across more questionable terrain to a sloping ledge. A bad step leads up to a bay with a thread belay amongst some boulders.

3) 5a, 35m. Move across the bay to gain the far arete. Above used to be the 'banana flake' - its integrity is demonstrated by its absence. The remaining rock is suspect to say the least. Start to the left of the arete. Climb to better rock and get some gear in thin cracks. Gain the exposed crystal ledge on the arete. Mantel up onto the next ledge. Above is a giant 'Jenga' tower. Ascend this to gain a bay of steep sloping scree. Belay at the back of this.

4) and 5) 70m. Layback up the crack at the back of the bay and take the easiest line up ledges above, stopping occasionally for a belay. Carry on until the fault-line of *Hamadryad* comes to meet you at a steep wall - belay.

6) Exit leftwards back to safety over a hut roof. It is best to ascend up towards Heaven Walls and follow an incline back down over the top of Yellow Wall to Serengeti.

FA. Joe Brown, Chris Davies, J.Smith 9.4.1971
FA. (P3 -replacement pitch after rockfall - Mark Dicken, T.Shaw 2002

⑲ The Gay Blade E6 6a

A bold outing up the dolerite vein in the arete which is a bit loose. Approach either by abseiling from above or climbing along *Opening Gambit* to the base of the dolerite pillar.

FA. Johnny Dawes, Bob Drury 2.7.1988

⑳ The Rock Bottom Line 7b+

Once the longest fully bolted sport route in the UK, but now surpassed by its neighbours to the right. It is still a great adventure from the very bottom to the top of the Quarryman Wall.

1) 6b, 30m. Climb the slab in the corner with some bridging. From the ninth bolt, carefully traverse right avoiding the scree ledge to a bolt belay.

2) 7a, 30m. The crack and flake-line are easy to start, but have a hard move over a bulge near the top to a ledge. Bolt belay.

3) 6b, 30m. Climb the slab/wall to a ledge at the foot of a short groove and possible belay ledge (two bolts). Continue up the arete past three bolts to the 'Matilda' ledge. Bolt belay.

4) 7b+, 25m. A beginners' Quarryman groove leads to a bolt belay below *Wonderful World...*

5) 7b, 20m. Belay a few feet further right. Take the flake and crack system up the attractive bulging wall. The thin crack doesn't take fingers very well. The crux is either a high step up right or left - take your pick.

FA. Ian Lloyd-Jones, Sion McGuinness 3.10.2011

㉑ Long in the Twll/The North Will Rise Again

. . . . 6c+

A long mid-grade, multi-pitch sport route that starts at the bottom of Twll Mawr.

1) 6b, 20m. The first pitch of *Rock Bottom Line*. Climb the slab in the corner with some bridging. From the ninth bolt carefully traverse right avoiding the scree ledge to a bolt belay, then walk right 10m to anchors.

2) 6a+, 30m. Climb slabs and faint grooves to a shallow blocky niche at 10m. Step right and continue to a ledge. Climb the wall on the left via thin/friable holds to an awkward step onto another ledge. Continue up the wall above between two flakes to a stance at the foot of a slanting ramp.

3) 6c+, 35m. Climb the rib and wall on the left to a shallow niche. Exit this with difficulty to gain a shallow groove on the left. Gain the ledge above the smooth part of the next wall by a dogleg right then back left. Continue up using a sharp rock fang on the right, then climb a shallow rib with sloping ledges. From the highest ledge, step left into a finger-crack. Mantel out of it and climb the short groove above to the stance.

4) 6b, 15m. Gain ledges on the left and climb grooves above to an awkward exit onto a sloping shelf at the base of a recess. Climb the right corner of the recess for a few metres, step left onto the back wall and climb it, passing a couple of ledges with difficulty. Gain a groove which leads to a large horizontal ledge. There is a belay about 3m left.

5) 3c, 8m. Walk about 5m right along the ledge to the fault-line of *Hamadryad*. Continue right and up to the stance. There are no bolts on this pitch.

6) 6a+, 20m. Climb the corner above the stance awkwardly. Continue up the rib to a ledge below the final steepening. Step left to regain the arete, then move back round to its right side for a final awkward exit onto the sloping ledge above.

FA. Colin Struthers, Harold Walmsley 27.3.2015

Combat Rock
p.162

**Exposed approach
to The Alcove**

New
York

Matilda

North Wall
p.170

Paris

Descent (map p.159, overview p.158)
- From the top of the wall, walk over
rough ground up to a grassy plateau
between Twll Mawr and Mordor. Head
upwards from here to pick up a rough
track which leads to the approach path
for Heaven Walls. Turn leftwards down
the slope here to wind down through
Serengeti and back to the main track.

South Wall
p.164

Approach from
South Wall tunnel

Hamadryad
p.170

Tân y Ddraig
p.170

110m
7b
7b+
65m
6b
40m
7a
6b
50m
6c+
6a+
6a+
3c
6b

17
16
15
9
19
21
18
20

A

Bus Stop Quarry
Dali's Hole
California
Australia
Serengeti
Never Never Land
Twll Mawr
Mordor - Lost World
Vivian Quarry
Rainbow Slab Area
Snakes and Ladders
Outlying

1 Hamadryad . . . . 🎌 🗻 🏞 👤 ☐ E3 5c

The original route on this section of wall sees little attention these days. It tackles the long diagonal groove in the face. Start down and left of this below a triangular slab. The first pitch begins at a large dolerite boulder.

1) 5a, 25m. The bold line up the lower wall feels serious. A stiff move off the scree gains a broken ledge system that heads up to the base of a slab. Bold technical climbing up its edge leads to a steep wall. Head back left to a bore-hole (cam) and mantel the sloping ledge to a block belay.

2) 5c, 30m. Move up to a ramp-line leading right to the crack. Follow this to a tree belay.

3) 5a, 35m. Continue up the crack passing a silver birch tree, with a small detour onto the left wall to avoid an annoying bush. Rejoin the crack and climb it to a stepped ledge and block belay.

4) 4b, 30m. Continue up the crack, trending left near the top to an easy exit from the wall as for *Opening Gambit*.

FA. Joe Brown, Claude Davies 10.4.1971
FFA. B.Davison, A.Cope 29.10.1988

2 Tân y Ddraig . . . . 🎌 ☐ 7a

An epic outing with some fine climbing, and a magnificent fifth pitch which makes it all worthwhile. It is also currently claimed to be the longest sport route in the UK. Start at the base of a brown slab between the starts of *The Desolation of Smaug!* and *Long in the Twll...*

1) 6b, 25m. Follow the seam/crack feature to an easing at the arete. Surmount the large flake before traversing a series of cleaned ledges which lead up to a bolt belay at the base of the large slab.

2) 6a+, 30m. Follow the line of bolts directly up the slab to reach a vertical groove. Bridge up this to gain a diagonal groove feature which leads to a shared belay with *Long in the Twll...*

3) 6a, 25m. Follow the ramp feature to a horizontal break, then traverse along the break, below the bolts, until it is possible to step down into *Hamadryad* just above a dead tree. Continue up and rightwards past a hidden bolt on a block ledge, until it is possible to clip the last resin bolt on the second pitch of *The Desolation of Smaug!*. Belay on the slopey ledge as for *The Desolation of Smaug!*.

4) 6b, 25m. Climb *The Desolation of Smaug!* to the third bolt, before traversing across blocky ledges to a fixed rope on a square-cut block. Extend this with a sling and down climb until it is possible to step around the corner. Two further bolts (best to extend with slings) protect the remainder of the traverse to a bolt belay directly below the stunning arete.

5) 7a, 35m. This is what all the traversing was for; a stunning well-positioned technical arete which provides great climbing all the way. It is possible to belay at the top of the arete or continue diagonally up and left, on great dolerite and in an awesome position, to a mantel and then a bolt belay on a large ledge.

6) 6a+, 30m. Traverse leftwards along the gangway for about 8m or so, until you reach the base of the green dolerite arete. Continue up the arete in a fine position with some funky holds, to a belay where you can relax and enjoy some stunning views.

FA. Ian Lloyd-Jones, Celt Lloyd-Jones, Callum Nelson 4.5.2015

Descent (map p.159, overview p.158) - From the top of the wall, walk over rough ground up to a grassy plateau between Twll Mawr and Mordor. Head upwards from here to pick up a rough track which leads to the approach path for Heaven Walls. Turn leftwards down the slope here to wind down through Serengeti and back to the main track.

North Wall

The massive and impressive North Wall of Twll Mawr was known for (and more often avoided because of) its highly adventurous routes. In recent years a few dedicated climbers have spent time, money and effort developing some amazing multi-pitch sport routes here. This has totally changed the character of the wall, making it a popular venue. Although these newer routes are fully bolted, the location and atmosphere mean that they should be regarded as adventurous sport climbing, with loose rock, long days and challenging rope management. There are currently four mutli-pitch sport routes here, including the two further left detailed on the Quarryman Wall section, and they have all vied for the coveted title of the longest sport route in the UK at some stage. Which one actually is the longest is open to question, but there is no doubt that all are superb challenges worthy of anyone's tick list. There are also a number of trad lines further right on the wall, some are new and all are pretty adventurous. Some of the routes suffer from seepage and are difficult or impossible in such conditions. However, the wall faces the morning sun and can also be too hot. As a result, you can climb on the face almost year round if there is a dry spell in the autumn, spring or even winter months.

Approach (map p.159, overview p.158) - Follow the main track through the upper quarries to the dip by Dali's Hole. Head over a gate on the right and down towards the Rainbow Slab Area. Go down one level and follow this leftwards towards the Llanberis Pass. At its end, take the tunnel and right fork into Twll Mawr. To reach the base of the routes, carry on and then scramble down into the depths of the giant hole.

3 The Desolation of Smaug! 🎌 🗻 ☐ 6c

A stunning adventure up the wall. Start below and to the left of *The Razor's Edge* terrace, which is identifiable by the large rusty chain on its right-hand side, below and slightly right of the striking crack/groove of *Hamadryad*.

1) 6b, 30m. Start at the foot of a blocky groove. Ascend this until it is possible to step right from a ledge and gain the start of a hanging groove. Enjoyable climbing up the groove leads to a step left at its top to the base of a blunt rib. Step onto the rib avoiding the loose blocks on the right, and continue up the rib to a bolt belay below a small pinnacle.

2) 6c, 30m. Climb up the pinnacle, where a steep step up and a pull gain the large slab. Trend up leftwards across the slab - at 3/4 height the climbing becomes testing. Continue up the steepening slab to gain the left arete, before stepping back right to gain the sloping belay ledge above.

3) 6c, 20m. Traverse airily right to the large rib. Continue upwards to a wide groove. Head up until it is possible to move out towards the continuation of the rib. Insecure climbing leads up the blunt rib to a belay at a small ledge.

4) 6a+, 15m. A hard steep start on blocky holds soon eases. Keep a look out for the two hidden bolts on the right. A sling on a flake may be useful if the exposure gets to you, but easy climbing soon leads to a belay next to a large pinnacle.

5) 6c, 15m. Traverse leftwards from the pinnacle until a step up gains the easy-angled slab. Continue upwards to the base of a slabby groove. A thought-provoking series of moves will hopefully gain the top of the groove. Continue up the easy-angled slab to a belay at the base of a groove.

6) 6b, 18m. A steep start soon leads to a short finger-crack in the corner. A confident approach will gain a ramp-line leading up leftwards to a ledge below the final short headwall.

FA. Ian Lloyd-Jones, Celt Lloyd-Jones 4.2014

Lots of sun — 35 min — Seepage

110m

6b

6a+

12

6c

6a+

7a

6c

6b

Quarryman Wall
p.166

60m

6a

50m

8

6c

6a+

5

4

6

Razor's
Edge
terrace

6b

6b

1

2

3

*Long in the
Twll/The
North Will Rise
Again - p.168*

Bus Stop Quarry · Dali's Hole · California · Australia · Serengeti · Never Never Land · Twll Mawr · Mordor - Lost World · Vivian Quarry · Rainbow Slab Area · Snakes and Ladders · Outlying

❹ The Antiquarian .... 🔧📷📖 ▢ **E5 6a**
Scramble up the chain to rack up on *The Razor's Edge* terrace.
1) 5b, 20m. Climb the pillar left of the V-groove. Cross the next rib on the left and quest up to the crack for some more reassuring gear. Rise until level with the *The Desolation of Smaug!* belay and traverse over to it.
2) 6a, 40m. Clip the first bolt of *The Desolation of Smaug!* then enter the groove. Follow this until pushed onto the rib and then follow this until the first of Joe Brown's bolts is spotted over by the corner on the right. Gain this and go up to the bolt at Joe's high point (the bolt is difficult to clip as it is bunged up with old tat). Continue in the corner until a slightly unnerving slopey traverse gains the big slopey ledge. Shuffle left on this to the *The Desolation of Smaug!* belay.
3) 6a, 50m. Climb the corner system directly above the belay to a decaying pink sling on a flake. Make a rising traverse left (cam slot), then go back right past a possible belay to climb directly up the corner system above. There is another possible belay here - either way plug the gear in the easy bits because it is about to run out. The corner starts to fill out into the right arete. Surmount the arete to join pitch 5 of *The Desolation of Smaug!* just before the crux. Follow this to the belay.
4) 6b, 20m. Finish as for *The Desolation of Smaug!* - p.170
FA. Calum Muskett, Mark Dicken 9.2014

❺ Twll Love .... 🔧🔧📷📖 ▢ **E5 6a**
Another trad offering. Scramble up the chain to rack up on *The Razor's Edge* terrace.
1) 5b, 30m. Start as for *The Antiquarian* at the crack. Ascend this until it runs out, then follow the slabby side of the corner above until a bolt is reached. Belay here with whatever else you can find.
2) 6a, 35m. Continue up the corner until it is possible to gain the slopey ledge on the left. Arrange gear and make a rising traverse back right. Make dynamic moves across the corner to snatch a clean ledge on the far side. Thrutch onto the ledge.
3) 6a, 25m. Follow the left arete of the corner behind the belay (poor gear), until you can make a committing step up to a sloping ledge (small cam hidden on the left). Take a large stride left and grapple onto undercuts, or boldly pull upwards to reach some poor gear. Scamper left to a good foothold and undercuts (wire in a corner). Undercut wildly leftwards to the penultimate bolt of *The Desolation of Smaug!* and mantel up to the belay.
4) and 5) as for *The Desolation of Smaug!* - p.170
FA. Mark Dicken, Ben Ryle 9.2014

❻ The Razor's Edge ... 🔧📷📖 ▢ **E3 6b**
More adventure climbing on the North Wall. Start by pulling up the chain to the sloping terrace.
1) 6b (5c/1pt), 40m. Move into the chimney and exit right, where a short traverse to a dead tree belay is possible. Move back into the overhanging fault-line. Climb up this until it gets too steep by a bolt on the right. Gain the sloping ledge above either with a point of aid (5c) or by gymnastics alone. Struggle past the next bolt to exit the steepness rightwards. Traverse 12m on a ledge to a corner with a block and bolt belay.
2) 4c, 30m. Climb the corner then the slabby ramp-line leading up and right to a bolt belay.
3) 5b, 30m. A hard pitch to follow. Head up for 10m to the right of steeper rock. A spike up and right protects a move down and round the sharp arete - The Razor's Edge. From the ledge on the other side, follow a slanting line of holds to a stance above the steepness, big cams in pockets.
4) 4a, 50m. Climb up and left to the col.
FA. Joe Brown, Chris Davies 5.1971
FFA. Stevie Haston, Tim Carruthers 7.1982

❼ The Baron ..... 🔧📷📷📖 ▢ **E5 6b**
Is it ruined or improved by the bolts on the third pitch?
1) 5c, 40m. Follow *The Razor's Edge* to the first bolt and continue straight up to the off-width bomb-bay chimney. Pull out left to a slab and belay above on a ledge.
2) 5a, 20m. Follow the seam up to the *Twll Love* belay.
3) 6b, 45m. Go up the crack until on top of the pedestal, where gear and some techy fingertip jams allow a lurch onto the jug on the right arete. Follow the arete (bolts) to where it rejoins the crack and continue up the dolerite band to belay on a ledge.
4) 4c, 20m. Head up and right as for *The True Finish*.
FA. Calum Muskett, Mark Dicken 1.5.2015

❽ The True Finish .... 🔧 ▢ **E4 6b**
A more direct finish to *The Razor's Edge*.
1) 6b (5c/1pt), 40m. As for *The Razor's Edge*.
2) 5a, 15m. The open groove above leads to a block belay.
3) 5c, 45m. An awkward step on the left quickly leads to a black slabby recess. As the angle steepens, so does the difficulty. On the left side is a bore-hole thread runner. Move left onto the centre of the slab and make a foot-traverse to gain a crack up the centre. Follow the crack to a huge block belay.
4) 4c, 20m. Head up and right along a gangway to the col and then up right over a fence. Alternatively, climb the right wall of the col to reach a rowan tree belay (5a).
FA. Chris Dale, Graham McMahon 7.1989

❾ Burning Bush .... 🔧📷📷📷 ▢ **E7 6b**
The parallel line to the left of *Bushmaster* starting up the groove round to its left. The route starts 10m right of the chain of Razor's edge, at a rib just right of a rusty pipe.
1) 6a, 35m. Follow the rib as it rises leftwards until it reaches a corner. Surmount this and scramble up to the bolt and shot-hole in the bay above - possible belay. Climb the groove boldly to good gear near the top and some tricky exit moves to a good belay.
2) 5b, 40m. Continue in the same line to belay in the corner down and right of the roofs.
3) 6b, 40m. Traverse left from the belay and get some gear in a thin groove in the arete. Climb up and left into a bold and insecure groove, which leads back to the right to a good rest before the roof. Assemble some poor small wires and skyhooks before tackling the V-groove in the roof. Very committing moves up the groove lead to some good but hard-to-place gear, then an easier pull over the roof and a pleasant finish.
FA. Calum Muskett, Steve Long, Mark Dicken and Gabriel Lees 3.7.2015

❿ Bushmaster .... 🔧📷📖 ▢ **E3 6b**
A standard 'North Wall adventure'. Start below and left of the 25m long corner with yellow flanking walls, above which a thin crack-line continues for two-thirds the height of the wall - take a lot of microwires!
1) 5a, 32m. The loose crack in the left wall leads to a stance on easier-angled rock.
2) 6b, 45m. Move up and right to the start of a thin crack-line that marks the way up the slab. Follow the crack, taking care in places, to an awkward move left to a good rest. Move back right and continue on your way up the crack. Small wires and technical weirdness lead to a sloping ledge occupied by gorse and scree. Traverse right to a block belay.
3) 5a, 40m. Gain the vegetation on the ledge up and to the left. Ledge shuffle up and left to gain the left facing corner crack that ends at a pinnacle. Head up the grooves behind the pinnacle to the belay on a large ledge.
4) 5a, 15m. Head up and right taking the line of least resistance to the heathery summit and a rowan tree belay.
FA. Joe Brown, Chris Davies 27.3.1982

Bus Stop Quarry · Dali's Hole · California · Australia · Serengeti · Never Never Land · Twll Mawr · Mordor - Lost World! · Vivian Quarry · Rainbow Slab Area · Snakes and Ladders · Outlying

Lots of sun | 38 min | Seepage

110m

60m

35m

② ⑧ ⑦ ⑤ ④ ⑥ ⑨ ⑩ ⑬

Razor's Edge terrace

① ② ③

Descent (map p.159, overview p.158) -
From the top of the wall, walk over rough ground up to a grassy plateau between Twll Mawr and Mordor. Head upwards from here to pick up a rough track which leads to the approach path for Heaven Walls. Turn leftwards down the slope here to wind down through Serengeti and back to the main track.

Bus Stop Quarry | Dali's Hole | California | Australia | Serengeti | Never Never Land | Twll Mawr | Mordor - Lost World | Vivian Quarry | Rainbow Slab Area | Snakes and Ladders | Outlying

⑪ Taith Mawr . . . . 🖊️🔧 💗🔧 👤🔧 ⬜ **E4 6a**

A long and arduous girdle across the North Wall. ED2 ABO, might be a better grade for this expedition. Start by abseiling to the Quarryman ledge, or climbing up *Opening Gambit* (p.168).

1) 4c, 25m. As for *Opening Gambit* pitch 2.

2) 5c,18m. As for *Opening Gambit* pitch 3, to the 'possible' belay on the arete, requiring big cams, slings, hooks and hope.

3) 5b, 25m. Traverse right to the end of the ledge and drop down 1m onto a continuation ledge. This ends in a ledge with a shot-hole, folded nut/tricam. Continue to traverse right with hands on a rail of flakes that takes skyhooks. Finally reach a vertical crack and some gear. Drop down and continue traversing to a hanging flake. Ascend this to belay in the groove of *Hamadryad*.

4) 5b, 40m. A poorly-protected pitch. Follow *Hamadryad* until level with the 'Bastard Bush of Twll Mawr'. Traverse below this to gain a big ledge on the right arete of the *Hamadryad* groove. Climb up a series of sloping ledges, slightly right of the arete, until level with a gorse infested ledge in a corner on the right. This is your belay - bring secateurs.

5) 5a, 40m. Climb the groove behind the belay until it is possible to step up right onto a sloping ledge. Slither right to a big flat hold and continue until a jug allows upward movement - more slopey slithering rightward below a perched block and around a rib into the groove beyond. Move up onto the ledges on the right, gain the dolerite arete and mantle to the belay of *The True Finish*.

6) 4a, 20m. Walk along and down to *The Razor's Edge* belay.

7) 6a, 30m. Now it gets serious. Check the time and seepage, as the next two pitches are inescapable. Down climb *The Razor's Edge* a few metres to the first significant sloping ledge. To your right is a series of sloping holds terminating in a gap, above and beyond which there is a slate spike and another slightly higher foot ledge. Lasso the spike and rock over onto the ledge (poor cam and a rounded jug above). Bridge out towards the arete on huge footholds and limbo under the holdless headwall to gain the jug on the arete. Protect your second then scamper round to belay in the corner below.

8) 5c, 30m. Climb above the belay until it is possible to pull out right onto a sloping ledge (shot-hole protection). Head right around the sharp arete and pop for the jug in the right wall. Campus to the ledge (pro), and continue down a bad step to a vegetated ledge. Belay on the far right at a crack.

9) 4b, 45m. Drop down to the heathery terrace. Traverse above the belay of *Bushmaster*, above the tunnel entrance, and up towards the chimney of *Scorpion*. Drop down right and proceed to the huge perched block at the end of the terrace. Surmount this and belay on the ledge above.

10) 4a, 10m. Head left until you can gain the Khyber Pass.

FA. Mark Dicken, Jon Byrne (P1-P4) 5.10.2008, (P5-P8) 19.2.2007, (P9-P10) Mark Dicken (solo) 28.1.2008

⑫ The Punter's Retreat . . . 👤🔧 💗🔧 ⬜ **E3 5b**

A handy exit if you have bitten off more than you can chew on *Taith Mawr*, or if you got benighted, scared or both! From the belay at the end of pitch four of *Taith Mawr*, leave the bay heading left to gain a series of sloping ramps leading to a blocky tower with a V-shaped cam slot on its right-hand side. Ascend this tower and head up to a steep bay with a stepped arete in its middle. Climb the arete, shuffle left and ascend to a vegetated shelf. Gain the shelf on the right and bumble left around the arete to an easier exit.

FA. Mark Dicken, Jon Byrne 5.10.2007

Opening Gambit - p.168

Quarryman Wall p.166

A

⑪

The Rock Bottom Line - p.168

⑬ Scorpion . . . . 💗🔧 👤🔧 ⬜ **XS 5b**

More choss on the right of the wall. The initial rock used to be covered by scree.

1) 4c, 20m. Start 5m right of *Bushmaster* and ascend the stack of blocks of your choice up the ramp-line to gain a vague groove feature. Follow this to below a nasty looking arete and belay in the groove.

2) 5a, 30m. Head up the short groove and step across the chasm! Follow the shelf to the corner on the left. Climb the left side of the blocky prow in the corner to a small tree. Move right onto a gentle ramp that zig-zags up to The Balcony. Belay at the tunnel entrance that used to lead to Mordor by *The Beast In Me* but has now been blocked by a rock fall meaning that there is no easy escape from here!

3) 5b, 25m. Scramble above the tunnel to the bottom of the big rift. Climb this with much excitement to a sloping ledge covered in spiky dog rose. Reach out left in a wild position to gain a good hold on the left arete. Climb this to another tunnel and a boulder belay.

4) 5a, 15m. Continue up towards the steep and juggy headwall and gain the grassy col and rowan tree belay. Escape down the rusty chain on the right to the Khyber Pass.

FA. Joe Brown, Chris Davies 17.4.1981

The Khyber Pass

110m

12

Bastard Bush of Twll Mawr

60m

8

1

6

4

9

The Balcony

32m

15

14

13

10

Descent (map p.159, overview p.158) - From the top of the wall, walk over rough ground up to a grassy plateau between Twll Mawr and Mordor. Head upwards from here to pick up a rough track which leads to the approach path for Heaven Walls. Turn leftwards down the slope here to wind down through Serengeti and back to the main track.

15 **Bonza Crack** . . . . ⛓ ⬜ HVS 5b
This route is situated high on the side of Twll Mawr. It used to be approached by walking across to the base until a colossal rockfall left the start way up the cliff! The route was then gained from a tunnel that starts from the base of the second set of ladders down from the Khyber Pass to overlook Twll Mawr. This also collapsed recently so now an abseil approach is required, to a belay of unknown quality in the tunnel mouth. If you get there the route follows a fine crack-line up a slab, but the dubious history and approach means that the route is probably best avoided.
FA. N.Lowry, T.Woodhead 25.8.1996

14 **Island of Stability.** . . ⛓ 🐾 ✂ ⬜ 6c
A narrow and reasonably sound dolerite pillar between *Scorpion* and *Bonza Crack* gives a long and excellent and well-bolted sport route with good positions and interesting climbing.
FA. Harold Walmsley, Ian Lloyd-Jones 25.8.2016

Bus Stop Quarry · Dali's Hole · California · Australia · Serengeti · Never Never Land · Twll Mawr · Mordor - Lost World · Vivian Quarry · Rainbow Slab Area · Snakes and Ladders · Outlying

Bus Stop Quarry

Dali's Hole

California

Australia

Serengeti

Never Never Land

Twll Mawr

Mordor - Lost World

Vivian Quarry

Rainbow Slab Area   Snakes and Ladders

Outlying

Mordor - The Lost World

Bus Stop Quarry

Dali's Hole

California

Australia

Serengeti

Never Never Land

Twll Mawr

Mordor - Lost World

Vivian Quarry

Rainbow Slab Area

Snakes and Ladders

Outlying

Mark Reeves high on the fine arete of *The Hand of God* (5c) - *p.189* - on Heaven Walls in The Lost World.

The Lost World has a reputation as a loose hole full of adventurous routes that frequently fall down, only usually visited for *Snakes and Ladders*. However, the new sport routes on Heaven Walls, The Balcony and The Cuttings are mostly on good rock and relatively easy to get to. These developments make the area much more appealing to most climbers and provide the awesome atmosphere found in the bigger and more remote sections of the quarries.

	No star	1 star	2 star	3 star
Mod to S / 4c	-	-	-	-
HS-HVS / 5a-6a+	7	8	2	-
E1-E3 / 6b-7a	5	6	3	1
E4 / 7a+ and up	6	4	3	1

The Lost World and Mordor are about as 'out there' (or should that be 'in there') and surreal as any area of the quarry. These two great excavations sit above the even bigger hole of Twll Mawr and require complex approaches relying on ladders, tunnels and the odd abseil. Although the classics are few and far between, the routes that are worth climbing more than deserve the effort it takes to reach them. Recent developments have also increased the appeal of the place with a set of good mid-grade sport routes being added to the upper section of The Lost World. This is also home to one of the stages of Snakes and Ladders (p.284).
Sadly the rock is not great and a number of routes have fallen down, often in a quite spectacular way. This particularly applies to the east side of both Mordor and The Lost World and any routes there should come with a bit of a health warning.

Conditions

This is a remote area which doesn't see that much traffic. The depth of the holes will give shelter from the wind and they are also well shaded in hot weather, making it a cool retreat. It can be slow to dry after rain and early in the season. The higher walls with the sport routes around The Balcony and The Cutting are more exposed and likely to dry quickly. The Balcony and Heaven Walls tend to get a decent amount of sun.

Pete Robins working the colourful, technical and demanding *The Wall Within* (7c) - p.187 - in The Lost World.

Bus Stop Quarry

Dali's Hole

California

Australia

Serengeti

Never Never Land

Twll Mawr

Mordor - Lost World

Vivian Quarry

Rainbow Slab Area

Snakes and Ladders

Outlying

Bus Stop Quarry | Dali's Hole | California | Australia | Serengeti | Never Never Land | Twll Mawr | Mordor - Lost World | Vivian Quarry | Rainbow Slab Area | Snakes and Ladders | Outlying

Approach

Mordor - The Lost World is situated in the upper quarries, and best approached from Deiniolen and Dinorwig via the A4244, which connects Llanberis to the coast road. Turn off the A4244 to Deiniolen and on through Dinorwig to parking at the road end near Bus Stop Quarry.

For Mordor - Walk along the main track through the quarry to Twll Mawr. Just beyond Twll Mawr where there is a long incline, head up this to a winding house. Go up one more level above the massive rockfall/landslip to above a drystone slate tower. Drop down scree by a pipe past the tower to a grassy level - a good reference point to explore from. Now descend two ladders to the Khyber Pass where you can reach all the routes in the lower quarry.

The Lost World - For the routes on The Druid Face, approach as for Mordor and go through the tunnel near *Geronimo's Cadillac* (p.184).

Heaven Walls, The Balcony and The Cutting - These higher areas are best approached from Serengeti or Australia. Go up the incline behind Yellow Walls and continue past a ruined building then drop down slightly into a broad cutting. Follow this rightwards to the point where it overlooks The Lost World - this is Heaven Walls. The Cutting and The Balcony are up the scree slope, one level from the broad cutting. Alternatively, go up the Stairs of Cirith Ungol from Australia to the Pen Garret Hut, which is on the same level as the The Cutting and The Balcony.

The Balcony
p.190

Heaven Walls
p.188

The Druid Face
p.186

Tunnels that lead to a bolt belay above The Wall Within

Slate tower

Mordor
p.182

Descend two ladders

Khyber Pass

Long incline beyond Twll Mawr

Twll Mawr - North Wall
p.170

Australia Col

Stairs of
Cirith Ungol

East Face
p.120

Pen Garret
Hut

Dali's Hole
p.62

California
p.70

Tunnel

The Cutting
p.191

The Balcony
p.190

Gate in
a dip

Approach
from Bus Stop
parking

Yellow Wall
p.134

Heaven Walls
p.188

The Druid Face
p.186

Nuremburg
p.143

Seamstress Slab
p.132

Patellaectomy
p.150

Air
vent

Never Never Land Slab
p.144

Mordor
p.182

Rainbow Slab Area
p.232

Khyber
Pass

North Wall
p.170

Quarryman Wall
p.166

South Wall
p.164

Watford
Gap

Combat Rock
p.162

Golgotha
p.160

GPS 53.127975
-4.108359

Dinorwig

Bus Stop

Vivian

Australia

California

Dali's Hole

Twll Mawr

Rainbow

2km

N

200m

N

Bus Stop Quarry · Dali's Hole · California · Australia · Serengeti · Never Never Land · Twll Mawr · Mordor - Lost World · Vivian Quarry · Rainbow Slab Area · Snakes and Ladders · Outlying

Tunnel to bolt belay above The Wall Within

20m

Khyber Pass

The line of Tick's Groove

(map p.181, overview p.180)

Mordor

The walls around the Khyber Pass have a few sport routes and some adventurous trad routes. The approaches can be as exciting as actually climbing them. **Approach (map p.181, overview p.180) -** Head along the main track through the quarry to Twll Mawr. Head up the long incline just beyond to the winding house. Go up one more level above the massive rockfall to above a drystone slate tower. Drop down scree by a pipe past the tower to a grassy level - a good reference point to explore from. Now descend two ladders to the Khyber Pass. Another ladder leads to the next level down for the lower routes. Walk all the way around the hole. The bottom level is down an even worse set of ladders - it is worth leaving a fixed line for back-up as you ascend and descend the ladders.

The long-standing project of Tick's Groove, E6 6b, to the left of Prometheus Unbound, was finally climbed by a strong team. Within months it had fallen down! (FA. James McHaffie, Alex Mason, Mark Reeves 10.2013)

❶ Prometheus Unbound _____ **E5 6c**
The bottom half has fallen down. It tackled the arete past several bolts. You might be able to abseil in for the top section.
FA. Chris Dale, Anita Grey, John Silvester 5.1987

❷ The Wall Without . . . _____ **E4 6a**
The greenstone arete left of the first descent ladders into the Khyber Pass. Climb to a thread at 5m and continue up left on better holds. Hut belay.
FA. Ray Kay, Martin Crook, John Tombs, Noel Craine 6.1998

❸ Three Steps to Heaven, One Step to Hell
. . . . _____ **E4 5c**
Follow *The Wall Without* to the first ledge/thread. Move right around the arete to the top of a stepped ledge. Now climb boldly to the top, wondering whether the thread will stop you.
FA. Mark Reeves, Ieuan Roberts 1.5.2000

❹ Harold Void . . . . _____ **E2 5b**
The arete right of the ladders over the big drop of Twll Mawr.
FA. Mark Dicken, Calum Muskett 10.4.2010

❺ XXXposure . . . . _____ **6a+**
The exposed arete left of *Dragon Slayer*.
FA. Ian Lloyd-Jones, Phil Targett (both led) 6.7.2007

❻ Dragon Slayer . . . . . _____ **7a**
Opposite the ladders. Follow the arete past five bolts (scary second clip) to a lower-off.
FA. D.Taylor, Pete Robertson, Malcolm Davies 9.1996

❼ The Beast in Me . . . _____ **7b**
The off-width groove system leaving the tunnel of the penultimate belay of *Scorpion*. Approach by the abseil from above *Dragon Slayer* reached by the rusty chain. Climb the bolted off-width groove to a ledge, then boulder out the wall above before making your way to the summit using a jam or two (cam). Some head scratching past a bolt eventually leads to welcome jugs.
FA. Mark Dicken 24.9.2013

Bus Stop Quarry · Dali's Hole · California · Australia · Serengeti · Never Never Land · Twll Mawr · Mordor - Lost World · Vivian Quarry · Rainbow Slab Area · Snakes and Ladders · Outlying

Maupin Rey Route, E3 5c, *followed a groove system, much of which has fallen down! (FA. Ray Kay, Nick Peblow, Martin Crook 10.1998)*

8 Josy Puss E5 6a
A strong groove and crack-line.
1) 6a, 40m. The substance of the route, taking the groove and crack to a belay ledge.
2) 5a, 7m. Traverse right to the arete and climb it to top.
Descent - Tricky! Probably the best option is to abseil down to the Khyber Pass.
FA. Ray Kay, John Tombs 10.1989

9 Rosen the Chosen E2 5b
Start from the bottom of the hole, next to the ladder.
1) 5a, 45m. Climb to the top of a large block then head diagonally rightwards along a ramp to a belay on the arete.
2) 5b, 15m. *A bold pitch up the arete and crack.*
Descent - Walk rightwards and across to the approach path to Heaven Walls.
FA. Ray Kay, Martin Crook (AL) 26.9.1998

10 Full Metal Jack Off . . . . . 7a+
The smooth corner at the bottom of the hole.
FA. Paul Pritchard, Geraldine Westrupp 26.9.1996

11 Journey to the Centre of the Earth
. . . . 6a+
A good climb in an amazing setting, although the adventure comes from descending a series of rusty ladders to get to the climb. The route itself is well-bolted and quite steep.
FA. Paul Pritchard, Dave Kendal, Adam Wainwright 30.9.1996

12 The Porphyry Chair . . . . 6c+
10m right of *Journey to the Centre of the Earth* is a line of seven bolts to a lower-off. There is a strange sitting move by the sixth bolt that provides the inspection point.
FA. Paul Pritchard, Adam Wainwright, Tom Leppert 19.7.1996

A winter route **White Mate, V 5** *can occasionally form on the waterfall between* The Porphyry Chair *and the ladders.*

13 Fellowship of the Ring E4 5c
Start by a tree on the left of the bay and follow a loose groove system up and right.
FA. Tom Luddington, Mark Reeves, Mark Payne 1999

14 Lord of the Pies E1 5c
The pleasant corner to a lower-off.
FA. Mark Payne, Mark Reeves 1999

15 Lord of the Rings . . . E4 5c
Climb the crack in the slab to a ledge. This is followed by a bold section leading up to the sharp arete above via several bolts.
FA. Mark Reeves, Tom Luddington 1999

Descent (map p.181, overview p.180) - Head upwards to pick up a rough track which leads to the approach path for Heaven Walls. Turn leftwards down the slope to wind down through Serengeti and back to the main track.

18 Geronimo's Cadillac . . . . HVS 5a
A serious undertaking. Start to the right of the tunnel.
1) 4c, 35m. Climb the line of least resistance to a groove below the col. Head left to the tree to belay.
2) 5a, 20m. Climb the chimney to a bad belay on spikes.
3) 25m. Walk along to another chimney and climb it.
FA. Ray Kay, Stevie Haston 4.1987

16 Young Man Afraid of Horses . E5 6a
A line to the left of the tunnel which leads to The Lost World.
1) 5a, 27m. Climb a thin crack to ledges and a groove.
2) 5a, 37m. Trend right to slabs and climb a crack to ledges.
3) 6a, 18m. A serious and loose pitch up a groove to the top.
FA. Stevie Haston, Ray Kay 4.1987

17 Wild Horses E3 5c
An odd route where exploring the tunnels can enable you to bypass the first pitch by gaining the col.
1) 5c, 38m. Climb past an iron spike and head right into a groove. Continue up grooves to the col.
2) 5c, 30m. Climb the arete via a peg runner.
FA. Ray Kay, Martin Crook, Dave Holmes 18.9.1998

35m

65m

Lots of sun   50 min

Col

35m

Tunnel to The Lost World

Bus Stop Quarry

Dali's Hole

California

Australia

Serengeti

Never Never Land

Twll Mawr

Mordor - Lost World

Vivian Quarry

Rainbow Slab Area

Snakes and Ladders

Outlying

Alan James climbing *The Gravity Hill* (6a) - *p.190* - on The Balcony.
This is one of a number of new sport routes established on the walls at the
top of The Lost World, increasing its appeal to a wider range of climbers.

Abseil approach
from above

A 25m

The Lost Level

Recently exposed
clean face

Tunnel approached
from level above
the Khyber Pass

A 30m

The Druid Face

This impressive hidden hole has been troubled by massive rockfalls over the years, which have kept development to a minimum and removed most of the earlier routes. The hole itself is also slowly filling up which has shortened some of the routes on both sides. Two recent rockfalls have removed most of the routes, but the upper pitch of *Northwest Face of the Druid* can still be climbed. Although this wall is obviously unstable, it does appear that the latest rockfall has left a big, solid and very impressive face so maybe there will be some major new routes here after things have settled down.

Approach (map p.181, overview p.180) - From above the first set of ladders that lead down to the Khyber Pass (p.182), either walk through a tunnel and abseil in down *The Wall Within* (30m). Alternatively, descend to the Khyber Pass and carry on down the next set of rickety ladders. Walk round to the opposite side of the level. Just past the debris there is a tunnel through to The Lost World - see p.184.

For the 'Lost Level' - From above the first set of ladders that lead to the Khyber Pass, head back up the path passing the drystone tower and walk up the side of the quarry. A degree of hunting will find the top of the level.

Old routes on this face are: **A Small Rusty Nail on a Large Mantelpiece, E5 6a**, *(FA. Ray Kay, Trevor Hodgson, Dave Towse 8.8.1998);* **The Coolidge Effect, E4 6a**, *(FA. Mark Reeves, Llion Morris, Dave Hollingham 1999;* **The Tampon Trip, XS**, *(FA. Paul Jenkinson, Mike Thomas 2.10.1987);* **North West Face of the Druid, E6 6a**, *(FA. Trevor Hodgson, Steve Chesslett 1.5.1987)*

❶ Northwest Face of the Druid (P4)

. . . . E2 5b

The original line took three hard pitches to get to The Lost Level. These collapsed taking half the 'Lost Ledge' with them but the crack can be reached still by traversing in. Take care though since there is still loose rock.
FA. Trevor Hodgson, Steve Chesslett 1.5.1987

❷ Lost Crack. E5 6b

The unforgiving crack direct from the base of *Northwest Face of the Druid (P4)* crack.
FA. George Smith 1998

❸ The Wall Within

. . . . 7c

A stunning sport route that is both weird and run-out in places. Recent rockfalls have made it a bit shorter but the main climbing still remains. The crux leads to memorable undercutting, then a tricky layback sequence arrives at a good foothold. The climbing eases thereafter, but is still awkward in places. *Photo on p.179.*
FA. George Smith 1996

Tunnel from Mordor

Approach along the left wall to the arete of Geographical Celibate - p.189

Bus Stop Quarry · Dali's Hole · California · Australia · Serengeti · Never Never Land · Twll Mawr · Mordor - Lost World · Vivian Quarry · Rainbow Slab Area · Snakes and Ladders · Outlying

Heaven Walls

A great area with plenty of routes. The two new sport routes *Saruman* and *Sauron* and the classic crack of *Dinorwig Unconquerable* are more than worth the journey. Combined with the developments at The Cutting and The Balcony, there is quite a lot of climbing to be had up here. If you are doing routes with a lower-off, remember that you do eventually need to top out since there is no way off the starting ledge except abseiling down and going out through Mordor.

Approach (map p.181, overview p.180) - Heaven Walls is best approached from the incline to the left of Yellow Wall, above Serengeti (p.128). Continue up past a ruined building, then drop down slightly into a gorge. Follow this rightwards to an exposed view point of The Lost World and an abseil point just below. Alternatively, tackle the full length of The Stairs of Cirith Ungol (p.180) and you end up on The Balcony, from where it is an easy drop down the scree slope.

1 Saruman 7a
Climb the natural line of grooves and flake-cracks on the left-hand side of the impressive *Sauron* slab.
FA. Ian Lloyd-Jones, Sion McGuinness 5.5.2011

2 Sauron 8b
The crack-line in the blank wall 20m left of *Dinorwig Unconquerable*.
FA. James McHaffie 3.3.2008

Approach from Serengeti

40m

25m

Ladders

**Approach from
Stairs of Cirith Ungol**

The Balcony
p.190

22m

9

❸ **The Black Gates. . . .** E1 5a
The tripartite crack system on the face to the left of *Pain Killer*.
Start 2m left of the corner next to a large block. Climb leftwards
on hand jams to reach good holds and the base of the three
large cracks. Ascend the cracks using a variety of jamming
techniques to a lower-off. Large cams needed.
FA. James Taylor, Andrew Cherry 20.7.2014

❹ **Pain Killer . . . .** E3 6a
The corner left of *The Long and* ... is excellent though a little
green from neglect.
FA. Mike Raine, Steve Howe 15.10.1986

❺ **The Long and Winding Road**
. . . . E5 6b
A stunning route set in an airy position.
1) 6b, 25m. Climb up to the pedestal as for *Pain Killer* and lasso
the poor peg. 'Powerglide' up rightwards for a distant side-pull.
This desperate move has sent a few strong contenders packing.
Carry on up the wall in a fine position passing two bolts, to
reach a bolt and peg belay.
2) 5c, 14m. Pull to the top of the crag and wobble your way
right to the arete and a death scree scramble off the top.
FA. Mike Raine, John Silvester 7.5.1986

❻ **Dinorwig Unconquerable** E3 5c
Indian Creek comes to the slate quarries. Care is needed to pass
some blocks at the start of the crack.
1) 5b, 26m. Climb the corner-crack. Take as many thin hand-
sized cams as you can afford or borrow.
2) 4c, 15m. Move up and scramble off the loose scree above.
FA. Mike Raine, John Gladstone 6.4.1986

❼ **Gay Lightweights and Hetero Stumpies**
. . . . . E5 6a
The line of flakes leading up to the steep crack, just to the left of
the abseil as you look into the hole.
FA. Ed Stone, P.Johnstone 10.1987

❽ **The Barrel of Laughs . . . . . .** E1 5c
The rounded rib on the left wall of the cutting as you approach.
It is found opposite where you drop down into the cutting. Climb
up past the only remaining bolt. There were three variation
finishes, but the bolts are missing.
FA. Mike Raine, Steve Howe 15.10.1986

❾ **The Hand of God . . .** 5c
The bolted line is scrappy at first but leads to a nice exposed
slabby arete. *Photo on p.176.*
FA. Harold Walmsley 4.5.2018

*A final route in the base of the hole is approached from Mordor
as described on p.187.*

❿ **Geographical Celibate . . . . .** E3 6a
The pleasant arete/dolerite pillar in the base of The Lost World
hole used to be twice as long, but has been half buried by
rubble. Climb up past a few bolts and wires to the top.
FA. Mark Reeves, M.Paine 2001

10

Bus Stop Quarry · Dali's Hole · California · Australia · Serengeti · Never Never Land · Twll Mawr · Mordor - Lost World · Vivian Quarry · Rainbow Slab Area · Snakes and Ladders · Outlying

The Balcony

A remote location which has become an appealing destination for those after mid-grade routes in a wild setting. Combining the routes here with The Cutting and the East Face of Australia (p.120) gives plenty for a good day of sport climbing.

Approach (map p.181, overview p.180) -
The Balcony is best approached from the incline to the left of Yellow Wall, above Serengeti (p.128). Continue up past a ruined building then drop down slightly into a gorge. Heaven Walls are straight ahead here. For The Balcony, go up a steep scree track to reach the level above near the entrance of The Cutting. The Balcony is around to the right overlooking the main hole and above Heaven Walls. Alternatively, tackle the full length of The Stairs of Cirith Ungol (p.181) and you end up on The Balcony level.

To mid afternoon | 40 min

⑤ Balcony Climb . . . . □ **HVS 4c**
The walls and grooves just right of *The Illusion*. Start just right of a shallow right-facing corner. Climb the wall to an awkward exit onto a ledge. Step right and go up between the blocks above to stand on the right-hand block. Climb the groove a short way and exit right. Scramble carefully to the top
FA. Harold Walmsley, Rob Davies 30.7.2016

⑥ Wobbly Blocks Climb . . . . □ **5c**
Start at a smooth fin that guards access to a hanging groove. Gain the groove and another groove above.
FA. Harold Walmsley, Rob Davies 9.8.2016

The Cutting

18m

Heaven Walls
p.188

① The Abstraction Ladder . . . . . . □ **VS 4a**
Left of the bolts of *The Gravity Hill* is a dirty groove. This climb takes the stepped arete just left of the groove on blocky holds, moving left a little near the top. It was climbed without prior cleaning, so some of the holds may still be doubtful.
FA. Rob Davies, Harold Walmsley 30.7.2016

② The Gravity Hill . . . . □ **6a**
A good route which is steeper than it looks and has a tricky start. *Photo on p.185.*
FA. Harold Walmsley, Rob Davies 8.7.2016

③ Flying Blind . . . . □ **6a**
The wall via the right edge of a green scoop about halfway up. Persevere as good holds do turn up on the blind bits.
FA. Harold Walmsley, Rob Davies 8.7.2016

④ The Illusion . . . . □ **6a+**
Start up a shallow groove, then climb the narrow pillar above mostly by the right arete.
FA. Harold Walmsley 30.7.2016

⑦ Back in the Groove . . . . . □ **6b**
A poor man's *Quarryman* - and the rock isn't good. Locate a small boulder, in a recessed corner, just left of *The Abstraction Ladder*. At the edge of the terrace directly below this are two belay bolts invisible from above. Abseil from the block and bolts down the V-groove to a two-bolt stance - you can see the bolt runners from the top belay bolts before you go down. Climb back up the groove by bridging and awkward back-and-footing.
FA. Harold Walmsley, Rob Davies 23.6.2016

Not much sun | 40 min

The Druid Face
p.186

15m

The Cutting
Bus Stop Quarry
Dali's Hole
California
Australia
Serengeti
Never Never Land
Twll Mawr
Mordor - Lost World
Vivian Quarry
Rainbow Slab Area
Snakes and Ladders
Outlying

8 9 10 11 12 13 14

Alternative approach to
The Balcony - bad step

The Cutting

The narrow cutting behind the front face of The Balcony has some decent sport routes. It faces north so is very shady, catches the wind and can be green and slimy. **Approach (map p.181, overview p.180) -** The Cutting is best approached from the incline to the left of Yellow Wall, above Serengeti (p.128). Continue up past a ruined building then drop down slightly into a gorge. Heaven Walls are straight ahead here. For The Balcony, go up a steep scree track to reach the level above near the entrance of The Cutting. Alternatively, tackle the full length of The Stairs of Cirith Ungol (p.181) to end up on The Balcony level.

8 Cutting Back . . . . VS 4a
A line up a greenstone band about 3m right of the blunt rib at the far end. Climb easily up the lower half of the band to some small ledges, then take the upper scoop more steeply past a couple of well-placed pockets. Unprotected.
FA. Harold Walmsley 9.6.2016

9 Buenos Notches. . . . 🛈 6a
Climb the prominent sharp arete with numerous notches. These provide surprisingly easy progress on good holds until the final fingery move.
FA. Harold Walmsley 15.6.2016

10 Cutting the Corner 5c
The corner taken all the way. An interesting start shared with *Fin Fan* turns into easy ground on big flat holds. There is no lower-off, so belay by going over the top and down the other side.
FA. Harold Walmsley 30.7.2016

11 Fin Fan. . . . . 🛈 6a
The next arete to the right of *Buenos Notches* is very sharp in its upper reaches. Start delicately up the corner to its left. Then, after an easier section, move out right to the arete and climb it full frontal to the top.
FA. Harold Walmsley 15.6.2016

12 Thinking is Better than Pulling 🛈 6a
The left-hand route on the slab. Climb the left side of the lower rib to jugs. Make technical moves left and up. Climb the rib and groove above to a lower-off hidden over the top.
FA. Harold Walmsley, Rob Davies 30.7.2016

13 Battle Scars . . . . 🛈 5c
The central route on the slab starts up *Thinking is Better than Pulling* and follows it to the jugs. Here, bear slightly right to the top right-hand corner of the hanging slab. Continue up the blunt rib and grooves above.
FA. Harold Walmsley, Rob Davies 30.7.2016

14 Uncomfortably Numb . . . 🛈 6b
A good climb taking the right-hand line on the slab. Climb a flaky left-facing groove to gain the mid-height flakes. Climb these and the slabby wall above, stepping right in the middle, then straight up to finish.
FA. Harold Walmsley, Rob Davies 9.8.2016

15 Flat World. 6a
The right-hand rib of the south-facing wall of The Cutting just beyond the end. Climb the chimney and, at its top, step left on to the rib and move up. From the top ledge, climb the steep wall into a groove - care with a wedged flake. Head directly up the final pillar. Don't be tempted to climb right of the final pillar.
FA. Harold Walmsley 8.4.2018

Vivian Quarry

Bus Stop Quarry

Dali's Hole

California

Australia

Serengeti

Never Never Land

Twll Mawr

Mordor - Lost World

Vivian Quarry

Rainbow Slab Area Snakes and Ladders

Outlying

Mikey Goldthorpe on *The Monster Kitten* (E1 5b) - *p.207* - in Vivian Quarry. Photo: Mike Hutton
This photo may help answer the question as to whether you hand or foot traverse the flake?! The short and intense crack is a vital part of *The East Face of Vivian* link-up (p.226) but, even if you are not going to the top of Vivian Quarry, it is still worth doing if you find yourself having climbed *Mental Lentils* with some time and energy to spare. Gaining the first jug is the crux, after which sustained climbing leads to the memorable step right into *Ladder Resist*.

Bus Stop Quarry

Dali's Hole

California

Australia

Serengeti

Never Never Land

Twll Mawr

Mordor - Lost World

Vivian Quarry

Rainbow Slab Area

Snakes and Ladders

Outlying

	No star	⚜	⚜	⚜
Mod to S / 4c	-	-	-	-
HS-HVS / 5a-6a+	19	5	-	-
E1-E3 / 6b-7a	24	20	11	3
E4 / 7a+ and up	11	22	21	8

Back in 1981, Stevie Haston borrowed a knife from Pete's Eats cafe and went on to clean the most famous climb on slate. *Comes the Dervish* set the ball rolling on a wave of development that is still going on today. It was this route that inspired the subsequent 'slatehead generation' to scour the quarries in search of new climbs.

Being so close to Llanberis and full of great climbs has made Vivian Quarry a popular venue. Scattered around the quarry are many great slate climbs of all types and styles. There is the slab of *Comes the Dervish* with its famous trad classics, the finger-searing difficulties of the sport routes on the Nostromo Wall, the run-out bolted routes on the Conscience Slab and, just in case that wasn't enough, you have the bold deep water solos of the *Bathtime* wall on The Prow. On almost every level there is at least one route worthy of attention and for most climbers there will be many visits' worth.

Conditions

The best climbing in the quarry faces west and gets the afternoon/evening sun. It is usually well sheltered from the wind, making it a great venue when things are blustery in the mountains. This same shelter makes it a big suntrap, so it can become too hot in the summer.

Access

Climbing is not permitted on the Prow until after the Dive Centre has closed, and please keep away from the tunnel entrance above *Psychotherapy* on the Wendy Doll Terrace, because it has rare bats in it.

Approach

Vivian Quarry is in the lower quarries, which are best approached directly from Llanberis. Heading from Caernarfon on the A4086 which passes through Llanberis, turn left towards the Slate Museum opposite the Snowdon Mountain Railway, just before the end of the village. Park in the large car park at the museum where there is a parking fee to pay. There are no free alternatives as all parking is now charged in Llanberis. From the car park, head towards the quarry and over the level crossing. The Pool Level is reached through the tunnel right of the Dive Centre. All areas, other than the Dwarf Level, are accessed from a path that leads up the left-hand side of the quarry. This is reached by turning left at the Dive Centre and heading down the side of the cafe/station. Then head up a flight of steps to reach the small tarmac access road. Turn left and after 10m the path/stairway heads up the side of the quarry.

Bus Stop Quarry | Dali's Hole | California | Australia | Serengeti | Never Never Land | Twll Mawr | Mordor - Lost World | Vivian Quarry | Rainbow Slab Area | Snakes and Ladders | Outlying

200m

N

N

Bus Stop

Vivian

Australia

California

Dali's Hole

Twll Mawr

Llanberis

Rainbow

2km

Top Level
p.229

Valkyries Level
p.228

Truffle Hunter Area
p.220

Ritter Sport Area
p.222

Llanberis
Lake
Railway

Hot Knives Level
p.218

Love Minus Zero
p.210

Psychotherapy Area
p.200

Nostromo Wall
p.212

Comes the Dervish
p.214

GPS 53.122309
P   -4.115818

Conscience Slab
p.216

Bobby's Groove Area
p.204

The Dwarf Level
p.208

Mental Lentils Area
p.206

The Prow
p.198

Muscle Beach
p.197

Dive
Centre

National Slate
Museum

Path from
Llanberis

Bus Stop Quarry

Dali's Hole

California

Australia

Serengeti

Never Never Land

Twll Mawr

Mordor - Lost World

Vivian Quarry

Rainbow Slab Area

Snakes and Ladders

Outlying

Bus Stop Quarry

Dali's Hole

California

Australia

Serengeti

Never Never Land

Twll Mawr

Mordor - Lost World

Vivian Quarry

Rainbow Slab Area

Snakes and Ladders

Outlying

Top Level
p.229

Valkyries Level
p.228

Truffle Hunter Area
p.220

Ritter Sport Area
p.222

Hot Knives Level
p.218

Comes the Dervish
p.214

Love Minus Zero
p.210

Conscience Slab
p.216

Nostromo Wall
p.212

Wendy Doll Ledge
p.200

The Dwarf Level
p.208

Psychotherapy Area
p.200

Bobby's Groove Area
p.204

Mental Lentils Area
p.206

The Pool
Level

The Prow
p.198

From Dive
Centre

Muscle Beach
p.197

The Prow
p.198

Descent by abseil or past cafe.

10m

Muscle Beach

A short area on the Pool Level with a few mid-grade trad routes which are out of the sun. It is worth a look if you are after something off the beaten track.

Approach - As you enter the base of Vivian Quarry from the Dive Centre, this area is immediately on the left after the tunnel. Head through (or usually over) the gate and along to the beach.

Descent - Abseil off one of the trees or head back down the side of the railway cafe to the base.

1 Brinwell . . . . [ ] **HVS 6a**
The left-hand line on the smaller wall, about 10m left of the iron spike of *Earwig Ho 87*. Climb past a roof and a bolt to a tree.
FA. Paul Pritchard, Steve Chesslett 6.4.1988

2 Boody Building . . . . [ ] **HVS 6a**
The right-hand line of the small wall, past a roof and bolt to a tree.
FA. Paul Pritchard, Paul Johnstone 24.1.1988

3 Silvester Still-born . . . . [ ] **E1 5c**
Start just left of a bent iron spike. Pass a bolt to gain a niche, then on to the top.
FA. Paul Johnstone 1.1988

4 Earwig Ho 87 . . . . [ ] **E3 5c**
Climb straight up the wall above the bent iron spike, passing a bolt which wasn't there on the first ascent.
FA. Mike Raine, J.Turner 5.4.1987

5 Booby Building . . . . [ ] **HVS 5a**
The rightmost line on the wall. Start below another iron spike. Climb past this and a bolt to the top.
FA. Paul Johnstone, Paul Pritchard 26.1.1988

Bus Stop Quarry

Dali's Hole

California

Australia

Serengeti

Never Never Land

Twll Mawr

Mordor - Lost World

Vivian Quarry

Rainbow Slab Area | Snakes and Ladders

Outlying

The Prow

There are some hard and bold routes on the promontory in the pool, some of which are deep water solos. The wall gets some sun in the morning, although it is shielded by tree cover in the summer. There is a little seepage.

Approach (map on p.195, overview on p.196) - From the Dive Centre, turn left and walk along the side of the railway cafe. Head up through the woods to a tarmac road - the top of the promontory is straight ahead. Climb over the fence and abseil into your desired route. Routes 1 to 3 are approached from below Muscle Beach.

Access - No climbing on the prow when the Dive Centre is open.

❶ One Wheel on My Wagon 　　　　　 **E4 5c**
The dirty stepped ramp is easy but bold. Often soloed and the crux is above the water
FA. Stevie Haston, Mike Raine 23.4.1987

❷ Order of the Bath . . . . . . 　　　　 **E6 6b**
The girdle. Head up *One Wheel on My Wagon* for 6m. Step right into the crack of *Wishing Well*. Move up to a break and traverse right along it, past a bolt, to reach the spikes on *I Ran The Bath*. Continue along to a bolt and finish up *Soap on a Rope*.

❸ Wishing Well . . . . . 　　　　　 **E6 6b**
The curving crack-line. Gain the crack and follow this with difficulty to the top. A peg was used for protection on the first ascent, but it is now missing.
FA. Paul Pritchard 23.4.1986

❹ Sucked Away with the Scum 　　　　　 **7c**
. . . .
Abseil to a hanging belay on a bolt. Forge a strong line up the wall, passing three bolts, to a tricky finale.
FA. Paul Pritchard 27.4.1988

❺ I Ran the Bath . . 　　　　　 **E7 6b**
Abseil to a hanging belay on a bolt. Move up from a scoop to another scoop. The bulging wall above leads to a line of jugs leading leftwards to a groove.
FA. Paul Pritchard 27.4.1987

❻ Dope on a Rope . . . . 　　　　　 **E5 6a**
This was climbed as an indirect start to *Soap on a Rope* which works better as a start for *Bathtime*. Abseil down to the ledge on the right edge of the prow. Traverse out left and head up to join the *Soap on a Rope* spikes. Finish up *Bathtime*. *Photo on p.201.*
FA. Tony Kay, J.Taylor 8.1988

❼ Bathtime . . . . . . 　　　　　 **E5 6a**
Often tackled as a solo with the difficulty all below 12m! Be warned though - hitting the still water below is not soft! Abseil to the ledge on the edge of the wall. Climb the groove right of the arete and make a bold swing left to reach jugs. Move left to a crack which is followed to a ledge - crux. It is possible to escape right into *Soap on a Rope* from here. A diagonal line leads up and left to a mossy finish. Consider having a rope to pull yourself out if soloing this route.
FA. Paul Pritchard 4.6.1987

> Not much sun | 5 min | Sheltered | Abseil in | Restrictions

Approach past cafe

A 20m

⑩ ⑪ ⑬ ⑭ ⑮ ⑫

⑧ Soap on a Rope E4 6a
Another common solo, but it is also a reasonable lead. Start at the ledge on the edge of the wall. Head up the groove until you can swing left onto spike jugs on the wall. Mantel up on these. A hard move up and right regains the arete and the first bolt. Carry on up the arete past a second bolt to the top.
FA. Paul Pritchard, Paul Johnstone 22.1.1988

⑨ Blades of Green Tara . . . E2 5b
A pleasant ramble up the front face of the tower. Start down and right of *Soap on a Rope*, right by the water's edge. Climb the groove diagonally up and right to the arete. Move back diagonally left to gain a ledge - a small sapling and flake provide the protection. Move up and slightly right for a few metres until you can gain the arete. Finish up this.
FA. Malcolm Boater 6.1984

⑩ Surreal Mirror . . . . 6b+
A pleasant route up the right arete of the front face of the prow. The bolts were placed so they have little effect on *Blades of Green Tara*.
FA. Llion Morris, Mark Reeves 8.2014

⑪ Le Voleur 7c
Good climbing up the wall left of the groove of *Artichokes, Artichokes*. Abseil to a bolt belay just above the water.
FA. Steve Mayers 23.3.1992

⑫ Artichokes, Artichokes 7b+
The prominent corner offers some good sport. Start from the beach on the right of the prow, best reached by abseil from the prow. Traverse out left past a bolt to gain the base of the groove. Climb this past bolts with a run-out to a ledge. Move left and ascend the groove passing a peg.
FA. Paul Pritchard 6.4.1988

⑬ Four Wheel Drift E4 6a
A safe and hard start leads to bold and easy climbing above. Abseil to the beach and start from here. Climb the crack past a difficult move. Above this, find a line of jugs that lead to the top.
FA. Stevie Haston, N.Parker 8.1980

⑭ Sesame Street Comes to Llanberis
. . . . E3 5c
Abseil down to the base of a groove to the right of *Four Wheel Drift*. Head up the groove and move right across a slab before heading up to ledges. Continue past a bolt to good footholds. Lower off or top out.
FA. Paul Johnstone, Paul Pritchard 27.1.1988

⑮ Aubergines, Aubergines E1 5b
Abseil into the bay and start at the base of a crack. Climb the crack to reach an arete and trees above.
FA. Mark Boniface, I.Wallis 5.198

Bus Stop Quarry | Dali's Hole | California | Australia | Serengeti | Never Never Land | Twll Mawr | Mordor - Lost World | Vivian Quarry | Rainbow Slab Area | Snakes and Ladders | Outlying

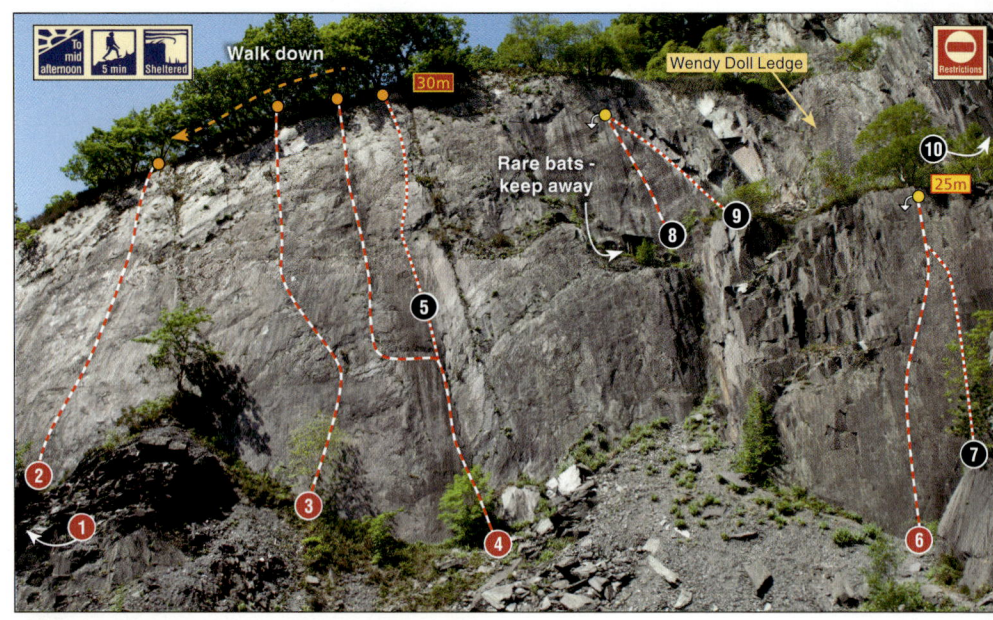

Walk down

30m

Wendy Doll Ledge

Rare bats -
keep away

25m

Psychotherapy Area

This east-facing wall doesn't see much attention and some of the routes are a bit loose and friable. *Psychotherapy* is worth seeking out though.
Approach (map on p.195, overview on p.196) - Pass the Dive Centre and walk round the Pool Level to the viewing platform, over the stile and all the way round.

1 Blue Touch Paper. E2 5c
To the left of the slab is a short clean arete whihas no gear
FA. Phil Targett 3.11.1989

2 Poetry in Motion E3 5c
A bold route up the clean sweep on the left side of the slab.
FA. Paul Jiggins, P.Dunkley 3.11.1986

3 Wave Out on the Ocean . E1 5a
Originally climbed with a rope with three knots for protection, but they never came back to bolt the route. As such the route is very bold up friable rock.
FA. Al Evans, S.Bennett 25.7.1990

4 The Blind Buddha. . . E2 5a
There are few runners on this route and maybe only one or two that would hold body weight! It is easy climbing but the rock is slightly friable. Start up the groove to a spike. Step down and move left to a ledge. Make some worrying pulls to gain a broken flake. From here, shuffle carefully upwards to reach the trees.
FA. Malcolm Boater, J.Clinton 6.1984

5 Stump Rogers E4 6b
A direct version of *The Blind Buddha*. Climb up the groove to the spike. Head up the smooth shield of rock above clipping a bolt. Hard moves to pass this lead to an easier but friable slab above.
FA. Bob Drury, Anne Amos 9.9.1986

6 Psychotherapy. E2 5c
A popular route which some rate as a sport route at 6a+. Climb the line of weakness to a bolt, then make a hard traverse right to gain the crack and a small wire. Carry on up the crack/ramp-line past a bolt on the right. Then, at the bolt above the ramp on the left, move up and left onto a headwall, and make for the large ledge below the lower-off. *Photo on p.202.*
FA. Andy Newton, Paul Pritchard 8.5.1988

7 Cat Flaps of Perception. E4 6a
Start up the stepped ramp (often damp) to the right of *Psychotherapy*. Climb the slab direct without any real protection to reach and follow the last few moves of *Psychotherapy*.
FA. Rob Mirfin, I.Davis 6.7.1993

Wendy Doll Ledge

This is the part-ledge above *Psychotherapy*. It is named after the long route *Wendy Doll* (p.226) which starts on the ledge below.
Approach - Gain the ledge by climbing a route below.
Access - No climbing near the tunnel where there are rare bats.

8 Working up a Lather. E4 6b
Way over on the left side of the level is a 'boilerplate' slab. This friable line climbs the slab past four bolts. Caution is required as there has been a rockfall and it has not been reascended.
FA. S.Jones, Paul Pritchard, Mike Thomas, Tony Kay 14.5.1988

9 Imperial Leather E4 6b
Has suffered a rockfall and not been reascended. Ascend the arcing line up past four bolts to the shared lower-off.
FA. Paul Pritchard, S.Jones, Tony Kay 11.5.1988

10 Spread 'em E4 5c
A left-facing V-groove above a sharp landing. Large cam useful.
FA. Cliff Phillips 25.8.1988

Mikey Goldthorpe gets a quick DWS ascent of *Soap on a Rope* (E4 6a) - *p.198*. Photo: Mike Hutton
Possibly one of the finest deep water solos in North Wales. The crux is close enough to the water to make it feel okay, but don't fluff the top arete since that would not be a nice experience! For the less brave, there are two bolts which permit more conventional ascents.

Bus Stop Quarry

Dali's Hole

California

Australia

Serengeti

Never Never Land

Twll Mawr

Mordor - Lost World

Vivian Quarry

Rainbow Slab Area

Snakes and Ladders

Outlying

Bus Stop Quarry

Dali's Hole

California

Australia

Serengeti

Never Never Land

Twll Mawr

Mordor - Lost World

Vivian Quarry

Rainbow Slab Area

Snakes and Ladders

Outlying

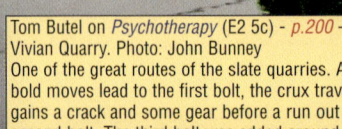

Tom Butel on *Psychotherapy* (E2 5c) - *p.200* - in
Vivian Quarry. Photo: John Bunney
One of the great routes of the slate quarries. A few
bold moves lead to the first bolt, the crux traverse
gains a crack and some gear before a run out to a
second bolt. The third bolt was added around 2007 to
protect a more direct finish straight up the final tower.

Bus Stop Quarry

Dali's Hole

California

Australia

Serengeti

Never Never Land

Twll Mawr

Mordor - Lost World

Vivian Quarry

Rainbow Slab Area

Snakes and Ladders

Outlying

Psychotherapy Area
p.200

12m

Bobby's Groove Area
This area is at the far end of the pool and has suffered a major rockfall - it has much unstable rock. Three routes are still climbable, but the others are worth avoiding.
Approach (map on p.195, overview on p.196) - Follow the tunnel to the side of the Dive Centre. At the end of the path, cross the stile and carry on to the bay at the back by a lot of debris!

❶ The Sponge that Walked Away
. . . . E1 5a
A poor route up the loose and blocky left ridge of the front face of the *Bobby's Groove* tower. Avoid.
FA. Cliff Phillips, D.Iwan Jones 19.6.1988

❷ Wendy Doll (P1) . . . . HVS 4c
This once popular three-pitch expedition has fallen out of favour, especially the first pitch. Climb the right ridge of the front face of the *Bobby's Groove* tower. The ridge that joins this to the ledge is falling down! Belay off a sapling. Pitch 2 is on p.226.
FA. Stevie Haston, N.Parker, Mick Howard 6.1981. The first route in Vivian.

❸ Two Bolts or Not to Be
. . . . 7b+
Although it has suffered a major rockfall, the route is still climbable. Make technical moves up to the first bolt. Some powerful moves reach the second, before a heart-stopping bold move leads to the easy slab.
FA. Simon Scully 9.5.1989

❹ Bobby's Groove . . 8a
The route remains climbable after the rockfall, and the hideously technical groove is still as baffling as it is good.
FA. Johnny Dawes 13.4.1988

❺ The Weetabix Connection . . . 6c+
This has not been reclimbed since the rockfall. It may be possible to climb the start before heading left to the lower-off on *Bobby's Groove*.
FA. Chris Jex, Leon Zablocki 26.2.1991

❻ The Golden Shower E3 6a
Has suffered a major rockfall. It should be avoided!!!!
FA. Nick Harms 3.11.1987

Mike Raine eyeing up the first bolt on *The Turkey Chant* (E2 5c) - *p.208* - on the Dwarf Level at Vivian Quarry.

This route was largely forgotten until it was re-equipped. A bolt was added to *Too Bald to be Bold* to make the link into the new belay easier and then a lower-off added to allow climbers to get down onto the Conscience Slab and head up the Dervish Slab. This was one of the crucial linking sections of what has become known as the *East Face of Vivian (aka Sunchaser Wall)* (p.226) - a great multi-pitch link-up giving sustained extreme grade climbing with an E2 and an E3 variation.

Outlying | Snakes and Ladders | Rainbow Slab Area | Vivian Quarry | Mordor - Lost World | Twll Mawr | Never Never Land | Serengeti | Australia | California | Dali's Hole | Bus Stop Quarry

❶ The Hong Jagged Route of Death

E3 5b

This is a serious outing and the rock is very loose. Start beneath the sabre-toothed ridge and climb this past a few hard moves after which it turns into choss. A riot shield is helpful for the belayer who will feel like they are facing a mob throwing stones.
FA. Cliff Phillips, Gwion Hughes, Nick Rice 12.4.1988

❷ Heinous Creature

E5 6a

The left-hand groove has no gear.
FA. Chris Dale 4.5.1986

❸ Sanity Fair

E3 5b

The arete between the two grooves is bold with the crux at the top. Move right to lower off *Sanity Claws*.
FA. Chris Dale 1.5.1986

Afternoon 3 min Sheltered

❹ Sanity Claws

E5 6a

The right-hand groove is harder than *Heinous Creature* but it does have some gear.
FA. Chris Dale 1.5.1986

❺ Fat Lad Exam Failure

E6 6b

Follow the seam up the centre of the slab to a flattened but still clippable bolt - worth checking before departure! Hard moves lead to a rest in the triangular pockets. Move right to the flake/rib and bolt, then follow it to the top. A horrendous scramble up scree leads to a bolt belay way back on the back wall.
FA. Nick Harms 28.4.1987

❻ Clap Please

E7 6c

A bold and dynamic pitch. Start below the centre of the wall. Climb diagonally right to a flattened peg/bolt. A hard traverse left leads to a bolt. Ignore the old bolt out left from a by-gone project. Traverse left for 2m and make more hard moves up to a crack and a good hold by a lower-off.
FA. Bob Drury, Alan McSherry 13.10.1986

Walk left

22m

❼ Dirt

E4 6a

A line of resin bolts marks the line up the right edge of the slab.
FA. M.Jones, Linn Kathenes 1996. Also claimed later as Glurp.

❽ Split the Dog

E3 5c

A meandering line up the broken rock. Start up the right side of the slab. Move left into a shallow groove and follow it to the top. Then move back right onto a large ledge. Climb the smooth groove above using the vertical shot-hole on the right wall before heading up ledges and crack to the top.
FA. Stevie Haston, Gwion Hughes, Mike Raine 4.1987

Bobby's Groove Area
p.204

Bus Stop Quarry · Dali's Hole · California · Australia · Serengeti · Never Never Land · Twll Mawr · Mordor - Lost World · Vivian Quarry · Rainbow Slab Area · Snakes and Ladders · Outlying

9 Dawes of Perception   E7 6c
Classic Dawes - bold and technical climbing. Gain the sabre teeth from the right and then climb the crack making sure you have arranged as much poor gear as possible before committing upwards. Scary moves to reach the sanctuary of the bolt are followed by desperate moves past it, to reach some cracks out left that lead to a hideous top-out.
FA. Johnny Dawes 1985

10 Mental Lentils   HVS 5b
A good route. Take a few wires to boost the bolts. Start to the right of a tree. Ascend the steep wall to a ledge. Move up to a wire at the base of the arete and foot traverse left to a bolt. From here, follow the line of weakness up and right past wires and a second bolt to the lower-off. If you are carrying on with *The Monster Kitten*, top out and belay off a bolt and tree.
FA. Jonathan Barbier 28.10.1986

11 Time Bandits   7b
A desperate boulder problem in the sky. Start up *Mental Lentils* and move out left to gain a bolt below a very thin slab. Try and pass this to reach the lower-off. Some gear is required for the section shared with *Mental Lentils*.

12 The Monster Kitten.   E1 5c
Start up *Mental Lentils* to belay at the base of the diagonal hairline crack. Climb this protected by small wires - do you hand or foot traverse it? Towards the top, the holds run out requiring a bold step right onto jugs. Finish straight up to the lower-off or top out and belay on the level above. *Photo on p.192.*
FA. S.Andrews, Sandy Britain 27.5.1986

13 Ladder Resist   E3 6a
Something of an ankle breaker. Make technical moves up polished rock to hopefully gain the high bolt. Above, the climbing eases but the gear disappears. Start up *Mental Lentils*.
FA. Nick Harms, Mo Anthoine 22.5.1988

14 Moving Being   E4 6b
Brilliant moves and a memorable run-out. Follow the crack to reach the crack/ramp that leads up and right past a bolt. Move along this to a niche and bolt. Traverse left with increasing difficulty to a dramatic slap for the left arete. Above, the climbing is much easier, but all there is for gear is a lonely microwire.
FA. Nick Harms, Jonathan Barbier 23.8.198

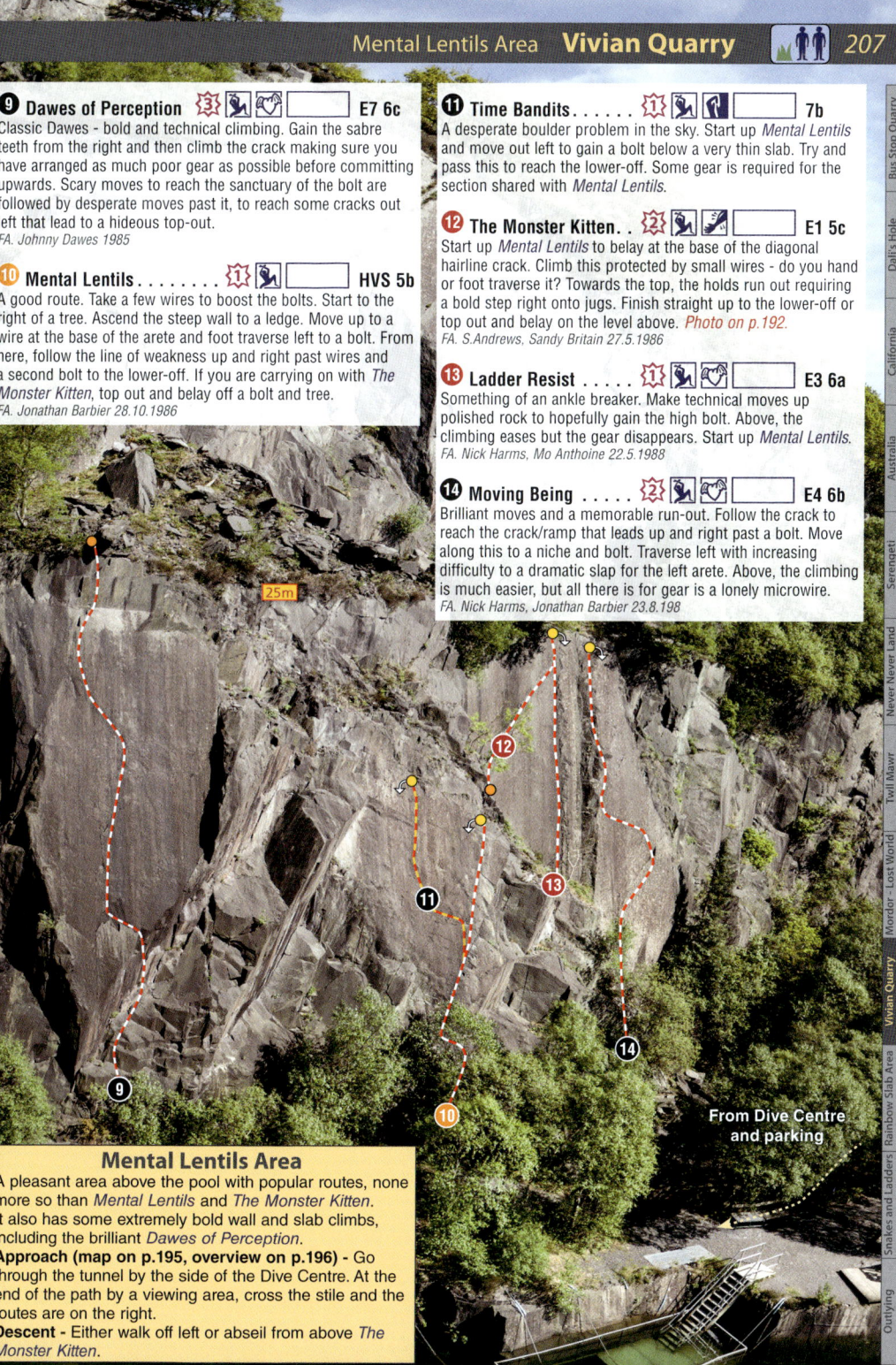

25m

Mental Lentils Area
A pleasant area above the pool with popular routes, none more so than *Mental Lentils* and *The Monster Kitten*. It also has some extremely bold wall and slab climbs, including the brilliant *Dawes of Perception*.
Approach (map on p.195, overview on p.196) - Go through the tunnel by the side of the Dive Centre. At the end of the path by a viewing area, cross the stile and the routes are on the right.
Descent - Either walk off left or abseil from above *The Monster Kitten*.

From Dive Centre
and parking

Bus Stop Quarry · Dali's Hole · California · Australia · Serengeti · Never Never Land · Twll Mawr · Mordor - Lost World · Vivian Quarry · Rainbow Slab Area · Snakes and Ladders · Outlying

The Dwarf Level

The next level up from the Pool level consists of clean slabs and the striking X cracks of *Sup 1* and *Sup 2*. However, the best routes are further right and *Too Bald to be Bold* is great, especially when combined with *Turkey Chant* or an even longer link-up - p.226.

Approach (map on p.195, overview on p.196) - The easiest approach is from below, by climbing *Mental Lentils* and *The Monster Kitten* - p.207. Alternatively, from the parking, walk towards the quarry and take the incline to the right of the Dive Centre. After about 20m, turn left and follow the path until you come to a tarmac access road. Ahead is small lay-by. Head up into the woods behind this and, after about 40m, the ground levels off. Cross the fence and take a vague quarryman's track that leads down to the level by an exposed polished scramble. **Descent -** Either walk off left or abseil from belay by *Too Old to Be Bold*.

❶ Watching the Sin Set 🎭🧗🪢 ☐ **E5 6c**
The slab left of the 'X' cracks is tackled by this thin and technical route past two bolts.
FA. Tony Kay, S.Jones, Nick Harms 7.1988

❷ Sup 1 . . . . 🎭🧗🪢 ☐ **E2 5a**
Teeter up the diagonal ramp for way longer than is pleasant. The gear is poor considering it is a crack. Continue, trying not to have a nervous breakdown as you pull onto the level above.
FA. Stevie Haston 1982

❸ Teliffant . . . . 🎭🧗🪢 ☐ **E4 6a**
Climb the line of weakness just left of the 'X' of *Sup 2* to a bolt. Tricky moves in a worrying position gain the ramp of *Sup 1*. Then head up the wall above via flakes and cracks to a lower-off.
FA. Gwion Hughes, Tony Kay, Cliff Phillips, Nick Rice 12.4.1988

❹ Sup 2 . . . . 🎭🧗🪢 ☐ **E2 5a**
The vertical mark of the giant 'X' is followed direct past a bolt with a tricky move to reach the ramp of *Sup 1*. Continue straight up to a scary top-out.
FA. Stevie Haston 1982

❺ The Shark that Blocked the Drain
. . . . 🎭🧗🪢 ☐ **E6 6b**
A bold route that was originally soloed after pre-practice. It will feel more like E7 to on-sight. Climb the slab up the front face of the little tower and veer right up cracks to a ledge.
FA. S.Jones 5.11.1987

❻ Wakey, Wakey, Hands off Snakey
. . . . 🎭🧗🪢 ☐ **E4 6a**
A terrifying excursion. Start by making your way up and left along a vegetated ramp-line to gain the corner and arrange some gear. Step back right and move onto the slab to reach a bolt. Move up and right along cracks which give poor gear but technically demanding climbing to eventually reach easier ground and the *Too Bald to be Bold* belay.
FA. Paul Barbier 22.8.1986

❼ On Shite . . . . 🎭 ☐ **E4 5c**
A terrifying direct finish. Follow *Wakey, Wakey, Hands off Snakey* to the bolt and continue straight up to the tree.
FA. S.Jones, Tony Kay 26.10.1987

❽ Too Bald to Be Bold . 🎭🧗🪢 ☐ **E2 5c**
An excellent third pitch for those who have done *Mental Lentils* and *The Monster Kitten* to get here. Start below a nose of rock and boldly follow a ramp-line on the right until you can reach leftwards by a prickly bush into a good crack on the main slab. Pull into the crack and follow it to a plinth. Arrange gear here and move up and left to a bolt. Go past this and up to a second bolt and then head up and right to the large ramp-line and another bolt. From here, either head up and left to the end of the level and a bolt belay, or head down the ramp to a ledge and double-bolt belay, then finish up the next route.
FA. K.Simpson, S.Winstanley 10.4.1989

❾ The Turkey Chant . . . . . 🎭🧗 ☐ **E2 5c**
Either climb the previous route or make a diagonal abseil into the belay. Head straight up from the belay on easy ground and make a reach out left to clip the first bolts. Past the bolt, move up and left to a ledge and reach a second bolt. Crux moves up and left lead to a two-bolt lower-off. One bolt is over the top of the crag. *Photo on p.205.*
FA. Paul Johnstone, Paul Pritchard 15.1.1988

Mental Lentils Area
p.206

Bus Stop Quarry · Dali's Hole · California · Australia · Serengeti · Never Never Land · Twll Mawr · Mordor - Lost World · Vivian Quarry · Rainbow Slab Area · Snakes and Ladders · Outlying

10 Dwarf in the Toilet

. . . . **E6 6b**

A great route with a stunning crux. Start up the steep crack to gain the hanging slab. Follow the crack until level with the first bolt. Spectacular moves lead left up the ramp past another bolt, where some blind groping round the final arete leads to a slab with a diagonal crack running up it. Follow this to the lower-off.
FA. John Redhead, Martin Crook 16.5.1986

11 Gideon's Way **E4 6a**

Follow *Dwarf in the Toilet* to the bolt on the right, then head up right along the ramp-line all the way to the top, where jugs lead back left to the *Dwarf in the Toilet* belay.
FA. Martin Crook, Noel Craine 14.6.1986

12 Sabre Dance **E3 5b**

A serious pitch up the black slanting ramp right of *Gideon's Way*. Follow the ramp for 14m, then traverse right (using a hidden shot-hole) to enter a groove on the far right. Follow this to a ledge. The steep corner above leads to the top.
FA. Chris Dale 10.5.1986

13 Bungle in the Jungle **E1 5b**

25m right of *Sabre Dance* a cluster of five birch trees provides the start. Climb these to avoid a blank wall and ramble up the broken ground to the top.

23m

The Monster Kitten - p.207

Bus Stop Quarry · Dali's Hole · California · Australia · Serengeti · Never Never Land · Twll Mawr · Mordor - Lost World · Vivian Quarry · Snakes and Ladders · Rainbow Slab Area · Outlying

Walk back down

25m   30m

Morning | 15 min | Sheltered

Love Minus Zero

The west side of the quarry on the Dervish Level has a decent wall with a couple of good bold routes. It is usually ignored by those walking past aiming for the main event.

Approach (map on p.195, overview on p.196) - From the parking, head towards the quarry, turn left at the Dive Centre and follow a path behind the station cafe. Head up the steps to a tarmac access road. Turn left and immediately on the right is a set of steps. Follow these up a level, and then another set of steps up a second level. The Dervish Level is over a fence just left of a building, These routes are found in the bay before the bad step across to the Dervish slab.

1 Lentil in a Stew . . . . HVS 5a
Start at the base of a flake that defines the left edge of the slab. Climb up to a spike and make a bold traverse right to the groove. Finish up this.
FA. Paul Barbier, R.Leishman 13.7.1986

2 Legs Together E2 5b
Delicate climbing up the left edge of the slab.

3 Legs Akimbo E2 5b
Interesting climbing in places. Start up *Legs Together*, then head up and rightwards around the arete to a horizontal traverse right. The holds then lead you back up and left via a high side-pull to a good ledge. Move rightwards to finish near *Feet Apart*.
FA. R.Ebbs 1.4.1978

4 Feet Apart E3 5b
A direct line up the slab. Climb up to and follow the flake up and left to a groove. Climb this to a niche below the bulge. Arrange gear, summon your bravery and move through the bulge on good holds. Once above the lip, you can either head straight up (very bold), or move up and left to a flake on *Legs Akimbo* and follow this to the top.
FA. Martin Barnicott 22.5.1986

5 Love Minus Zero E6 6a
A lonely lead up the pillar just right of the arete. Start at an iron spike. Move up and traverse right at 6m to a jug. Climb direct to another jug. Continue, eventually moving left to prominent jugs with relief.
FA. Chris Dale 7.5.1986

6 Down to Zero E3 5b
The compulsory warm-up prior to climbing *Love Minus Zero*. Start by a tree below the centre of the wall. Use the tree to help you get established, then move up to the left end of the ledge and continue more or less direct to the top.
FA. Chris Dale, Nick Thomas, John Tombs 6.5.1986

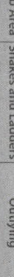
Bus Stop Quarry | Dali's Hole | California | Australia | Serengeti | Never Never Land | Twll Mawr | Mordor - Lost World | **Vivian Quarry** | Rainbow Slab Area | Snakes and Ladders | Outlying

Age Concern

Left of the Dervish slab is a poor section of rock with few routes of interest.

Approach (map on p.195, overview on p.196) - From the parking, head towards the quarry, turn left at the Dive Centre and follow a path behind the station cafe. Head up the steps to a tarmac access road. Turn left and immediately on the right is a set of steps. Follow these up a level, and then another set of steps up a second level. The Dervish Level is over a fence just left of a building. These routes are found in the bay before the bad step across to the Dervish slab.

7 Yak Kak . . . . **XS**
The back left-hand corner of the bay is best avoided as it is a route of little substance both figuratively and literally.
FA. Stevie Haston 4.5.1986

8 Age Concern . . . . **HVS 5a**
The corner on the right side of the bay. Climb up the groove and head up the V-corner above. Eases towards the top.
FA. Colin Goodey, Sue Goodey 8.5.1988

9 Bong to Lunch . . . . **HVS 4c**
A bold offering which has been scoured by rockfalls. Start below the crest of the buttress. Ascend the groove until it peters out. Trend left via some flatties to the crest, and gain the top slab just right of *Age Concern*. Follow the scooped slab which leads to the top via a crack on the left.
FA. Stevie Haston 1983

10 The Moon Head Egg Monster From Allsup
. . . . **E1 4c**
Start up *Frustrated Lust* to the ledge, then step back left onto the slab. Climb this past two large and very loose flakes. Probably best ignored.
FA. N.Smith, A.Bond 8.1988

11 Frustrated Lust . . . . **HVS 5a**
Climb broken ground to a short wall. Climb this to a ledge. Finish up the corner to the left of the hanging slab.
FA. Stevie Haston 1983

Walk back down

20m

20m

From mid morning · 16 min · Sheltered

Nostromo Wall

A great area with some demanding routes that give an amazing view back down to Llanberis. Sadly the easiest route is *Child's Play*, a great but technical 7b+. If that sounds a bit easy then you can try the chimney slot of *Gin Palace* or one of John Redhead's sculpted creations.

Approach (map on p.195, overview on p.196) - From the parking, head towards the quarry, turn left at the Dive Centre and follow a path behind the station cafe. Head up the steps to a tarmac access road. Turn left and immediately on the right is a set of steps. Follow these up a level, and then another set of steps up a second level. The Dervish Level is over a fence just left of a building. Walk round and make an airy step to below the Dervish slab. Nostromo Wall is on the left after the step.

❶ Nostromo . . . . 🎽 📷 ☐ **E4 6b**

The dogleg crack-line on the left end of the wall is very loose.
Start by the bad step, where a desperate start and a pile of
boulders leads to a ledge at 12m. Move awkwardly right to gain
the slanting crack and follow it to the top, or reach right to a
lower-off.
FA. Martin Crook, Dave Towse 2.10.1983

The route **Nostrodamus, E4 6b,** *started up Nostromo and then
tackled the steep arete above and left. This has collapsed.*

❷ Menopausal Discharge

. . . . 🎽 📷 📷 ☐ **8a+**

A good route, that was chipped, although the crux is performed
off more of a scratch for a foothold.
*FA. John Redhead 9.6.1986. Originally called a rather tasteless Menstrual
Discharge, then renamed Mysoginist's Discharge for the 1987 guide. It
even got a direct version by Andy Pollitt called Kleinian Envy! It has finally
settled on the name given here.*

❸ Young and Easy Under the Apple Boughs

. . . . 🎽 📷 ☐ **E4 6a**

The awkward dogleg crack up the centre of the wall. Start up the
crack (easy at first), until you pass the two bolts on *Colditz*. Both
are clippable, but make little difference to this route. Just past
here the climbing gets hard as a result of recent hold loss. A
determined and balanced approach is needed to gain improving
holds above the dogleg. One more perplexing move leads to
easier climbing and the top. Lower off from the ledge above.
FA. John Redhead, Martin Crook 2.5.1986

❹ Colditz . . . . 🎽 📷 📷 ☐ **7b+**

Climb the initial wall to gain the crack just below the apex. Reach
out left to clip a bolt and gain the start of the challenging groove.
Head up this to a seemingly impossible move. Think dynamic
moves to slopers!
FA. Sean Myles, Mark Pretty 17.4.1991

❺ Manic Strain . . . 🎽 📷 📷 📷 ☐ **8a**

Another chipped route, which was 'designed' for tall climbers;
shorter people find it much harder. Even for the tall it is
ridiculously thin with big moves.
FA. John Redhead 24.4.1986

❻ Gin Palace . . . . 🎽 📷 📷 📷 ☐ **7c**

An amazing route - a **7b+** chimney into a hard and sustained
headwall. Some will walk up the slot, others will just be totally shut
down by it, and vice-versa with the headwall. *Photo this page.*
FA. Craig Smith 25.6.1986

❼ Child's Play . . . . 🎽 📷 📷 ☐ **7b+**

Bridge up the groove until you can launch up the wall. The initial
sequence is not obvious.
FA. Bob Drury 2.6.1986

❽ Hymen Snapper . . . . 🎽 📷 📷 ☐ **E5 5c**

Follow the groove that *Child's Play* starts up to a loose and
serious finale.
FA. Stevie Haston, Lee McGinley 8.1982

Caroline Ciavaldini on the 'woman-eating' crack of *Gin Palace* (7c) -
this page. The sport grade is a bit of a joke! Photo: David Simmonite
A brutal testpiece that repels more people than it attracts with its
extreme back-and-footing.

Abseil descent

36m

Bad step to
Conscience Slab

The Full
Monty - p.

Comes the Dervish

A great area with many classic routes, in a commanding position above the rest of the quarry and Llanberis. The slab is a haven of trad slab climbing with some very bold propositions and some more moderate classics like *Comes the Dervish*, which started the slate revolution of the 1980s and *Last Tango in Peris*.

Approach (map on p.195, overview on p.196) - From the parking, head towards the quarry, turn left at the Dive Centre and follow a path behind the station cafe. Head up the steps to a tarmac access road. Turn left and immediately on the right is a set of steps. Follow these up a level, and then another set of steps up a second level. The Dervish Level is over a fence just left of a building. Walk round and make an airy step to below the Nostromo Wall to the Dervish slab.

1 Reefer Madness . . . ⬡ 🧗 🧗 ▢ **E3 5c**
The left-hand corner of the slab is technical and the gear is hard to find. At and above the overlap the rock becomes very loose.
FA. Stevie Haston, Paul Trower 5.1982

2 For Whom the Bell Tolls
. . . . ⬡ 🧗 🧗 ▢ **E6 6b**
A bold outing. Thankfully the crux is low down, but there is still a lot of sustained and unprotected climbing all the way to the overlap. Climb up the hairline crack 3m to the right of the corner. At the overlap move right into *Menstrual Gossip* and the first decent gear since the ground.
FA. Andy Pollitt, Martin Crook, J.Taylor 29.4.1984

3 Menstrual Gossip . . . ⬡ 🧗 💙 ▢ **E6 6b**
The vague line of scoops that appears to be a 'weakness' in the slab about 3m to the left of *Comes the Dervish*. Climb up to a poor wire at 10m then continue up past where it at least feels safe to do so, to another good wire placement. Head up to the overlap and follow easy ground up and right to gain the *Comes the Dervish* belay.
FA. John Redhead 5.85

4 Comes the Dervish
. . . . ⬡ 🧗 🧗 🧗 💙 ▢ **E3 5c**
A stellar route, and one deserving of its reputation. Follow the crack-line up for 8m to the first good runner. Easier climbing leads to the kink in the crack, passing this is the crux. Good holds lead up to the overlap, which is easier to pass than it looks. Above, the gear is small and the climbing run-out. A steady head leads to the belay. *Photo on p.9.*
FA. Stevie Haston 2.1981

5 Belldance . . . . ⬡ 🧗 🧗 💙 ▢ **E5 5b**
Follow *Comes the Dervish* to a good jug above its dogleg crux. The safety minded will climb up and place a high side runner in the overlap and return to this point. Step out and into *Flashdance* and head slightly down and further right to a good ledge below a downward-facing tooth in the overlap. Make a desperate few moves up to gain the overlap at the point of the tooth. Move slightly right and make an airy step over the lip. It is hard and loose to climb direct - most people step right and place gear in *Last Tango*, then climb just left of this until they can regain the diagonal crack on the left that leads to the *Comes the Dervish* belay.
FA. John Redhead, Dave Towse 19.3.1984

6 Last Tango in Peris . . . . . . ⬡ ▢ **E2 5b**
Another classic line. Start up the parallel diagonal cracks near the arete and head up and right to a ledge. Some moves over a widening crack lead to another ledge on the arete. Follow the crack, leading up and left to the overlap. Move over this via the left-hand groove, and follow the line of weakness up a vague crack to a bolt belay.
FA. Mel Roberts, Cefin Edwards 12.5.1985. Finally given its original name.

7 Flashdance . . . . ⬡ 🧗 💙 ▢ **E5 6a**
An extremely bold and memorable outing up a vague line of scoops that link *Last Tango in Peris* and *Comes the Dervish*. From *Last Tango in Peris*, make moves up to a diagonal crack and the last good gear until *Comes the Dervish*. Move on up the scoops to a poor sideways wire placement, then make very nervy moves to a good ledge just short of *Comes the Dervish*, before reaching the crack with a massive sigh of relief. Finish up *Comes the Dervish*.
FA. Andy Pollitt, Tim Freeman 8.1983

8 Flashdance/Belldance ⬡ 🧗 💙 ▢ **E6 6b**
This seering link-up of two routes gives a route of much substance. Many people start off with this in mind and end up finishing up *Comes the Dervish*!

9 Breakdance . . . . ⬡ 💙 ▢ **E7 6b**
Climb *Flashdance* to the first good diagonal wire slot above *Last Tango in Peris*. Then head directly up the slab past a lonely resting spot. Arrange as many skyhooks as you can and make a series of desperate moves in a 'do or die' situation to gain the overlap just left of *Last Tango in Peris*. Finish up this with ease.
FA. Adam Wainwright 1.1.1989

10 Poledance . . . . ⬡ 💙 ▢ **E6 6b**
Climb *Flashdance* to the first good diagonal crack/wire slot above *Last Tango in Peris*. Rock up onto the crack and step right. Climb the slab above via a scary sequence of moves aiming for start of the *Last Tango in Peris* hand traverse. From here, move up and right to gain the arete and crack of *Wendy Doll* and follow this to the top.
FA. Mark Reeves, Llion Morris 15.9.2011

11 Wendy Doll (pitch 3) . . . . . . 🧗 ▢ **E1 5b**
This pitch is prone to rockfall and may have changed. It is advised to start up *Last Tango in Peris* and continue to the ledge on the arete at half-height. From here gain the crack in the arete and climb it to the top.
FA. Mick Green, S.Kelly 9.1973

12 Swinging By The Bell . . . ⬡ 💙 ▢ **E5 6a**
Climb *Last Tango in Peris* to the start of the hand traverse. Break out across the wall and follow a line of weakness slightly downwards to gain *Comes the Dervish*. You can head up here, but the route continues out left and then up to gain the overlap as for *Menstrual Gossip*.
FA. Dave Towse, Mel Roberts 20.3.1984

13 The Missing Link . . . ⬡ 🧗 💙 ▢ **E2 5c**
A contrived but interesting addition to link the top of the Dervish slab to the next levels, used to make *The East Face of Vivian* possible from bottom to top (p.226). Walk along the ledge leftwards from the Dervish belay, making sure no one is below you, to below the first bolt. Climb up a vague crack past two bolts and a 1.5 cam to reach a two-bolt lower-off. When doing the link you can 'swing' from here to the next level.
FA. Mark Reeves, Llion Morris 2011

Bus Stop Quarry | Dali's Hole | California | Australia | Serengeti | Never Never Land | Twll Mawr | Mordor - Lost World | Vivian Quarry | Rainbow Slab Area | Snakes and Ladders | Outlying

Conscience Slab

A great area with several amazing routes, in a commanding position above the rest of the quarry. Sadly there has been some rockfall around the slab, but most routes are still climbable and the rock seems to have stabilised.

Approach (map on p.195, overview on p.196) - From the parking, head towards the quarry, turn left at the Dive Centre and follow a path behind the station cafe. Head up the steps to a tarmac access road. Turn left and immediately on the right is a set of steps. Follow these up a level, and then another set of steps up a second level. The Dervish Level is over a fence just left of a building. Walk round and make an airy step to below the Nostromo Wall to the Dervish slab. Make an even worse step than on the Dervish approach to get across the gap here. You can use a cows tail to protect off bolts or lead across.

1 **The Gully** . . . . 🪨 ☐ **VS 5a**
The gully is choss and best avoided.
FA. John Tombs 5.6.1986

A couple of other routes taking lines across the slab were recorded here - **Slate's Slanting Crack, E2**, *and* **Foetal Attraction, E4**. *These have been superseded by the better direct routes.*

2 **The Full Monty** . . . . 🔆🔲 ☐ **6a+**
A long 30m pitch which is quite bold in places.
FA. Mike Raine, Andy Newton 23.12.2006

3 **Mister, Mister** . . . . 🔆🔲 ☐ **6b**
Follow the *The Full Monty* to where bolts lead out left to a lower-off.
FA. Mike Raine, Andy Newton 23.12.2006

4 **The Sweetest Taboo** . 🔆🪨🔲 ☐ **E4 6a**
The original route of the slab gives some great bold climbing although it is not climbed very often these days. Start up the slab 3m left of the ramp-line. Make a difficult move left at 6m to a good hold, then climb back right past a bolt. Finish direct.
FA. Mike Raine, Johnny Dawes 1.5.1986

5 **Menage a Trois** . . . . 🔆🪨🔲 ☐ **E4 6b**
A direct finish to *The Sweetest Taboo*. Head straight up the wall trending rightwards past three bolts.
FA. Mike Raine 24.7.1987

6 **Is it a Crime?** . . . . 🔆🔲 ☐ **E3 5c**
Follow the ramp-line at the bottom of the slab for 6m - good wire as a side runner. Step left onto a good spike runner. Now make a few bold moves, first left, then up, to the first bolt. Head up and right to a second bolt. Exciting moves past this lead to a crack which is followed to a third bolt, before you pass the old belay chain. A new lower-off has been added up and left.
FA. Mike Raine, Chris Dale 10.5.1986

7 **Never as Good as the First Time**
. . . . 🔆🪨 ☐ **E3 5c**
Start up *Is it a Crime?* to its first bolt, and then step left and make a bold move up to gain a large flake. Follow the crack-line rightwards to the finish of *Is it a Crime?*.
FA. Mike Raine, Chris Dale 10.5.1986

8 **Never as Sweet** . 🔆🪨🔲 ☐ **E4 6a**
A combination of routes that makes a great outing which is less scary than the start of *The Sweetest Taboo*. Start up *Never as Good as the First Time* to the flake and finish up *The Sweetest Taboo*.

9 **That Obscure Object of Desire** 🪨 ☐ **VS 4b**
The rising break-line is easy but has little in the way of gear. Climb up to the loose ground and a break that heads back left. Follow this to the lower-off on *Is It A Crime?*.
FA. Mike Raine 22.4.1986

10 **The Spark That Set the Flame**
. . . . 🔆🔲 ☐ **E5 6b**
The faint crack-line leads through a slight overlap. No real gear to speak of.
FA. Bob Drury 1985

11 **Smokeless Zone** . . . . . . 🔆🪨🔲 ☐ **E4 6b**
A thin bolted slab to a lower-off.
FA. Claude Davies, Matt Wells, Phil Targett, Clive Stephenson 9.12.1986

12 **You Can Dance if You Want to** . . ☐ **HVS 5a**
The right arete is climbed up to the lower-off on *Smokeless Zone*.

13 **Vivander** . . . . 🪨 ☐ **HVS 5a**
An obscure route with a nasty finish. Start in the bay right of the slab. Head up over bulges behind the tree and past a bore-hole thread. Move left into a loose gully, then back right to the top via some scree.
FA. Cliff Phillips, Paul Barbier 18.5.1986

A route - **Throttle With Bottle, E2 5c** *- has been reported as a groove in a small slab above the Conscience Slab, somewhere?*

Bad step

The Dwarf Level
p.208

Outlying Snakes and Ladders Rainbow Slab Area Vivian Quarry Mordor - Lost World Twll Mawr Never Never Land Serengeti Australia California Dali's Hole Bus Stop Quarry

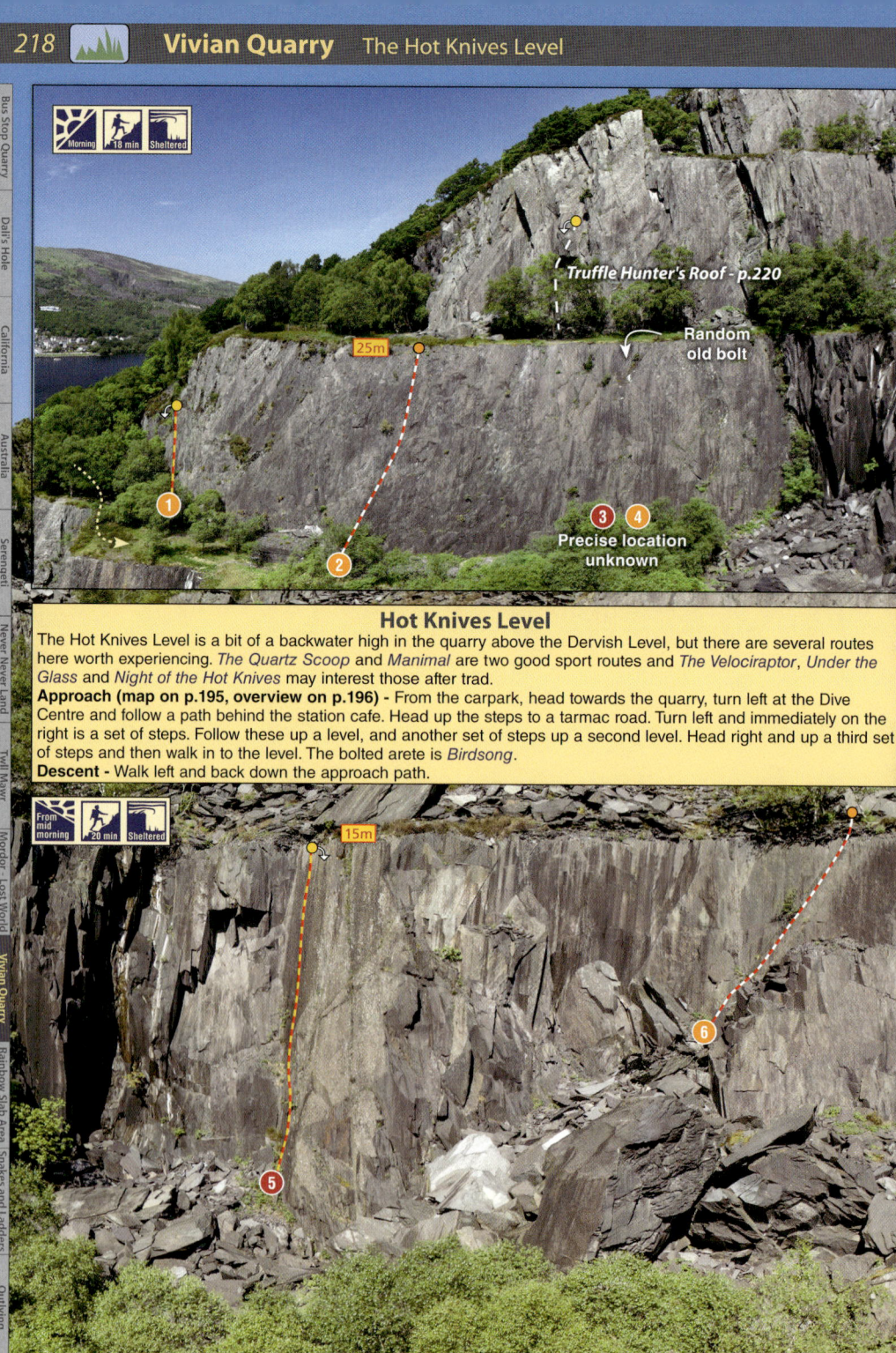

Truffle Hunter's Roof - p.220

Random old bolt

25m

Precise location unknown

Hot Knives Level

The Hot Knives Level is a bit of a backwater high in the quarry above the Dervish Level, but there are several routes here worth experiencing. *The Quartz Scoop* and *Manimal* are two good sport routes and *The Velociraptor*, *Under the Glass* and *Night of the Hot Knives* may interest those after trad.

Approach (map on p.195, overview on p.196) - From the carpark, head towards the quarry, turn left at the Dive Centre and follow a path behind the station cafe. Head up the steps to a tarmac road. Turn left and immediately on the right is a set of steps. Follow these up a level, and another set of steps up a second level. Head right and up a third set of steps and then walk in to the level. The bolted arete is *Birdsong*.

Descent - Walk left and back down the approach path.

15m

1 Birdsong . . . . 🔩 [ ] 6a+
A nice route up the arete on the left-hand side of the level. There is a strange crux at the top.
FA. Phil Targett, Ian Lloyd-Jones 13.5.2008

2 Binman . . . . 🔩 [ ] HVS 5a
Start a few metres right of a hut, near the left end of the long friable wall. Climb up, trending right at first, then finishing more direct. A serious route!
FA. Malcolm Boater 6.1984

3 Abus Dangereux . . . . . . 🔩 [ ] E2 5b
More friable and serious climbing, though the precise line taken is unclear. Start near the middle of the wall at a vague groove. Climb the thin cracks. A single decent runner in the whole 22m ensures focus! Seldom if ever repeated.
FA. Matthieu Mounier, Matt Nuttall 17.7.1991

4 Fallout . . . . 🔩 [ ] VS 4c
A line somewhere on the right of the wall. Climb a groove, step left and continue past a peg to the top. Probably unrepeated.
FA. John Tombs, Paul Barbier 10.5.1986

5 Manimal . . . . 🔩2 [ ] 6c
At the back of the bay is a nice clean steep slab with four bolts. Some wires can be placed in a crack before the first bolt. The rock at the bottom needs care, but the wall above is worth it!
Photo on p.227.
FA. G.Sewell, J.Cleford 4.3.1992

6 Baby Nina Soils her Pants . . . . . [ ] VS 4b
The right-slanting rib left of *Night of the Hot Knives*.

7 Night of the Hot Knives . . 🔩 [ ] E3 5c
The right-slanting groove gets more demanding with height. The crux is the finish over some suspect rock. You might want to pre-place a long sling around the tree on the level above.
FA. Martin Crook, Dave Cuthbertson 3.1.1986

8 Tribal Blow . . . . . . [ ] E6 6b
The slanting crack right of *Night of the Hot Knives* is committing and technical. It used to have a peg, but this has gone - now you only get some poor wires.
FA. Bob Drury, Sandy Britain 24.4.1986

9 Solvent Abuse . . . . [ ] E3 5b
A clone of the thin ramp of *Sup 1*, but harder. Climb the rib past a poor skyhook placement to a reasonable top-out.
FA. Martin Crook and a cast of thousands 27.4.1986

10 Under the Glass . . . . [ ] HVS 5a
A pleasant route up the dolerite tower on the right of the bay. Climb the slab and rib to a triangular pocket, then finish up a groove on the right.
FA. Cliff Phillips 25.5.1986

11 The Velociraptor . . . . [ ] E2 5c
A pleasant if short route. Climb the corner to a triangular pocket out left on the slab. Then head up the slab past two bolts.
FA. T.McClean and party 19.1.1992

Walk back down

15m

Bus Stop Quarry
Dali's Hole
California
Australia
Serengeti
Never Never Land
Twll Mawr
Mordor - Lost World
Vivian Quarry
Snakes and Ladders Rainbow Slab Area
Outlying

Truffle Hunter Area

The west side of the Ritter Sport Level only really has one route of interest plus a few loose trad routes.
Approach (map on p.195, overview on p.196) - From the carpark, head towards the quarry, turn left at the Dive Centre and follow a path behind the station cafe. Head up the steps to a tarmac access road. Turn left and immediately on the right is a set of steps. Follow these up a level, and then another set of steps up a second level - The Dervish Level. Head left and then right and up a third set of steps - The Hot Knives Level - and continue up another set of steps to reach the level.

❶ Truffle Hunter's Roof ⚡2️⃣ 🪨🧗 ☐ **6b+**
The bolted roof accesses the parts most slate doesn't reach. Gain the roof with surprising difficulty, then lean miles out to good holds on the lip. Traverse right and get stood up using biceps, elbows, heels, buttocks and any other available body part. The lower-off is just up and right. *Photo opposite.*
FA. Paul Johnstone, Dave Cuthbertson, K.Read 11.12.1987

❷ Satires of Circumstance . . . . 🧗 ☐ **E2 5b**
A total choss-fest. Ascend the shattered groove right of *Truffle Hunter's Roof.* Switch back up and left where the rock at least appears more substantial. The slabby groove then leads up, but it is best to go across to the lower-off on *Truffle Hunter's Roof* if you have got this far.
FA. Paul Jenkinson, Mark Boniface 20.4.1988

❸ Jumping the Gun . . . . 🧗 ☐ **E1 5b**
Climb the short groove to reach the bulge. Pass this leftwards to the slab. Follow the crack up and left before veering back right up another crack to the top.
FA. Malcolm Campbell 27.5.1986

❹ Puff Puff . . . . 🧗 ☐ **E2 5c**
Start as for *Jumping the Gun*, but move right through the bulge to gain the crack/groove on the right of the slab. Follow this to its top, then step right and finish up a crack left of an arete.
FA. J.Banks, L.Naylor 29.5.1986

Walk back down

Bus Stop Quarry

Dali's Hole

California

Australia

Serengeti

Never Never Land

Twll Mawr

Mordor - Lost World

Vivian Quarry

Rainbow Slab Area

Snakes and Ladders

Outlying

Bus Stop Quarry

Dali's Hole

California

Australia

Serengeti

Never Never Land

Twll Mawr

Mordor - Lost World

Vivian Quarry

Snakes and Ladders

Rainbow Slab Area

Outlying

Pete Robins cruising across the lip of *Truffle Hunter's Roof* (6b+) - *opposite* - a fantastic route that traverses the lip of a roof high in the quarry. It was re-equipped in 2007 and is one of the better 6b+ routes in the quarries due to its unique angle - it is not a slab or a wall! A clipstick helps reach the first bolt. Getting this far is not too bad, but the really tricky bit remains!

Bus Stop Quarry

Dali's Hole

California

Australia

Serengeti

Never Never Land

Twll Mawr

Mordor – Lost World

Vivian Quarry

Rainbow Slab Area

Snakes and Ladders

Outlying

Owen Samuels on the striking layback crack of *Ritter Sport* (E3 5c) -
p.225 - an after-work classic of the upper Vivian Quarry levels.
The Ritter Sport Level is good for long evenings after work as the sun
stays on this face until late. *The Madness* at E1 is a classic bold slab,
but it is *Ritter Sport* that stands out, with its steep layback start up the
prominent flake. This has recently been joined by *Major Whiff* which
complements the aromas of *Private Smells* and *General Odours*.

Bus Stop Quarry

Dali's Hole

California

Australia

Serengeti

Never Never Land

Twll Mawr

Mordor - Lost World

Vivian Quarry

Rainbow Slab Area

Snakes and Ladders

Outlying

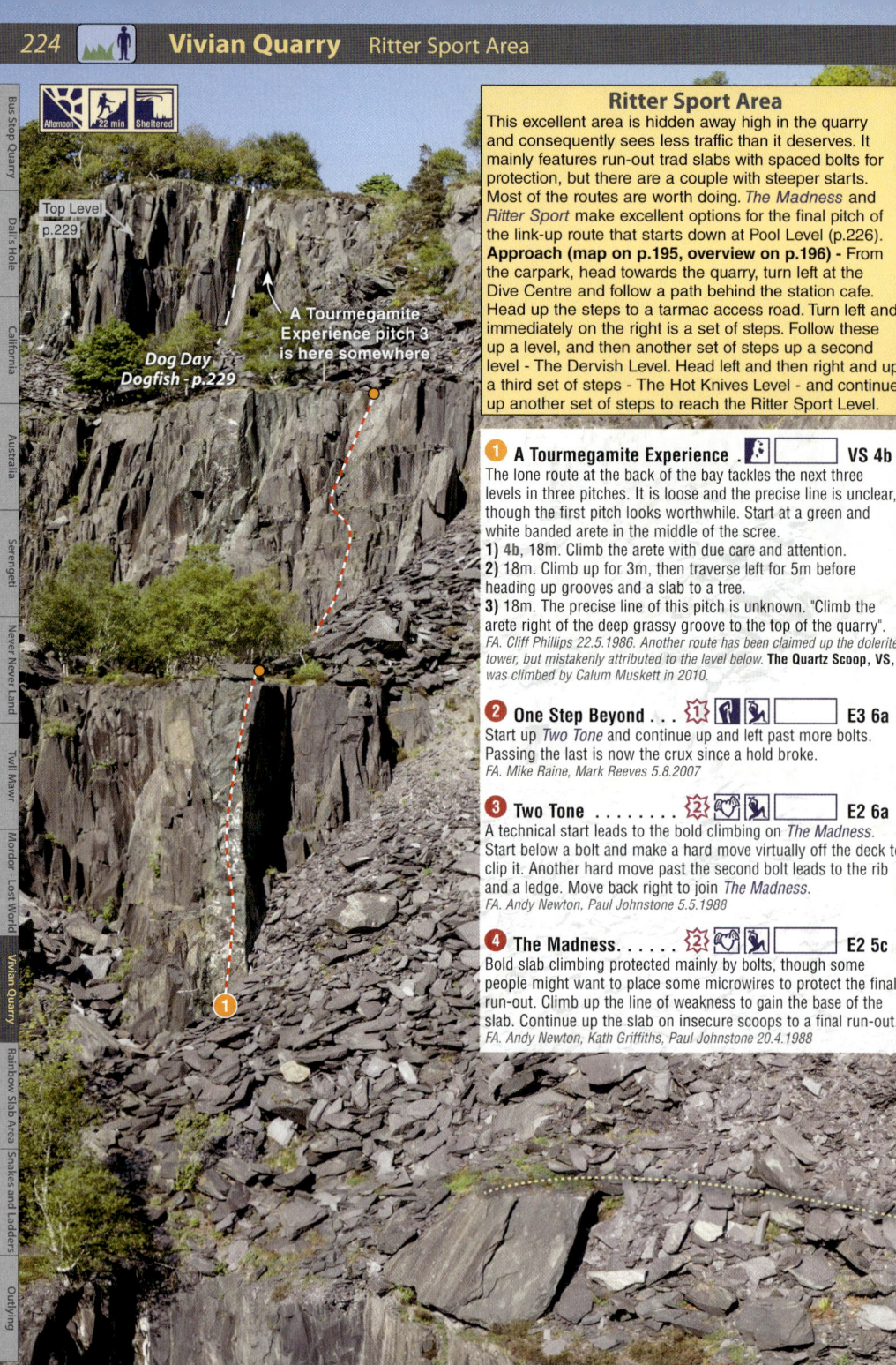

Afternoon | 22 min | Sheltered

Top Level
p.229

A Tourmegamite
Experience pitch 3
is here somewhere

Dog Day
Dogfish - p.229

Ritter Sport Area

This excellent area is hidden away high in the quarry and consequently sees less traffic than it deserves. It mainly features run-out trad slabs with spaced bolts for protection, but there are a couple with steeper starts. Most of the routes are worth doing. *The Madness* and *Ritter Sport* make excellent options for the final pitch of the link-up route that starts down at Pool Level (p.226). **Approach (map on p.195, overview on p.196) -** From the carpark, head towards the quarry, turn left at the Dive Centre and follow a path behind the station cafe. Head up the steps to a tarmac access road. Turn left and immediately on the right is a set of steps. Follow these up a level, and then another set of steps up a second level - The Dervish Level. Head left and then right and up a third set of steps - The Hot Knives Level - and continue up another set of steps to reach the Ritter Sport Level.

1 A Tourmegamite Experience .   **VS 4b**
The lone route at the back of the bay tackles the next three levels in three pitches. It is loose and the precise line is unclear, though the first pitch looks worthwhile. Start at a green and white banded arete in the middle of the scree.
1) 4b, 18m. Climb the arete with due care and attention.
2) 18m. Climb up for 3m, then traverse left for 5m before heading up grooves and a slab to a tree.
3) 18m. The precise line of this pitch is unknown. "Climb the arete right of the deep grassy groove to the top of the quarry".
FA. Cliff Phillips 22.5.1986. Another route has been claimed up the dolerite tower, but mistakenly attributed to the level below. **The Quartz Scoop, VS,** *was climbed by Calum Muskett in 2010.*

2 One Step Beyond . . .   **E3 6a**
Start up *Two Tone* and continue up and left past more bolts. Passing the last is now the crux since a hold broke.
FA. Mike Raine, Mark Reeves 5.8.2007

3 Two Tone **E2 6a**
A technical start leads to the bold climbing on *The Madness*. Start below a bolt and make a hard move virtually off the deck to clip it. Another hard move past the second bolt leads to the rib and a ledge. Move back right to join *The Madness*.
FA. Andy Newton, Paul Johnstone 5.5.1988

4 The Madness. **E2 5c**
Bold slab climbing protected mainly by bolts, though some people might want to place some microwires to protect the final run-out. Climb up the line of weakness to gain the base of the slab. Continue up the slab on insecure scoops to a final run-out.
FA. Andy Newton, Kath Griffiths, Paul Johnstone 20.4.1988

Bus Stop Quarry · Dali's Hole · California · Australia · Serengeti · Never Never Land · Twll Mawr · Mordor - Lost World · Vivian Quarry · Rainbow Slab Area · Snakes and Ladders · Outlying

5 **Silly on Slate** . . . . ⚀ ⬜ HVS 4c
The bold dirty groove on the right of the slab.
FA. Norman Clacher, Trevor Hodgson 4.4.1986

6 **Private Smells** . . ⚀ 🔲 🔲 🔲 ⬜ E5 6b
A good but bold and scary line. Start up the rib next to *Silly on Slate*, place a wire on the left and make a reach right to clip the first bolt. Then head straight up passing a few more bolts, each of which proves hard to clip.
FA. Paul Pritchard, Nick Harms 10.1987

7 **General Odours** . . . . ⚁ 🔲 🔲 ⬜ E4 6a
A great route, that is technical and unobvious at first so really tricky to on-sight. Start as for *Private Smells* and then make a bold and perplexing foot-traverse rightwards to gain a bolt out right. Above the slab is slightly easier, but rope-drag becomes an issue.
FA. Paul Johnstone, Andy Newton 1988

8 **Private Smells Direct** . . . . . . 🔲 ⬜ E5 6b
A desperate direct to *Private Smells* passing a manky bolt that appears to be too low to protect you anyway.
FA. Paul Pritchard 31.12.1987

9 **Major Whiff** . . . . ⚁ 🔲 🔲 ⬜ E3 5c
Worth 'sniffing out' one evening. Start right of *General Odours* at a counter flake-line to *Ritter Sport*. Layback the flake passing two bolts, then make a flick left to reach a small cam slot. A committing rockover left gains the slab and a bolt on *General Odours*. Continue up this past a bolt, then traverse right to the *Ritter Sport* lower-off.
FA. Dave Rudkin, Tim Neill 3.5.2017

10 **Major Sport** . . . . ⚀ 🔲 🔲 ⬜ E2 5c
A less bold combination of the two routes on either side. Start up *Major Whiff* and then move into *Ritter Sport* at the pinnacle.

11 **Ritter Sport** . . . . ⚁ 🔲 🔲 ⬜ E3 5c
Start up the right-hand flake. Make a tricky move to reach the first bolt. Layback up to the top of the pinnacle. A committing reach up and right leads to better holds and the slab. Follow the ramp rightwards to a small spike. A crack now leads back left - follow this to a lower-off. *Photo on p.222.*
FA. John Redhead, Andy Newton 25.4.1986

Bus Stop Quarry | Dali's Hole | California | Australia | Serengeti | Never Never Land | Twll Mawr | Mordor - Lost World | Vivian Quarry | Snakes and Ladders | Rainbow Slab Area | Outlying

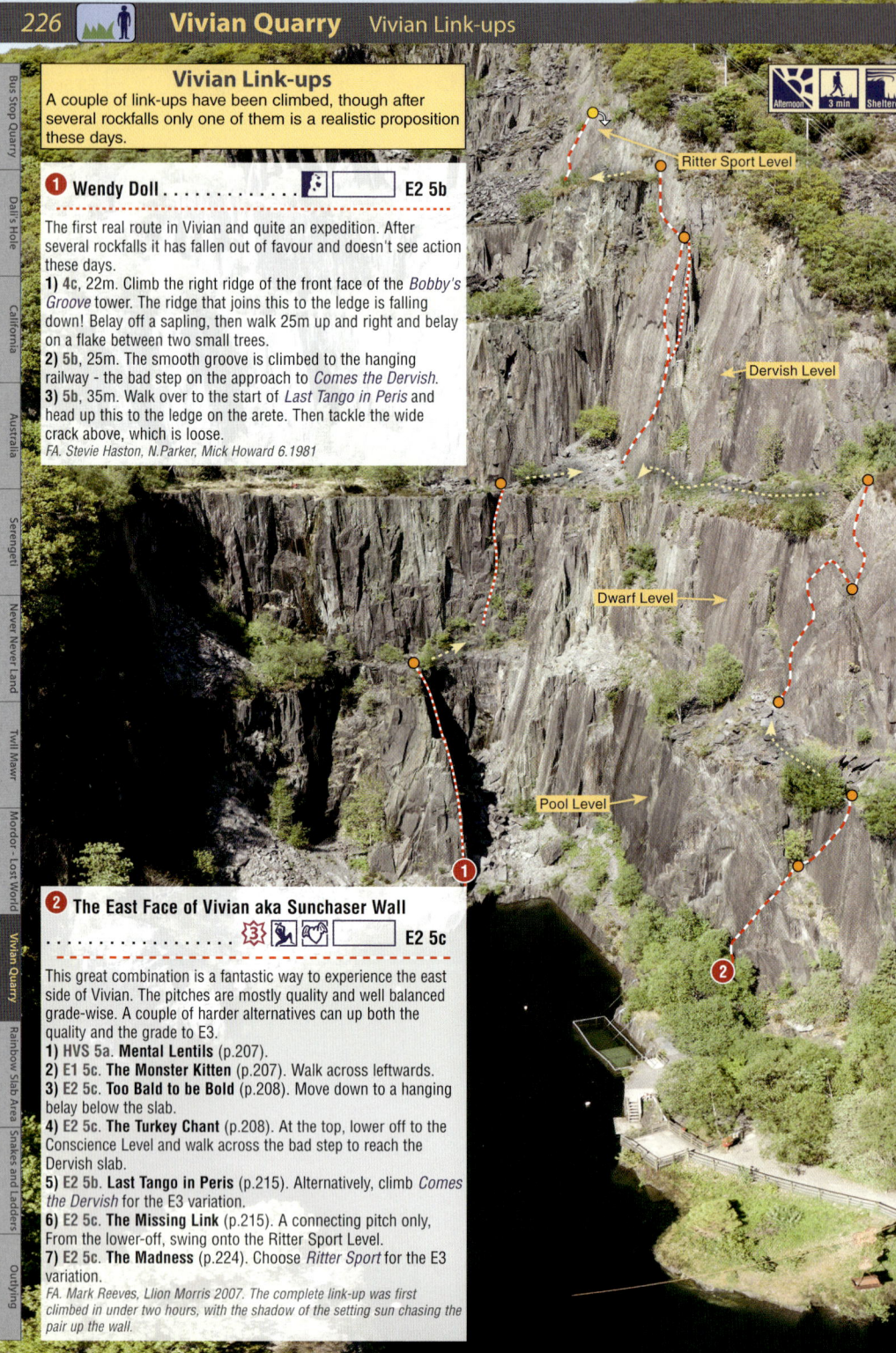

Vivian Link-ups

A couple of link-ups have been climbed, though after several rockfalls only one of them is a realistic proposition these days.

1 Wendy Doll **E2 5b**

The first real route in Vivian and quite an expedition. After several rockfalls it has fallen out of favour and doesn't see action these days.

1) 4c, 22m. Climb the right ridge of the front face of the *Bobby's Groove* tower. The ridge that joins this to the ledge is falling down! Belay off a sapling, then walk 25m up and right and belay on a flake between two small trees.

2) 5b, 25m. The smooth groove is climbed to the hanging railway - the bad step on the approach to *Comes the Dervish*.

3) 5b, 35m. Walk over to the start of *Last Tango in Peris* and head up this to the ledge on the arete. Then tackle the wide crack above, which is loose.
FA. Stevie Haston, N.Parker, Mick Howard 6.1981

2 The East Face of Vivian aka Sunchaser Wall
. . . .   **E2 5c**

This great combination is a fantastic way to experience the east side of Vivian. The pitches are mostly quality and well balanced grade-wise. A couple of harder alternatives can up both the quality and the grade to E3.

1) HVS 5a. **Mental Lentils** (p.207).

2) E1 5c. **The Monster Kitten** (p.207). Walk across leftwards.

3) E2 5c. **Too Bald to be Bold** (p.208). Move down to a hanging belay below the slab.

4) E2 5c. **The Turkey Chant** (p.208). At the top, lower off to the Conscience Level and walk across the bad step to reach the Dervish slab.

5) E2 5b. **Last Tango in Peris** (p.215). Alternatively, climb *Comes the Dervish* for the E3 variation.

6) E2 5c. **The Missing Link** (p.215). A connecting pitch only, From the lower-off, swing onto the Ritter Sport Level.

7) E2 5c. **The Madness** (p.224). Choose *Ritter Sport* for the E3 variation.
FA. Mark Reeves, Llion Morris 2007. The complete link-up was first climbed in under two hours, with the shadow of the setting sun chasing the pair up the wall.

Ritter Sport Level

Dervish Level

Dwarf Level

Pool Level

Bus Stop Quarry · Dali's Hole · California · Australia · Serengeti · Never Never Land · Twll Mawr · Mordor - Lost World · Vivian Quarry · Rainbow Slab Area · Snakes and Ladders · Outlying

Bus Stop Quarry

Dali's Hole

California

Australia

Serengeti

Never Never Land

Twll Mawr

Mordor - Lost World

Vivian Quarry

Snakes and Ladders | Rainbow Slab Area

Outlying

Ben Alsford on the thin and technical *Manimal* (6c) - *p.219* - on the Hot Knives Level of Vivian Quarry, a great route with a perplexing crux.

Top Level

Valkyries Level

Ritter Sport Area
p.222

Comes the Dervis
p.21

Hot Knives Level
p.218

Nostromo Wall
p.212

Ritter Sport Area p.222

Comes the Dervis p.21

Hot Knives Level p.218

Nostromo Wall p.212

To mid afternoon | 25 min

25m

Afternoon | 26 min

15m

1 2 3

4

Walk back down

20m

Valkyries Level

A minor area up high in the quarry has two routes of interest for the enthusiast.

Approach (map on p.195, overview opposite) - From the carpark, head towards the quarry, turn left at the Dive Centre and follow a path behind the station cafe. Head up the steps to a tarmac access road. Turn left and immediately on the right is a set of steps. Follow these up four levels to The Valkyries Level.

① **Pas da Dutchy** . . . . ⬚ **6a**
The slab on the left at the entrance to the level.
FA. Pete Robins 1.2.2007

② **Pas de Chevre** . . . . . ⬚ 🔲🔲🔲 **7b**
Sustained and complex moves lead up the arete.
FA. Nick Harms 18.5.1988

③ **Ride of the Valkyries** . . . ⬚🔲 ⬚ **E2 5c**
The open slab right of *Pas de Chevre*, just past the fence. Start below the centre of the slab and climb boldly up a shallow groove to a scoop. Continue past two horizontal breaks and a peg with increased interest.
FA. Lew Hardy, Ian Stevens, Chris Ayres 5.1987

④ **Power Tool Resurrection** . ⬚🔲 ⬚ **7a**
This triangular slab is situated on the opposite side and reached by a precarious scramble from either the Valkyries Level, or below from the top of the Ritter Sport Level. The route tackles the right-hand side of the slab past some old bolts.
FA. Terry Taylor 1992

Top Level

Up in the gods, the highest level has little of interest, especially since the only sport route has been de-bolted.
Approach - Go up one more level above Valkyries.
Descent - Walk back down the to the approach path.

⑤ **Goodbye Natterjack Toad** . . . . . ⬚ **HVS 5a**
The central groove and rib on the left wall past two bolts to a single bolt lower-off.
FA. Terry Taylor, Alun Hughes 1993

⑥ **Faulty Towers** . . . . 🔲🔲 ⬚ **E2 5c**
Loose and frightening climbing. Start up the crack on the left side of the pillar and gain the loose arete. Follow this to the upper wall and climb direct to the top.
FA. T.Dale, Chris Dale 20.4.1987

⑦ **Caleduwlch** . . . . ⬚🔲 ⬚ **E4 6a**
The slanting crack to the left of the tower leads to a groove and a loose arete to finish.
FA. Pat Littlejohn, P.Judge 15.11.1991

⑧ **Dog Day Dogfish** . . . . ⬚ **VS 4c**
A forgotten VS. It was bolted in 2010 to give a **5b** sport route. It was then de-bolted so it is a trad route again at VS. The old studs run up the left wall of the V-groove.
FA. John Tombs, A.Shaw 17.9.1989. It was renamed The Lost Tomb after being bolted.

Bus Stop Quarry

Dali's Hole

California

Australia

Serengeti

Never Never Land

Twll Mawr

Mordor – Lost World

Vivian Quarry

Rainbow Slab Area

Snakes and Ladders

Outlying

Rainbow Slab Area

A climber starts up the run-out section on *Pull My Daisy* (E2 5c) -
p.245 - with a long way to go to the next runner. Photo: Mike Hutton
Though it is by far the most popular route on the Rainbow Slab, this
route takes no prisoners. The initial crack is sustained which leaves
you with a reasonable rest at the pipe inserted at half-height. Don't
linger here too long though since you will end up questioning how
solid the pipe is - not a good idea since you have to climb a further
10m with it as your main runner.

Bus Stop Quarry

Dali's Hole

California

Australia

Serengeti

Never Never Land

Twll Mawr

Mordor - Lost World

Vivian Quarry

Rainbow Slab Area

Snakes and Ladders

Outlying

	No star	🔆	🔆🔆	🔆🔆🔆
Mod to S / 4c	1	1	-	-
HS-HVS / 5a-6a+	20	6	10	-
E1-E3 / 6b-7a	22	18	13	4
E4 / 7a+ and up	15	12	25	21

The Rainbow Slab Area is one of the best known locations in the slate quarries. It is home to the iconic feature of an immaculate slab of rock with the eponymous ripple arcing across it. This is one of the finest single slabs of rock in the country and it has been developed with a set of routes to match.

The rest of the area doesn't quite match up to this stunning slab although there are still plenty of good routes dotted about. Getting to them can be quite complex as some of the levels are only reachable by abseil.

The Rainbow Slab itself is mostly old-school trad classics with minimal or no bolting giving run-out and technical routes requiring deft footwork, strong fingers and a very steady head. Elsewhere in the area there is more sport climbing on offer which tends to be on vertical and featured terrain.

Conditions

This area is reasonably well sheltered and can provide dry climbing when the mountain crags are out of condition. It generally gets morning and midday sun and is hot if there is no wind. Some of the walls, especially the Colossus Wall, suffer from seepage after rain.

Access

The Rainbow Slab Area is on land owned by First Hydro Company who have to comply with the Mines and Quarries Act. There is no formal permission to climb or walk in the quarries away from the public footpaths. There have been few problems here over the years, but the area is in direct view of the First Hydro offices so a sensible approach is required. Please keep numbers down to a reasonable level, watch your language and, if you do take a classic 15m lob off the *Rainbow of Recalcitrance*, remember to dust yourself off like nothing happened!

Do not climb below the levels described here or on the tower above the First Hydro buildings with the exception of the Plateau Slab - p.272.

Dave Rudkin on the extremely popular *Horse Latitudes* (6a+) - *p.238* - on the Bela Lugosi Slab. This route used to be an E3 solo that nobody really climbed, although a young Leo Houlding did once solo it in one of the first pairs of Five Ten approach shoes, much to onlookers' horror. Its first ascensionist was happy for the line to be retro-bolted and since then it has rightly become one of the most popular 6a+ routes in the quarries.

Bus Stop Quarry

Dali's Hole

California

Australia

Serengeti

Never Never Land

Twll Mawr

Mordor - Lost World

Vivian Quarry

Rainbow Slab Area

Snakes and Ladders

Outlying

Bus Stop Quarry

Dali's Hole

California

Australia

Serengeti

Never Never Land

Twll Mawr

Mordor - Lost World

Vivian Quarry

Rainbow Slab Area

Snakes and Ladders

Outlying

Bus Stop Quarry

Dali's Hole

California

Australia

Serengeti

Never Never Land

Twll Mawr

Mordor - Lost World

Vivian Quarry

Rainbow Slab Area

Snakes and Ladders

Outlying

Approach

The Rainbow Slab Area is in the lower quarries but can be approached from three points.

From Llanberis (Rainbow and Cig-Arete Areas) - Park in the Slate Museum (fee), or Dolbadarn Castle, and walk down the First Hydro private road for 20m, to where a public footpath is signed on the left. Follow this as it weaves up through the woods and turns into a walled zig-zagging path up through scree. The path flattens off at a bridge by a winding house. Turn right (towards Llanberis Pass) after the metal bridge and follow the flat enclosed path as it curves left. As the wall ends, cross the fence and follow the level path until it goes left round a corner, shortly after which you reach some buildings on the left. Drop down one level to the top of the Rainbow Slab or go up one level to the Manatese Level.

GPS 53.127975 -4.108359

Dinorwig

Australia

Vivian

Bus Stop

California

Dali's Hole

Twll Mawr

Llanberis

Rainbow

N

GPS 53.107282 -4.095477

Nant Peris

Nant Peris

2km

National Slate Museum

GPS 53.122309 -4.115818

Path from Llanberis

Zig-zag path through scree

First Hydro private road

Castell Dolbadarn

From above (Manatese and German Schoolgirl Levels) - Park as for Bus Stop Quarry and follow the main track into the quarries. Just after the gate that leads up to Australia is a second gate on the right. Climb over this and follow the path down a few bends to a point on the Manatese Level, above the German Schoolgirl Level.

200m

N

From Nant Peris (Plateau Slab and Peppermint Tower) - Park in the lay-by before the village with 'NANT PERIS' written in slate. Cross the road and walk 50m toward the village and turn left onto a footpath that leads along a tarmac road and across the end of the lake. Turn left along the lake through a gate and head up the main track through the quarry. At the second level a plain leads out left from the track by a long gate. Cross the plateau (under Plateau Slab - p.272) to the right of the main tower and head down the track to a black fence. Head through the gate and on to join the other approach below the quarryman's path up to the Cig-Arete Level.

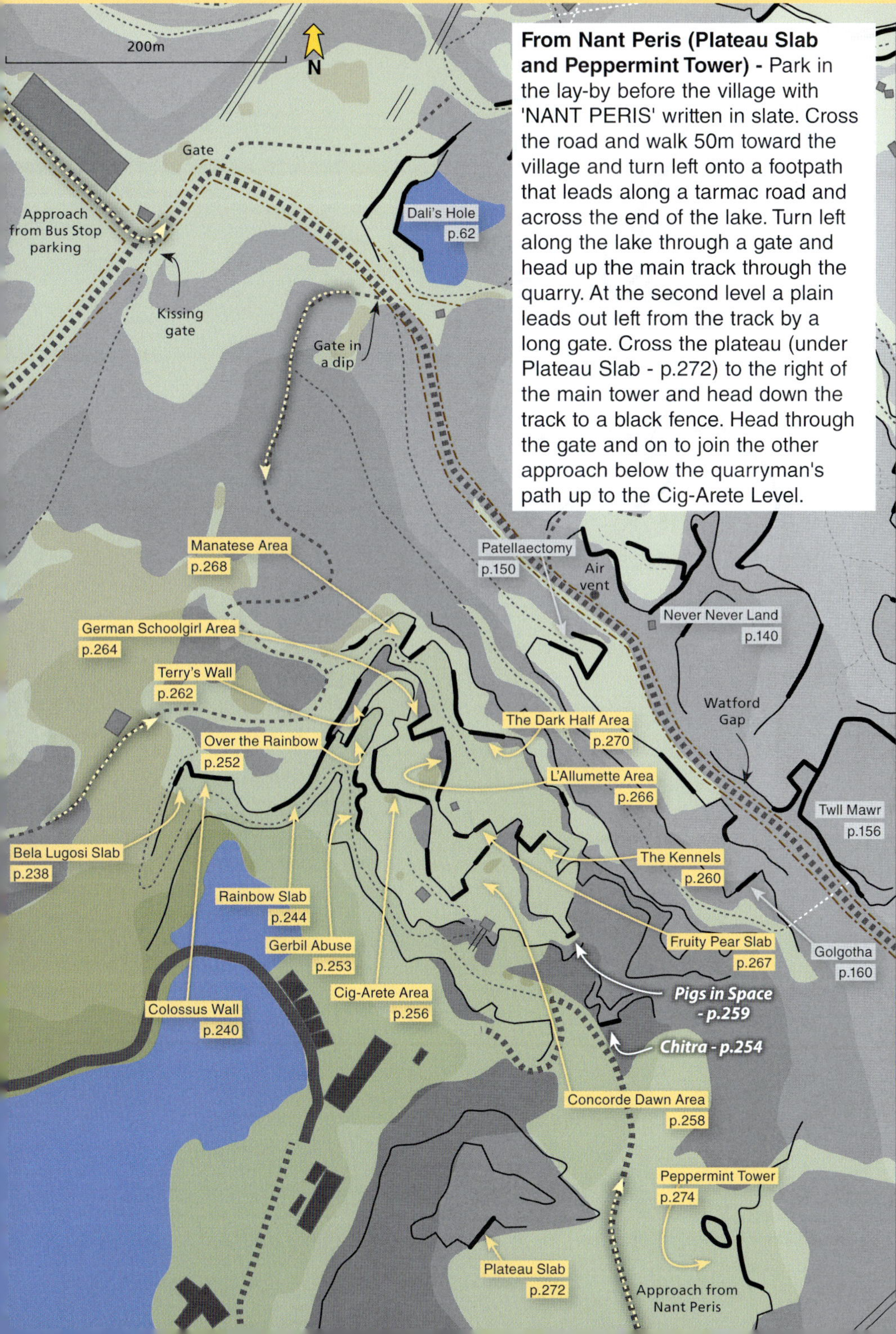

Gate

Approach from Bus Stop parking

Kissing gate

Dali's Hole
p.62

Gate in a dip

Manatese Area
p.268

German Schoolgirl Area
p.264

Terry's Wall
p.262

Over the Rainbow
p.252

Bela Lugosi Slab
p.238

Rainbow Slab
p.244

Gerbil Abuse
p.253

Colossus Wall
p.240

Cig-Arete Area
p.256

Patellaectomy
p.150

Air vent

Never Never Land
p.140

Watford Gap

The Dark Half Area
p.270

L'Allumette Area
p.266

The Kennels
p.260

Twll Mawr
p.156

Fruity Pear Slab
p.267

Golgotha
p.160

Pigs in Space - p.259

Chitra - p.254

Concorde Dawn Area
p.258

Peppermint Tower
p.274

Plateau Slab
p.272

Approach from Nant Peris

Bus Stop Quarry · Dali's Hole · California · Australia · Serengeti · Never Never Land · Twll Mawr · Mordor - Lost World · Vivian Quarry · Rainbow Slab Area · Snakes and Ladders · Outlying

Bus Stop Quarry

Dali's Hole

California

Australia

Serengeti

Never Never Land

Twll Mawr

Mordor – Lost World

Vivian Quarry

Rainbow Slab Area

Snakes and Ladders

Outlying

Australia
p.80

Main path dip
by Dali's Hole

Manatese Area
p.268

Buildings described
in approach

Terry's Wall
p.262

From Slate
Museum parking

Ⓐ

Colossus Wall
p.240

Bela Lugosi Slab
p.238

Rainbow Slab
p.244

Over the Rainbow
p.252

**No climbing on the levels below
the Rainbow Slab**

Never Never Land
p.140

Twll Mawr
p.156

German Schoolgirl Area
p.263

The Dark Half Area
p.270

Tunnel approach to
Twll Mawr - p.158

Golgotha
p.160

L'Allumette Area
p.266

The Kennels
p.260

Fruity Pear Slab
p.267

*Pigs in Space
- p.259*

Chitra - p.254

Cig-Arete Area
p.256

Concorde Dawn Area
p.258

**From Nant
Peris**

The 'Quarryman's Path'

Gerbil Abuse
p.253

**No climbing on the levels below
the Rainbow Slab**

Bus Stop Quarry

Dali's Hole

California

Australia

Serengeti

Never Never Land

Twll Mawr

Mordor - Lost World

Vivian Quarry

Snakes and Ladders

Rainbow Slab Area

Outlying

Bus Stop Quarry

Dali's Hole

California

Australia

Serengeti

Never Never Land

Twll Mawr

Mordor - Lost World

Vivian Quarry

Rainbow Slab Area

Snakes and Ladders

Outlying

Bela Lugosi Slab

The Bela Lugosi Slab is a friendly slabby wall with four great routes that are very popular. It gets plenty of morning sun and tends to dry quicker than the adjacent Colossus Wall.

Approach (map p.235, overview p.236) - From the buildings described on the main approach, walk about 20m further on to a path that leads down scree just over a fence on the right. Follow this path down to the grass. You are now stood on top of Colossus Wall. Turn right and follow a small cliff-top path that drops down gradually to the level below, then walk back left to the base of the crag.

1 **Nearly but not Quite** . . . . [ ] E1 5c
The open vegetated corner to the left of the slab.

2 **Horse Latitudes** . . . . [ ] 6a+
An excellent route up the arete. The lower arete is fine, the exposed upper arete, originally climbed separately as *The Horsin' Around Finish,* is the crux. *Photo on p.22 and p.232.*
FA. Martin Crook, Iwan Jones, Bob Drury, D.Jones 15.6.1985
FA. (Horsin' Around Finish) Andy Holmes, Steve Long 20.5.1986

3 **Bela Lugosi is Dead** . [ ] E1 5b
Another great route, this time trad - small wires and cams will help a lot. The runners do run out below the wide crack, so it is advisable not to pass any on your way. *Photo opposite and p.22.*
FA. Martin Crook, Nick Walton 28.5.1984

4 **Alive and Kicking** . . . [ ] E1 5b
More good climbing although it is a little run out, and the bolts are very hard to clip if you are short. Virtually a 6a+ sport route.
Photo on p.22.
FA. Gwion Hughes, Iwan Jones 6.4.1986

5 **Catrin** . . . . [ ] E2 5c
One that has a trad grade as gear is usually placed to reach the first bolt. Climb up the flake to the tree, then move left past a bolt to a tiny groove. Follow this past a second bolt, and exit to the lower-off on *Alive and Kicking.*
FA. Llion Morris, Mark Reeves 10.3.2007

6 **Frogs** . . . . [ ] HS 4a
The right corner of the slab is often damp. In a cold winter it has formed *Combined Colours* a grade IV ice route.
FA. Allen Williams, Andy Popp 6.4.1986

Niall Campbell leading the great *Bela Lugosi is Dead* (E1 5b) - *opposite*.
One of the best E1s in the slate quarries, named after a record by
Bauhaus, a post-punk band heralded as the harbingers of gothic rock.
Bela Lugosi died many years before the route was climbed but was
a goth icon, almost individually personifying the modern image of
Dracula and vampires through his work as a horror film actor.

Bus Stop Quarry

Dali's Hole

California

Australia

Serengeti

Never Never Land

Twll Mawr

Mordor - Lost World

Vivian Quarry

Rainbow Slab Area

Snakes and Ladders

Outlying

Bus Stop Quarry

Dali's Hole

California

Australia

Serengeti

Never Never Land

Twll Mawr

Mordor - Lost World

Vivian Quarry

Rainbow Slab Area

Snakes and Ladders

Outlying

❶ Nifty Wild Ribo E1 5a
An uninspiring line somewhere up the back of the recess.
FA. Cliff Phillips, Sandy Britain 26.2.1987

❷ Shazalzabon E5 6b
The system of groves protected by a mix of trad gear and bolts.
1) 6b, 23m. Bridge up then rock over left onto a spike. Layback up the central fin using wide bridging to the belay.
2) 6b, 20m. Climb the groove to the bulge then stretch right to an undercut and make a stiff pull to easier finishing moves.
FA. Bill Gregory, I.Barton, Dave Gregory 7.1990

❸ Jack of Shadows . . .   E4 6a
Usually in the shadows, this route tackles a groove-system up the left-hand side of the Colossus Wall.
1) 6a, 23m. Start up a rib, passing two bolts. Continue up with difficulty to transition into the groove on the right. Ascend this past more bolts until you are forced out right at the top of the groove. Perplexing moves and long reaches lead up past another bolt to a sloping ledge and belay.
2) 5c, 18m. Climb the left-hand side of the corner past three bolts. This is steeper and more difficult than it first appears!
FA. Owain Jones, R.Whitwell 22.6.1986

❹ Light and Darkness E5 6b
Squeezed in between *Jack of Shadows* and *Big Wall Party*, up the front face of the pillar.
1) 6b, 25m. Make a steep pull up onto the overhanging face of the pillar and move up to the first bolt on the left. Head up left on undercuts, past the second bolt, to reach a chimney. Climb this and exit left onto a ledge. Move right past the third bolt and ascend a groove, exiting right onto *Big Wall Party* at the jugs. Leave *Big Wall Party* and move back left under the overhang using a finger jug on the lip, small cam on the left. Make your way up the left side of a slim groove - all rather awkward - to the belay.
2) 6b, 18m. From the right end of the ledge, move onto the face cautiously and make a reach for the distant ledge above, this is the *Big Wall Party* belay. Strenuous climbing leads up the steep overhanging corner-crack above the ledge to the top.
FA. Chris Dale, Nick Dixon 17.7.1986

❺ Big Wall Party . . .   E5 6b
A tough proposition. Start just right of the slate wall.
1) 6b, 28m. Head up the left edge of the front face via a crack-line and slopey holds to a large jug at 8m. Move left and go up to a bolt. The next two bolts are passed with great difficulty before you can trend left to reach a wire on the arete. Move back right and head up to another bolt, before a big move up and left to reach a hold on the arete. Continue on to the ledge and two-bolt belay (optional). Move back right onto the front face and make a long move to the ledge above - belay here.
2) 6b, 16m. Lean out right and make a few precarious moves to gain the crack on the front face. Climb this to the top.
FA. John Allen, Paul Williams 5.7.1986

❻ Major Headstress . . .   E5 6a
Classic sustained and reachy climbing. Start just right of the arete by a crack. Climb this to a niche at 8m and clip the bolt above. Move up to the V-groove and climb its left arete on good holds with a long reach for the second bolt. More fingery climbing leads you on past a couple of reaches to a third bolt. Layback past this and traverse right to better holds and another bolt. Ascend the groove (tricky for the short) and mantel onto a ledge (harder for the tall). Step right to join *Ride the Wild Surf* and finish up its thrilling groove in the headwall.
FA. Paul Williams, Colin Gilchrist 5.6.1986

❼ Ride the Wild Surf . .   E4 6a
The best line on the wall and a total pump-fest. Start near the centre of the wall at the large flake. Climb up to a bolt on the left and then another on the right. Move back left to get stood in the 'Chipadeedoodah' hold. Layback strenuously to gain a jug/small ledge, then continue up the groove/small corner, passing a number of bolts to reach a small roof. Boldly climb the 6m run-out to the next bolt, then move right into a groove and summon up all your reserves for the final headwall!
Photo on p.242.
FA. Paul Williams, D.Jones 26.4.1986

❽ Wall of Flame E5 6a
Climb *Great Balls of Fire* to the niche on its traverse right towards *Colossus*. Step out left and climb confidently to the next bolt 6m above. Now make a hard move left into a groove below a small capping roof (bolt out left). Make a long exposed reach over the roof to a good hold. Traverse left to the foot of a short problematic groove. Climb this to a ledge and make a heart-stopping traverse out left past a bolt to a peapod-shaped groove. Struggle up this to an escape left onto good holds. Move left to the arete and finish up this.
FA. Paul Williams, Dave Lawson 1.5.1986

❾ Great Balls of Fire E4 6a
More sustained climbing on a harder counter line to *Colossus*. Start just left of *Colossus* below a slim groove. Climb this past two bolts to a tricky section leading to another bolt. From here trend right to gain a niche in *Colossus* and move right again to the base of a smooth V-groove. Thrutch up this and then take the stepped groove-line leading up and right to the top.
FA. Paul Williams, John Allen 12.4.1986

❿ Colossus. E3 5c
A great route, although it often seeps on the crux, and is more like E5 when that is wet. A selection of trad gear and a lot of quickdraws is useful. Start by a large boulder below a line of weakness that goes the full height of the wall. Make difficult and polished moves to reach the first ledge, and follow the curving line of weakness up and right to another ledge at 12m. A step left, followed by an awkward pull up, leads to better holds. Then climb a crack to a pinnacle. From its top, move up and left into a niche, before it is possible to move back right to below a slanting V-groove capped by a roof. Move up into the V-groove, exiting it to the foot of a crack left of the small roof. Hard moves up this (crux) lead to good flat holds. Traverse left to an airy mantelshelf, then follow the ledges up and right to the top.
FA. Paul Williams, Andy Holmes 27.3.1986

⓫ Colostomy. E4 6a
A girdle of the Colossus Wall.
1) 6a, 23m. *Jack of Shadows* pitch one.
2) 6a, 30m. From the ledge, move right onto the front face and head up to a ledge to arrange protection. Climb down and climb/pendulum across to a good hold on *Major Headstress* (bolt). Climb up and right to join *Ride the Wild Surf* at a groove, reverse *Wall of Flame* rightwards before moving into *Colossus* at the slanting V-groove. Move right into *Great Balls of Fire* and follow this to the top.
FA. Grant Farquhar, Graham Ettle 9.1988

⓬ OM 69 Runner Bean . . . . . .   VS
Start where 'OM 69' is painted onto a white cylinder protruding from the ground. Climb the rib just to the right to a large block. Jam up the block above to a ledge. Finish up the slabby rib.
FA. Cliff Phillips 26.10.1984

Walk back down

50m

11

8

1
2
3
4
5 6
7 9
10
12

Bus Stop Quarry
Dali's Hole
California
Australia
Serengeti
Never Never Land
Twll Mawr
Mordor - Lost World
Vivian Quarry
Snakes and Ladders
Rainbow Slab Area
Outlying

Colossus Wall

The Colossus Wall is a steep and uncompromising nearly-vertical wall with some stunning lines. They mostly give sustained climbing with decent protection, but not good enough to be considered full sport routes. The wall seeps after bad weather and, despite facing southwest and getting afternoon sun, it is sometimes slow to dry.

Approach (map p.235, overview p.236) - From the buildings described on the main approach, walk about 20m further on to a path that leads down scree just over a fence on the right. Follow this path down to the grass. You are now stood on top of Colossus Wall. Turn right and follow a small path that drops down gradually to the level below, then walk back left to the base of the crag.

Bus Stop Quarry

Dali's Hole

California

Australia

Serengeti

Never Never Land

Twll Mawr

Mordor - Lost World

Vivian Quarry

Rainbow Slab Area

Snakes and Ladders

Outlying

Bus Stop Quarry

Dali's Hole

California

Australia

Serengeti

Never Never Land

Twll Mawr

Mordor - Lost World

Vivian Quarry

Rainbow Slab Area

Snakes and Ladders

Outlying

A Japanese climber from a BMC International Meet enjoying *Ride the Wild Surf* (E4 6a) - *p.240* - on the amazing Colossus Wall.
The BMC International Meets in North Wales used to be a regular celebration of all things trad and sport in the area. Often many of the delegation would ask to visit the slate for its unique character and atmosphere.

Walk back down on
the main approach

38m

45m

Approach

Rainbow Slab

The huge expanse of perfect quality slate behind the Dinorwig power station holds a justifiable position as the jewel in the crown of climbing in the Llanberis quarries. It is one of the finest pieces of rock in the country and has a set of routes to match. *Pull My Daisy* is the entry level route at E2, and even that has a big run-out. The rest are all harder and bolder (but also infinitely memorable) leads of the highest quality. The slab faces southeast, getting sun until early afternoon. It turns into a slippery water slide if there is any rain, but dries quickly. The right-hand side seeps after prolonged rain.

Approach (map p.235, overview p.236) - From the buildings above the area on the main approach, follow the path down and right across the top of the crags to the end of the level. Walk back along the base past the Colossus Wall. When you turn the next corner, the slab is revealed in all its glory.

❶ Freak yer Beanbag E5 6b
Start by a 'death razor' below the orange wall, just before you turn the corner to the Rainbow Slab. Climb the groove and thin crack with a hard layback section - crux. Carry on to a hand-traverse leftwards past a spike. Finish up a groove.
FA. Paul Pritchard, Phil Dowthwaite, S.Edmonson 19.7.1986

❷ Cabbage Man meets the Flying Death Leg
. . . .   E2 5c
A poor route. Start on the left edge of the main slab and climb a corner until a step left and up gains a scoop. Move left and finish up *Freak yer Beanbag*.
FA. Paul Pritchard, Gwion Hughes, 3.11.1986

❸ Red and Yellow and Pink and Green, Orange and Purple and Blue E1 5a
A solo that is committing as the easiest line is hard to follow. There is some poor gear at 25m which may slow you down a bit, both up and down. Start in from the arete. Follow some holds up and right with an awkward reach to gain a good ledge. Move back up and left to a more broken area of rock and poor runners. From the left of the ledge, make a committing move to a good hold and follow more positive holds to the top.
FA. Mark Lynden 6.1984

❹ The Richard of York Finish   E3 5b
Follow *Red and Yellow...* to the broken ledges at 25m. Gain the lower of two scoops from the right-hand side of the ledges. A shallow fault-line leads up right to the top. *Photo on p.250.*
FA. Mark Lynden, W.Lockley 7.1984

❺ Eros E2 5b
Start up *Red and Yellow...* to the first good ledge, then head straight up until level with the pipe on *Pull My Daisy*. Traverse across to clip this and carry on up *Pull My Daisy*.
FA. Mark Lynden, Steve Long, John Silvester, Dave Towse 7.1984

❻ Pull My Daisy   E2 5c
An excellent and memorable route with a run-out section that will put hairs on your chest! Start below a crack and climb edges up and left, then back right, to reach the first gear in the crack. Follow the crack, sometimes on the wall to the left or right, to gain the pipe. Make bold moves to a shot-hole below a tower, then move left to a groove and follow it easily to a belay on a large flat ledge. *Photo on p.230.*
FA. Mark Lynden, John Silvester 7.1984

❼ Chewing the Cwd   E5 6b
Similar in character to, but not as spectacular as, *Rainbow of Recalcitrance*. Start up *Pull My Daisy* to the spike. Step up and right to gain more good gear. Now follow the faint ripple up and right briefly until you can step back right into the continuation of the *Pull My Daisy* crack move up to easier ground.
Release from Excrement, E6 6b - From the pipe, move up and right to the faint ripple and follow this in a terrifying position to belay on the prow, as for *Poetry Pink*.
FA. Paul Pritchard, T.Jones, Mike Thomas 14.2.1987

❽ Naked Before the Beast
. . . .   E6 6b
A route that takes no prisoners. Start where the rainbow feature peters out. Follow the crack just to its left up for 18m, where a hard step right onto a good hold/ledge, gives access to the rainbow itself. Move back up and left to regain the hairline crack. This gives almost no gear. Significant commitment and hard work lead to the relative sanctuary above.
FA. Dave Towse, John Redhead 7.1984

❾ The Cure for a Sick Mind
. . . .   E6 6b
Poetry Pink on steroids and one of the best lines on slate for the tall! It is said to be 8a if you pre-place a long draw on the third bolt. Start just right of the base of the rainbow and move up to the break. Climb up and left then straight back right to gain the second bolt. Move left to join *The Rainbow...* at a ledge below the crux. Climb this and head up in an alarming position to clip a bolt. Run it out to the prow then easier climbing to the belay. *Photo on p.11.*
FA. Paul Pritchard, T.Jones, Mike Thomas 14.2.1987

❿ Poetry Pink E5 6b
A stunning route that is the entry-level E5 on this slab, but should not be underestimated.
1) 6a, 30m. Start below the tower. Move up and then left to better holds that lead to the break and gear. Delicately mantel up to the bolt. A hard sequence of moves above this eventually leads to a decent three-finger edge. Beyond this every move gets easier as you run it out to where a mantelshelf leads to the second bolt. Blowing it here requires Usain Bolt as a belayer. Move up and left onto the rainbow, then teeter right to jugs. Ascend to the groove past microwires and micro cams. Belay on the prow on the left.
2) 5b, 12m. Step right and follow the groove to the top, or take the second pitch of *Released from Treatment* (p.248).
FA. John Redhead, Dave Towse 7.1984

⓫ Memorable Stains E4 6a
The left arete of the prow past three bolts is exposed and tricky.
FA. Paul Pritchard 14.12.1987

⓬ Bungles Arete . .   8b
The prominent right arete is extremely difficult.
FA. Sean Myles 12.1990

⓭ The Very Big and the Very Small
. . . .   8b+
Three bolts mark the way. You will be forgiven if you don't see any holds, but they are there - tiny matchstick edges. This was rumoured to be the hardest slab in the word until James McHaffie climbed the *Meltdown* in Twll Mawr (p.166). *Photo on p.13.*
FA. Johnny Dawes 3.7.1990

Bus Stop Quarry · Dali's Hole · California · Australia · Serengeti · Never Never Land · Mordor - Lost World · Twll Mawr · Vivian Quarry · Rainbow Slab Area · Snakes and Ladders · Outlying

14 Very Big Cop Out . . . E5 6b
As for *The Very Big and the Very Small* up to the second bolt. Stand up in the break below the second bolt and stretch out left for what feel like jugs to finish up *Poetry Pink*.
FA. Calum Muskett 11.2017

15 Raped By Affection
. . . . E7 6c
The first bolt at 22m is enough to put most people off. It has been on-sighted and must be one of the boldest leads this side of Cloggy. Start 7m left of the rib of *Cystitis By Proxy* above a really bad landing. A tricky sequence off the ground leads to a break at 6m. A vague broken depression leads to the rainbow past poor skyhooks and microwires. The bolt just above the rainbow is something of the ultimate ''gripper clipper''. Move up to a traverse line and either make a massive span, or jump, up and left for a good crimp. Above is the second bolt. From here, step right and then straight up to the top.
FA. John Redhead, Dave Towse 7.84

16 Cystitis By Proxy E5 6b
A tricky pitch that is bolder since the microwire placements have blown out. It can be split at the flakes/ledges at half-height. Start by some ledges just before the scree, below a vague rib. Ascend the rib to a shattered crack, get in as much gear as possible because there isn't much more! Carry on up the shattered crack until the climbing gets hard and a foothold can be seen out left. Make a very committing move left onto the foothold, after which good holds lead to the broken ledges. Take the right-hand line of two bolts, passing the second via a tricky move out of the letter-box - crux. Above, easier but bold climbing leads up and right to the top. *Photo on p.249.*
FA. Dave Towse, John Redhead 29.6.1986

17 Ringin in Urea's E6 6b
The direct variant on *Cystitis By Proxy*. Start up *Cystitis By Proxy* and, from just above the overlap, head straight up to a boss of rock and the first bolt. Tricky moves up past this lead to the next bolt and then onto the rainbow where you can join *Splitstream* to the top.
FA. Nick Harms 11.10.87

18 Splitstream E5 6b
A great route - probably the best of the E5s on this slab. It is hard to read low down as there is no real line to follow. Start 10m right of *Cystitis By Proxy* at the first 'landing pad'. Climb the slab to a horizontal break at 10m. Continue on for 5m to a leftwards traverse and some microwires. Move up to a bolt runner, make a desperate move past this, and then follow a left-trending line to the broken ledges. Take the left bolt line. At the first bolt, traverse left for 4m to below the bolt and move up to this. From here, either step left and head direct, or take a diagonally rising line leftwards to the top. *Photo on p.30.*
FA. (first half) Dave Towse, John Redhead 5.4.1986
FA. (finish) Dave Towse, Andy Newton 26.4.1986

19 Stiff Syd's Cap . . E6 6c
The crack that runs halfway up the right side of the slab. Start just right of *Splitstream* beneath the crack. Move up to a good slot (sideways runner), continue up towards the crack over a slight bulge to a break and the start of the crack. Climb up past a few well spaced runners and the two bolts to a tricky reach for the traverse line and head over to the top two bolts on *Cystitis by Proxy* and climb that to the top. *Photo on p.249.*
FA. John Redhead, Dave Towse 5.4.1986

20 Prick up Urea's E6 6c
A direct finish to *Stiff Syd's Cap*, from the second bolt move out left to a mantel. Continue up to another bolt which is difficult to clip and even harder to pass. Continue onto the top via *Released from Treatment*.
FA. Nick Harms, Paul Barbier 1.12.1987

21 DOA E6 6c
The left of three discontinuous cracks on the right of the slab is climbed past a bolt to a lower-off. Often wet.
FA. Bob Drury, John Allen 4.7.1986

22 Drury Lane E6 6b
The thin central crack has a hard start followed by some bold climbing above. It is often wet.
FA. Bob Drury, John Allen 4.7.1986

23 Jai'a'n E6 6b
The right discontinuous crack past five bolts of dubious quality. Worth re-equipping. Often wet.
FA. Nick Harms, Mo Anthoine 6.4.1988

Walk back down on the main approach

45m

Bus Stop Quarry

Dali's Hole

California

Australia

Serengeti

Never Never Land

Twll Mawr

Mordor - Lost World

Vivian Quarry

Rainbow Slab Area

Snakes and Ladders

Outlying

Walk back down on
the main approach

To mid afternoon | 35 min | Sheltered | Seepage

38m

45m

24 Released From Treatment

E6 6b

Two great pitches, both with safe big air potential!
1) 6b, 35m. Follow *Pull My Daisy* to the pipe. Move up and
right to a crack and good runners. A hard traverse right leads
to the crack of *Naked Before the Beast* and a microwire. More
hard climbing right past a bolt to eventually leans to the jugs of
Poetry Pink. Follow this to the belay on the prow.
2) 6b, 25m. Step back down right into the groove, and traverse
out to a bolt on *Raped By Affection* level with the belay. Carry on
traversing until below a second bolt on *Spiltstream*, move up to
this, and then step right above the crux of *Cystitis By Proxy* and
head all the way to the right of the slab.
2a) 6a, 20m. Less of a traverse and easier to second. Follow the
original to above the crux of *Cystitis By Proxy* and finish up this.
2b) 5c, 20m. A surprisingly easy version but very bold. From the
first bolt traverse right to just before *Splitstream*, then climb over
the top of its second bolt on good holds. Step right above the crux
of *Cystitis By Proxy* to follow this to the top.
FA. Dave Towse, John Redhead, Andy Newton 26.4.1986

Bus Stop Quarry

Dali's Hole

California

Australia

Serengeti

Never Never Land

Twll Mawr

Mordor - Lost World

Vivian Quarry

Rainbow Slab Area

Snakes and Ladders

Outlying

25 Rainbow of Recalcitrance

. . . . 3 🖐️🦶🏻🪨 ▢ **E6 6b**

One of the finest 'lines' on British rock which is as amazing as it is frightening.

1) 6b, 40m. Start where the rainbow feature peters out. Follow the crack just to its left up for 18m, where a hard step right onto a good hold/ledge gives access to the rainbow itself. Difficult climbing up the initial rib hopefully allows you to get stood on the rainbow. Teeter right to the jugs on *Poetry Pink,* in what is now an outrageously run-out position. Most people head up and get the gear in the high flake on *Poetry Pink*, then move back down. Carry on right, with a gripper clipper to reach a bolt, to the belay on the ledges - bolt and flake.

2) 6a, 22m. Head along the now-fading ripple to a bold and tricky clip, then move up and left to the lower of two black grooves. Finish up this and work your way left to the belay.
FA. John Silvester, Mark Lynden 7.1984

Bus Stop Quarry

Dali's Hole

California

Australia

Serengeti

Never Never Land

Twll Mawr

Mordor - Lost World

Vivian Quarry

Rainbow Slab Area

Snakes and Ladders

Outlying

Dave Evans on the ridiculously run-out *Richard of York Finish* (E3 5b) - *p.245* - on the Rainbow Slab.
A moment of utter madness as Dave, having just reached the first runners at 20m, prepares to run it out to just below the top of the slab.
This was the author's first route on slate back in 1993. He had come up to Bangor to visit a friend, was lowered down the slab and top-roped this route in a light snow shower. For some reason he fell in love with the quarries that day and returned to study and climb at Bangor a year later.

Bus Stop Quarry

Dali's Hole

California

Australia

Serengeti

Never Never Land

Twll Mawr

Mordor - Lost World

Vivian Quarry

Rainbow Slab Area

Snakes and Ladders

Outlying

Over the Rainbow

Although overshadowed by its venerable neighbour, this wall actually has a couple of good rebolted routes - *Over The Rainbow* and *Cwms The Dogfish*. The wall faces east and gets morning sun.

Approach (map p.235, overview p.236) - Walk right from the Rainbow Slab (p.244).

Descent - Scramble up the rock to the left side of the pipe - about Diff - and the then walk around to the abseil on the Rainbow Slab.

❶ Over the Rainbow E5 6a
A great and steady route up the greenstone pillar.
1) 5c, 17m. Gain the dogleg crack - large cams helpful. Follow it up to a scree-covered ledge and bolt belay.
1) 6a, 17m. Go up and right onto the exposed. Follow this and the slab on the right past four bolts to the top.
FA. Mike Raine, Malcolm Campbell 14.4.1987

❷ Cwms the Dogfish . .   8a
A fine steep slab yields only to an enigmatic sequence and great determination.
FA. Nick Harms 3.8.1988

❸ The Race against Time . .   E3 5b
A serious route up the prominent pillar in the bay. Start on the left-hand side of the bay below a thin rightward slanting flake-crack, just to the right of the main flake system. Climb to a point just below the top of the flake-crack, step left on a good foothold. Continue up the right-hand side of the large pillar with no gear to a triangular foothold at its tip - good gear in the break. Make a long pull off the ledge and finish direct.
FA. Sandy Britain, P.Gilliver 25.5.1988

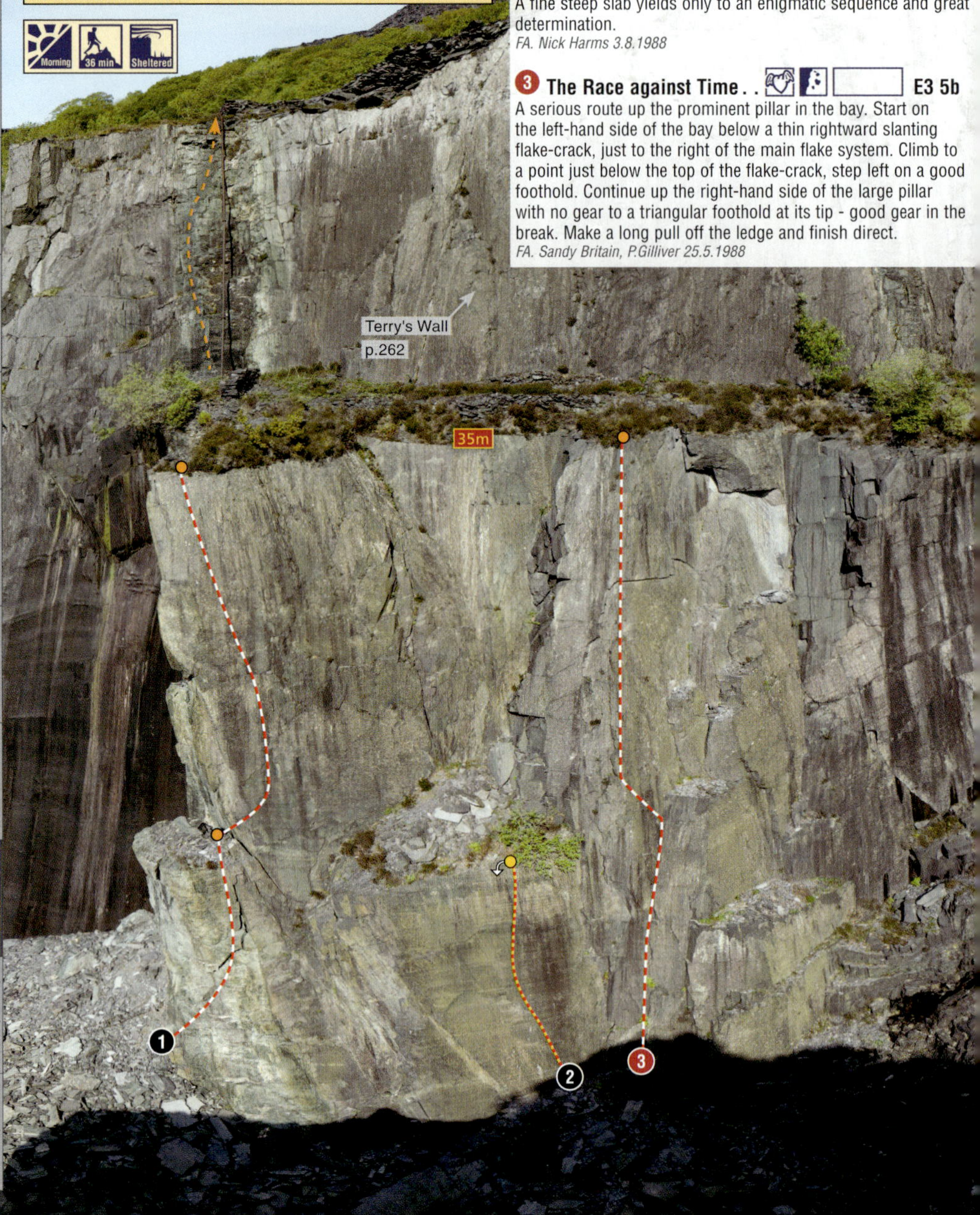

Terry's Wall p.262

35m

Cig-Arete Area
p.256

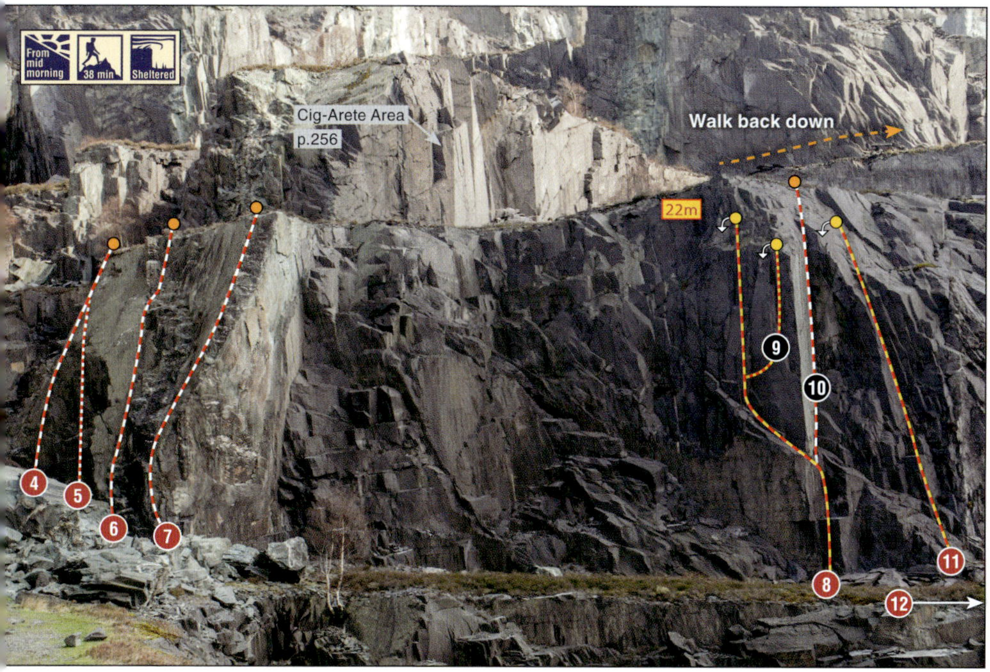

Walk back down

22m

9

10

4

5

6

7

8

11

12

Gerbil Abuse

This small but steep area is dominated by the striking arete of *Vermin on the Ridiculous*. Though bolted as sport routes, many of the bolts are desperate to clip and the routes are hard to on-sight but make good redpoints. **Approach (map p.235, overview p.236) -** Beyond the end of Rainbow Slab (p.244) is a scree-filled gully. This area is just beyond the scree.

4 **How Hot is Your Chilli?**. . . . . ⬛ E2 6a
The steep start up the left-hand arete has suffered rockfall. Start to the right and move up and left to gain a ledge. Climb the wall, using the arete, to a large thread runner. Step right and climb cracks to the top.
FA. Steve Lumley 21.6.1987

5 **F Hot** . . . . ⬛ E2 5c
Climb up steep rock to join *How Hot is Your Chilli?* on the top slab.
FA. Keith Hawker 20.6.1987

6 **Hooded Cobra** . . . . ⬛ E1 5b
The hanging slab to the left of the *Little Urn* arete. Start 3m left of the curving arete, just left of the dolerite band. Move up left then more directly up the slab to reach the top.
FA. Lew Hardy, Chris Parkin 8.7.1986

7 **Little Urn** . . . . ⬛ E3 5b
The slanting arete opposite the right-hand end of Rainbow Slab. Care is needed with loose rock at the bottom. From the foot of the arete, climb steeply at first past a hollow spike to a good cam slot and positive flat holds to a large flat hold. Move back to the arete and follow it delicately to the top.
FA. Martin Barnicott 27.5.1986

8 **Gerbil Abuse** . . . . ⬛ 6c+
A tricky route which is hard to lead ground up. A clipstick and a redpoint approach improve this route. Climb up to the arete, then make an interesting move left onto the ramp and walk up this to a smaller arete/groove. Move up this with difficulty.
FA. Mike Thomas, Mark McGowan 2.4.1986

9 **Vermin on the Ridiculous**
. . . . ⬛ 7b+
A tricky route, with a radical sideways dyno. Climb *Gerbil Abuse* to the arete/groove, then make a hard move right to the main arete. Finish up the groove.
FA. George Smith 16.8.1986

10 **The Homicidal Hamster from Hell**
. . . . ⬛ E5 6c
Start up *Vermin on the Ridiculous*, then move right to the corner and climb it past a bolt.
FA. Paul Pritchard 23.10.1987

11 **The Spleenal Flick** . . . . . ⬛ 6c+
The hanging ramp-line is steeper than it looks. *Photo on p.255.*
FA. Nick Harms 27.9.1987

12 **Dangling by the Diddies** . . . . . . ⬛ E2 5b
50m right of *The Spleenal Flick* is an overhanging arete which lies between the five vertical bore-holes and the iron pipe, close to the wall on the path. From the base of the arete climb the groove, step down left, then surmount bulges to reach a sapling at half-height. Move diagonally right to the hanging flake and make a 'dangling' mantel into a niche. Move over the next bulge, step right and finish direct.
FA. Cliff Phillips, Nick Thomas 15.10.1986

Bus Stop Quarry · Dali's Hole · California · Australia · Serengeti · Never Never Land · Twll Mawr · Mordor - Lost World · Vivian Quarry · Rainbow Slab Area · Snakes and Ladders · Outlying

Morning | **45 min** | **Sheltered**

22m

13 **3.15 to Yuma** . . . . 1 ☐ **E4 6a**
On the same level as *Gerbil Abuse* past the gate. Start at the
foot of *Chitra*. Bounce off the rail tracks onto the juggy rib on
your left and gain the arete which leads to a chunky auburn
thread. Step right and stretch for the dogleg crack which leads
(awkwardly) up rightwards to the convenient *Chitra* lower-off.
FA. Tim Neill, Lou Wilkinson 10.2014

14 **Chitra** . . . . 3 ☐ **7c**
This was a great route, but rockfalls seem to be filling in the
start. Thin, technical and bouldery climbing up the leaning wall.
FA. Nick Harms 27.3.1989

13

14

George Smith repeating a freshly re-equipped *The Spleenal
Flick* (6c) - *p.253* - on the Gerbil Abuse area.
The rising ramp-line looks easier than it is and catches a
few people out. Even more so its neighbours *Vermin on the
Ridiculous* and *Gerbil Abuse*, both of which have typical
slate 'gripper clippers' and some committing moves.

Bus Stop Quarry

Dali's Hole

California

Australia

Serengeti

Never Never Land

Twll Mawr

Mordor - Lost World

Vivian Quarry

Rainbow Slab Area

Snakes and Ladders

Outlying

Bus Stop Quarry

Dali's Hole

California

Australia

Serengeti

Never Never Land

Twll Mawr

Mordor - Lost World

Vivian Quarry

Rainbow Slab Area

Snakes and Ladders

Outlying

Cig-Arete Area

A great sport climbing area, with a better grade spread than much of the climbing hereabouts. The angular walls face roughly southeast and get plenty of sun. The rock is compact and dries quickly.

Approach (map p.235, overview p.236) - From the Rainbow Slab (p.244) walk past a small slate wall until you reach the quarryman's steps. Go up one level by a winding house. The climbing is back left.
It is also possible to approach from Nant Peris (p.235).

6 The Colour Purple . . . . . 🔲 🔲 🔲 E1 5c
This used to have a desperate start, but (for once!) rockfall has made entering the groove much easier.
FA. Martin Crook, Johnny Dawes 9.7.1986

7 Nik-Arete . . . . 🔲 🔲 🔲 6c
The left arete of the wide groove left by a rockfall.
FA. Pete Robins, Adam Wainwright, Mark Reeves 25.3.2007

8 Waiting on an Angel . . . . 🔲 E1 5b
The main corner up the rock scar past a bolt and some wires.
FA. Mark Dicken 7.12.2002

1 The Mu Mu . . . . . . 🔲 🔲 🔲 7c+
In the bay left of *Overtaken by Department C*.
FA. Adam Hocking 2005

2 Overtaken by Department 'C'
. . . . 🔲 🔲 6a
A pleasant route up a narrow seam of emerald dolerite. A couple of tricky moves past the last bulge lead to a thin slab.
FA. Ian Lloyd-Jones, John Roberts, Peter White 15.6.2008

3 Taken Over By Department 'C'
. . . . 🔲 🔲 🔲 7a
The thin wall by the graffiti that gives this route its name. Challenging climbing leads to a reasonable break. A final committing sequence gains a lower-off.
FA. Nick Harms, Gwion Hughes, 8.9.1986

4 Jaded Passion . . . . . 🔲 🔲 🔲 E5 6a
The crack is desperate and poorly protected.
FA. Mike Thomas, S.Jones 8.9.1986

5 Sleight of Hand . . . . 🔲 🔲 🔲 6c
A desperate lunge for the initial ledge is followed by an interesting groove to a lower-off.
FA. Mike Thomas 8.9.1986

9 Cig-Arete . . . . 🔲🔲🔲 **7b**

Technical contortions and powerful moves up the wall/arete may lead you to the lower-off. This has been the scene of much frustration but the sequence, when you have it, is reasonable. The route starts from the blocks on the left, stepping onto the right wall. *Photo on p.1 and p.43.*
FA. Johnny Dawes, Chris Dale 8.6.1986

12 Gwion's Groove . . . . 🔲🔲 **6a+**

A reasonable route with a few bold moves. Link the start of *Where Are My Sensible Shoes?* to the top of *Drowning Man* via a small ramp-line.
FA. Mark Dicken, Sandy Dicken 20.3.2007

13 Drowning Man . . . . 🔲🔲 **6b**

A nice route up a groove on the right of the wall. Make some steep moves to gain the groove. Wrestle up this - harder than it looks, especially if seeping after rain. At the top of the groove, gain the ramp-line that leads up and right to the final corner.
FA. Rob Deane, Perry Hawkins 15.12.1987

Descend by abseil from tree

15m

10 The Listening and Dancing

. . . . 🔲🔲🔲🔲🔲 **E5 6b**

Some fierce face climbing that is quite bold as it has no fixed gear. Climb the wall and place some cams on the left and right. Bold moves lead to the slanting bore-hole - runner at its top. (It is also possible to reach out left to the bolt on *Cig-Arete*). Move up to a wire slot before breaking out right on positive slots and crimps to reach better holds just before the top.
FA. Trevor Hodgson, Mike Thomas 15.9.1986

11 Where are my Sensible Shoes?

. . . . 🔲🔲🔲 **7b**

A great route, with a couple of difficult sections that are hard to read. Climb up and get stood up on a good ledge to clip the second bolt. Hard moves right past this lead to a sustained section past several bolts. The direct finish is the same grade, but involves a very hard pull; most people move right and traverse back left to the lower-off.
FA. Mike Thomas 17.9.1986

14 Coming up for Air. . . 🔲🔲🔲🔲 **E5 6b**

Feels like 7a+ climbing, but is a bit bold for a sport grade. Climb up to the metal spike and head onto the horn of rock and a bolt. Commit up leftwards to a good hold and another bolt. Battle up to and into the niche and exit rightwards to a lower-off.
FA. Perry Hawkins, Ed Stone 23.2.1988

15 Tongue in Situ . . . . 🔲 **E1 5c**

Climb the first bulge to an alcove. Move onto a vertical razor and swing right onto a 'tongue' - don't look too closely at how it is attached! Move onto the slab, then up and left on blocky steps to the top near a tree.
FA. Cliff Phillips 30.9.1986

16 Saved by the Whole . . . . 🔲 **HVS 5a**

Start just right of a steep chossy arete. Go up onto some ledges and traverse right for 4m. Head up the groove and then move left into a larger groove. Continue up this. Leaving it at the top provides the crux and name of the route.
FA. Cliff Phillips 29.9.1986

Bus Stop Quarry | Dali's Hole | California | Australia | Serengeti | Never Never Land | Twll Mawr | Mordor - Lost World | Vivian Quarry | Snakes and Ladders | Rainbow Slab Area | Outlying

Bus Stop Quarry
Dali's Hole
California
Australia
Serengeti
Never Never Land
Twll Mawr
Mordor - Lost World
Vivian Quarry
Rainbow Slab Area
Snakes and Ladders
Outlying

Concorde Dawn Area

The rest of the Cig-Arete level has several developed sections giving routes of variable quality. *Satisfying Frank Bruno*, *The Untouchables* and *Concorde Dawn* are all brilliant hard sport routes. The rest mostly fall into the adventurous esoteria category.

Approach (map p.235, overview p.236) - Walk under the Rainbow Slab and along to an incline leading back up left to the next level. The first routes are to the left, *Unchain My Heart* is straight ahead and the *Pigs in Space* area is to the right. It can also be approached from Nant Peris (p.235).

Approach to The Kennels - p.260

15m

---

1 **Satisfying Frank Bruno** 7b+
The pocketed wall has some powerful moves and getting the sequence correct is crucial.
FA. Paul Pritchard 7.1988

2 **Pocketeering...** 7a+
A desperate problem above the start of *Satisfying Frank Bruno*.
FA. Paul Pritchard 7.1988

3 **The Untouchables ..** 8a
This short and intense route has been highballed at f7B.
FA. Johnny Dawes 24.7.1988

4 **Unchain My Heart .....** E3 5c
A route created with 'designer danger'. Start up the slab to the right of the crack and gain the spike on the left arete. Committing moves up right from here gain good edges just below and right of a flake and a bolt. Make a heart-in-your-mouth move to gain the flake and bolt. Continue to the top.
FA. Rob Deane, Paul Johnstone, Iwan Jones 7.2.1988

5 **Envy.................** VS 4c
Start just right of *Unchain My Heart* and climb direct to a step on the right arete to join *Emerald Eyes*.
FA. Rob Deane, Iwan Jones 12.2.1988

6 **Emerald Eyes ....** VS 4b
A steady climb up the green dolerite dyke which makes up the right arete of the slab.
FA. Rob Deane (solo) 12.2.1988

7 **Pork Torque..............** E2 5c
A line through the undercut corner to the right of the arete. A tricky start gains the corner, which leads more easily to the top.
FA. Rob Deane, Perry Hawkins, Steve Howe 7.2.1988

8 **Home is Where the Heart is**
.... E5 6b
The enticing crack-line to the left of *Concorde Dawn* is sustained and technical until you can move out right to easier ground.
FA. Drew Fineron 5.2015

9 **Concorde Dawn ....** 8a
A desperate start leads to more desperate climbing to reach and pass the first break. It doesn't get any easier until a desperate finale to reach a hold on the right side of the nose.
FA. Rob Mirfin 27.8.2006

10 **Snuffler ....** VS 4c
The left arete of the *Pigs in Space* slab.
FA. R.Liddle, L.Dow, K.Turner 26.4.1993

11 **Pigs in Space ....** HVS 4c
The centre of the green dolerite tower.
FA. Lew Hardy, Chief Superintendent J.Peck, Detective Constable G.Briggs 3.6.1986

12 **Is Marilyn Monroe Dead? .....** HVS 5b
The right arete of the slab.
FA. R.Liddle, L.Dow, K.Turner 26.4.1993

The next two routes are actually on the German Schoolgirl Level, but can only be reached from below.

13 **Buxton The Blue Cat.........** VS 5b
The left arete of the slab up and right of *Pigs in Space*.
FA. R.Liddle, L.Dow, K.Turner 26.4.1993

14 **Nothing...................** VS 4c
The insignificant slab up the scree facing Nant Peris.
FA. R.Liddle, L.Dow, K.Turner 26.4.1993

Bus Stop Quarry | Dali's Hole | California | Australia | Serengeti | Never Never Land | Twll Mawr | Mordor - Lost World | Vivian Quarry | Snakes and Ladders | Rainbow Slab Area | Outlying

The Dark Half Area
p.270

Fruity Pear Slab
p.267

The Kennels

Concorde Dawn Area
p.258

*Pigs in Space
- p.259*

Incline to Cig-Arete level

15m

① ② ③

The Kennels

This big cube of rock is actually on the German Schoolgirl Level but is best approached from the Cig-Arete Level below. It has three excellent hard sport routes.

Approach (map p.235, overview p.236) - From the top of the incline leading to the Cig-Arete level, turn right and into the second bay about 30m away below the *Pigs In Space* tower. Head up the scree, turn left, and walk along the level to the routes.

❶ Rowan 7c
The right-facing groove, directly above the winding house on the level below.
FA. Pete Robins, Ben Bransby 18.4.2007

❷ The New Slatesman
. . . . 8b
The arete right of *Rowan*. *Photo opposite.*
FA. Pete Robins 25.2.2008

❸ Doggy-Style 7c
The steep wall. Climb an immaculate holdless corner to a bivy-ledge, then the bouldery headwall above.
FA. Pete Robins 6.6.2007

Bus Stop Quarry
Dali's Hole
California
Australia
Serengeti
Never Never Land
Twll Mawr
Mordor - Lost World
Vivian Quarry
Rainbow Slab Area
Snakes and Ladders
Outlying

James McHaffie getting close to making the first ascent of *The New Slatesman* (8b) - *opposite*. This was the scene of a climb-off between James McHaffie and Pete Robins. On this occasion it was won by Pete, who attributed his victory to bouldering. It apparently has two 7a moves - the one to hang the hold where Caff's right hand is in this picture is possibly the hardest individual move in the quarries.

Terry's Wall

This loose wall has little to recommend it (apart from giving a nice view of the Rainbow Slab).
Approach (map p.235, overview p.236) - From the buildings mentioned in the main Rainbow Slab approach, head up one level to large left-hand bend. Terry's Wall is below the bend and gained by abseiling off a fence post and a block. The best place to do this is near the lower end of the wall, down the side of a pipe that disappears over the edge.

1 Skinning the Ladder . . . . . . HVS 5a
A line near the base of the abseil, a little to the right of the iron spikes. Ascend the loose wall, weaving in and out of spikes which are used for protection only. Move out left at the top.
FA. Mark Boniface, A.Shaw 17.3.1987

2 Big Bendy Buddha . . . . VS 4c
Start 5m left of the sharp corner at the top of the face. Ascend the cracks for 12m and then take the traverse line right into the base of the sharp corner. Finish up this.
FA. A,Whittall 17.8.1986

3 Lesser Mortals . . . . HVS 5a
A bold offering. Climb direct to the corner that *Big Bendy Buddha* finishes up.
FA. Sid Siddiqui, Iwan Jones, P.Stone 17.8.1986

4 Vertigo . . . . VS 4c
The best route here is a serious lead that requires a steady head. Climb the green dolerite pillar on jugs.
FA. Terry Taylor 26.4.1986

5 Run for Fun . . . . VS 4c
Start 3m right of *Vertigo* and climb the right side of the pillar.
FA. Terry Taylor 23.5.1986

6 Contextual Stiffy E3 6a
An okay route. Start at the top of the pile of slate. Follow the diagonal crack to the flake. Step left across the wall to the bolts. Follow a thin groove to the top.
FA. Jay Hartford 14.5.2017

7 Stacked Deck E3 6a
Start much further right towards the back of the bay. Climb large flakes for 5 metres before a short traverse right joins the base of a second crack. Follow this to the lower-off. A bolder variation **(E1 5a)** continues up and left before the traverse to the lower-off.
FA. Jay Hartford 14.5.2017

Many routes have been climbed between Terry's Wall and The German Schoolgirl Area. The rock is still actively falling down so best to avoid **Torrents of Spring, Cornucopia, Sprint for Print, Senile Delinquent, Bring out the Gimp** *and* **Sunk Without a Trace.**

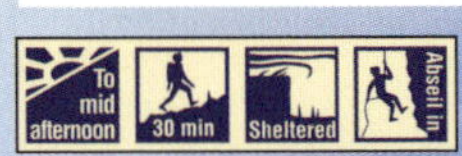

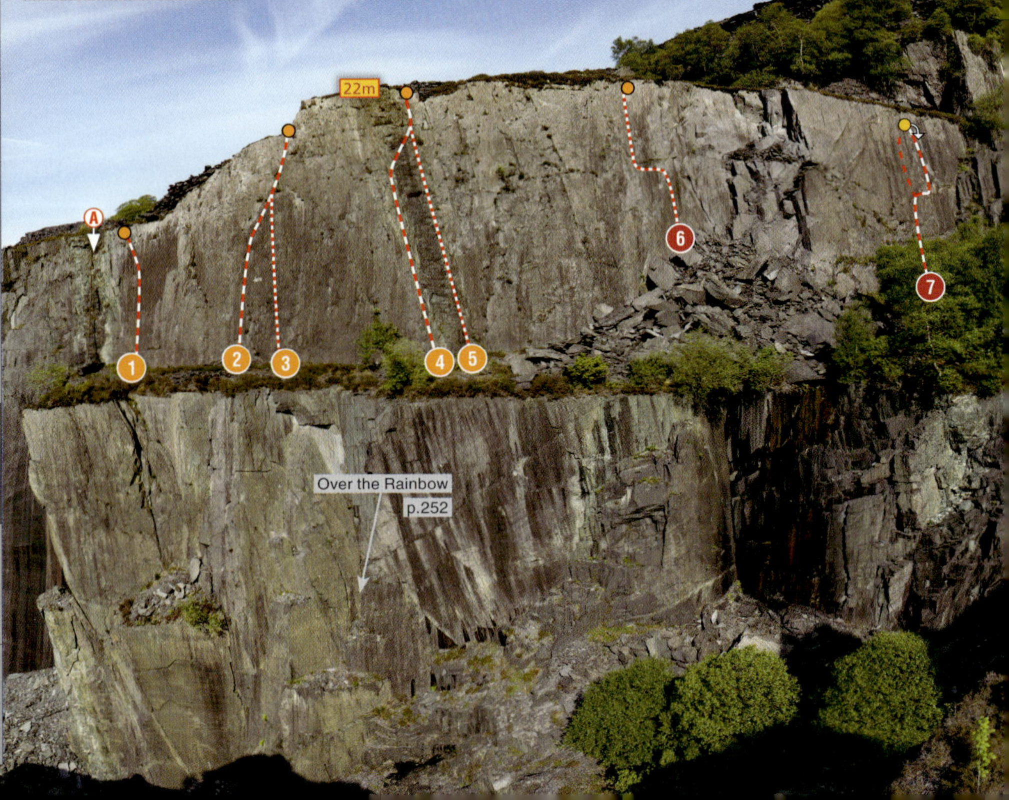

Bus Stop Quarry

Dali's Hole

California

Australia

Serengeti

Never Never Land

Twll Mawr

Mordor - Lost World

Vivian Quarry

Rainbow Slab Area

Snakes and Ladders

Outlying

Steve Parry on the immaculate corner of *The German Schoolgirl* (E2 5c) - *p.265* - on an upper level of the Rainbow Slab Area. Named after the first ascensionist caught sight of a group of German school kids that were wandering around the quarries that day.

German Schoolgirl Area

An isolated prow with a couple of slate classics and some good sport routes. It offers sun or shade on either side.

Approach (map p.235, overview p.236) - From the buildings described on the main approach, follow the path up to the first large turn left. Cross the fence and follow a path on the right that leads round to a promontory, with a large block and bolt belay. Abseil off here to access the routes.

Evening | 35 min | Sheltered | Abseil in

20m

A

Original start

1

2

Bus Stop Quarry | Dali's Hole | California | Australia | Serengeti | Never Never Land | Twll Mawr | Mordor - Lost World | Vivian Quarry | Rainbow Slab Area | Snakes and Ladders | Outlying

20m

Bus Stop Quarry
Dali's Hole
California
Australia
Serengeti
Never Never Land
Twll Mawr
Mordor - Lost World
Vivian Quarry
Rainbow Slab Area
Snakes and Ladders
Outlying

❶ The Dark Destroyer . 🔲 🪨 💪 ☐ **7c+**
The original start is now defunct after a hold came off, or at least it is much harder! Instead, start up the crack of *The Mau Mau*. Where this route steps right into the right-hand crack, carry on up the left crack for a few moves and make a bold step left to reach a good hold and the bolts. Thin and powerful climbing leads up to the lower-off.
FA. Mark Pretty 13.4.1991

❷ The Mau Mau . . . . . 🔲 🪨 🔷 ☐ **E4 6a**
Seriously strenuous. Start at the dogleg crack. The crack is easy to the ledge at 10m, after which it is much harder and sustained. Eventually you are forced out onto the wall on the left.
FA. Paul Williams 20.5.1986

❸ Ari Hol Hi . . . . 🔲 ☐ **E4 6a**
A worthwhile but serious outing. Start on the front of the pillar. Climb up to the huge ledge and follow a crack to a large block on the left. Step right to a groove and climb this to a ledge on the left. Swing up right to a triangular ledge. Move up to a sloping ledge with difficulty and then walk off left to finish.
FA. Crispin Waddy, D.Crilley 6.1987

❹ Rock Dancer's Daughter 🔲 🦁 ☐ **7a+**
The innocuous looking groove just left of the arete has its awkward moments.
FA. Mark Delafield, Colin Goodey, Del Smith 6.1991

❺ Silver Shadow . . . . 🔲 🦁 ☐ **E4 6a**
The arete is challenging but can be protected by clipping some extra bolts out left.
FA. Richie Brookes, M.Murray 3.3.1987

❻ True Clip . . . . . . 🔲 🪨 🦁 ☐ **7b+**
A desperately thin wall climb up the line of bolts to the left of *German Schoolgirl*.
FA. Nick Harms 19.9.1988

❼ German Schoolgirl . . . . . 🔲 🦁 ☐ **E2 5c**
The immaculate corner has a hard start to get to a ledge on the right at about 5m. The route eases above. *Photo on p.263.*
FA. Martin Crook, Nick Walton 18.8.1984

❽ Spong . . . . 🔲 🦁 🦁 ☐ **7c+**
An amazing route, with either a very hard high step or a dyno between good holds.
FA. Nick Dixon 4.1989

L'Allumette Area

The section to the right of the German Schoolgirl Area has several routes: the tricky groove of *L'Allumette* is the best. It faces southwest, gets afternoon sun and is relatively sheltered.

Approach (map p.235, overview p.236) - From the German Schoolgirl Area, head right along the base of the wall to a groove above a bad step.

1 Werp . . . . HVS 5a

The right-to-left line up the low-angled slab.

2 Monster Hamburger Eats the Alien Baby

. . . . 6c

Start up the ramp as for *Werp*, then take the groove up the face to reach a final groove.

FA. Nick Harms, Paul Barbier 9.1988

3 The Coming of Age E4 6a

Start at the dolerite dyke to the left of the bad step. Climb a thin crack in the right side of the tower. It looks like it has been affected by rockfall over the years.

FA. Paul Jenkinson, Nick Harms 20.10.1988

4 L'Allumette 7a

A great test for the lover of the weird and enigmatic. From the bolt belay enter the groove, then attempt to leave it to a ledge.

FA. Johnny Dawes, Paul Pritchard 7.1.1987

5 Brain Death E2 5a

The right-to-left rising ramp-line. The potential of a factor two fall should only add to the appeal. Head up past a spike to the *L'Allumette* lower-off.

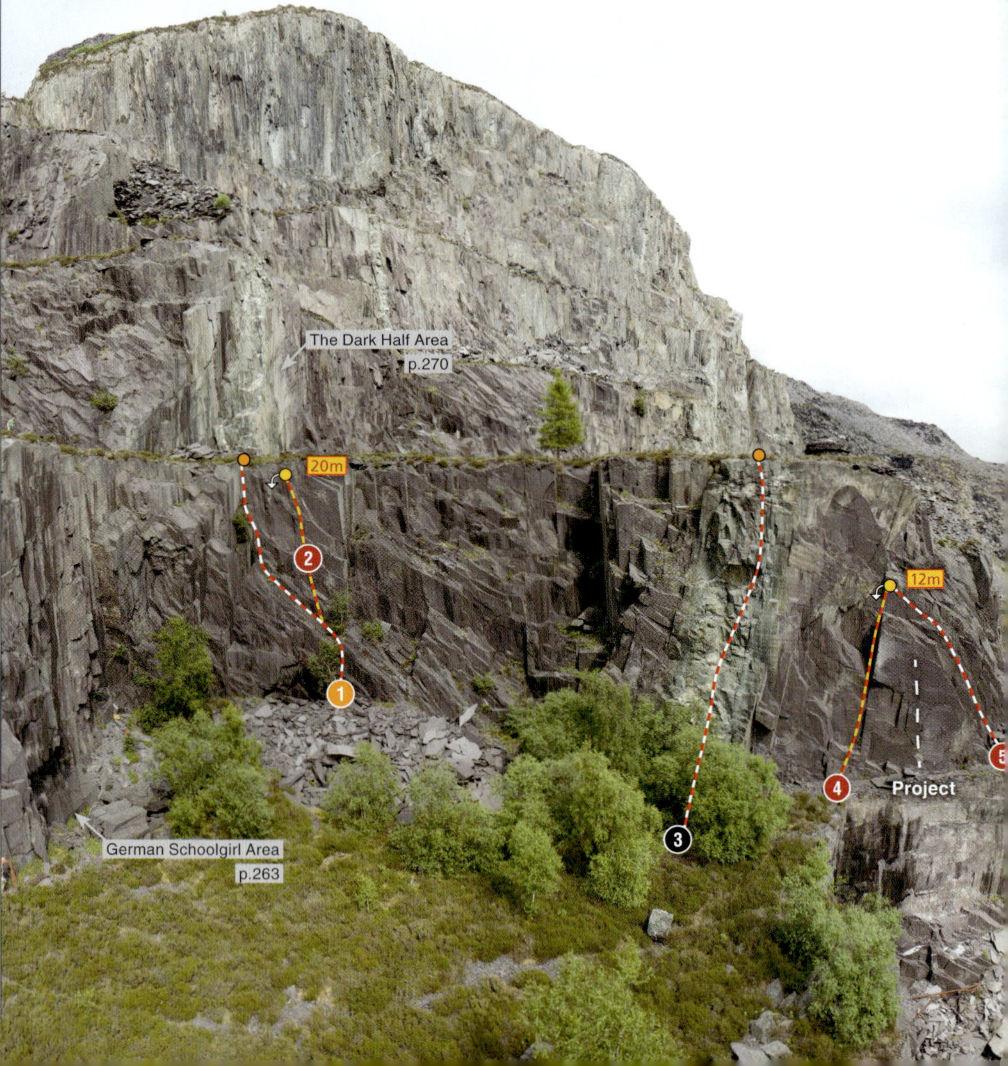

The Dark Half Area
p.270

German Schoolgirl Area
p.263

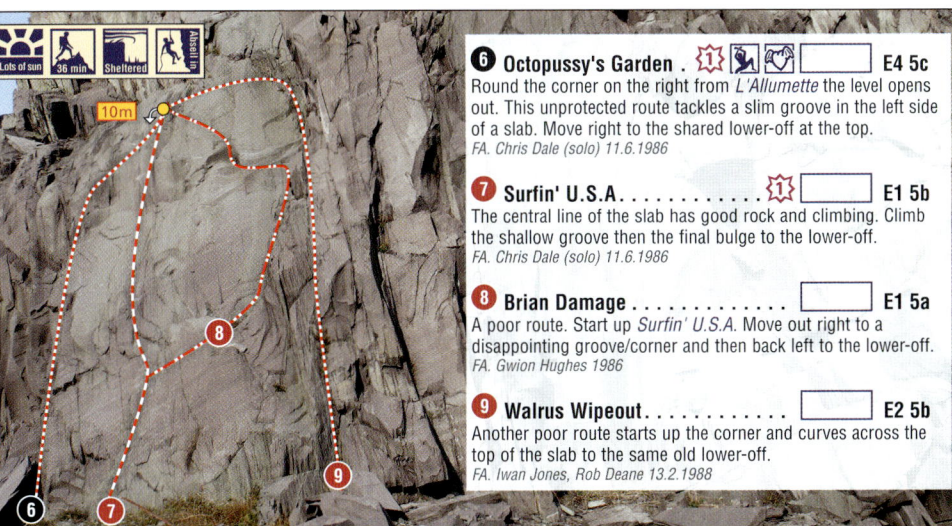

6 Octopussy's Garden . E4 5c
Round the corner on the right from *L'Allumette* the level opens out. This unprotected route tackles a slim groove in the left side of a slab. Move right to the shared lower-off at the top.
FA. Chris Dale (solo) 11.6.1986

7 Surfin' U.S.A. E1 5b
The central line of the slab has good rock and climbing. Climb the shallow groove then the final bulge to the lower-off.
FA. Chris Dale (solo) 11.6.1986

8 Brian Damage E1 5a
A poor route. Start up Surfin' U.S.A. Move out right to a disappointing groove/corner and then back left to the lower-off.
FA. Gwion Hughes 1986

9 Walrus Wipeout E2 5b
Another poor route starts up the corner and curves across the top of the slab to the same old lower-off.
FA. Iwan Jones, Rob Deane 13.2.1988

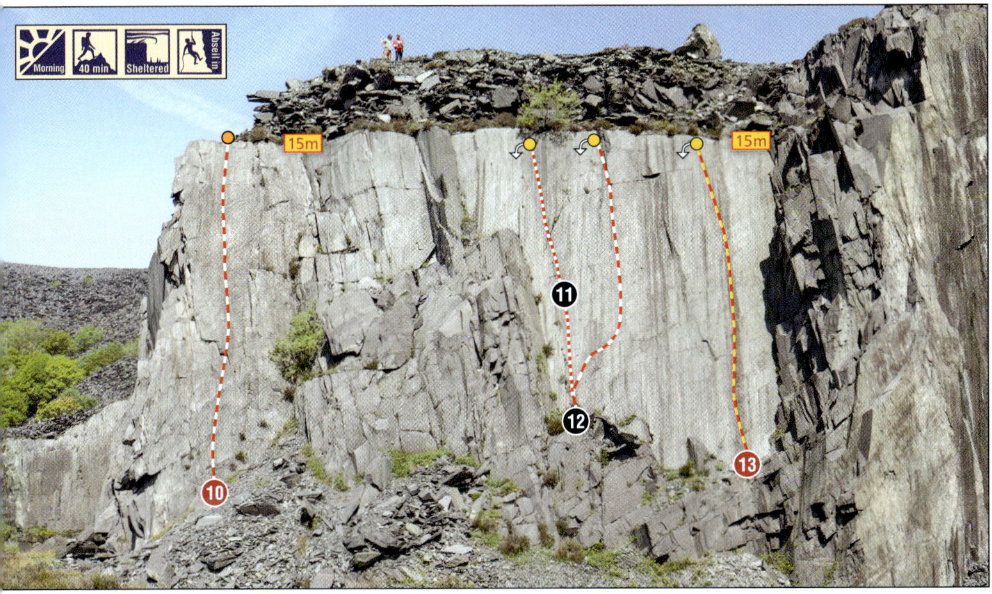

Fruity Pear Slab
The far end of the level, facing Llanberis Pass.

10 Scratching the Beagle E1 5b
Climb the thin crack in the left-hand slab.
FA. Rob Deane, Perry Hawkins 30.9.1987

11 A Mere Trifle E6 6b
Head up the thin crack just left of the bore-hole to a peg. Climb up to a vague groove, past a microwire placement. Another thin crack leads to the bolt belay and lower-off - phew!
FA. Nick Harms, Mo Anthoine 18.9.1988

12 Fruity Pear in a Veg Shop Romp E6 6b
Climb rightwards into a groove. A poor stacked (?) peg in the shallow shot-hole protects the crux that follows. Then head straight up to a scary finish.
FA. Nick Dixon, Martin Crook 14.7.1986

13 Fruity Pear Gets Just Deserts 7a+
Start beneath the line of bolts. Pass the first to a rest, climb up to the second, then step left and up to the lower-off.
FA. Nick Harms, Mo Anthoine 18.9.1988

Bus Stop Quarry | Dali's Hole | California | Australia | Serengeti | Never Never Land | Twll Mawr | Mordor - Lost World | Vivian Quarry | Snakes and Ladders | Rainbow Slab Area | Outlying

Manatese Area

This level is used to access German Schoolgirl level, although it sees much less attention. It has several good hard routes, including the trad line of *Manatese*.

Approach (map p.235, overview p.236) - From the buildings mentioned in the main Rainbow Slab approach, head up one level to large left-hand bend. Cross the fence and follow a path on the right that leads round. The first route is almost immediately on the left.

1 Tumbling Left E1 5b
The first slab encountered on the approach. Climb the left line past two bolts to a lower-off.

2 Walls Come Tumbling Down . E1 5b
Climb the right-hand line on the slab past two bolts to a lower-off.
FA. Chris Jex, Ian Lloyd-Jones 11.5.1991

❸ Manatese . . . .  **E4 6a**
The dogleg crack up the steep wall has become a lot harder since the mid-way pillar fell down, but it is now a better route. Move leftwards up the crack to where it bends. Pull straight into the upper crack. Climb this to its end, then the steep wall to the lower-off.
FA. Rich Lyon, Al Wells, Mike Cluer 16.5.1986

❹ The Master Craftsman (Il Miglior Fabbro) .
. . . . **7c+**
Fairly intense climbing although only short.
FA. Mark Katz 19.1.2000

❺ Womaninstress **E2 6b**
A thin crack leads to a ledge at 4m. After this, follow ledges over choss to the top.

❻ God Betweens Money **E4 6a**
Just around the corner from the *Manatese* wall is a barrel-shaped slab. Climb this to a lower-off
FA. Allen Williams (solo) 14.7.1986

The next routes are further right on some tiered slabs.

❼ Occam's Razor **E1 5b**
Start opposite *God Betweens Money*, by a pyramidal boulder. Move up to a rounded arete and climb past a bolt onto an easy-angled slab. Scamper up the slab to the top - no more runners.

❽ Pit and the Pendulum . . . . **HVS 5a**
Climb easy-angled terrain aiming for the white groove at the top above the hidden pit.
FA. Iwan Jones, T.Mitchell 4.1988

❾ Snowdon Lady . . . . **HS**
Start below and left of a small oak. Go up to the left of a tree, then diagonally left to the top. Named after the strange portrait of the lady that can be seen by some on the hillside opposite this wall. Turn round.... can you see her? Try looking above a lone tree by the wall that runs across the slope.
FA. Iwan Jones (solo) 7.2.1986

❿ Lone Pine . . . . **HS**
Climb to the right of the oak tree trending left to a steep finale.
FA. Iwan Jones (solo) 7.2.1986

⓫ Heaven Steps . . . . **VS 5a**
Follow *Lone Pine* until a few metres past the tree. Move out right to the arete and tackle the short fist crack.

Walk off left

30m

15m

⑥ ⑦ ⑧ ⑨ ⑩ ⑪

Bus Stop Quarry
Dali's Hole
California
Australia
Serengeti
Never Never Land
Twll Mawr
Mordor - Lost World
Vivian Quarry
Rainbow Slab Area
Snakes and Ladders
Outlying

The Dark Half Area

Further along the level is a clean triangular wall with the hard slate classics of *The Dark Half* and *Heatseeker*.
Approach (map p.235, overview p.236) - From the buildings mentioned in the main Rainbow Slab approach, head up one level to large left-hand bend. Cross the fence and follow a path on the right that leads round. The first route is almost immediately on the left.

❶ Green Ernie E5 6a
Climb up to the large ledge. Continue close to the corner avoiding the holds and the bolt on the right.
FA. Martin Barnicott 27.5.1986

❷ Paradise Lost Indirect E2 5c
A great route up the left arete of *The Dark Half* buttress. Gain the original route from the left, avoiding the really hard moves - a bit of gear is required to reach the first bolt.
FA. Rick Newcombe, Harold Walmsley, Paul Bolger 11.1989

❸ Paradise Lost Direct . . . 6c+
A harder start past old bolts on suspect rock.
FA. Chris Davies 13.4.1991

❹ Paradise Lost 6c
Start to the right of the arete and trend leftwards to the arete. The bolts are on the right-hand side, but most of the climbing takes place on the left. Sustained climbing past another two bolts leads to the lower-off.
FA. Nick Harms, S.Young 11.1989

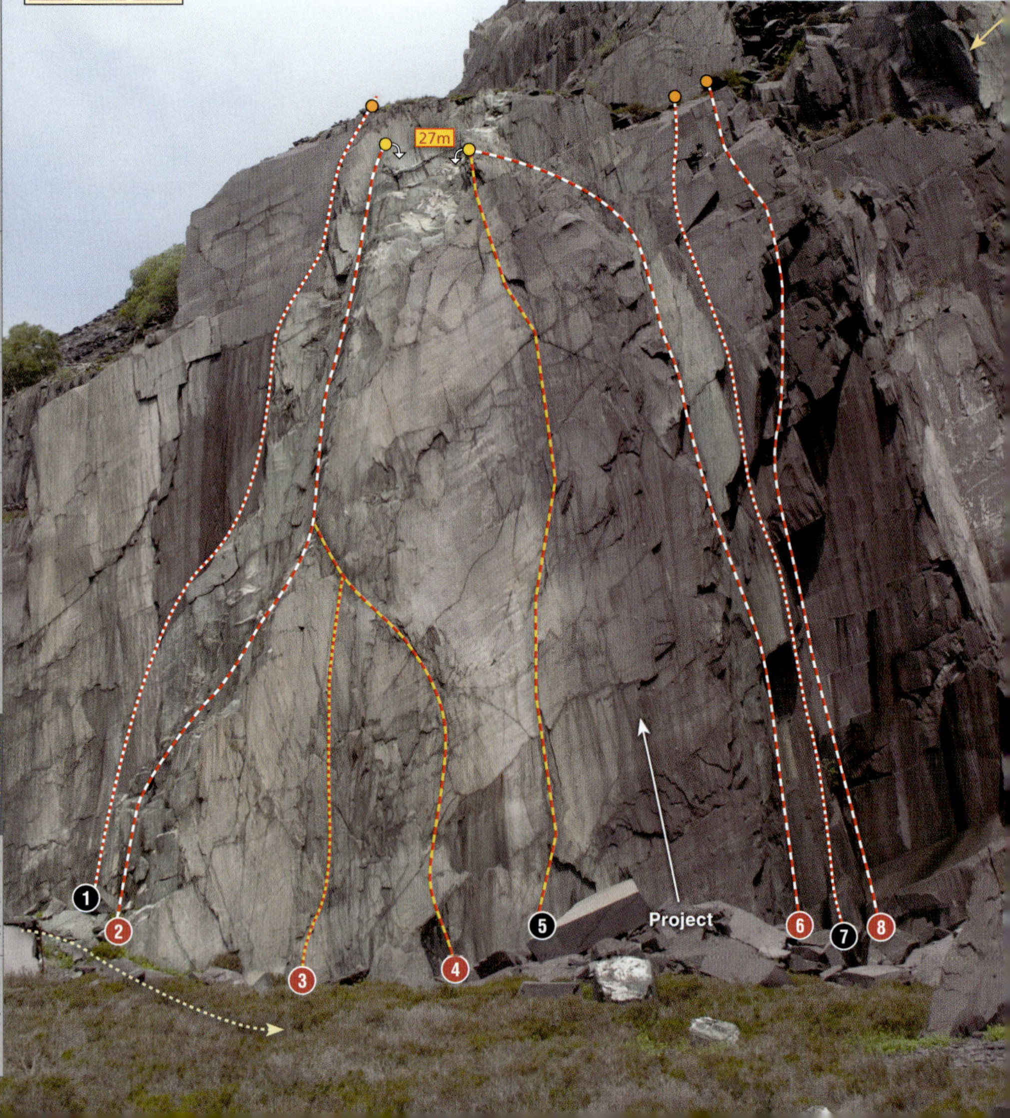

27m

Project

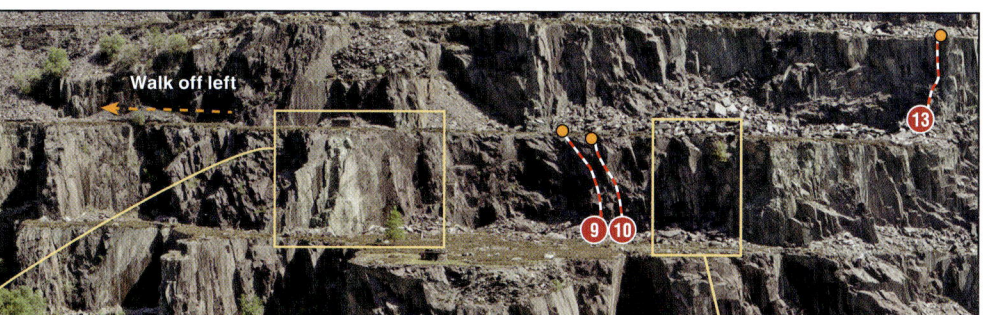
5 The Dark Half 8a
One of the most popular hard routes in the quarries, and rightly so. The correct sequence of shapes, grunts and ferocious pulls will lead you to the lower-off.
FA. Nick Harms 27.11.1990

There is a project line just to the right of The Dark Half - it is more than likely much harder than 8a!

6 Angel on Fire E2 5c
A hidden gem. Climb the groove in the arete, following it up and left at the top to *The Dark Half* belay.
FA. Paul Williams, Johnny Dawes 5.6.1986

7 Celestial Inferno E4 6a
The groove just right of *Angel on Fire* has a small roof to negotiate at half-height. Good jams appear after the roof. Exit up and right to belay on a old building.
FA. Paul Williams, Martin Barnicott 6.6.1986

8 Chariots of Fire E2 5c
The next groove right is steep and often damp. Head up the groove and make alarming moves right over a seemingly detached block to gain a chimney. Move up the steep crack above to reach the final obstacle. Negotiate the overhang and climb up and left to belay on the old building.
FA. Joe Brown, D.Jones 26.6.1989

9 The Grey Slab E1 5b
50m right of *Angel on Fire* is a slanting gangway. Start below the top of gangway. Move up then right to get to the base of the gangway, then leftwards up this to the top.
FA. Anita Grey, Chris Dale 5.1987

10 Captain Black and the Mysterons
. . . . E2 5b
Start 3m right of *The Grey Slab*, Climb up the shattered crack to the ramp that cross *The Grey Slab* low down. From here climb directly to the top.
FA. Iwan Jones, Steve Howe 1988

11 Heatseeker 7c
The bolted arete is amazing.
FA. Perry Hawkins 13.4.1988

12 Y Rybelwr E4 6a
Climb a groove to a peg, go left to a second groove (peg), then left to the main groove. Four bolts and gear lead up to the top.
FA. Ian Lloyd-Jones 11.5.1991

The next level up has one lonely route. At the far end is an attractive looking bow-shaped off-width crack. Don't be taken in by its good looks.

13 667 Neighbour of the Beast
. . . . E3 5c
The off-width bow-shaped crack. It turns out not to be that attractive to climb and the belayer should avoid belaying at the base of the route. Probably the best quote from one of the first ascent team was, "To be honest I am surprised the route is still here!"
FA. Will Perrin, Mark Reeves 6.6.2000

Bus Stop Quarry
Dali's Hole
California
Australia
Serengeti
Never Never Land
Twll Mawr
Mordor - Lost World
Vivian Quarry
Rainbow Slab Area
Snakes and Ladders
Outlying

Plateau Slab

This outlying slab has been developed with sport routes at friendly grades. The routes have a bit of a 'done one, done 'em all' feel about them, but don't let that put you off. It is situated on the Llanberis Pass side of a tall tower known as the Trango Tower, and is directly above some of the power station buildings - access is a bit sensitive.

Approach (map p.235) - The wall can be approached from the main areas by walking right from the Rainbow Slab, past the bottom of *Gerbil Abuse* and on through a gate. Head up the track to the plateau and the slab is on the tower on the right, facing up Llanberis Pass.

It is more usual to approach from Nant Peris. Park in the lay-by just before Nant Peris with a slate display saying 'NANT PERIS'. Walk up the road 50m toward the village, then turn left onto a footpath that leads along a tarmac road and across the end of the lake. Turn left along the lake through a gate and head up the main track through the quarry. At the second level, a plateau leads out left from the track by a long gate. Head across this to where the slab is facing you on the left.

🚫 **Access -** The First Hydro power station is directly below the back of the Plateau Slab and climbing is banned on the rest of the tower. Only careful negotiation let climbers develop the limited climbing on this slab. Please keep to the described routes and refrain from making new developments.

1 🔵 **1981** . . . . VS 5a
Left of the Plateau Slab is a clean finger-crack that has good gear and a couple of nice moves. Belay above it, then walk right to gain one of the lower-offs on the slab.
FA. Claire Mason, D.Bright 19.5.2012

2 🔵 **Colin's Arete** 4c
Start just on the left arete.
FA. Colin Goodey 8.2012

3 🔵 **Circus Skills** 6a
Climb a zig-zagging line on the left side of the slab.
FA. Tesni Lloyd-Jones, Celt Lloyd-Jones 5.5.2012

4 🔵 **Monster Munch** . . . . 6c+
The thin seam.
FA. Ian Lloyd-Jones, Ray Wood, Kieran Forrest 13.5.2012

5 🔵 **White Tiger** 6a
The second thin seam.
FA. Celt Lloyd-Jones, Ian Lloyd-Jones 5.5.2012

6 🔵 **Slate Ninja** 6a
A line of five Petzl bolts.
FA. Celt Lloyd-Jones, Ian Lloyd-Jones 5.5.2012

7 🔵 **Celtic Warrior** . . . . 6a+
The next line of weakness.
FA. Celt Lloyd-Jones, Tesni Lloyd-Jones 5.5.2012

8 🔵 **Magic Carpet** 5a
The line left of the groove.
FA. Celt Lloyd-Jones, Tesni Lloyd-Jones 5.5.2012

9 🔵 **Carpe Diem** 5c
The groove shares a lower-off with *Teenage Dreams*.
FA. Colin Goodey 8.2012

10 🔵 **Teenage Dreams** 6b
Climb to the highest point on the slab.
FA. Tesni Lloyd-Jones, Kieran Forrest 13.5.2012

11 🔵 **Plateau Corner** 5c
The corner is much better than it looks.
FA. Colin Goodey 8.2012

12 🔵 **Pick and Mix** 6a
The ubiquitous girdle does manage a lot of climbing by borrowing bolts on other routes. Start up *Circus Skills* and finish on the *Teenage Dreams* lower-off.

15m

Peppermint Tower

Another attraction in this remote area is the Peppermint Tower, which has a few good esoteric routes: *Jugs Mawr* is a fantastic steep trad route, unlike anything on slate; *Honorary Limestone* is a top quality sport route.

Approach (map p.235) - The wall can be approached from the main areas by walking right from the Rainbow Slab, past the bottom of *Gerbil Abuse* and on through a gate. Head up the track to the plateau and the slab is on the tower on the right, facing up Llanberis Pass.

It is more usual to approach from Nant Peris. Park in the lay-by just before Nant Peris with a slate display saying 'NANT PERIS'. Walk up the road for 30m toward the village, then turn left onto a footpath that leads along a tarmac road and across the end of the lake. Turn left along the lake through a gate and head up the main track through the quarry. At the second level a plateau leads out left from the track by a long gate. Head across the plateau and the Peppermint Tower is over on the right.

Peppermint Tower

From Plateau Slab

❶ Circles are Sound **E5 6b**
This is the arete on the actual tower facing the Rainbow Slab. Climb the right side of the arete for 8m without any gear. Move left around the arete and across the slab beneath an overlap to a corner system in the arete. It is best to abseil off the *El Juego Grande* lower-off just below the summit.
FA. Chris Dale (solo) 8.6.1986

❷ Greedy Girls . . . . **HVS 4c**
The scrappy green dolerite face. Start 5m left of the overhanging nose. Climb up and traverse rightwards over the top of the nose. From here, follow the arete with care to the top.
FA. Chris Dale (solo) 16.4.1986

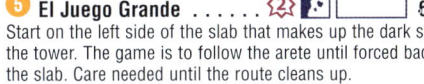
3 The Descent . . . . VDiff
Start to the left of *Jugs Bach* and climb up to the arete. Turn right and continue near the crest until over the top of the lower-off on *Jugs Bach*, then turn left again to reach the summit. From here you can lower off *El Juego Grande*.

4 Jugs Bach 5b
The line of bolts opposite *Jugs Mawr* on the Peppermint Tower. Follow the bolts to a ledge. The move to the next bolt is scary. Continue to a steep finale and a lower-off. Take care when pulling ropes since rocks can be dislodged from the ledges. *Photo on p.276.*
FA. Mark Reeves, Simon Lake 20.4.2018

5 El Juego Grande 6a
Start on the left side of the slab that makes up the dark side of the tower. The game is to follow the arete until forced back onto the slab. Care needed until the route cleans up.
FA. Mark Reeves, Simon Lake 20.4.2018

6 Jugs Mawr E3 5c
Just behind the tower is a little hidden gulch. Climb the steep dolerite dykes on big holds past a couple of pegs. These can be backed-up with good gear. There is a single-bolt lower-off. Alternatively, traverse to the lower-off on *Honorary Limestone*.
FA. Geoff Turner, Al Wells, James Wilson 18.6.1988

7 Honorary Limestone . . 7a
A good route. Climb up past five bolts to a groove. At its top, don't head direct - traverse left along a break to a ledge shared with *Jugs Mawr* and then come back right to clip the bolt. The remainder of the route is technical but not desperate.
FA. Ian Lloyd-Jones 22.3.2012

8 Midnight Arete . . . . . 7a+
The arete left of *Midnight Drives* is bolted in an old-school fashion. Start up the groove. Move out to the arete a long way below the first bolt. The climbing to get there is easy-ish - passing it is the crux. More run-out easy climbing reaches the crimpy and sustained headwall, then on to the lower-off.

9 Midnight Drives E2 5b
Climb the slab between the two aretes to a small ledge. Move into the left corner and thrutch to the top.
FA. J.Beasant 16.9.1988

10 Chinook Arete 7a
The right-angled arete to the right of *Midnight Drives*. If you enjoyed *G'Day Arete* you will probably enjoy this one - some cool moves.
FA. Ian Lloyd-Jones 22.3.2012

11 Song of the Minerals . . 7b
The blunt arete of the tower is thin.
FA. Paul Barker 1999

12 Come Inside . . . 5.9
No climbing from 1 February to 31 July each year owing to possible nesting birds. A hideous off-width - huge cams, big-bros and car jacks may be required, although there are some chockstones which may be home to a nesting chough. In strong winds rock can be blown into the slot, funnelling down on you from above - now that is hard rain!
FA. Tim Badcock, Steve Sinfield 1999

13 Strawberry Jam E2 5c
Right of *Come Inside* is another large crack. The initial 'well-tested' block bars the way.
FA. Dan Ely, Dan Hale 7.7.2012

14 "HELP!" (it's raining jugs) E4 5c
Climb *Strawberry Jam* past the dangerous block and place the last of your protection. Then head right up the narrow ramp, running it out to the top past much loose rock which will rain down on your belayer.
FA. Dan Ely, Dan Hale 7.7.2012

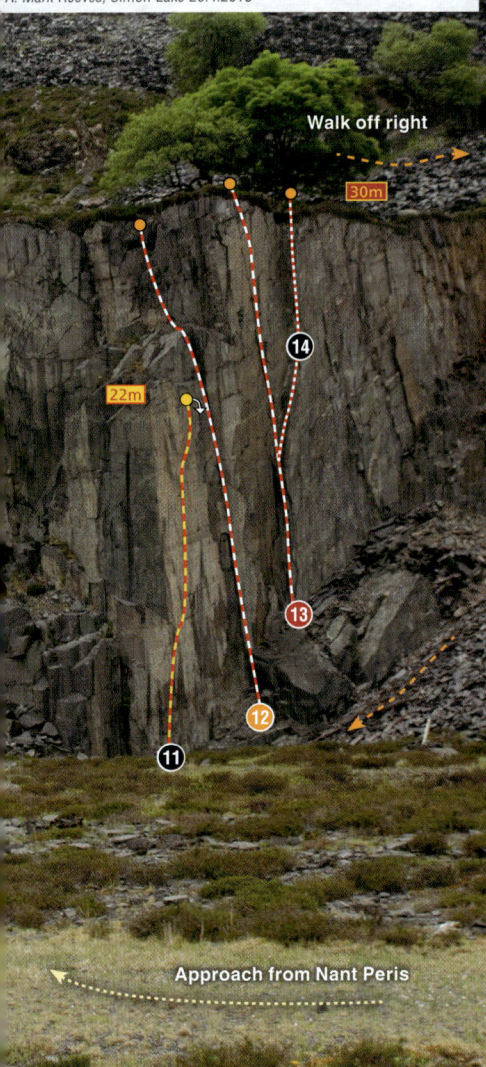

Walk off right

30m

22m

14

13

12

11

Approach from Nant Peris

Bus Stop Quarry · Dali's Hole · California · Australia · Serengeti · Never Never Land · Twll Mawr · Mordor - Lost World · Vivian Quarry · Rainbow Slab Area · Snakes and Ladders · Outlying

Bus Stop Quarry

Dali's Hole

California

Australia

Serengeti

Never Never Land

Twll Mawr

Mordor - Lost World

Vivian Quarry

Rainbow Slab Area

Snakes and Ladders

Outlying

Simon Lake on the second ascent of *Jugs Bach* (5c) - *p.275* - a
fine addition to the Peppermint Tower. Photo: Mike Hutton
The Peppermint Tower had somehow avoided development
despite the obvious dolerite tower on its east face. Both new
bolted routes on the tower are really good and well worth a
look if you have climbed on the Plateau Slab. They are also two
of the latest additions to the quarries, showing that the eagle-
eyed can still find new routes of quality at reasonable grades.

Bus Stop Quarry

Dali's Hole

California

Australia

Serengeti

Never Never Land

Twll Mawr

Mordor - Lost World

Vivian Quarry

Rainbow Slab Area

Snakes and Ladders

Outlying

Bus Stop Quarry

Dali's Hole

California

Australia

Serengeti

Never Never Land

Twll Mawr

Mordor - Lost World

Vivian Quarry

Rainbow Slab Area: Snakes and Ladders

Outlying

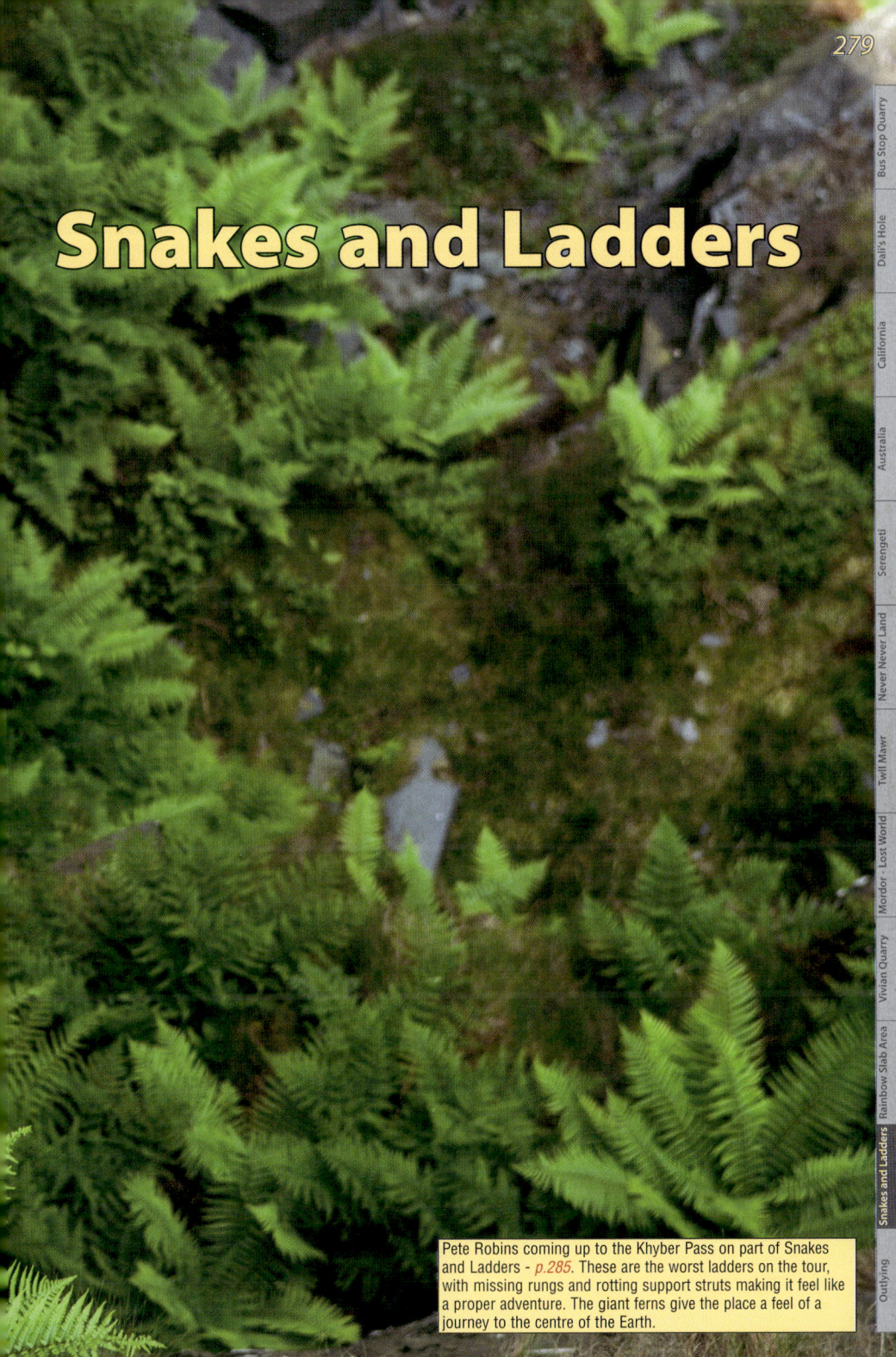

Snakes and Ladders

Bus Stop Quarry

Dali's Hole

California

Australia

Serengeti

Never Never Land

Twll Mawr

Mordor - Lost World

Vivian Quarry

Rainbow Slab Area

Snakes and Ladders

Outlying

Pete Robins coming up to the Khyber Pass on part of Snakes and Ladders - *p.285*. These are the worst ladders on the tour, with missing rungs and rotting support struts making it feel like a proper adventure. The giant ferns give the place a feel of a journey to the centre of the Earth.

Snakes and Ladders is the name given to a popular tour of the quarries through tunnels and up and down ladders, taking in three of the main areas. It is similar to a via ferrata, although not one that has been prepared as such. There is some modern fixed gear to help with abseils and protect some sections, but most of the metalwork has been abandoned for at least the last 60 years and is in a rickety state.

The tour has evolved over the years. It started with climbers exploring the myriad of tunnels and holes in search of new routes and ways between the quarries, but it is only in recent years that Snakes and Ladders has become 'a thing'.

This section contains a description to follow a specific route however, if you have extra time, it is worth exploring the many tunnels and levels to see where they take you. It is a great way to get a feel for what it was like to work in these great quarries and experience some of the more remote and serene places at the same time.

Safety

A word of caution. This is a decaying industrial landscape and the places you go have not been prepared for via ferrata use with lanyards and safety cables. Some of the ladders are very old and rickety and it is worth protecting yourself accordingly for the event that something might give way on you. Rockfalls in the remote areas of the quarry are not uncommon, so don't linger under the big loose faces. There are also major rockfalls from time to time, but these tend to only be in very rough weather. A major collapse in The Lost World has covered the base with huge blocks in recent years.

Climbing Level

With these safety warnings in mind, basic rock climbing knowledge, and the ability to climb and abseil are required for the tour. It is advised that at least one member of the party is an experienced climber. You can skip the first section in California which is around HVS 5a. For more experienced climbers the tour is possible as a wet weather day, where you can include the California section if you are up to it, or do it in reverse with a section of abseiling to avoid the difficult climbing.

Gear

Snakes and Ladders requires nothing more than you would find on a normal rack: Harness, helmet, belay device, 60m rope, 4 slings and at least one screwgate for each person. A few quickdraws and a headtorch are advisable for some of the longer tunnels.

Approach

The upper quarries are best approached from Deiniolen and Dinorwig via the A4244, which connects Llanberis to the coast road. Turn off the A4244 to Deiniolen and on through Dinorwig to parking at the road end near Bus Stop Quarry. Head along the main track until it opens out by a large cutting shed on the left, then continue to a kissing gate by a left bend in the track. Pass through here and follow the main track towards a large incline. Where the track bends right, hop over the gate in front of you and follow the path up and right for one level - Dali's Hole is down and to your right. Traverse around to the opposite side of Dali's Hole and follow a small track back down into the hole to a tunnel on the left. This is the entrance to California.

Bus Stop Quarry
Dali's Hole
California
Australia
Serengeti
Never Never Land
Twll Mawr
Mordor - Lost World
Vivian Quarry
Rainbow Slab Area
Snakes and Ladders
Outlying

200m

N

Approach missing California section

The Salt Pans
p.98

The Rognon
p.88

Fruitbat Level
p.104

East Face
p.120

*Snakes and Ladders
- Australia - p.282*

Australia
Col

Stairs of
Cirith Ungol

Great
Bores
Tunnel

Pen Garret
Hut

Approach
from Bus Stop
parking

Tunnel
of Love

Dali's Hole
p.62

*Snakes and
Ladders -
California
- p.282*

California
p.70

Tunnel

The Lost World
p.188

Serengeti
p.126

*Snakes and
Ladders - The
Lost World
- p.282*

Air
vent

Never Never Land
p.144

Mordor
p.182

Khyber
Pass

Rainbow Slab Area
p.232

Watford
Gap

Twll Mawr
p.156

Return back
to main track

Bus Stop Quarry
Dali's Hole
California
Australia
Serengeti
Never Never Land
Twll Mawr
Mordor - Lost World
Vivian Quarry
Rainbow Slab Area
Snakes and Ladders
Outlying

Bus Stop Quarry · Dali's Hole · California · Australia · Serengeti · Never Never Land · Twll Mawr · Mordor – Lost World · Vivian Quarry · Rainbow Slab Area · Snakes and Ladders · Outlying

California exit tunnel

Tunnel of Love

Dali's Wall p.65

California approach tunnel

Sun and shade

20 min

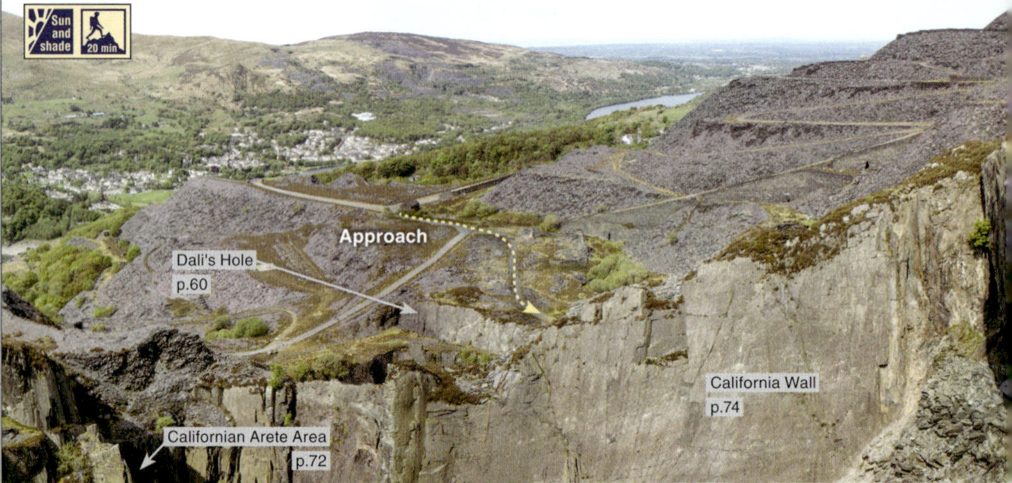

Approach

Dali's Hole p.60

California Wall p.74

Californian Arete Area p.72

❶ Snakes and Ladders - California ☐ HVS 5a

The first section tackles the enticing hole mid-way up the magnificent blank slab in California. It involves some tricky climbing, but can be done in reverse if the weather is poor or the climbing team are not up to it.

Follow the normal approach to California to the base of the left-hand side of the main California Wall (p.74). Make a short hard move to the chain and hand-over-hand up this until you get your feet onto good holds where you can rest. Carry on up to a bolt belay in the tunnel mouth. Walk through the tunnel and abseil of the chain on the tree.

In Reverse - You can scramble up to the tree in the California exit tunnel and go through this to pop out halfway up the California Wall. Abseil down past the chain and then go back out through the California approach tunnel.

Walk back along the approach to the Tunnel of Love, on the right of Dali's Wall (p.65).

❷ Snakes and Ladders - Australia

. . . . ⚡🐑 ☐ **Mod**

The Australia section tackles the wide open base before coming round onto the East Face. Here two tiers of ladders lead up to the Pen Garret Hut. Go through the Tunnel of Love from the California section which exits at the base of Australia under the route Darkness Visible (p.87). Scramble across the base and to the left of the Rognon to arrive at the Salt Pans. Head right towards the left side of the East Face of Australia to an iron ladder. Climb this, head right to the next ladder and then up this to the Pen Garret Hut.

To start Snakes and Ladders with this section, follow the approach to The Salt Pans on p.98.

The Salt Pans
p.98

The Rognon
p.88

Looning the Tube
p.90

Tasmania
p.87

East Face
p.120

Pen Garret
Hut

Ladders

Ladders

❷

Bus Stop Quarry · Dali's Hole · California · Australia · Serengeti · Never Never Land · Twll Mawr · Mordor - Lost World · Vivian Quarry · Rainbow Slab Area · Snakes and Ladders · Outlying

Bus Stop Quarry

Dali's Hole

California

Australia

Serengeti

Never Never Land

Twll Mawr

Mordor – Lost World

Vivian Quarry

Rainbow Slab Area

Snakes and Ladders

Outlying

Mark Reeves making the committing abseil in to the base of The Lost World from the Heaven Walls. Photo: Alan James

③ Snakes and Ladders - The Lost World

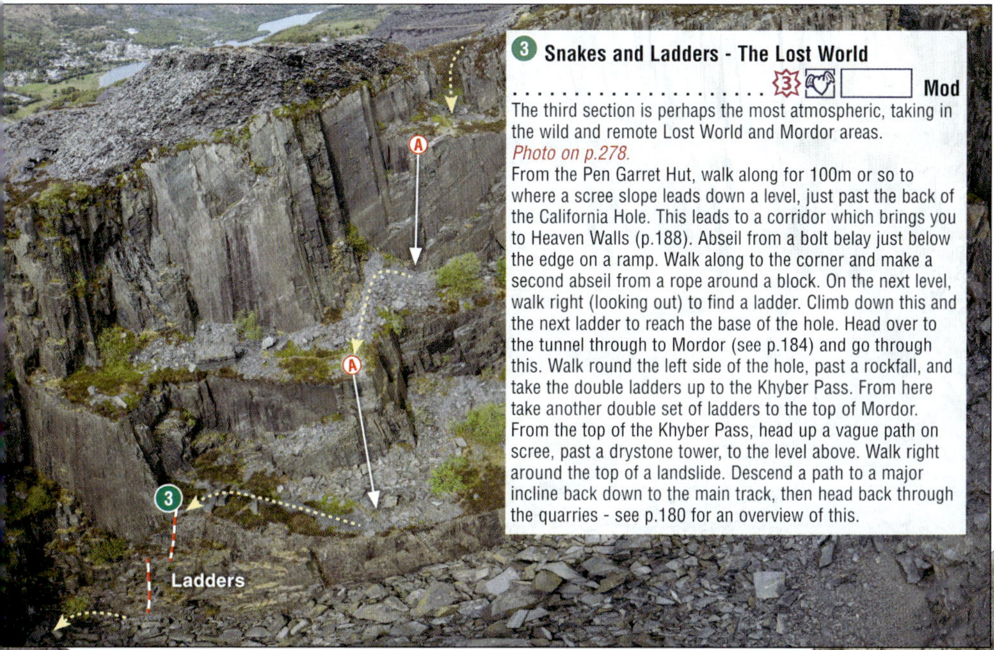

. . . . ③ 🏔️ ☐ **Mod**

The third section is perhaps the most atmospheric, taking in the wild and remote Lost World and Mordor areas.
Photo on p.278.

From the Pen Garret Hut, walk along for 100m or so to where a scree slope leads down a level, just past the back of the California Hole. This leads to a corridor which brings you to Heaven Walls (p.188). Abseil from a bolt belay just below the edge on a ramp. Walk along to the corner and make a second abseil from a rope around a block. On the next level, walk right (looking out) to find a ladder. Climb down this and the next ladder to reach the base of the hole. Head over to the tunnel through to Mordor (see p.184) and go through this. Walk round the left side of the hole, past a rockfall, and take the double ladders up to the Khyber Pass. From here take another double set of ladders to the top of Mordor. From the top of the Khyber Pass, head up a vague path on scree, past a drystone tower, to the level above. Walk right around the top of a landslide. Descend a path to a major incline back down to the main track, then head back through the quarries - see p.180 for an overview of this.

Ⓐ

Ⓐ

③

Ladders

Extension or mini loop with abseil down The Wall Within

Khyber Pass

Ladders

The Lost World Extension - There are some tunnels to explore here. You can extend the tour with an extra loop by walking along the top level and through the tunnel to find the abseil point above *The Wall Within* (p.186). Abseil down here back to the base of The Lost World and repeat the tunnel and ladders from here again.

Bus Stop Quarry · Dali's Hole · California · Australia · Serengeti · Never Never Land · Twll Mawr · Mordor - Lost World · Vivian Quarry · Rainbow Slab Area · Snakes and Ladders · Outlying

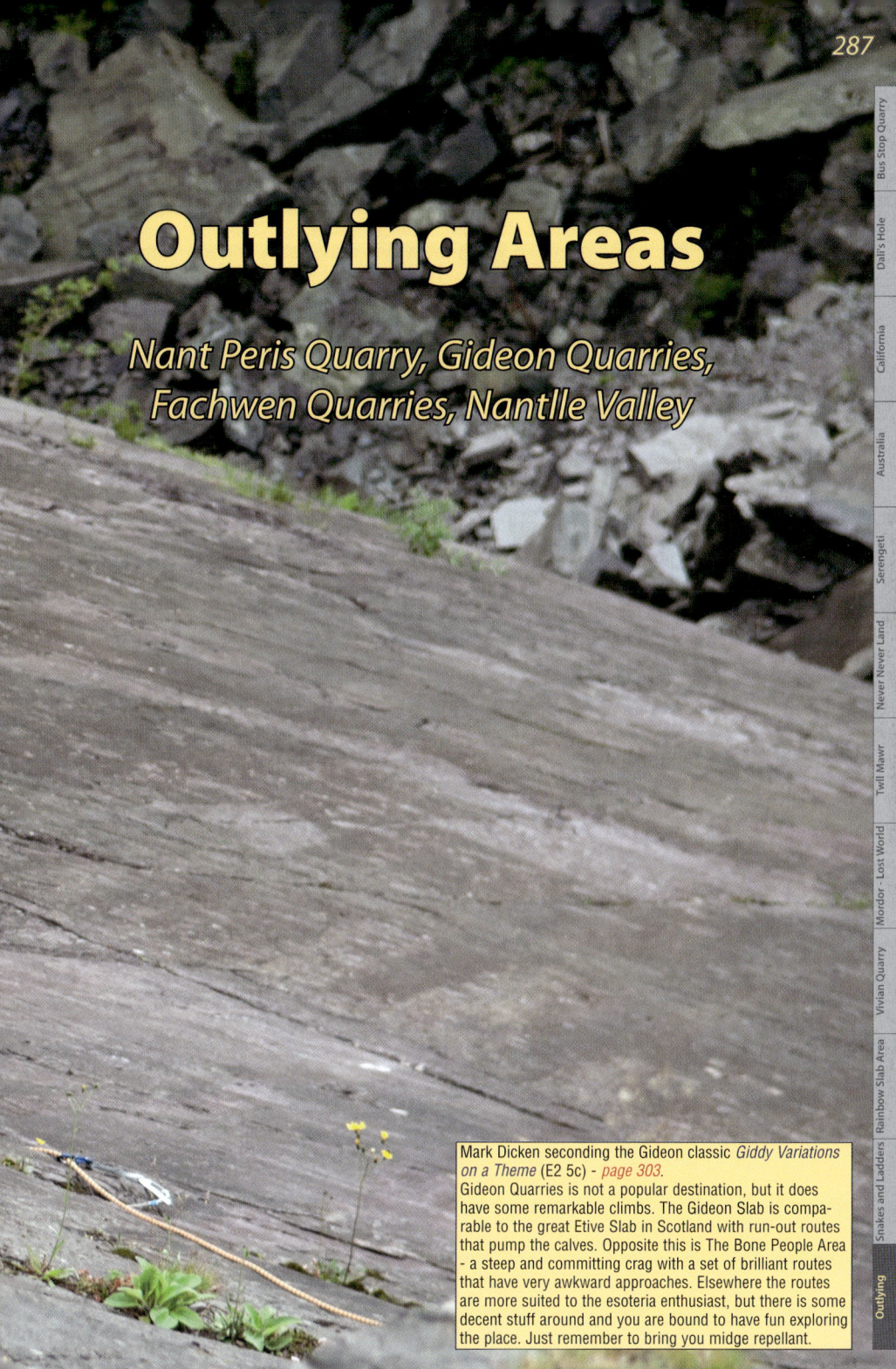

Outlying Areas

Nant Peris Quarry, Gideon Quarries, Fachwen Quarries, Nantlle Valley

Bus Stop Quarry

Dali's Hole

California

Australia

Serengeti

Never Never Land

Twll Mawr

Mordor - Lost World

Vivian Quarry

Rainbow Slab Area

Snakes and Ladders

Outlying

Mark Dicken seconding the Gideon classic *Giddy Variations on a Theme* (E2 5c) - *page 303*.
Gideon Quarries is not a popular destination, but it does have some remarkable climbs. The Gideon Slab is comparable to the great Etive Slab in Scotland with run-out routes that pump the calves. Opposite this is The Bone People Area - a steep and committing crag with a set of brilliant routes that have very awkward approaches. Elsewhere the routes are more suited to the esoteria enthusiast, but there is some decent stuff around and you are bound to have fun exploring the place. Just remember to bring you midge repellant.

	No star	🏵	🏵🏵	🏵🏵🏵
Mod to S	-	-	-	-
HS to HVS	-	-	-	-
E1 to E3	4	-	-	-
E4 and up	2	-	-	-

This small quarry above Nant Peris was developed in the late 70s by some slightly over-enthusiastic climbers desperate for new routes. The main Llanberis quarries hadn't really been opened up then, so you can excuse them to an extent!

The routes are included here just so you know what is available and for completeness. The rock on all the routes is very loose and most have probably never seen a second ascent.

Conditions

One redeeming feature is that it does face north which can mean it is cool in hot weather. It also means that it would be slow to dry if you were ever sat waiting!

Approach

Park in the lay-by just west of Nant Peris with a slate display saying 'NANT PERIS'. From here a good track leads in the direction of the Llanberis Pass. Walk through a field until you are below the quarry. Head up the incline to the left until level with the base of the *Nice Guy* arete and follow the level across to it. Cross the scree to the base of other routes.

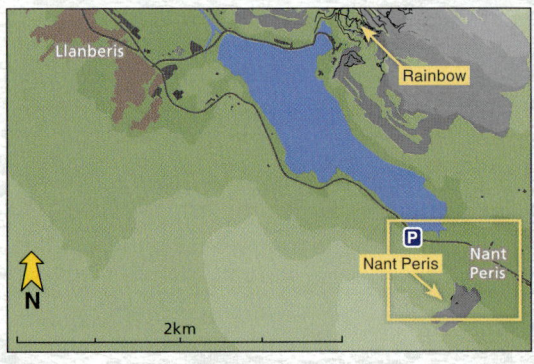

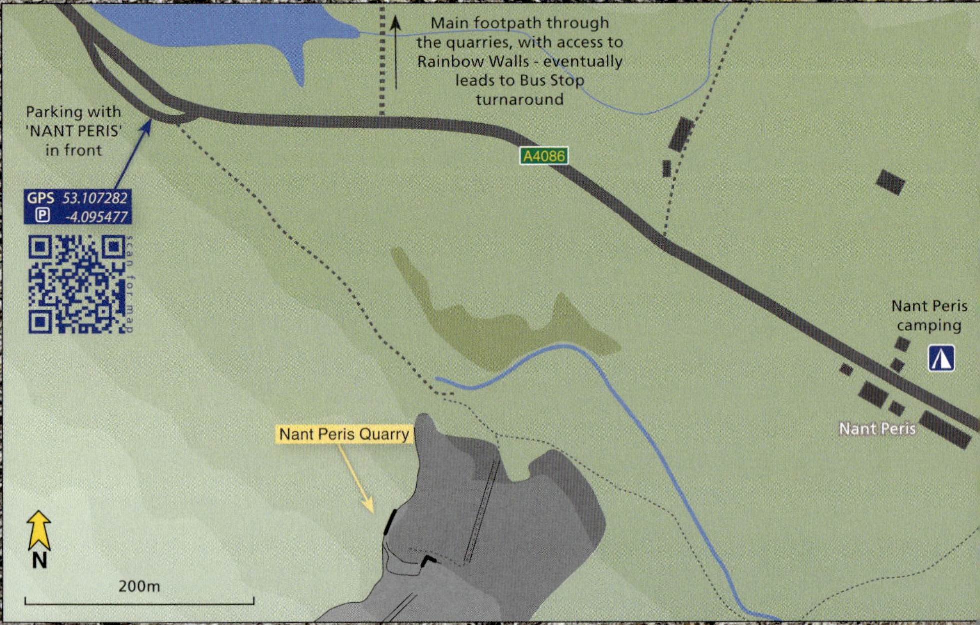

Side tabs:
Bus Stop Quarry · Dali's Hole · California · Australia · Serengeti · Never Never Land · Twll Mawr · Mordor - Lost World · Vivian Quarry · Rainbow Slab Area Snakes and Ladders · Outlying

1 Nice Guy............. E1 5a
On the east (left - looking in) side of the main quarry. Climb the arete without any real gear.
FA. Al Evans 23.7.1990

40m

2 The Hooligan........... E1 5a
The loose and vegetated corner system
FA. Paul Williams, Jimmy Jewel 11.3.1979

3 Vandal............. E2 5b
Generally solid climbing leads to a rubble-filled exit gully. Take the wide cracks up the corner to a roof, then the deteriorating groove above.
FA. Paul Trower, Callum Hudson 11.1978

4 The Deceiver........ E3 5c
The thin shield of rock that constitutes this route feels barely attached. Strenuous finger and hand-crack climbing leads up the wall - try not to pull off too much!
FA. Jimmy Jewel, Paul Williams 24.4.1979

The next two routes have been affected by a rockfall in the top half of the groove system.

5 The Poacher........... XS
The crack/corner has yet to be reascended!
FA. Jimmy Jewel, Paul Williams, M.Patterson 10.3.1979

6 Butcher............. XS
Climb the shallow groove to the tip of the fang, then follow the crack. Yet to be reascended!
FA. Paul Trower, Callum Hudson 11.1978

Bus Stop Quarry | Dali's Hole | California | Australia | Serengeti | Never Never Land | Twll Mawr | Mordor - Lost World | Vivian Quarry | Rainbow Slab Area | Snakes and Ladders | Outlying

	No star	⚜	⚜	⚜
Mod to S / 4c	-	-	-	-
HS-HVS / 5a-6a+	11	2	1	-
E1-E3 / 6b-7a	13	7	5	-
E4 / 7a+ and up	8	6	3	4

Bus Stop Quarry

Dali's Hole

California

Australia

Serengeti

Never Never Land

Twll Mawr

Mordor - Lost World

Vivian Quarry

Rainbow Slab Area

Snakes and Ladders

Outlying

The Gideon Quarries are a real slate backwater. This is partly due to the more erratic nature of the rock - whilst there is some good rock hidden in this working, there is also a lot of loose and friable choss. If adventure is your thing, there are some really fine routes and it is a great place to hide from the crowds on busy days.

The lowest working is home to the off-width challenges of *The Mancer Direct* and *Liquid Armbar*, if you fancy yourself as a wideboy or girl. Just above the road is Film Set Quarry and the great slabs of *The Second Coming* and *Near Dark (After Dark)*. The bridging testpiece *Gender Bender* is also worth a look, and *The Bone People* and *Synthetic Life* offer some steep climbing - for slate. The Gideon Slab classics are *Giddy Variations...* and *Pandora Plays Sax*, and right up at the back is *Cracking Up*. There are also several isolated sport routes worth hunting out.

Conditions

The conditions can be a little more damp than the Dinorwig side of the valley, due in part to the north-facing aspect of some walls and dense vegetation. Some areas face east/west, so you can also get the morning or evening sun.

Access

There have been serious problems here in the past, but access appears less problematic now providing climbers keep a low profile. The quarries are owned by Gwynedd Council who make it clear that there is no official access for public safety reasons. There are high fences and signs prohibiting access, but there have not been any reports of practical access problems for many years.

In early 2017 planning permission was granted for a new hydro-electric power station on the site. When work starts on this (unknown time-scale) it is likely that access to some of the quarries will be permanently lost, especially to Mancer and Film Set Quarries which will become flooded to produce a holding reservoir.

Due to nesting birds, some areas are restricted from 1 March until the end of June.

Mike Raine working *Autocrat* (6c) - *page 303* - in the Gideon Quarries.
Part of the mid-noughties new wave of sport routes, Mike's *Autocrat* lead the way for a flurry of new routes in the area.

Bus Stop Quarry

Dali's Hole

California

Australia

Serengeti

Never Never Land

Twll Mawr

Mordor - Lost World

Vivian Quarry

Rainbow Slab Area

Snakes and Ladders

Outlying

Approach

The area is accessed via a small road that leads up out of the back of Llanberis. From the High Street, turn up Goodman Street (which is at the crossroads occupied by the ultimate climbers' cafe, Pete's Eats). Head up this road. After about 300 metres and a steep section, the road flattens out and leaves the village. Carry on up the road which eventually widens out then closes up again with a high wire fence. The lower parking spot - for the main Gideon Quarry - is on the left by a gate. Continuing a little further you pass Film Set Quarry close to the road on the left. Just beyond this on the right is the plentiful upper parking, from where you can approach Film Set Quarry through a hole in the fence and Mancer Quarry from above down the path and road. It is also possible to approach Mancer Quarry from the main road below, by turning up the wide road marked 'Glyn Rhonwy'. Park as far up here as you can, then continue walking up the road on the right. This leads past the entrance gate to the Mancer Quarry.

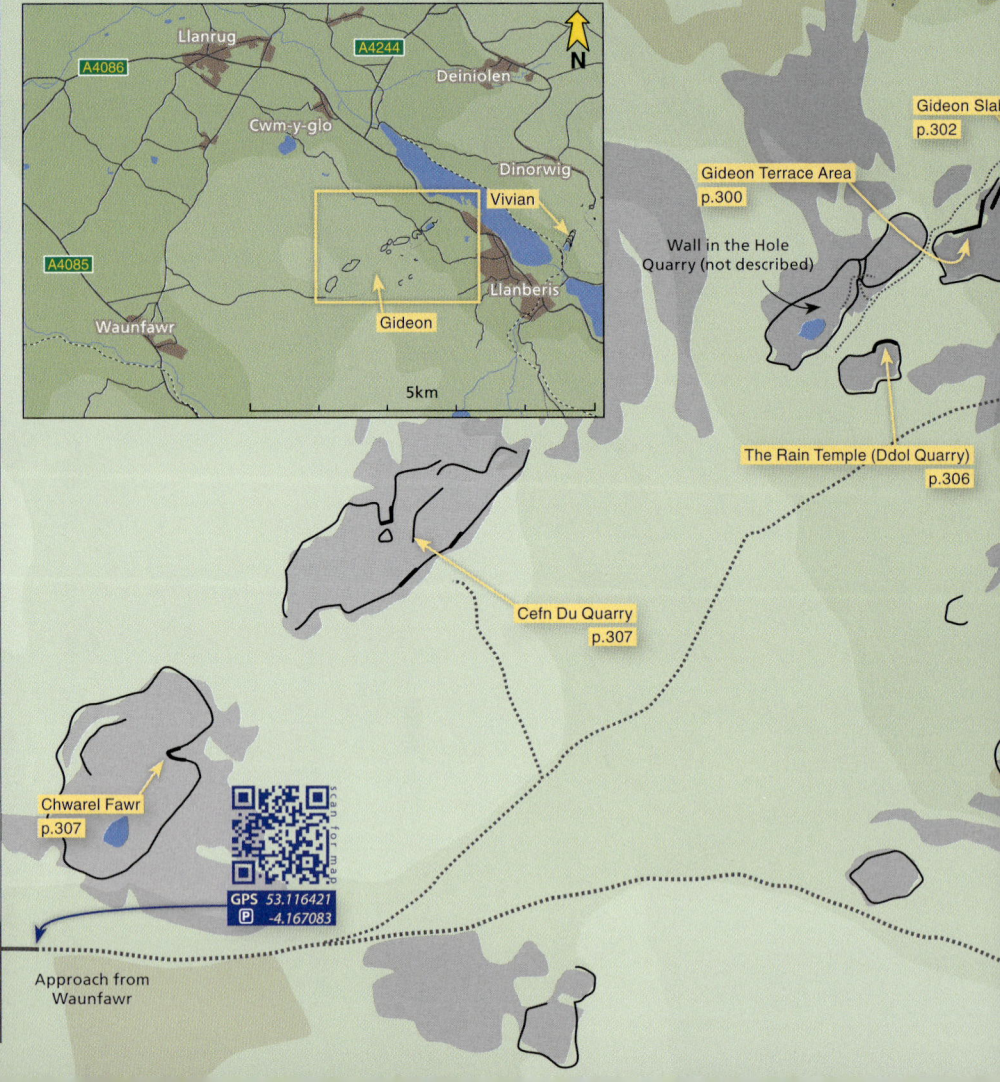

N

Llanrug

A4244

A4086

Deiniolen

Cwm-y-glo

Dinorwig

Vivian

A4085

Llanberis

Waunfawr

Gideon

5km

Gideon Slab
p.302

Gideon Terrace Area
p.300

Wall in the Hole
Quarry (not described)

The Rain Temple (Ddol Quarry)
p.306

Cefn Du Quarry
p.307

Chwarel Fawr
p.307

GPS 53.116421
-4.167083

scan for map

Approach from
Waunfawr

N

Llyn Padarn

Damocles Slab
p.297

Mancer Quarry
p.296

GPS 53.125877
P -4.146773

GPS 53.124869
P -4.136441

Film Set Quarry
p.298

Land that Time Forgot
p.298

GPS 53.123709
P -4.144355

Glyn Rhonwy

Bone People Area
p.304

Chwarl Plas Goch
p.306

Goodman Street

Llanberis

Shotgun Quarry
p.306

400m

Bus Stop Quarry

Dali's Hole

California

Australia

Serengeti

Never Never Land

Twll Mawr

Mordor - Lost World

Vivian Quarry

Rainbow Slab Area

Snakes and Ladders

Outlying

The Bone People Area
p.304

Gideon Terrace Area
p.300

Gideon Slab
p.302

To Chwarl
Plas Goch

To Shotgun
Quarry

Land that Time Forgot
p.298

Film Set Quarry
p.298

GPS 53.123749
P -4.144402
Lower
parking

Road to
nowhere

Bus Stop Quarry

Dali's Hole

California

Australia

Serengeti

Never Never Land

Twll Mawr

Mordor - Lost World

Vivian Quarry

Rainbow Slab Area Snakes and Ladders

Outlying

Upper parking

GPS 53.125886
Ⓟ -4.146790

Damocles Slab
p.297

Mancer Quarry
p.296

Bus Stop Quarry

Dali's Hole

California

Australia

Serengeti

Never Never Land

Twll Mawr

Mordor - Lost World

Vivian Quarry

Rainbow Slab Area

Snakes and Ladders

Outlying

Mancer Quarry

The lowest quarry is a bit esoteric and better known as a local wild swimming spot. There are a couple of decent routes for off-width aficionados, in the shape of *Liquid Armbar* and *Mancer Direct*. For the sport climber looking for a quiet slab, *Clippopotamus* may well do the trick.

Approach (map p.292, overview p.294) - From the parking by Film Set Quarry, walk along the road to a surfaced path through the fence on the north side of the road (right going uphill). Follow this path down to join the wide but redundant road. Walk along the left-hand side of the road until a path leads to a gate in the fence with a hole on its right. Go through here where a track leads down into the quarry. Mancer is best reached by following a vague track across the left edge of the quarry, until above the wall and abseiling in.

For *Clippopotumus*, follow the previous description and walk round the edge of the right side of the quarry to reach the top of the wall. Otherwise, from the upper parking, head over the fence to a faint path that leads perpendicularly away from the road on a flat promontory. Head along this for about 100m, until a large dolerite boulder is seen in the undergrowth down and right. Scramble down the scree to the block and pass it on the left. 10m further on is a small oak tree and just beyond this is an old fence on the right. Follow the fence until a gap appears - you are now above Damocles Slab.

🚫 **Access** - Nesting kestrels can be found in the tunnel high on the walls of the promontory, so do not disturb this area.

The Mancer Wall

The pool

Black Butte Wall projects

Main track

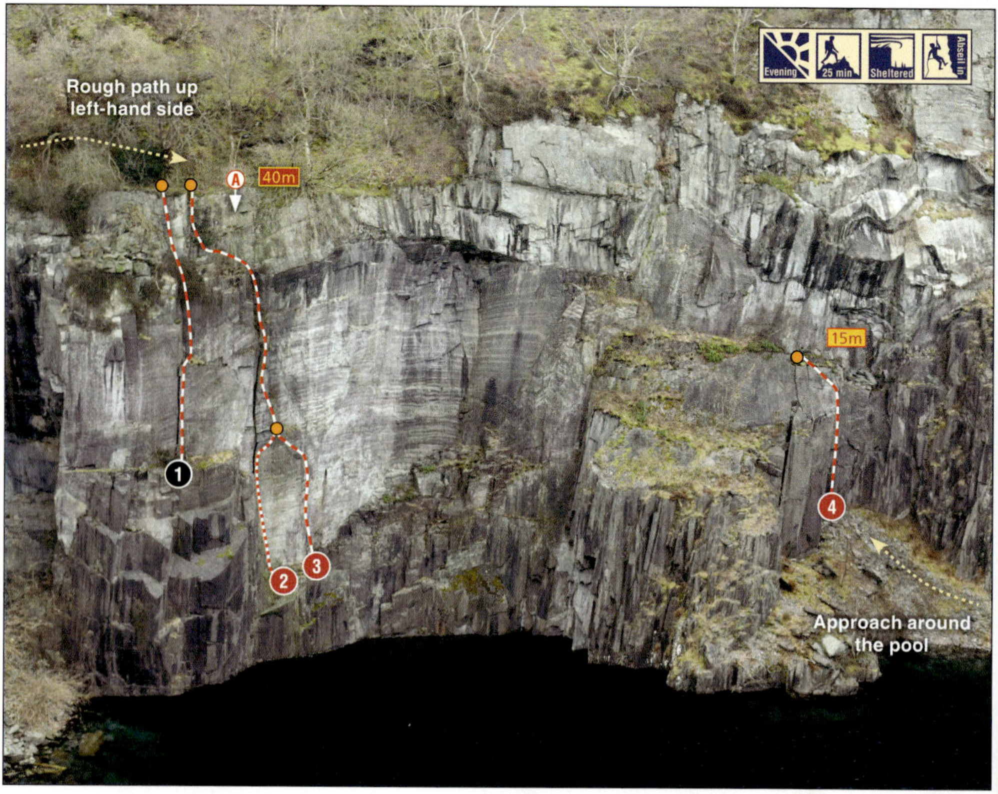

Rough path up left-hand side

A 40m

15m

1

2 3

4

Approach around the pool

The Black Butte Wall is on the left as you descend the main track into the quarry. It has two lines of bolts which are projects.

❶ Liquid Armbar . . . . 🔲 **E4 6a**
5.11 in off-width money - very big cams are essential. Abseil onto the ledge and squirm up the unrelenting crack. Collapse onto the halfway ledge to recompose yourself. The climbing above is only 5.9, but still awkward. Finish up ledges.
FA. Mark Dicken 9.2009

❷ The Mancer Original Start . . . 🔲 **E1 4c**
Abseil to the lower ledge. The lower part of the corner is avoided diagonally on the left, then regained with a exciting pull. A final hand-traverse right gains the belay. Big cams are required for the belay. Finish up pitch 2 of *The Mancer Direct*.
FA. Stevie Haston, Lee McGinley 8.1981

❸ The Mancer Direct . . . . . 🔲 **E3 5b**
Abseil to the lower ledge and brace yourself for battle.
1) **5b**, 18m. Fight your way up the 5.10 slot which only accommodates large cams, which are also needed for the belay!
2) **4c**, 21m. Ferret up behind the pinnacle (taking care not to push too hard) to reach its summit. Cracks and ledges lead to the top.
FA. Stevie Haston, Lee McGinley 9.1982

❹ Good Crack . . . . 🔲 **E3 6a**
A long walk round the pool leads to a short leftward-slanting finger-crack. Abseil off the tree.
FA. George Smith, Chris Parkin 6.1988

Damocles Slab
On the north side of the quarry is a white slab with no approach from below. A pair of disused fence posts above marks the spot to abseil from trees.

❺ I Don't Wanna Pickle . . . . . . 🔲 **E4 6a**
Abseil to a bolt belay above a prominent boulder and climb up to the first bolt. Traverse left to a creaking vegetated flake, pass a bolt, then climb up past a few more bolts and some shocking runners to the top.
FA. Mark Boniface 11.1988

❻ Blah de Blah de Blah! . . . . . . 🔲 **E4 5c**
Start as for *I Don't Wanna Pickle* and move left past a small corner then up to a second bolt. After a short distance, traverse right to the third bolt before finishing up a broken crack.
FA. Mark Boniface 11.1988

❼ Damocles . . . . 🔲 **HVS 5a**
A hard-to-reach bolt belay gives abseil access to this route - use a nearby tree to help. Climb the crack-line to the niche, passing this on its left. Climb on past bolts to regain the crack at the top.
FA. Nick Walton, Martin Crook 9.2008

The right-hand side of the wall has a lone route which can be reached by scrambling down a scree slope to the right of it.

❽ Clippopotamus . . . . 🔲 **6b**
A nice route worth seeking out.
FA. Martin Crook, Nick Walton, Andy Newton 9.2008

The Land that Time Forgot

This is the subsidiary quarry adjoining the Film Set Quarry and separated by a ridge of rock and the pinnacle of Don Quixote. You can make your way between the two workings by scrambling up to the ridge. It is easier to go from Film Set to The Land That Time Forgot than vice versa, as there is a short technical down climb coming from the opposite direction.

❶ Near Dark (After Dark) . . . . . ⛺① [   ] E2 5b
A decent route up a clean slab on spaced bolts. It is best approached from above by abseiling from trees behind the two bolt studs that mark the top of the route, the hangers of which have been removed.
FA. Andy Newton, Kath Griffiths 6.5.1990

❷ Bring me the Head of Don Quixote

. . . . [icons] [   ] E2 5a
The aiguille-like central tower is like a mini Cerro Torre, but sees few ascents. Approach by abseiling down *Near Dark (After Dark)* and then scrambling across to the central ridge that spilts the quarry. From the shoulder on the right, climb stacked blocks to gain the reddish groove on the right side of the tower and a pedestal. The first and last reliable runner is here. Move round to the left side of the tower. A ledge (exfoliating!) allows movement back right to mantel the earthy summit. To belay, pull up a rope, drop it down the far side and get your belayer to run round and tie it off to the ground. Belay off this, then abseil off in a similar way.
FA. Mark Dicken, C.Neale 2003

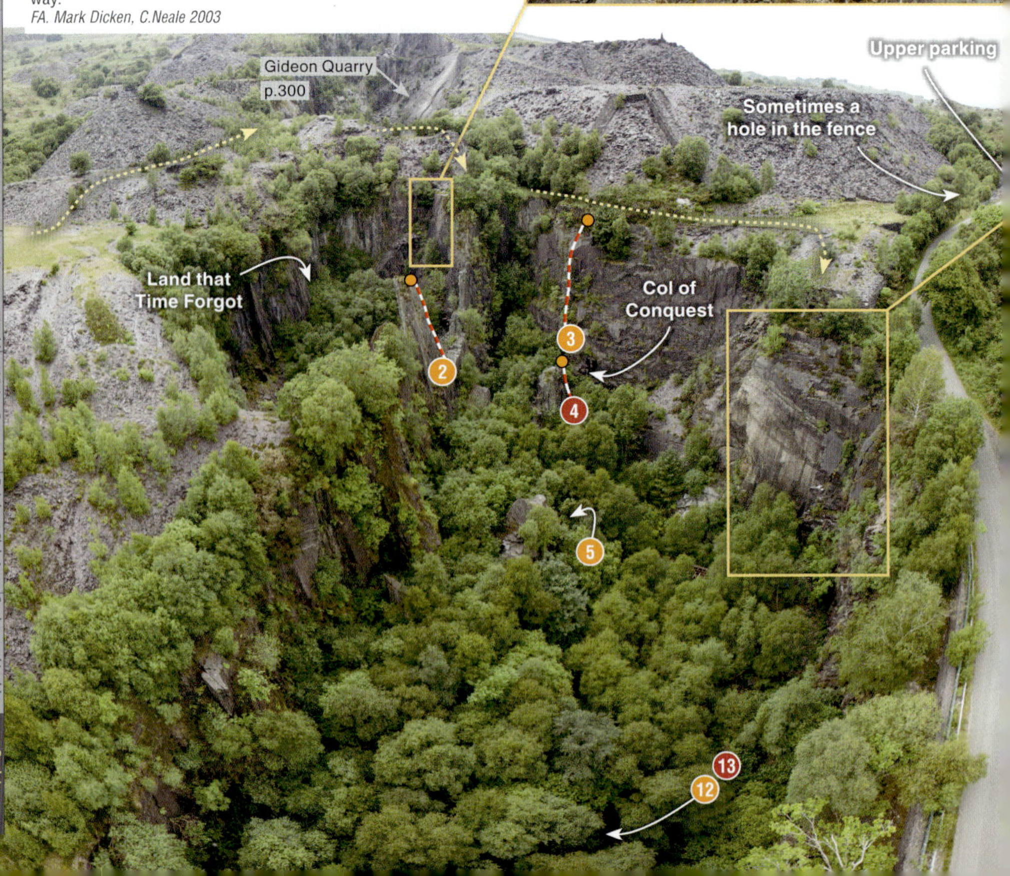

35m

The pinnacles in the quarry give a few points of interest for explorers seeking a summit experience.

❸ Old Fogies Never Die . . . . . . 🧗 ⬜ **VS 4b**
From the Col of Conquest, climb the dolerite rib to exit the quarry. On paper this is the easiest way out, but it is far better to use *Near Dark (After Dark)* as an exit.
FA. Cliff Phillips, Phil Bagnall 22.2.1989

❹ Arrampicata Speiligone . . . . 🧗 ⬜ **E1 5a**
From the Col of Conquest, ascend the small right-hand tower. Abseil from a bolt lower-off, which may be buried under vegetation by now?
FA. Cliff Phillips, Mark Boniface 1989

❺ Arse Over Tit . . . . 🧗 ⬜ **VS 4c**
This route reaches the summit of the other small tower in the base of the quarry. The arete facing *Arrampicata Speiligone* is climbed past a spike to further ironmongery on the top. Scramble off the far side.
FA. Cliff Phillips 2.5.1984

The best climbing is on the clean wave slab.

❻ The Second Coming . . . . 🏆2 🧗 ⬜ **E4 6b**
Similar to *Comes the Dervish,* but with an evil crux at the top. Start up the left-hand crack (better gear then *Monsieur Avantski*) to a good rest before the final bulge. This proves problematic to say the least! Above it turns into a scramble for the top.
FA. Stevie Haston, Martin Crook 4.1984

Film Set Quarry

This quarry is so named as it was a major location for a cult film 'The Keep'. It has a few good routes - the *Gender Bender* slab is the main point of interest and the isolated slab of *Near Dark (After Dark)*. It is extremely sheltered and the climbing gets plenty of sun but the dense vegetation means that it is slow to dry.

Approach (map p.292, overview p.294) - From the lower parking, follow the track into the quarry for 200m. Take a path on the right which leads up through the quarries. This takes you over the top of the Film Set Quarry. Make your way along the top to locate the abseil points. It can also be approached more directly from the upper parking where there is sometimes a hole in the fence that allows quick access to the top of the *Gender Bender* slab. It is best to leave the abseil rope in place and take prussiks in case you can't make it out through conventional means.

❼ Monsieur Avantski . . 🏆1 🐾 ⬜ **E4 6a**
The central crack is sustained and insecure with spaced gear - try not to pass anything by.
FA. John Silvester, A.Wilke 10.1984

❽ Gender Bender . . . . 🏆2 🧗 ⬜ **E3 6b**
Technical body-tearing bridging will suit yoga enthusiasts. Pass a testing mantelshelf and continue more easily above to top out on the left.
FA. Stevie Haston, Martin Crook, Andy Newton 4.1984

❾ Marital Aids . . . . 🧗 ⬜ **E5 6b**
The girdle. Climb *Gender Bender* to the mantelshelf, then follow the crack-line out left across the slab passing *Monsieur Avantski* and *The Second Coming.* Climb this to the bulge and traverse up and out to the arete to finish.
FA. Stevie Haston, Tim Downes 18.4.1984

❿ The Trash Heap Has Spoken
. . . . 🧗 ❤️ ⬜ **E1 5a**
Poor climbing on the right of the slab.
1) **5b**, 10m. Climb the short groove and traverse 10m right into a large corner-groove and belay.
2) **5a**, 15m. Climb up the groove with nothing in the way of gear.
FA. Cliff Phillips, N.Thomas 29.4.1984

⓫ The Trash Heap Speaks Again 🧗 ⬜ **VS 4b**
The stepped wall and easy-angled groove.
FA. Cliff Phillips, M.Thompson 2.5.1984

⓬ Mental Block . . . . 🧗 ⬜ **VS 4c**
On the opposite side of the quarry is a flake that is fixed to the wall with industrial bolts. This route climbs the arete left of this via four mantels, to a finish up the groove.
FA. Cliff Phillips 8.4.1984

If you follow the wall right for 100m or so you will reach a slender detached flake pinned to the wall by some old quarrymen bolts.

⓭ Layed Back Boys . . . . 🔧 ⬜ **E2 5b**
The bolted-on flake. Gain the flake and layback up the right side before either your arms or the rock explode.
FA. Stevie Haston, Paul Trower, A.Howard 3.1984

Bus Stop Quarry | Dali's Hole | California | Australia | Serengeti | Never Never Land | Twll Mawr | Mordor - Lost World | Vivian Quarry | Rainbow Slab Area | Snakes and Ladders | Outlying

Gideon Terrace Area

Some of the sport routes on Gideon Terrace are totally different to the rest of the climbing in this quarry. *Cracking Up* is a really fine route.

Approach (map p.292, overview p.294) - From the lower parking, climb over the gate and walk up the hill by a fence. As the tarmac path veers off left, move round the fence on the right and follow a zig-zag track on the right through some trees. You will then glimpse the massive Gideon Quarry working. Follow the path right in front of the quarry and then take a another zig-zagging path up the right side of the quarry to a hut. Here a small cutting leads through to Gideon Terrace. *Cracking Up* is further along the ledge.

🚫 **Access -** All routes in this area are restricted from 1 March to 30 June due to nesting birds. Check the BMC RAD for the latest information.

Bus Stop Quarry
Dali's Hole
California
Australia
Serengeti
Never Never Land
Twll Mawr
Mordor - Lost World
Vivian Quarry
Rainbow Slab Area
Snakes and Ladders
Outlying

❶ Cracked Up . . . . 🖐   **HVS 5b**
The off-width corner-crack left of *Cracking Up* is a great introduction to the slate off-width.
FA. Stevie Haston, Cliff Phillips 3.1984

❷ Cracking Up . . . . 🌟 🖐   **E2 5c**
A cracking pitch! A difficult move off the deck gains the ever widening crack. Following it to the top proves much easier the moment your fingers fit into it. It then goes through hands to beyond fist, but is mostly laybacked.
FA. Stevie Haston, Cliff Phillips 3.1984

❸ The Rothwell Incident. . . 🐦 🔖   **XS 5b**
The corner to the right is exciting if nothing else.
FA. Mark Reeves, D.Rothwell 1999

❹ Uhuru for Mandela . . 🌟 🐦 🔖   **E2 5c**
A nice line, though slightly contrived. Abseil to below the smooth slab and ascend to a bolt. Move up right to a small ledge with some difficulty. Bolder but easier climbing brings you to the overlap, where some protection spurs you on to loose rock above. Pass some bore-holes to easier climbing on improving rock back to the terrace.
FA. Mark Boniface, A.Garland 16.6.1988

⑤ Kenny's Wall 5c
Reasonable climbing. The lower-off is missing, so top out.
FA. Nick Walton, Martin Crook 9.2008

⑥ Ladybird Girl/Giddy One . E3 6a
The open groove-line yields a good route. Bolts and small wires protect, with a bolt belay at the top. The route was originally done without fixed gear at around E5.
FA. Stevie Haston, A.Haston 1987
FA. (Bolts) Chris Parkin, Chris Ayres 1990

⑦ The Hand of Morlock 6c+
Use a clipstick for the first bolt to avoid an ankle-snapping start. Otherwise it is more like a **E4 6a**.
FA. Tony Hughes, Oliver Cain 22.8.2007

⑧ Los Alamos 6c
Climb the wall past two bolts to a double-bolt lower-off. A long reach is required to start the sequence.
FA. Phil Targett,Tony Hughes 5.11.2011

⑨ The Mosquito E6 6c
There is no gear but it is around **7b** to top rope. Climb to the triangular protrusion. A techy sequence gains better holds leading to the lower-off.
FA. Calum Muskett 7.2.2010

⑩ The Gnarly SPAR Kid E2 6a
The blocky arete on the right edge of the wall. Make difficult moves past the first bolt to reach the second, then a series of pulls on big holds to the lower-off.
FA. Tony Hughes, G.Oldridge 5.9.2007

20m

Walk down

14m

To mid afternoon | 15 min | Sheltered | Restrictions

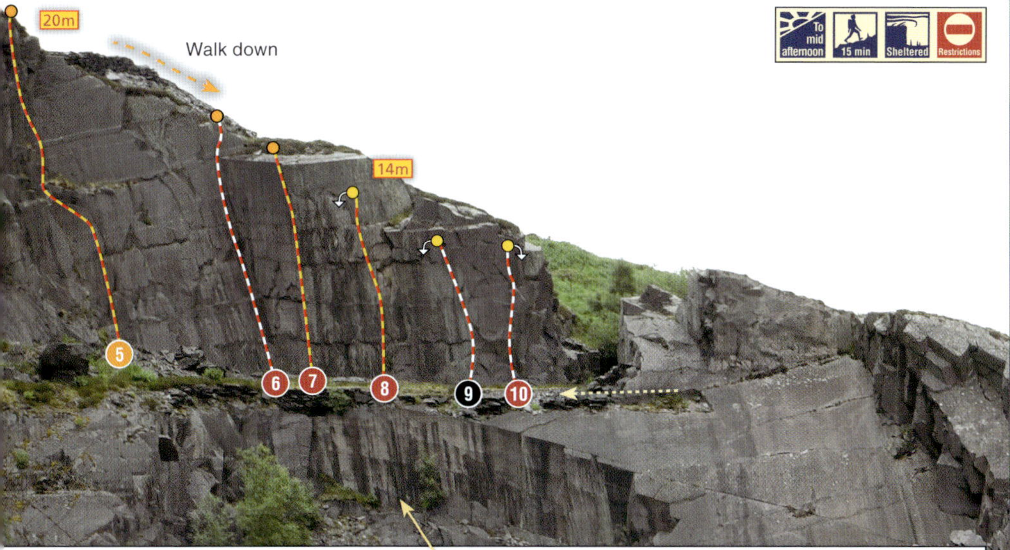

⑤ ⑥ ⑦ ⑧ ⑨ ⑩

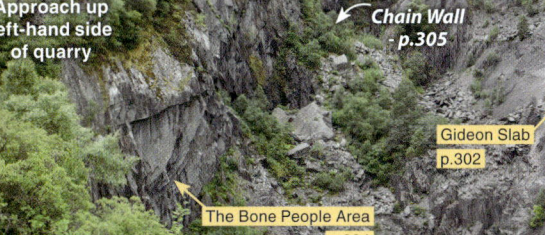

Approach up left-hand side of quarry

Chain Wall - p.305

Gideon Slab p.302

The Bone People Area p.304

Autocrat - p.303

Main approach

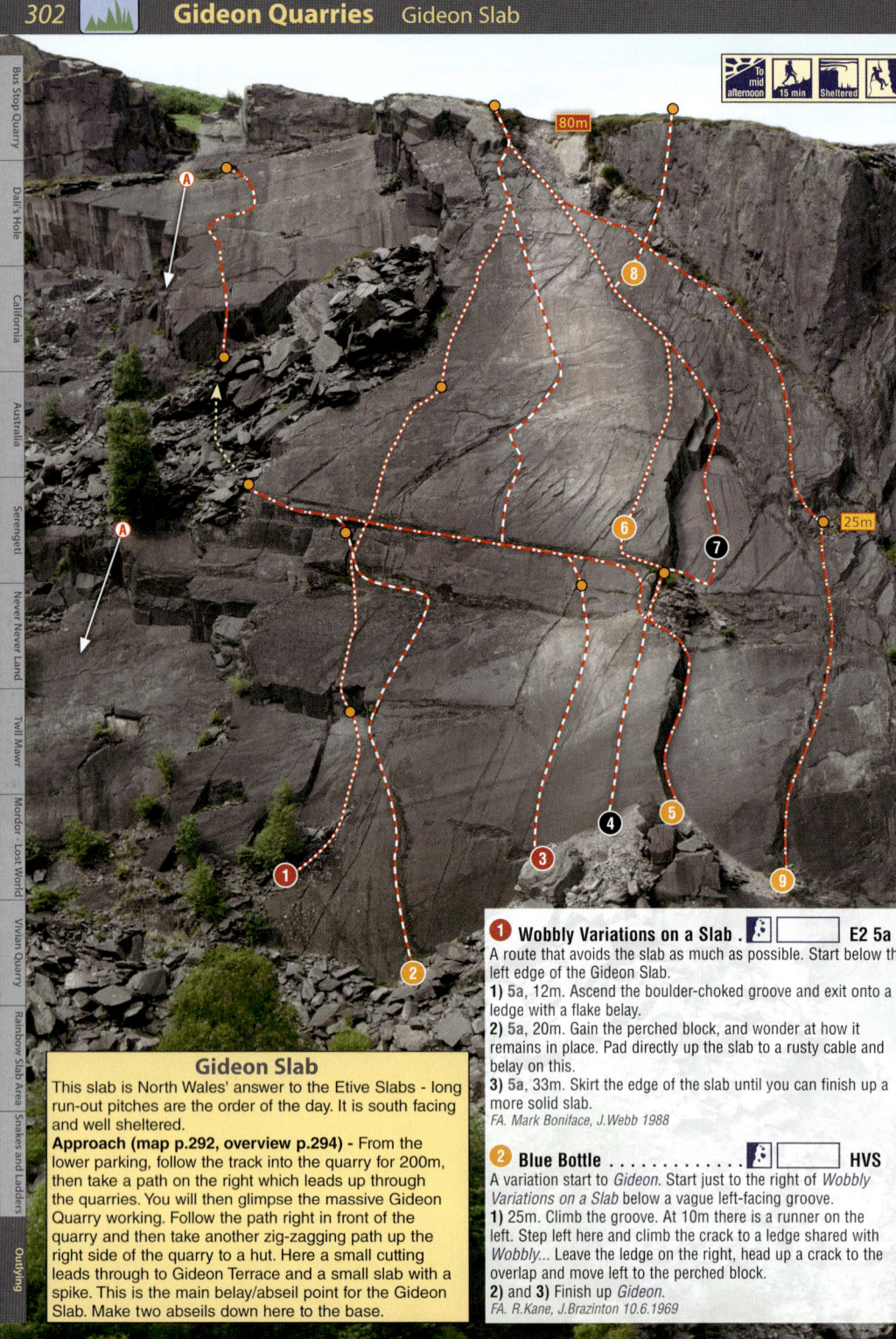

80m

25m

Gideon Slab

This slab is North Wales' answer to the Etive Slabs - long run-out pitches are the order of the day. It is south facing and well sheltered.

Approach (map p.292, overview p.294) - From the lower parking, follow the track into the quarry for 200m, then take a path on the right which leads up through the quarries. You will then glimpse the massive Gideon Quarry working. Follow the path right in front of the quarry and then take another zig-zagging path up the right side of the quarry to a hut. Here a small cutting leads through to Gideon Terrace and a small slab with a spike. This is the main belay/abseil point for the Gideon Slab. Make two abseils down here to the base.

1 Wobbly Variations on a Slab E2 5a
A route that avoids the slab as much as possible. Start below the left edge of the Gideon Slab.
1) 5a, 12m. Ascend the boulder-choked groove and exit onto a ledge with a flake belay.
2) 5a, 20m. Gain the perched block, and wonder at how it remains in place. Pad directly up the slab to a rusty cable and belay on this.
3) 5a, 33m. Skirt the edge of the slab until you can finish up a more solid slab.
FA. Mark Boniface, J.Webb 1988

2 Blue Bottle . . . . HVS
A variation start to *Gideon*. Start just to the right of *Wobbly Variations on a Slab* below a vague left-facing groove.
1) 25m. Climb the groove. At 10m there is a runner on the left. Step left here and climb the crack to a ledge shared with *Wobbly...* Leave the ledge on the right, head up a crack to the overlap and move left to the perched block.
2) and **3)** Finish up *Gideon*.
FA. R.Kane, J.Brazinton 10.6.1969

Bus Stop Quarry | Dali's Hole | California | Australia | Serengeti | Never Never Land | Twll Mawr | Mordor - Lost World | Vivian Quarry | Rainbow Slab Area | Snakes and Ladders | Outlying

❸ Giddy Variations on a Theme
. . . . ②🦉🖐️☐ **E2 5b**

A fine outing in the style. Start 6m left of *Gideon*, a few metres down from the apex of the scree/boulder cone. *Photo on p.286.*
1) 5b, 20m. Head up the seam that leads right of the ledge to a shot-hole. Either a very small tricam or folded medium wire provides some semblance of protection. Continue delicately up the slab with you heart in your mouth to reach a ledge and sapling - combined they almost give enough gear to belay off.
2) 5b, 60m. Move up to the fault-line of the *Gideon* traverse and head left along it for a few metres, until you are below a slim groove to the right of the chossy overlap. Place as much gear as you can here, skyhooks, microwires and anything else small you are carrying. Say a prayer and launch up the groove, then pad left to the main overlap via a large dimple. Move up the overlap to some wire placements. From here aim up and left of the apex of the slab, then finish direct up this.
FA. Cliff Phillips 21.2.1987

❹ Pandora Plays Sax Direct Start
. . . . ①🦉🖐️☐ **E4 6a**

Neglected and hard when mossy, so it might be worth giving it a spring clean if you abseil straight in. Start just left of the base of the arete near the top of the scree tower, below a crack. Climb the crack to gain the belay - more terrifying than it sounds. Finish up any of the routes from here.

❺ Gideon . . . . ①🎿☐ **HVS 4c**
The original slate route that failed to ignite much interest. It tends to avoid any real climbing, but is something of an adventure. Start at the base of a groove just right of the top of the scree cone.
1) 4c. 50m. Ascend the groove until forced left to a ledge on the arete. What remains of a manky peg and a wire offer some solace before you head left along the fault-line passing the perched block. This used to be the belay, but there is a better, less dangerous one around the left edge of the slab.
2) 13m. Scramble up the scree to a belay below the final slab.
3) 4c, 24m. Head up the middle of the slab to gain the a ledge. Move left and then back right before gaining the top of the slab.
FA. Al Harris, Eric Penman 7.1964

❻ Pandora Plays Sax . . . . ②☐ **HVS 4c**
A more direct and better version of *Gideon*.
1) 4c, 18m. As for the first pitch of *Gideon*. Climb to the vegetated ledge on the arete before the long traverse left.
2) 4c, 55m. Move up and left for 2m and gain the overlap via the rib. Follow this to a crack. Pad up the easy-angled slab, moving leftwards towards the top before the rock deteriorates, to gain the more solid slab left of the steep choss.
FA. Stevie Haston, Ray Kay 3.1987

❼ Ultra Cricket Zone . . . . 🎿☐ **E4 6a**
1) 6a, 18m. As for *Pandora Plays Sax Direct Start*.
2) 5c, 56m. Go down and right over stacked scree. Head up cracks that spilt the subsidiary slab (gear to the left). Head through the centre of the overlap and climb the rib until it peters out. Then trend left to finish up *Pandora Plays Sax* or the *Pandora's Box Finish* for the full effect!
FA. Trevor Hodgson, Martin Wragg, T.Jones 5.4.1987

❽ Pandora's Box Finish . . . . . . 🎿☐ **HVS 4b**
A direct finish to *Pandora Plays Sax*. Take the chossy groove.
FA. Ray Kay, H.Falconer 2002

❾ The Climbing Pains of Adrian Mole
. . . . 🎿☐ **HVS 5b**

Start 8m right of *Gideon* at the base of a slabby rib.
1) 5b, 25m. Scuttle up the rib until it is possible to gain a crack to the right. Head up this to a chossy ledge and flake.
2) 5b, 55m. Gain the leftwards-trending line of weakness below the overlap and follow it to a groove system that continues leftwards. Pass a ledge and tree to gain the *Pandora Plays Sax* slab and follow it to the top.
FA. Trevor Hodgson, A.Hodgson, T.Jones 29.3.1987

Autocrat Buttress
Abseil in to the next two routes from above.

❿ Autocrat . . . . ①🖐️☐ **6b+**
A fine route with some sustained sections and mega exposure. From the left side of the terrace, wander up the arete.
Photo on p.291.
FA. Mike Raine, Elfyn Jones 2008

⓫ Beating the Raine . . . . ①☐ **7b**
A tricky route that leads to a crescendo of difficulty.
FA. Calum Muskett 13.11.2010

Bus Stop Quarry
Dali's Hole
California
Australia
Serengeti
Never Never Land
Twll Mawr
Mordor - Lost World
Vivian Quarry
Rainbow Slab Area
Snakes and Ladders
Outlying

Grassy scramble
- take care

60m

The Bone People Area

The Bone People is one of the finest E4s in North Wales, but few people seem to know about it. Add in *Synthetic Life* and *The Bridge Across Forever* and you have three routes that are well worth exploring. Sadly the approach is quite hard work, which is the main reason that this wall sees little attention. It faces northwest and stays damp and mossy after rain or in the colder months, but does catch the late afternoon sun.

Approach (map p.292, overview p.294) - From the lower parking, follow the track into the quarry for 200m then take a path on the right which leads up through the quarries. You will then glimpse the massive Gideon Quarry working. Carry on up the zig-zagging path on the left to a large dolerite drystone wall above the left side of the quarry. Above that wall is a hut made of large dolerite blocks. Follow the grass along the edge of the quarry until you reach a grassy plateau. It is possible to make a heart-in-your-mouth scramble down to the tree and abseil in from here - a 60m rope will just reach the ground. You may wish to either abseil off trees on the grassy plateau down to the tree or, at the very least, be roped up as you scramble down. Moving between routes is extremely difficult and treacherous in places, so it is best to abseil in to the base of your chosen route.

Access - There may be nesting peregrines from 1st March - 30th June. This restriction can change so check the BMC RAD.

❶ Synthetic Life . . . . 🔟 📷✂📏 [ ] 7a+

One of the new wave of super sport routes of exceptional quality on perfect granite-esque dolerite. It has four distinct cruxes - apparently a bit like a 7a+ version of *The Plum* at Tremadog. Abseil down *The Bone People* with a 60m rope and swing in to the bottom of the route. The route has been equipped with an intermediate abseil anchor so that it is possible to climb on a single 50m rope with some careful ropework. The lower slab suffers from seepage and it would be a good idea to take a brush. Start at the base of a narrow ramp/groove behind the huge boulder. Climbing up the ramp/groove to a hard move leftwards across the top of the slab. Pull through the roof and traverse back right. Technical moves lead to a blind reach above the roof. Make a sideways dyno to a jug, then move up the rib and the slab towards an overlap. Difficult moves through this lead to delicate climbing left across the upper slab until below the final groove. A final long reach and a stiff pull if you are tall, or more technical climbing for the short, leads to a bolted abseil anchor.
FA. Pete Harrison, Chris Parkin 21.5.2010

❷ The Bone People 🔟 📷✂📏 [ ] E4 6a

One of the finest E4s in North Wales, but its remote location means not many people know this. The first pitch is slabby and serious, the second well protected and exposed. Start by abseiling in - a 60m rope only just reaches the ground.
1) 5c, 20m. Start at some blocks at the back of a corner-groove. Pull up left past a bolt to reach a cam placement. Move leftwards to another bolt and make a committing move left to gain the arete. Head up to the bolt belay.
2) 6a, 20m. Make a hard pull right through the bulge. An awkward move left after the second bolt reaches the third. Head up past a side-pull and a few more bolts to an exposed groove. Belay just above this on a mossy slab.
3) 4b, 10m. Try not to slip as you edge across to your abseil rope, which will aid progress up the mossy exit.
FA. John Silvester, Chris Dale 6.1988

❸ The Bridge Across Forever

. . . . 🔟 📷✂📏 [ ] E5 6b

Another forgotten classic.
1) 5c, 20m. As for *The Bone People*.
2) 6b, 33m. Climb *The Bone People* to the second bolt, then swing onto the exposed right wall. Pass two bolts to a sloping foothold and continue up a small groove to the roof. The crux is gaining the right arete at the roof.
FA. Chris Dale, Trevor Hodgson 2.7.1988

❹ Senior Citizen Smith

. . . . 🔟 📷✂📏 [ ] E6 6b

An outrageously good route up the well-protected overhanging horizontal crack, connecting two run-out slabs. The end of the crux has big fall potential, but it is into clean air - with a soft catch the swing into the side-wall should be manageable. Climb the left side of the slab past a 5c rockover - a low runner on the right won't keep you off the ground, but will stop you from going down the slope. Continue up to some microwires at 8m. At the top of the slab, arrange bomber gear as far left as you can before launching out across the overhanging wall - a brilliant sequence of powerful moves. The upper slab leads to a bolted abseil station.
FA. Pete Harrison, Pete Robins 29.6.2010

❺ Chain Wall . . . . 🔟 📏✂ [ ] M8+

The extremely steep dry tooling wall is approached by abseiling to the base of *Uhuru for Mandela* (p.300) and then descending the slope. Sustained mixed climbing featuring figure 4s and desperate footwork starts from a boulder with aid from a metal spike. A clipstick is required to clip the first bolt prior to departure. The location is shown on p.301.
FA. Ramon Marin, M.Pritchard 10.10.2009

Not much sun | 20 min | Sheltered | Abseil in

Bus Stop Quarry · Dali's Hole · California · Australia · Serengeti · Never Never Land · Twll Mawr · Mordor - Lost World · Vivian Quarry · Rainbow Slab Area · Snakes and Ladders · Outlying

Bus Stop Quarry | Dali's Hole | California | Australia | Serengeti | Never Never Land | Twll Mawr | Mordor - Lost World | Vivian Quarry | Rainbow Slab Area | Snakes and Ladders | Outlying

Shotgun Quarry

A small quarry with a couple of routes and a long-standing project which could be quite good.

Approach (map p.292) - Start by the gate on the Gideon approach). Walk up the tarmac path and take a path on the left after 100m. Follow this for 250m to a fenced off area on the right. Go through the fence and down a narrow slate corridor into the quarry.

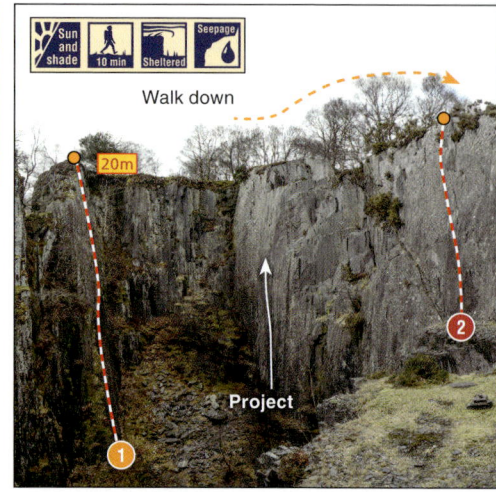

Walk down

Project

❶ **Clegir Arete**. . . . . 🔲 **HVS 5a**
The tower on the left of the quarry, past three bolts and a peg. A bramble section warrants the use of secateurs mid-route.
FA. Al George, B.Lewis, J.Banks 17.7.2002

There is a project on the clean wall. The line is abseiled by local outdoor centres, but is still loose.

❷ **Scraping the Twin Barrels** . . . 🔲 **E1 5b**
The slabby wall on the right side of the quarry above a small gangway. On the left is a point spike - belay off this.
FA. Chris Watkins, Rob Greenwood 18.4.2009

Chwarl Plas Goch

A small quarry with a couple of technical sport climbs.
Approach (map p.292) - Start by the gate on the Gideon approach. Walk up the tarmac path and after 150m, take a path on the left opposite where the main Gideon approach goes right. Walk along here to a purple spoil heap. Head up this and follow the path directly up to the entrance to this small quarry.

❸ **Admire or Ignore** . . . . . . 1️⃣ 🧗 🔲 **7c**
The left-hand groove is harder than it looks.
FA. Pete Robins 5.2014

❹ **Demon Landlord** . . . . . . 2️⃣ 🧗 🔲 **6c**
The right-hand groove is well bolted. It dries slowly.
FA. Martin Crook 2014

The Rain Temple (Ddol Quarry)

This is the smaller quarry to the east of the Wall in the Hole Quarry. A single clean slab is situated on its north side but it is rapidly returning to nature. It does have a single sport route though and at a friendly grade.
Approach (map p.292) - Follow the approach to Gideon Terrace (p.300). From just before the corridor, head up a faint path up the left side of an old decaying fence. At the top, a metal gate gives access to the left edge of the Wall in the Hole Quarry - see below. Another gate gives access to more open hillside. 100m further on and left is The Rain Temple quarry. Abseil from above the route leaving your rope in place to aid the vegetated top-out.

❺ **Cabin Fever**. . . . . 🔲 **5c**
A cleaned line on the rock.
FA. Martin Crook, Nick Walton 8.2008

Wall in the Hole Quarry - *This bigger open quarry passed on the approach to The Rain Temple has three loose routes.* **Twisted Nerve, E4 6b,** *past two bolts in the lower part;* **Friendly Argument, E2 5b,** *on the east wall of the upper section;* **A Big Wall Climb, XS,** *up the back south wall of the upper hole.*

Cefn Du Quarry

High up on the Gideon side is a wide working which has a few routes and a lot of loose scree.

Approach (map p.292) - Drive towards Caernarfon on the A4086. As you enter Llanrug, turn left by the Glyntwrog Inn, heading towards Waunfawr. Carry on to a little hamlet that is marked as the start of Waunfawr. At a crossroads by a white house, take the left turn signed as a dead end and head uphill. After 2km, there is a carpark on the left, just as the tarmac turns into a rough track. Park and follow the track on foot. Where the track forks, take the left fork to the fence line. Follow this up and left before it comes back right at a gate and a beautiful old slate stile. Cefn Du Quarry is below you. Access to the quarry is from the lower end, which is best reached along its right edge where a grassy valley leads into the quarry.

6 The Reclining Bloon E4 6a
A booming start past a metal spike leads to the bolted corner. Difficult climbing on questionable rock with threatening emasculation leads to a lower-off.
FA. Martin Crook 9.1996

7 The New Salesman E4 6b
The pillar. Climb the right arete past some bolts to the overlap. A difficult tussle leads left to a ledge in the centre of the face. Move right and climb the arete boldly to a lower-off.
FA. Chris Parkin 7.1990

8 Carneddau Flash Goggles . . . E1 5a
The white slab *"which resembles in some lights the Piz Gemmli Flat Iron, this similarity is unfortunately short lived."* From the bottom left-hand side, pad up to the loose fin and on to the top.
FA. Martin Crook 9.1996

9 The Wriggler E1 5a
On the opposite side of the quarry is Mount Doom - a buttress with a band across it and a wizard's hat atop.
1) 20m. Shuffle along a ledge passing shot-holes (occasional cam) to a bolt belay.
2) 5a. 30m. Move up left through the prominent band of rock (cam). Move back right to a bolt and continue up past some thin moves. A line of jugs leftwards heads to the next bolt. Continue on to the summit and a bolt belay well back.
FA. Mark Dicken, Ioan Doyle 30.10.2008

Chwarel Fawr

The highest working offers shelter and tranquillity but nothing really worth climbing.

Approach (map p.292) - Park as for Cefn Du. From the carpark, head straight up the hill almost perpendicular to the road and cross the fence to reach the edge of the hole. Heather stomp up left along the edge to where it levels off. Descend to a lower level and pick your way down scree to the base of the route - all rather exciting! There is a long tunnel approach from Cefn Du Quarry, but this is loose and dangerous.

10 Way Down in the Hole . . E1 5a
Hidden in the depths, this rambling journey is loose and mossy in places. It is best avoided.
1) 5a, 5m Move up the slate pedestal and reach out to clip the bolt. Continue past this to a chain and thread belay. Re-belay on a bollard below the dolerite tower.
2) 5a, 12m. Climb the exposed left arete to a belay.
3) 4a, 10m. Traverse off left passing a bad step with a block/bucket seat belay.
FA. Mark Dicken, Joe Sterling 21.12.2008

Bus Stop Quarry | Dali's Hole | California | Australia | Serengeti | Never Never Land | Twll Mawr | Mordor - Lost World | Vivian Quarry | Rainbow Slab Area | Snakes and Ladders | Outlying

Bus Stop Quarry

Dali's Hole

California

Australia

Serengeti

Never Never Land

Twll Mawr

Mordor - Lost World

Vivian Quarry

Rainbow Slab Area

Snakes and Ladders

Outlying

Fachwen is the area of ancient woodland that lies to the northwest of Vivian Quarry. Several test workings were made during the mining of the area. The quarries are vegetated and loose and have no appeal to climbers, though keen locals have stumbled on the odd route whilst walking round the hillside. These have been included for completeness. If it is warm then this place can feel like a tropical jungle, complete with its fair share of biting insects. On top of this water seeps from what seems like everywhere.

Approach

Park in the Vivian Quarry carpark (Pay and Display). Follow the white posts across and up to the quarry hospital. The last building in the hospital complex is the old morgue, compete with slate slab for keep the bodies cool! Carry on along this path as it rises slowly up the side of the lake to a viewpoint where it descends to the ruins of an old mill by a slate bridge.

Allt Wen - From the bridge by the ruined mill, go down a path on the left just past the bridge to the railway tracks and turn left (southeast), back on yourself, to a cutting above the railway. You must not do this when the Lakeside Railway is operating during the day. It usually stops at 5pm.

Muriau Gwynion Bach and Mawr - From the slate bridge, carry along up the track marked by white posts to the first house on the left - this is part of 'Cae Mabon', a woodland community project that often has great storytelling evenings and other earthy activities. Opposite this, a yellow path leads off through a kissing gate. About 30m further along the track, where a green fence with writing on it starts, is a hint of a quarry above the track. A stile above the track gives access to the quarry. If you reach the communal carpark for 'Cae Mabon' on the left, you have gone too far for Muriau Gwynion Bach. Muriau Gwynion Mawr is further along the track where another flattened parking area is found on the left. Just past this, the track goes over a bridge and the quarry is down and to your right.

Chwarel Terfyn - Carry on along the path marked by white posts past the Muriau Gwynion quarries as far as the signpost to Padarn Cafe. Descend through the cafe grounds to a station halfway down the lake. The quarry is behind the station buildings, behind some bins and barbed wire. Some care is needed with access due to the proximity of the railway.

Map labels:
500m
Padarn cafe
Muriau Gwynion Mawr
Muriau Gwynion Bach
N
Cae Mabon
Chwarel Terfyn
Slate bridge
Old ruined mill
Allt Wen Quarry
Llyn Padarn
Llanberis Lake Railway
GPS 53.122309 -4.115818
Llanberis
National Slate Museum

Backdrop: Muriau Gwynion Bach at its most glorious

Allt Wen Quarry

The cutting above the railway has a lonely loose route with a chossy top-out.

1 Psychic Sidekick **E2 6a**
On the left of the cutting up the edge of the slab. A clean groove leads up to an earth and rubble exit.
FA. Phil Targett 20.11.1990

Muriau Gwynion Bach

A hidden cutting which is rather peaceful. It even has its own picnic meadow, although if the midges are out it is you who will be dined on! It is the best of the quarries on this hillside, so start here and see what you think before venturing elsewhere.

2 The Woodflower **E3 6b**
On the left wall as you face into the quarry is a layback feature and a bolt. Use the layback and an undercut to reach the top. If you are as tall as the first ascensionist, slam-dunk an edge via a running jump and mantel to the top.
FA. George Smith, Martin Crook 6.1987

3 Brewing Up with Morley Wood   **E1 5b**
A reasonable route up a mighty flake in the back of the quarry. Follow this wide offering past kettles, stones, rams' skulls and any other wide gear you have, to reach the top.
FA. George Smith, Martin Crook 6.1987

4 Unknown Slab **E2 5b**
On the right side of the quarry is a slab with a single bolt.

Muriau Gwynion Mawr

The largest of the Fachwen holes is spoiled by vegetation, poor rock quality and the large puddle/bog at the bottom of the hole. The easiest approach is from the corner nearest to the flattened communal parking. Scramble down the right side of the quarry (looking in) and rock hop around to the left, just past the tunnel.

5 If You Want . . . .   **HVS 5b**
A clean slab has a bolt in the middle and tree on top.
FA. A.Shaw, Mark Boniface 4.1989

Chwarel Terfyn

Round the back of the station building halfway down the lake. Screened off by bins and barbed wire, this hole is rarely climbed in and has nothing really to offer. Access maybe questionable, but so too is the climbing!

6 Steve Lineman **E1 5b**
On the right side just past the fence are a couple of yellow bolts.
FA. Mark Boniface 11.1989

7 The Niche . . . .   **HVS 5b**
A juggy line through slime and algae to the top - fun hey?

Bus Stop Quarry

Dali's Hole

California

Australia

Serengeti

Never Never Land

Twll Mawr

Mordor - Lost World

Vivian Quarry

Rainbow Slab Area

Snakes and Ladders

Outlying

The Nantlle Valley is the forgotten area of slate climbing, almost totally ignored by the Slateheads save for a dedicated few who explored these holes and found a small set of rather adventurous routes. Ray Kay's *The Purple Tailed Love Fish* was a classic of its genre, but has sadly fallen down. All that remains now across the various holes are a few forgotten trad routes. Some of these look like they might be worth repeating, but in the main these quarries are something of a unknown backwater. They may well yield some exciting new routes to anyone wanting to explore. While some may well be climbable on trad gear, turning up with a drill and some bolts would probably help create more interest from other climbers. Also, some areas look good but would need lower-offs way below the top of the crag to avoid deadly top sections. An additional drawback is that many of the holes are flooded and require an abseil to a ledge or hanging belay to start the routes.

Approach
From Caernarfon, head south on the A487. Turn off left and left again at a second roundabout into Penygroes. Go down the main street and turn right by the Co-op down Victoria Road, or the next one down County Road. Either way you end up leaving the village on the B4418 towards Talysarn. At the T-Junction in Talysarn, turn left then right through the village and follow the road to the slightly pointless roundabout. Park considerately here and walk straight ahead down a track which leads into the quarries.

Conditions
The rock is generally loose and the climbing is adventurous. The damp nature of the holes also means that some areas can be very mossy and lichenous.

Access
The main Dorothea Quarry pool is reputedly over 100m deep and popular as an unofficial scuba diving location, often used on weekends. It is best to avoid *Trev's Slab* when divers are in the pool although they may not mind. The pool has a gruesome reputation for fatal diving accidents because of its depth and the ease with which divers can get into difficulty.

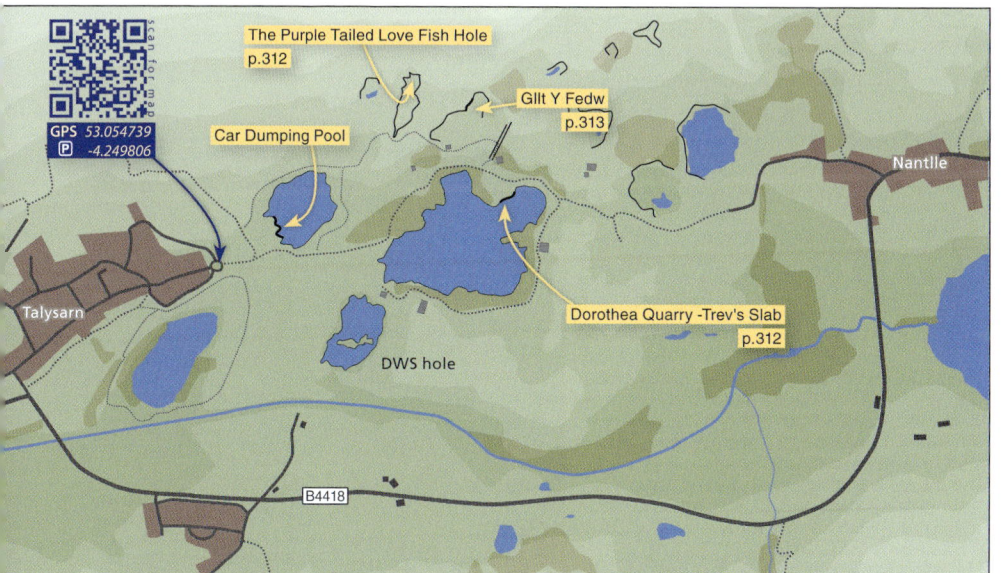

Car Dumping Pool

Delightfully named! This pool has a couple of claimed routes but not much else to offer.

Approach - Walk east from the parking and this is the pool immediately on the left, as you pass the sliding gate. *The Dogger* is below the mound just by the track, but the route can be viewed by bushwhacking around the left side of the quarry to above the tower. This is the second buttress of four on this side.

Buttress 2 -
Graffitied Tower

Buttress 3

Buttress 4

1 The Dogger . . . . **HVS 5a**
From the approach track, the first buttress is accessed by abseiling from trees on a mound above the track. The route is obvious from the viewpoint of the second buttress (which is easily identifiable by steps covered in graffiti). Abseil to a ledge just above the water. Climb the strenuous finger-flake and crack above, stepping right to finish. Small cams are useful.
FA. Jamie Macdonald, J.Lawley 2.5.2010

2 I Wish My Wife Was This Dirty . **VS 4a**
The fourth buttress is situated opposite a man-made wall and is approached by a scree slope on its north side. Start at the crack below a large metal spike. Climb the crack using the arete if required.
FA. Jamie Macdonald, J.Lawley 2.5.2010

GPS 53.054739
-4.249806

The Purple Tailed Love Fish Hole
p.312

Gllt Y Fedw
p.313

Car Dumping Pool

Nantlle

Talysarn

Dorothea Quarry -Trev's Slab
p.312

DWS hole

B4418

Bus Stop Quarry · Dali's Hole · California · Australia · Serengeti · Never Never Land · Twll Mawr · Mordor - Lost World · Vivian Quarry · Rainbow Slab Area · Snakes and Ladders · Outlying

Bus Stop Quarry | Dali's Hole | California | Australia | Serengeti | Never Never Land | Twll Mawr | Mordor - Lost World | Vivian Quarry | Rainbow Slab Area | Snakes and Ladders | Outlying

Dorothea Quarry - Trev's Slab

This infamous hole has a single route. It is also a popular unofficial scuba diving location which reputedly has a depth of more than 100m. Sadly it also has a gruesome reputation for fatal diving accidents.

Approach (map p.311) - Head into the quarry and walk along the main track, past a weird abandoned building in the woods, to arrive at Dorothea Quarry. There is a large carpark area on the right.

1 Trev's Tribute . . . . [   ] E2 5b

Carry on along the path and Trev's Slab in on the right below. It is best viewed by continuing to the far end of the pool and looking back from a hillock above the 'No Tombstoning' signs. Abseil from the bolt at the top of the slab to a hanging belay above the waterline. Bust some moves out right and up to gain the right arete of the slab. Follow the bolts to the top.

FA. Simon Beal, Andy Scott 5.2.2008

Approximate line of
The Purple Tailed
Love Fish

Steep wall
hidden from view

The Purple Tailed Love Fish Hole

This is a deep and impressive hole, though the route *The Purple Tailed Love Fish* has suffered a rockfall. Other areas might be of interest to sport climbers or dry-toolers.

Approach (map p.311) - Immediately on the left, as you pass the sliding gate is the Car Dumping Pool. Circumnavigate this either way to reach a plateau above the steep back wall. Head up a path and when it levels out, strike out towards the large hole.

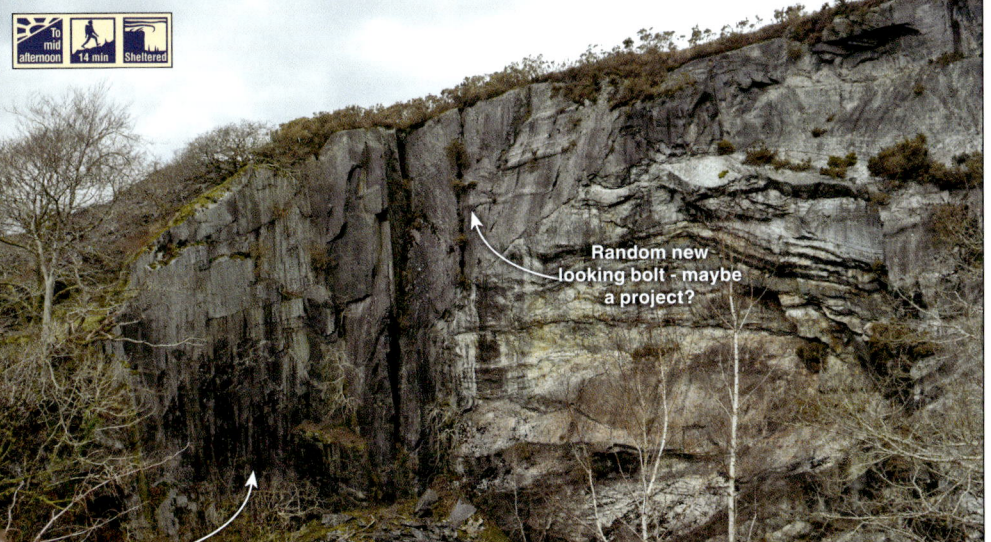

To mid afternoon
14 min
Sheltered
Random new looking bolt - maybe a project?
Mini Colossus Wall

Gllt Y Fedw

This hole actually has some routes, although no-one knows what they are and they are ripe for re-equipping.
Approach (map p.311) - Head into the quarry and walk along the main track to arrive at Dorothea Quarry with a large carpark area on the right. From this flattening, turn off left and head up towards a vegetated incline that leads up between drystone slate walls. At the top of this, turn left and walk through a ruined house - Gllt Y Fedw is below you.

The following routes are bolted, but have been neglected. It will take a steady explorative person to repeat them, though they look good enough to re-equip with a proper lower-off. There are other possibilities in this quarry.

2 **Gllt Y Fedw Slab Left** . . . . . . E4 ?

3 **Gllt Y Fedw Slab Right** . . . . . E4 ?

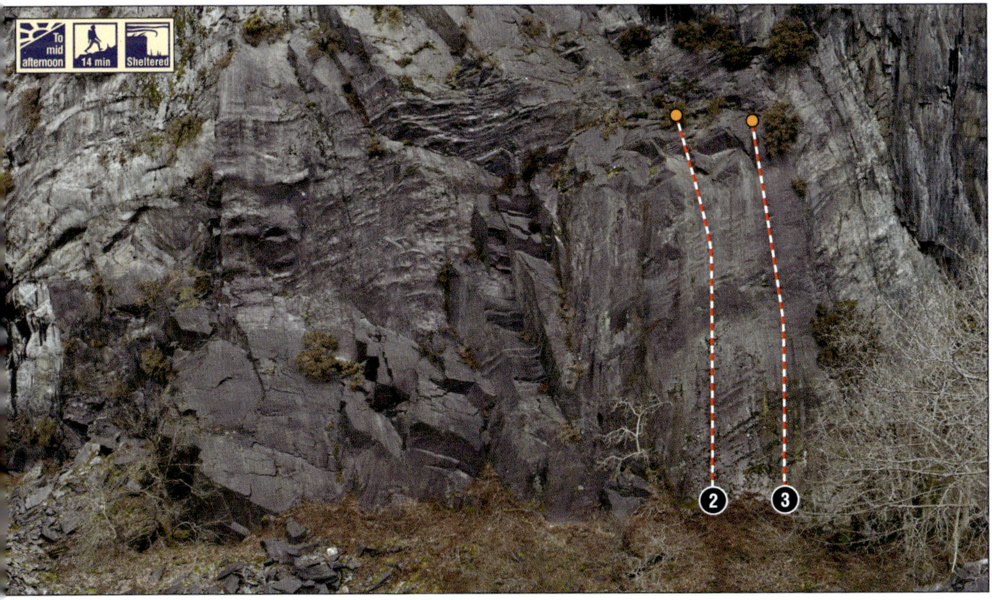
To mid afternoon
14 min
Sheltered
2
3

Bus Stop Quarry
Dali's Hole
California
Australia
Serengeti
Never Never Land
Twll Mawr
Mordor - Lost World
Vivian Quarry
Rainbow Slab Area
Snakes and Ladders
Outlying

Bus Stop Quarry · Dali's Hole · California · Australia · Serengeti · Never Never Land · Twll Mawr · Mordor - Lost World · Vivian Quarry · Rainbow Slab Area · Snakes and Ladders · Outlying

Bus Stop Quarry | Dali's Hole | California | Australia | Serengeti | Never Never Land | Twll Mawr | Mordor - Lost World | Vivian Quarry | Rainbow Slab Area | Snakes and Ladders | Outlying

Bus Stop Quarry · Dali's Hole · California · Australia · Serengeti · Never Never Land · Twll Mawr · Mordor - Lost World · Vivian Quarry · Rainbow Slab Area · Snakes and Ladders · Outlying

Left margin tabs (vertical): Bus Stop Quarry | Dali's Hole | California | Australia | Serengeti | Never Never Land | Twll Mawr | Mordor - Lost World | Vivian Quarry | Rainbow Slab Area | Snakes and Ladders | Outlying

Bus Stop Quarry
Dali's Hole
California
Australia
Serengeti
Never Never Land
Twll Mawr
Mordor - Lost World
Vivian Quarry
Rainbow Slab Area
Snakes and Ladders
Outlying

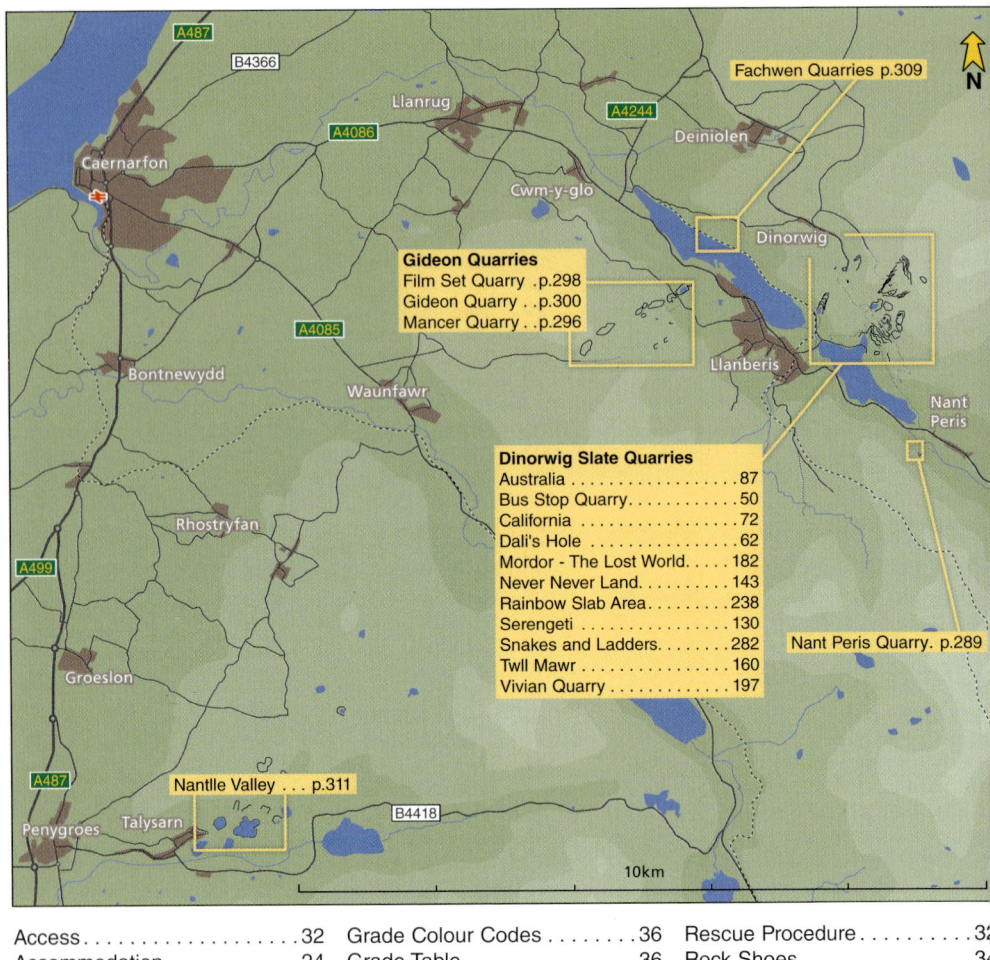

Fachwen Quarries p.309

N

Gideon Quarries
Film Set Quarry . .p.298
Gideon Quarry . .p.300
Mancer Quarry . .p.296

Dinorwig Slate Quarries

Nant Peris Quarry. p.289

Nantlle Valley . . . p.311

10km